ENCYCLOPEDIC DICTIONARY OF
SEMIOTICS, MEDIA, AND COMMUNICATIONS

Semiotics, media, and communications are three closely linked fields. Briefly stated, semiotics, the science of signs, looks at how humans search for and construct meaning; communication studies is concerned with how meaning is conveyed; and media studies considers the ways in which messages are transmitted and received. This dictionary is designed to help students and general readers unlock the significance of the terms commonly used in these fields.

Being interdisciplinary in nature, semiotics, media studies, and communication studies draw from ideas and terminology derived from other disciplines. Hence, this dictionary also encompasses basic concepts from the fields of anthropology, archeology, psychology, psychoanalysis, linguistics, philosophy, artificial intelligence, computer science, and biology. Collected here are definitions and descriptions of terms, concepts, personages, schools of thought, and historical movements that appear frequently in the literature.

The basis of each entry is a simple definition, which often includes the term's origin and important cross-references. Illustrations are provided where necessary, along with historical sketches of movements or schools of thought. The commentary on personages consists of brief statements about their contribution and relevance. Thus, the dictionary not only defines what a term means, but often delves into its history, applications, and broad implications.

This is a compact, practical guide that will be invaluable to students in semiotics, media, and communication studies. Because of its interdisciplinary approach, it will also provide a wide range of scholars with a handy reference to disciplines other than but related to their own.

(Toronto Studies in Semiotics)

MARCEL DANESI is Professor and Director of the Program in Semiotics and Communication Theory at the University of Toronto.

MARCEL DANESI

Encyclopedic Dictionary of Semiotics, Media, and Communications

UNIVERSITY OF TORONTO PRESS
Toronto Buffalo London

© University of Toronto Press Incorporated 2000
Toronto Buffalo London
Printed in Canada

ISBN 0-8020-4783-1 (cloth)
ISBN 0-8020-8329-3 (paper)

Printed on acid-free paper

Toronto Studies in Semiotics
Editors: Marcel Danesi, Umberto Eco, Paul Perron, Thomas A. Sebeok

---

Canadian Cataloguing in Publication Data

Danesi, Marcel, 1946–
Encyclopedic dictionary of semiotics, media, and communications

(Toronto studies in semiotics)
Includes bibliographical references and index.
ISBN 0-8020-4783-1 (bound)   ISBN 0-8020-8329-3 (pbk.)

1. Communication – Dictionaries.   2. Semiotics – Dictionaries.   3. Mass media –
Dictionaries.   I. Title.   II. Series.

P87.5.D36 2000   302.2'03   C00-930589-0

University of Toronto Press acknowledges the financial assistance to its publishing program of
the Canada Council for the Arts and the Ontario Arts Council.

University of Toronto Press acknowledges the financial support for its publishing activities of
the Government of Canada through the Book Publishing Industry Development
Program (BPIDP).

CONTENTS

Preface
vii

Dictionary
3

Bibliography
245

Index
259

PREFACE

The human race is a species consumed by a quest for *meaning*. This search has led it to create myths, art, science, language, and all the other *meaningful* activities that define its evolution. The study of how humans search for and make meaning comes under the rubric of *semiotics*, defined as the science of *signs*. The study of how meaning is conveyed to others comes, instead, under the rubric of *communication science*. And the study of how the transmission of messages is carried out, and how it affects its receivers, comes under the category of *media analysis*. These three fields are thus concerned with what is perhaps the most fundamental condition of human life – the capacity for making and using words, gestures, drawings, and so forth for thinking and communicating.

As fascinating and as relevant to understanding the contemporary world as the work in these fields is, the writing in their respective scholarly literatures is often too technical, laden with jargon, and highly abstruse. To unlock the relevance and significance of the work within these fields, a terminological *key* is required, especially by those who are new to them. The purpose of this dictionary is to provide such a key. It constitutes a collection of basic terms, concepts, personages, schools of thought, and historical movements that come up recurrently in *semiotics*, *media analysis*, and *communication science*. The dictionary has been envisaged with students taking beginning courses in such fields as semiotics, psychology, linguistics, mythology, education, literary studies, cultural anthropology, communication studies, and media analysis in mind, so that they can have a practical reference manual at their disposal to help them make sense of the technical writing they are expected to comprehend and interpret. For this reason, the entries included here are laid out with an easy-to-follow style and are often illustrated with practical examples.

Content

Semiotics, media analysis, and communication science are interdisciplinary fields, and are thus cluttered with notions that are used in other disciplines. Hence, the choice of items for this dictionary was expanded to include not only the basic ideas coined within these fields, but also those that theorists and practitioners have taken from other fields – from anthropology, archeology, psychology, psychoanalysis, linguistics, philosophy, artificial intelligence, computer science, and biology.

I must warn the user of this dictionary, however, that to keep the proportions of this volume within the limits of a compact practical reference work, I have had to limit my choices to the main items that recur in the relevant literature. Nevertheless, I have tried to cast as broad a net as possible, so as to gather within one cover the bulk of the ideas that the beginning student or interested general reader will need to know in order to decipher the relevant literature.

Organization

Each term is defined in a straightforward fashion. The etymology is provided for most of the terms. This gives the reader useful information on the source and original meaning of the term. Entries are frequently exemplified practically under the heading *Illustration(s)*. Occasionally additional commentary may be needed. This is included under the heading *Note*, which either illustrates further the meaning or uses of an entry, or else provides a historical sketch of a movement, school of thought, etc. – hence the stipulation *Encyclopedic Dictionary* in the title. These *notes* are designed to give the reader the bare facts, so that she/he can follow the historical allusions made in the relevant literature to events and personages. Cross-references to other articles in the dictionary are indicated by an asterisk. When mentioned in an article, terms having an entry of their own in the dictionary are often italicized. The commentary provided for each of the personages consists of a brief statement about his/her relevance and/or contribution to the field. Only those personages to whom the technical literature regularly alludes have been included in this dictionary.

Bibliography

A bibliography of relevant works is included at the back. This constitutes a personal choice of works intended as a further source of reference and a general reading list.

Acknowledgments

I wish to thank the editorial staff at University of Toronto Press for all their advice, support, and expert help in the making of this dictionary. I am especially grateful to Dr Ron Schoeffel and Anne Forte, without whom this volume would never have come to fruition. I am indebted to the three reviewers of the first draft of the manuscript for all their useful and helpful comments. Without the thorough and insightful copy-editing of John St James this work would have been much less complete. Needless to say, I alone am responsible for any infelicities that remain in the volume.

I thank Victoria College of the University of Toronto for having allowed me the privilege of teaching and coordinating its Program in Semiotics and Communication Theory over many years. In that regard, I would especially like to mention Dr Rose-anne Runte and Dr Eva Kushner, the presidents under whom I have worked, and Dr Alexandra Johnston, Dr William Callahan, and Dr Brian Merrilees, the Principals of the College with whom I have had the pleasure of coordinating the program. I am also thankful to Lynn Welsh, Julie Berger, Susan MacDonald, and Joe Lumley for their constant help and support over the years. Another debt of gratitude goes to the many students I have taught. Their insights and enthusiasm have made my job simply wonderful! They are the impetus for this dictionary.

Marcel Danesi
University of Toronto, 1999

ENCYCLOPEDIC DICTIONARY OF
SEMIOTICS, MEDIA, AND COMMUNICATIONS

DICTIONARY

At painful times, when composition is impossible and reading is not enough, grammars and dictionaries are excellent for distraction.

Elizabeth Barrett Browning (1806–61)

A

abduction
[< Latin AB 'away' + DUCERE 'to lead']
[see also *deduction, *induction]
Term used by Charles *Peirce to designate the kind of reasoning whereby a concept is formed on the basis of an existing concept or model; an abduction is essentially a 'hunch' as to what something entails or presupposes.

Illustration: A classic example of an abduction is the model of atomic structure originated by the English physicist Ernest Rutherford (1871–1937). Rutherford guessed, essentially, that the inside of an atom had the structure of an infinitesimal solar system, with electrons behaving like planets orbiting around an atomic nucleus.

abecedary
[uncommon synonym for *alphabet]

Abelard, Peter
[1079–c. 1142]
Medieval French philosopher and theologian, whose fame as a teacher made him one of the most celebrated figures of the 12th century. Abelard taught that the *Platonic forms – abstract mental images – were patterns extracted from particular objects.

Abelard also taught that truth is attainable only by carefully weighing all sides of any issue.

absence of language in advertising
[see *advertising, absence of language in]

abstract art
[< Latin AB 'from' + TRAHERE 'to draw']
20th-century visual art style characterized by the use of abstract, symbolic images (rather than direct, realistic ones) conveying moods, feelings, and impressions.

Illustration: The abstract art movement gained its early momentum in 1908 when Pablo Picasso (1881–1973) painted landscapes as assemblages of constituent little cubes. These paintings, which were called cubist (see *cubism), impel the viewer to reconstruct the landscape in his/her imagination.

abstract concept
[see *concept, abstract]

abstract expressionism
[< Latin AB 'from' + TRAHERE 'to draw']
Mid-20th-century art movement promoting the spontaneous expression of feelings and emotions through the physical act of painting itself, rather than through realistic representation.

Note: Influenced by European avant-garde artists who had immigrated to the United States during the 1920s, 1930s, and 1940s, the expressionist movement found its main home in New York City. Expressionist paintings consisted mainly of 1. shapes resulting from the gestures made by the artist's hand, called action paintings; 2. compositions of colors and shapes for their own sake, called color field paintings.

Well-known abstract expressionists include Jackson Pollock (1912–56), Willem de Kooning (1904–97), Mark Rothko (1903–70), and Robert Burns Motherwell (1915–91).

abstract image
[see *image, mental]

acculturation
[< Latin AD 'to' + COLERE 'to till']
[term introduced into anthropology in the late 19th century]
Process by which continuous contact between two or more distinct societies causes cultural change.

Note: Acculturation unfolds in one of two ways: 1. the beliefs, conventions, customs, and codes of the societies in contact may merge, producing a single culture; 2. one society may completely absorb the cultural patterns of another, transforming them radically.

acoustic phonetics
[< Greek AKOUEIN 'to hear'; and PHONĒ 'sound']
[see also *articulatory phonetics]
Branch of *phonetics dealing with the nature of the wave patterns produced by the individual sounds of languages.

Note: The origin of acoustic phonetics can be traced to the publication of *Sensations of Tone* (1863) by the German physicist Hermann *Helmholtz. Acoustic phoneticians use spectrographs, kymographs (machines that trace pressure curves), X-ray machines, and other instruments to record speech waves, so that they can identify the recurrent patterns produced by speech sounds. A branch of acoustic phonetics, known more specifically as *auditory phonetics,* deals instead with how speech sounds are perceived physically and psychologically.

acronym
[< Greek AKRON 'head' + ONOMA 'name']
Word formed from the initial letters of a series of words, and usually pronounced as such.

Illustrations: 1. WAC = <u>W</u>omen's <u>A</u>rmy <u>C</u>orps; 2. radar = <u>r</u>adio <u>d</u>etecting <u>a</u>nd <u>r</u>anging; 3. laser = <u>l</u>ight <u>a</u>mplification by <u>s</u>timulated <u>e</u>mission of <u>r</u>adiation; 4. UNESCO = <u>U</u>nited <u>N</u>ations <u>E</u>du<u>c</u>ational, <u>S</u>cientific, and <u>C</u>ultural <u>O</u>rganization.

acrostic
[< Greek AKRON 'head' + STIKHOS 'line of verse']
[also called *word square]
Puzzle whose solution requires that a word or saying be reckoned from the first or last letters of words in lines of prose or verse, taken in some order.

Illustrations: 1. <u>L</u>ike a thick haze, <u>o</u>nce you're in it, <u>v</u>ery rarely does it, <u>e</u>vaporate away. What is it? Answer: l + o + v + e = love (= an acrostic derived from the initial letter of the first word of each of the given phrases). 2. A colo<u>r</u>, sometimes called ceris<u>e</u>, that is characteristic of bloo<u>d</u>. What color is it? Answer: r + e + d = red (= an acrostic derived from the last letters of the three clue words).

actant
[term coined by French semiotician A.J. *Greimas]
Prototypical character role that manifests itself cross-culturally in all kinds of *narratives: e.g. a *hero,* an *opponent,* a *helper,* etc.

Illustration: In the novel *Madame Bovary* (1857), by the French writer Gustave

Flaubert (1821–80), the following actants can be discerned: *subject actant* = Emma, *object actant* = happiness, *sender actant* = Romantic literature, *receiver actant* = Emma, *helper actant* = Léon, Rodolphe, *opponent actant* = Charles, Yonville, Rodolphe, Homais, Lheureux.

Note: An actant may surface as a single character, as several characters, as an event, or as a theme. Several actants may also surface as one and the same character, event, or theme. In a mystery novel, for instance, the *hero* may have several enemies, all of whom function actantially as a single *opponent*. In a love story, a lover may function actantially as both *object* and *sender*. An actant is, in effect, *who* or *what* perpetrates or endures specific *actions* in a narrative. Greimas claimed that actants relate to each other in a binary fashion: *subject* vs. *object*, *sender* vs. *receiver*, *helper* vs. *opponent*, etc.

actantial theory
[see *actant]

action painting
Painting resulting from the spontaneous splashing of paint on to a canvas; the painting that results is supposed to emphasize the emotional nature of the act of painting itself.

Note: The term *action painting* was first used to describe the works of the Dutch-American painter Willem De Kooning (1904–97), because he made paintings with highly vigorous and dynamic brush strokes.

adage
[< Latin ADAGIUM 'saying']
[also called *aphorism]
Saying that purports to set forth a general truth, gaining credence either through constant use or on account of the authority of the person who coined it.

Illustrations: 1. 'A good husband makes a good wife' (John Florio, c.1553–1625); 2. 'It ain't over 'til it's over' (Yogi Berra, 1925–).

adaptation
[< Latin AD 'to' + APTARE 'to fit']
Physical adjustment made by an individual organism or an entire species to its environment.

Illustration: Mimicry in animal behavior – the ability to become inconspicuous to predators by blending into the environment or to simulate the coloration of a species distasteful to predators – is the best-known manifestation of adaptation.

addressee
[< Latin AD 'to' + DIRIGERE 'to lay straight, direct']
1. receiver of a message; 2. person(s) to whom a message is directed.

addresser
[< Latin AD 'to' + DIRIGERE 'to lay straight, direct']
1. sender of a message; 2. person(s) who initiate(s) a communication.

adjective
[< Latin AD 'to' + IACERE 'to throw']
Part of speech used in association with a *noun or other substantive, limiting, qualifying, or specifying its meaning.

Illustrations: 1. *This is an enjoyable book.* 2. *Alexander is smarter than you think.* 3. *Sarah has a brilliant mind.* 4. *Theirs is a happy family.*

Note: In English an adjective is recognizable by certain suffixes, such as -*able*, and -*ous*, or by its position in noun phrases (directly before the noun). It can also have one of three forms: positive (*clear, beautiful*), comparative (*clearer, more beautiful*), superlative (*clearest, most beautiful*).

Adler, Alfred
[1870–1937]
Austrian psychiatrist who rejected Sigmund *Freud's belief that sexuality was the prime motivator of behavior and the source of most neuroses. Adler stressed the sense of inferiority (to which he gave the name *inferi-*

ority complex), rather than sexual drives, as the motivating force in human life. Adler's works include *The Theory and Practice of Individual Psychology* (1918) and *The Pattern of Life* (1930).

Adorno, Theodor
[1903–1969]
German philosopher, sociologist, and musicologist who applied Marxist concepts (see Karl *Marx) to the study of human nature and modern society. His books include *Minima Moralia: Reflections from Damaged Life* (1951), *Jargon of Authenticity* (1964), a critique of philosopher Martin Heidegger and others who denied the possibility of objective truth, and *Negative Dialectics* (1973), in which Adorno examined the crucial role played by art in human life.

adverb
[< Latin AD 'in relation to' + VERBUM 'word']
Part of speech used in association with a verb, an adjective, or another adverb, specifying or modifying its meaning.

Illustrations: 1. *He runs <u>rapidly</u>*. 2. *They are <u>very</u> happy with their children.*

advertising
[< Latin ADVERTERE 'to direct one's attention to']
The making of public announcements designed to promote the sale of specific commodities or services.

Note: A poster found in Thebes dated back to 1000 BC is considered to be the world's first advertisement. In large letters it offered a whole gold coin for the capture of a runaway slave. Throughout history poster advertising in marketplaces and temples has constituted a common means of promoting and disseminating information about the barter and sale of goods and services.

In the Middle Ages, advertising was entrusted largely to town criers – citizens who read public notices aloud, shouting the praises of the wares of the merchants who hired them. After the invention of the movable-type printing press in Europe around 1440, merchants started hanging printed posters outside their shops and inserting announcements in books, pamphlets, and newspapers. In the 17th century, the *London Gazette* became the first newspaper to reserve a section exclusively for advertising. So successful was this venture that shortly thereafter new agencies came into being for the specific purpose of creating newspaper ads for merchants and artisans. Advertising spread rapidly in the 18th century, proliferating to the point that the British writer and lexicographer Samuel Johnson (1709–84) felt impelled to make the following statement in *The Idler*: 'Advertisements are now so numerous that they are very negligently perused, and it is therefore become necessary to gain attention by magnificence of promise and by eloquence sometimes sublime and sometimes pathetic.'

The first *advertising agency* was founded by Philadelphia entrepreneur Volney B. Palmer in 1841. By 1849 Palmer had opened offices in New York, Boston, and Baltimore in addition to his Philadelphia office. With improved transcontinental transportation, distribution, and communications systems, mail-order houses appeared on the scene in the United States in the 1870s. Book publishers, seed companies, railroads, and steamship lines were among the early users of nation-wide advertising.

In the last two decades of the 19th century many American firms began to market packaged goods under *brand names. Previously, such everyday household products as sugar, soap, rice, and molasses had been sold in neighborhood stores from large bulk containers. The first brand names of soap products date from about 1880, and include *Ivory, Pears', Sapolio, Colgate, Kirk's American Family*, and *Packer's*. Along with *Bon Ami, Wrigley*, and *Coca-Cola*, such products quickly became household names. Encouraged by the effectiveness of brand naming in enhancing a product's familiarity, between 1890 and 1920 industrial corporations started using persuasive advertising en masse, not simply to inform people about the availability and qualities of their products, but to influence how they should be perceived. The advent of radio in the 1920s, subsequently, brought about the use of a new psychologically powerful form of advertising – the *commercial*. Based on the compelling logic of narrative, the persuasive qualities of the human voice, and the allure of musical jingles, the radio commercial became a highly effective vehicle for promoting product recognizability.

In the first decade of the 20th century psychologists were hired by advertising agencies to help create messages and campaigns designed to influence consumption behavior. The founder of American behavioral psychology, John B. Watson (1878–1958), for instance, was hired by the J. Walter Thompson advertising agency to devise persuasive tactics for promoting the marketability of certain products. After the Second World War, advertising developed into a business so huge that it became a symbol of America itself in the eyes of the world. With the advent of television after the war, the advertising industry logically adapted the idea of the radio commercial to the new visual medium.

Today, advertising constitutes much more than just a persuasive 'sales pitch.' It has become a dominant form of social discourse. The advertiser's implicit messages, styles of presentation, and pervasive visual grammar are everywhere, surreptitiously shaping the lifestyle behaviors of individuals, as well as subliminally suggesting how people can best satisfy their innermost urges and aspirations. Advertising has succeeded, as the semiotician Roland *Barthes warned, in building an unbroken, imagistic bridge between the product and the consumer's consciousness, thus inculcating a highly consumerist lifestyle and world-view in society at large.

advertising, absence of language in
[< Latin ADVERTERE 'to direct one's attention to']
Advertising technique consisting in the intentional omission of language, suggesting, by implication, that the product 'speaks for itself.'
Illustrations: 1. In print advertisements, products are sometimes shown without any written commentary, with only their brand names being revealed. 2. In TV commercials, scenes revolving around products are sometimes shown without dialogue or explanation, with only the brand names being revealed.

advertising, consumer
[see also *advertising]
Advertising directed towards the promotion of products and services.

advertising, trade
[see also *advertising]
Advertising directed at dealers and professionals through appropriate trade publications and media.

advertising, use of alliteration in
[< Latin ADVERTERE 'to direct one's attention to']
[see *alliteration]
Common advertising technique consisting in the making of statements or jingles in which the initial consonant sound of a brand name is repeated. This increases the likelihood that a product's name will be remembered.
Illustrations: 1. *The Superfree sensation.* 2. *Guinness is good for you.* 3. *Marlboro man.*

advertising, use of formulas in
[< Latin ADVERTERE 'to direct one's attention to']
Common advertising technique consisting in the use of formulaic speech to enhance recognition of a product. Formulas are meaningless or trivial statements that sound

truthful or authoritative by virtue of the fact that they are self-evident.

Illustrations: 1. *Triumph has a bra for the way you are!* 2. *A Volkswagen is a Volkswagen!* 3. *Coke is it!*

advertising, use of the imperative form in
[< Latin ADVERTERE 'to direct one's attention to']
Common advertising technique consisting in the use of the imperative form of verbs to create the effect that an unseen authoritative source is giving advice.

Illustrations: 1. *Trust your senses!* 2. *Join the Pepsi Generation!* 3. *Have a great day, at McDonald's!*

advertising, use of jingles in
[< Latin ADVERTERE 'to direct one's attention to']
Common advertising technique, based on a simple musical tune, intended to enhance recognition of a product. The easy rhythm and flowing melody contribute to memory of the product by association.

Illustrations: 1. *Snap, crackle, and pop!* 2. *Breakfast of champions!*

advertising, use of persuasion techniques in
[< Latin ADVERTERE 'to direct one's attention to']
Advertising techniques designed to persuade consumers to buy or endorse a product.

Illustrations: 1. *Repetition* is the technique whereby the content of radio and television commercials is reiterated in the print media (newspapers, magazines, posters, displays, etc.) in order to capture the attention of a large segment of potential customers. 2. *Brand naming* is designed to gain the consumers' allegiance to, and confidence in, a product. 3. The *something-for-nothing* lure is a technique designed to grab the attention of potential consumers: *Buy one package and get a second one free; Send for free sample; Trial offer at half-price; Finish this sentence and win $1,000,000,000 in cash, an automobile, or a trip to Florida for two; No money down;* etc. 4. *Humorously contrived* ads and commercials convey friendliness and, thus, help to portray a product as agreeable. 5. Endorsements of products by celebrities make them appear reliable. 6. *Appeals to parents* induce them to believe that giving their children certain products will secure them a better life and future. 7. *Appeals to children* to 'ask mummy or daddy' to buy certain products increase the likelihood that parents will 'give in' to their children's requests. 7. *Scare copy* techniques are designed to promote such goods and services as insurance, fire alarms, cosmetics, and vitamin capsules by evoking the fear of poverty, sickness, loss of social standing, and/or impending disaster.

advertising, use of repetition in
[< Latin ADVERTERE 'to direct one's attention to']
[see also *advertising, use of persuasion techniques in]
Common advertising technique consisting in the recycling of sales pitches on radio and television commercials in print media such as newspapers, magazines, posters, outdoor displays, etc. in order to grab the attention of a large market segment for the product.

Illustrations: 1. The *Pepsi Generation* pitch (for *Pepsi Cola*) of a few years back was presented through radio and TV commercials, and reiterated through print advertising. 2. The *This Bud's for you* pitch (for *Budweiser* beer) was similarly presented through radio and TV commercials, and reiterated through print advertising.

advertising, use of secretive statements in
[< Latin ADVERTERE 'to direct one's attention to']
Common advertising technique consisting

in the use of statements designed to create the effect that something secretive is being communicated, thus capturing people's attention by stimulating curiosity.

Illustrations: 1. *Don't tell your friends about…* *… 2. Do you know what she's wearing? 3. Who's that behind the wheel?*

advertising, use of the something-for-nothing lure

[< Latin ADVERTERE 'to direct one's attention to']
[see also *advertising, use of persuasion techniques in]
Advertising technique consisting in offering a potential buyer a 'something-for-nothing' deal so as to entice him/her to purchase the product (even if on a trial basis).

Illustrations: 1. *Buy one and get the second one free! 2. Send for your free sample! 3. Trial offer at half-price! 4. Finish this sentence and win $100,000 in cash, an automobile, or a trip to the Caribbean for two! 5. No money down!*

advertising agency
[see *advertising]

aesthesia
[< Greek AISTHESIS 'perception, sense-impression']
1. total sensory and emotional reaction to a physical stimulus, an idea, or a work of art; 2. heightened sensitivity to beauty.

aesthetic theories
[see *aesthetics]

aestheticism
[< Greek *aisthesis 'perception, sense-impression']
1. devotion to, or pursuit of, the expression of beauty in art; 2. belief that beauty is the basic objective of life from which all others, especially moral ones, are derived; 3. view that artists have no social obligation other

than to strive for the representation of beauty in their art.

Note: One of the best-known aestheticists of modern times was the Irish-born writer Oscar Wilde (1854–1900), who turned the 'art-for-art's-sake' philosophy of aestheticism into a lifestyle that many have since emulated. As an aesthete, the eccentric Wilde wore long hair, filled his room with various art objects, and lived a 'devil-may-care' life. Wilde's aestheticism was ridiculed in the comic periodical *Punch* and satirized in the Gilbert and Sullivan comic opera *Patience* (1881). Nonetheless, his wit and flair won him many devotees.

aesthetics
[< Greek AISTHESIS 'perception, sense-impression'; this term was introduced into philosophy in 1753 by the German philosopher Alexander Gottlieb *Baumgarten]
The study of beauty and meaning in art and of the psychological responses to it; aesthetics deals in particular with the question of whether beauty and ugliness are objectively present in art works, or whether they exist only in the mind of the individual.

Note: The Greek philosopher *Plato laid out one of the first substantive theories of aesthetics, claiming that the experience of art was guided by 'ideal forms' of beauty pre-existing in the mind. In his *Republic*, Plato wanted to banish some types of artists from his ideal republic because he thought their work was so emotionally powerful that it encouraged immorality. He especially disliked certain kinds of musical compositions, believing that they engendered laziness or incited people to behave immoderately.

*Aristotle saw art as the imaginative attempt to separate intrinsic pattern from the matter of objects, such as the human body, so as to impose it on some other substance, such as marble (in sculpture). Aristotle held that the major function of art was to provide a means of attaining happiness. In his *Poetics*, he argued that tragic drama, for instance, so stimulates the emotions of pity and fear, which he considered morbid and unhealthy, that by the end of the play the spectator is purged of them. This catharsis makes the audience psychologically healthier and thus more capable of achieving happiness.

The 3rd-century Roman philosopher *Plotinus believed that artistic representation revealed the essence of an object more intrinsically than the direct experience of the object did. He argued that true art raised the soul to a religious contemplation of universal forms of beauty present in all objects. Throughout the Middle Ages the role of art was, in fact, interpreted in purely religious terms, but by the Renaissance art was reappraised as having both religious and secular functions.

The first modern theory of aesthetics was formulated in the 18th century by the German philosopher Alexander Gottlieb *Baumgarten, who defined the experience of art as the sensory recognition of perfection. In the same century, playwright and critic Gotthold Ephraim Lessing (1729–81), archaeologist and antiquary Johann Joachim Winckelmann (1717–68), and philosophers Immanuel *Kant and Johann Gottlieb Fichte (1762–1814) explored such issues as art's limitations, the nature of artistic expression, the moral dimension of art, and the relation of art to the structure of the mind. The German poet, dramatist, philosopher, and historian Johann Christoph Friedrich von Schiller (1759–1805) saw art as the means through which the individual's sense of personal liberty and morality gained expressive form.

In the 19th century aesthetic theories proliferated. G.W.F. Hegel believed that art, religion, and philosophy were the vehicles through which the human spirit manifested itself. Arthur Schopenhauer (1788–1860) claimed that art provided a means of escaping the painful world of daily experience.

Friedrich *Nietzsche (1844–1900) asserted that art allowed humans to cope with their sorrowful plight, transforming their pointless experiences into consequential events. Political theorist Karl *Marx (1818–83) maintained that art was great only when it supported the causes of its society. The French impressionist painters rejected the idea of art as imitation of Nature. As a result they became more concerned with how to convey feelings on canvas than with how to represent objects with a high degree of fidelity. The French philosopher Victor Cousin (1792–1867), subsequently, derived the principle of 'art for art's sake' from Kant's view that art has its own esoteric reason for being. This idea has undergirded most Western theories of art ever since.

In the 20th century, French philosopher Henri *Bergson saw the aesthetic experience as an intuitive apprehension of reality unmediated by rational thought. The Italian philosopher and critic Benedetto *Croce viewed it as the innate sense of truth without reflection. The American poet George *Santayana argued that the pleasure derived from experiencing a work of art was motivated by an intrinsic quality in the art work itself, rather than being a purely subjective response to the work. American educator John *Dewey viewed aesthetic experiences as being separate from, and more meaningful than, normal fragmentary human experiences. Austrian psychoanalyst Sigmund *Freud (1856–1939) believed that art revealed hidden psychic conflicts and was, thus, a powerful means for discharging tensions. French philosopher Jean-Paul Sartre (1905–80) saw art as an expression of the individual artist's need to seek answers to the question of existence. British critic I.A. *Richards saw art as giving order and coherence to experience. American philosopher Susanne *Langer developed the distinction between the symbols used in conventional language and the more 'holistic' ones used in nonverbal art forms as a basis for under-

standing why art is so emotionally powerful. Others have commented on the conditioning effects of tradition, fashion, and
other social pressures on aesthetic tastes,
noting, for example, that in the early 18th
century the plays of William Shakespeare
were once viewed as barbarous and ob-
scene.

affix
[< Latin AFFIXUS 'fastened']
Form in a language that is added to a word
or other form.

Illustration: Illogical is interpreted as one
word, but it is decomposable into smaller
units: the basic form, *logic*, which has a
dictionary meaning, and two *affixes* – the
negative prefix *il-*, which has a functional
meaning ('opposite of'), and the suffix *-al*,
which also has a functional meaning ('the
act or process of being something').

Note: There are four types of affixes: 1. *prefixes*, which are attached before a form;
2. *suffixes*, which are attached after a form;
3. *infixes*, which are inserted within a form;
4. *circumfixes*, which are added around a
form. *Pre-*, *-un*, and *a-* are examples of prefixes: e.g. *preannounce*, *undo*, *amoral*. The
endings *-ly*, *-ness*, and *-ity* are examples of
suffixes: e.g. *friendly*, *cleanliness*, *equality*. An
example of an infix is the form *-mi-* in the
Bantoc word *fumikas* 'to be strong' (spoken
in the Philippines): this is decomposable
into the basic form *fukas* 'strong' and the
infix *-mi-* 'to be.' An example of a circumfix
is found in the Chicksaw language (a Native
American language spoken in Oklahoma),
where the word *iklakno* 'it isn't yellow', is
made up of the root form *lakn-* 'it is yellow'
and the circumfix *ik-* + *-o* 'it is not.'

age of equals
[see also *age of the gods; *age of heroes]
Final stage in Giambattista *Vico's theory of
the cultural cycle in which common people
rise up against the 'heroes' of the previous

stage and win equality; but in the process
society begins to disintegrate as people
become more deceitful. Vico claimed that
this state of deceitfulness is not a final hope-
less event, for it invariably leads to cultural
regeneration and to the rediscovery of
the basic ethical, moral nature of human
existence.

age of the gods
[see also *age of equals; *age of heroes]
Early stage in Giambattista *Vico's theory of
the cultural cycle in which cultures are born
as attempts by groups of early peoples to
understand natural phenomena such as
thunder and lightning. Not possessing the
scientific knowledge to understand or 'explain' such events, early humans ascribed
them to awesome and frightful 'gods' –
hence the designation 'age of the gods.'
Religion, burial rites, the family, and other
basic institutions are established as attempts
to appease the gods.

age of heroes
[see also *age of equals; *age of the gods]
Middle stage in Giambattista *Vico's theory
of the cultural cycle in which a dominant
class of humans – the 'heroes' of the developing culture – subjugate the common people, who both fear and admire the heroes.

agnosia
[< Greek AGNOSIA 'ignorance']
Loss of the ability to interpret sensory
stimuli, such as sounds or visual images.

agraphia
[< Greek A- 'without' + GRAPHEIN 'to write']
Disorder marked by a loss of the ability to
write.

Alcuin
[AD 735–804]
Medieval English scholar and ecclesiastic,
whose letters provide valuable information
about the social life and educational prac-

tices of 8th-century Europe. Alcuin's hand-writing style led to the development of the *Carolingian*, a script that influenced the handwriting of the early Italian Renaissance typesetters, from which modern type is derived.

algorithm

[< Middle Latin ALGORISMUS, after Arabic mathematician al-Khwarazmi, 9th-century AD]

Systematic, step-by-step method of solving a certain kind of problem or of representing a procedure.

Illustration: A three-step algorithm for multi-plying two general algebraic expressions, $(x + a) (x + b)$, where a and b represent two given numbers and x a variable, is the fol-lowing: 1. multiply the two x's in each ex-pression: $= x^2$; 2. to this, add the sum of the product of the 'middle' and 'outside' factors $(ax + bx) = x^2 + (a+b)x$; 3. finally, add the product of the last two factors $(ab) = x^2 + (a+b)x + ab$.

aliquid stat pro aliquo

[Latin for 'something that stands for some-thing else']

St *Augustine's definition of the sign as something that, over and above the impres-sions it makes on the senses, causes some-thing else (what it stands for) to come to mind as an image or concept.

allegory

[< Greek ALLOS 'other' + AGOREUEIN 'to speak in assembly']

Narrative or poem in which the plot, the characters, and the settings have a purely symbolic meaning.

Illustrations: 1. *Le roman de la rose*, written in the 13th century by French poets Guillaume de Lorris and Jean de Meung, is a widely known allegory of human love. 2. In the West, the art of allegorical writing reached its apotheosis during the Middle Ages in the

work of the Italian poet *Dante Alighieri, especially in his *Divine Comedy* (1321), and a little later in the work of the English poet Geoffrey Chaucer, especially in his *Canter-bury Tales* (1387–1400).

alliteration

[< Latin AD 'to' + LITTERA 'letter']

Repetition of the initial sound (usually a consonant or consonant cluster) in two or more words of a phrase, expression, line of poetry, etc.

Illustrations: 1. s̲crolls of s̲ilver s̲nowy s̲entences (Hart Crane, 1899–1932); 2. *Their t̲ale of t̲error their t̲urbulence t̲ells!* 3. s̲ing-s̲ong; 4. n̲o-n̲o.

alliteration in advertising

[see *advertising, use of alliteration in]

allomorph

[< Greek ALLOS 'other' + MORPHĒ 'form']

Actual form that a *morpheme (minimal unit in a language) takes in a phrase or sentence.

Illustration:

1.	2.
a boy	*an apple*
a picture	*an egg*
a girl	*an olive*

From a comparison of the forms in 1 and 2, it can easily be seen that the indefinite arti-cle morpheme in English has two forms: 1. *a* before a word beginning with a consonant; 2. *an* before a word beginning with a vowel.

allophone

[< Greek ALLOS 'other' + PHONĒ 'sound']

Actual pronunciation that a phoneme (basic sound unit) takes in a word.

Illustration: In English the phoneme /l/, represented by the alphabet letter l, is ar-ticulated in two different ways. When the /l/ occurs at the end of a syllable or word – as in *kill, bill, pull, doll*, etc. – it is articulated by raising the back part of the tongue to-wards the soft palate (back part of the palate); when it occurs in all other positions – as in *life, last, filter, pluck*, etc. – it is articulated with the tip of the tongue touching the top portion of the upper teeth. These two articulations are called *allophones*. (Note that English orthography does not distinguish between the two allophones.)

allusion
[< Latin ALLUSIO 'a playing with']
Indirect reference to a theme, plot, character, idea, etc. in a conversation, play, narrative, discourse, etc.

Illustrations: 1. 'Without naming names, the chairperson criticized the troublemakers.'
2. 'In this poem there is an allusion to classical mythology.'

alphabet
[< Greek ALPHA + BETA, the first two letters of the Greek alphabet]
System of characters (marks, figures, letters, symbols, etc.) for representing speech sounds.

Note: Alphabets are distinguished from *syllabaries* and from *pictographic* and *ideographic* systems of representation. A syllabary provides characters for representing separate syllables; a pictographic system provides characters for representing picturable things; an ideographic system provides characters for representing non-picturable (abstract) ideas.

Early systems of writing were of the pictographic and/or ideographic type. As common picture signs were written down in abbreviated form (for the sake of expediency), the stage was set for the transition from pictographic to alphabetic representation. Instead of drawing, say, the full head of an ox, pictograph users started drawing only its bare outline. This abbreviated pictograph eventually became a new symbol standing for the word *ox* (*aleph* in Hebrew), and a little later just for the initial sound in the spoken word itself (the *a* in *aleph*).

The last stage occurred around 1700–1000 BC, when the Phoenicians created such an abbreviation system for recording consonant sounds. The first letter of the Phoenician alphabet represented the glottal consonant at the beginning of the word *aleph*. The Greeks later adopted the Phoenician system, but since they had no glottal consonant in their language, they reassigned the Phoenician character to representing the vowel *alpha*. They then called each symbol by words – *alpha, beta, gamma*, etc. – which were imitations of Phoenician words: *aleph* 'ox,' *beth* 'house,' *gimel* 'camel,' etc.

The Greek alphabet spread throughout the Mediterranean world, giving rise to the Roman one, which became the basic alphabet of all the languages of Western Europe following the Roman conquests. About AD 860 Greek missionaries converted the Slavic tribes to Christianity and devised for them an alphabetic system of writing known as Cyrillic. The Cyrillic alphabet is used currently in Russian, Ukrainian, Serbian, and Bulgarian writing. The Arabic alphabet, another offshoot of the early Semitic one, probably originated around the 4th century AD and is generally used by the Islamic world.

Although alphabets were born as systems for representing sounds, alphabetically recorded languages are, paradoxically, often highly unphonetic, largely because alphabetic systems tend not to change in tandem with the spoken language. This leads to the presence of anomalous written forms such as the English words *knife, knot, knight, knock*, etc., the spelling of which reflects the pronunciation of an earlier period, when the *k* before *n* was pronounced.

alterity
[< Latin ALTER 'other']
[also called otherness]
Movement emphasizing ethnic, racial, and sexual diversity in philosophy, the arts, and

the sciences. This movement was given impetus by Michel *Foucault's accusation in the 1980s that the 'Other' – i.e. the person of different race, sexual orientation, etc. – had been excluded for too long from the center of Western society's representational activities.

ambiguity
[< Latin AMBIGERE 'to wander around']
Ambivalence or multiplicity of meaning of a word, statement, work of art, etc.

Illustration: The sentence *The pig is ready to eat* is ambiguous because, depending on *context, it can refer to 1. the actual animal called a *pig* (a mammal of the family *Suidae*), which looks hungry and is thus *ready to eat*; 2. a cooked *pig* that is *ready to be eaten*; 3. a *person* who appears gluttonous and over-anxious *to eat*.

amphibology
[uncommon synonym for *ambiguity]

anachronism
[< Greek ANA 'against' + CHRONOS 'time']
Word, statement, work of art that is, or seems to be, out of its proper time.

Illustration: The question *Whither is the washroom?* uttered today would sound oddly antiquated, because words such as *whither*, *hither*, and *thither* are anachronisms, belonging to an earlier period of vocabulary usage in English, having now been largely replaced by *where*, *here*, and *there* (except in poetical or rhetorical usage).

anaglyph
[< Greek ANA 'against' + GLYPHEIN 'to carve']
1. ornament carved in low relief; 2. picture consisting of two slightly different perspectives of the same object in two contrasting colors that are superimposed on each other, producing a three-dimensional effect when viewed through two correspondingly colored filters or lenses.

anagram
[< Greek ANA 'back' + GRAMMA 'letter']
Word or phrase made from another word or phrase by rearranging its letters.
Illustrations: 1. *won = now*; 2. *dread = adder*; 3. *drop = prod*; 4. *stop = pots*.

Note: The medieval doctrine of cabalism attached great importance to anagrams, believing that they predicted the destiny of persons. A famous anagram is the one formed from the name *Florence Nightingale*: 'Flit on, cheering angel.'

analog computer
[see *computer]

analogy
[< Greek ANA 'against, back, throughout' + LOGOS 'word, reckoning']
1. similarity in some respects between two words, statements, concepts, etc. that are otherwise unlike; 2. process by which words, constructions, etc. are formed or created on the model of already-existing patterns in a language; 3. process of making an inference from certain resemblances between two or more things to a probable further similarity between them.

Illustrations: 1. *Energize* was formed from *energy* by analogy with *apologize* from *apology*. 2. Old English *handa* became *hands* on the model of other plural forms ending in -s.

analytic language
[< Greek ANA 'throughout' + LYSIS 'a loosing']
[see also *synthetic language]
Language that is characterized largely by the fact that it depends on word order, rather than on word structure, to convey sentence meanings.

Illustration: In English, an analytic language, the two sentences *The boy loves the girl* and *The girl loves the boy* mean different things. On the other hand, in classical Latin, the sentence *The boy* (PUER) *loves* (AMAT) *the girl* (PUELLAM) could have been rendered in any one of six ways – Puer amat puellam; Puer puellam amat; Amat puer puellam; Amat puellam puer; Puellam puer amat; Puellam amat puer – because the ending on each word would have indicated what relation the word had to the others: PUER is in the nominative case and is thus the subject of the sentence, no matter where it occurs in it; PUELLAM is in the accusative case (nominative = PUELLA) and is thus the object of the sentence, no matter what its position is in the sentence.

analytic philosophy
[< Greek ANA 'throughout' + LYSIS 'a loosing'; PHILOSOPHOS 'lover of wisdom']
20th-century philosophical movement, dominant in Great Britain and the United States since the Second World War, dealing primarily with how language encodes concepts.

Note: The founders of this movement were the British philosophers G.E. Moore (1873–1958) and Bertrand *Russell. Moore and Russell claimed that the primary task of philosophy was to determine how language encoded truth or falsity on the basis of its logical structure. Such ideas attracted to Cambridge the Austrian philosopher Ludwig *Wittgenstein, who subsequently became a central figure in the movement. The world, Wittgenstein argued, is ultimately composed of simple facts, which it is the purpose of language to encode. Metaphysical, theological, and ethical statements, therefore, were factually meaningless. Paradoxically, Wittgenstein repudiated his own views in his posthumously published *Philosophical Investigations* (1953), arguing in that work that once attention is directed to the way language is actually used in ordinary discourse, the rich fluidity of linguistic meanings makes it obvious that propositions do much more than encode simple facts. Philosophy, concluded Wittgenstein, should thus focus its efforts on resolving problems that arise as the result of the inbuilt *ambiguity in language.

Philosopher John *Austin subsequently maintained that, in fact, the starting point for philosophical inquiry should be an analysis of the extremely fine distinctions drawn in the *speech acts that are performed during ordinary conversation. Willard Quine (1908–) also argued that speaking one way rather than another is a thoroughly pragmatic decision, not an ontological one. Contemporary analytic philosophers now maintain that attention to the logical structure of language and to how language is used in everyday discourse should be the starting point for resolving philosophical problems.

analytical engine
[< Greek ANA 'throughout' + LYSIS 'a loosing']
Calculating machine invented by British mathematician Charles *Babbage in 1833, of which only a part was ever built. Babbage's engine was, in effect, the first general-purpose digital *computer, although it was conceived long before electronics technology appeared. It had the capacity to perform various mathematical operations, using punched cards as a form of permanent memory.

anaphora
[< Greek ANA 'back' + PHEREIN 'to bear']
[see also *cataphora]
Reference to a word or phrase in a statement or conversation occurring earlier in it.

Illustrations: 1. *Alexander saw Sarah just before bumping into her* (*her* = anaphoric pronoun referring back to *Sarah*). 2. *Mark saw himself in the mirror* (*himself* = reflexive anaphoric pronoun referring back to *Mark*). 3. *I bought a toy yesterday; it was for my grandson* (*it* = anaphoric pronoun referring back to *toy*).

anchorage
Term coined by Roland *Barthes referring to the effect captions play in constraining the meaning of a photograph, a figure, etc. in print media.

Illustration: The drawing of a cat on a stool in an ad, when viewed without a caption, has a myriad interpretive possibilities:

However, if the caption *Looking for a Companion* were added to it, then the only interpretation that the drawing would elicit is that of an appeal for pet adoption. The caption is thus said to *anchor* the interpretation of the drawing.

animal communication
[see *communication, animal]

animation
[< Latin ANIMA 'soul']
[see also *cartoons]
Sequencing of a series of drawings that creates the illusion of continuous motion when the drawings are shown rapidly in succession.

Note: Animation toys, such as 'flipbooks,' have been around for centuries. Film animation became a cartoon genre at the beginning of the 20th century, after the invention of motion pictures.

animism
[< Latin ANIMA 'soul']
Belief that all objects possess a soul or life force.

Note: The German physician and chemist Georg Ernst Stahl (1660–1734) coined this word to describe his theory that the soul is responsible for organic development. Since the late 19th century, however, the term has mainly been associated with anthropology and the British anthropologist Sir Edward Burnett *Tylor, who described the origin of religion and primitive beliefs in terms of animism. Tylor asserted that many tribes without written traditions believe that spirits are the cause of life in both living beings and objects. Such peoples picture spirits as phantoms, resembling vapors or shadows, that move from person to person, from the dead to the living, and among plants, animals, and lifeless objects.

annals
[< Latin ANNALIS 'yearly']
1. written chronological record of the events of successive years; 2. periodical or journal in which the records and reports of a learned field are compiled on a yearly basis.

annotation
[< Latin AD 'to' + NOTARE 'to write']
[also called emotive connotation; see also *denotation; *connotation]
1. furnishing critical commentary or explanatory notes to a word, statement, work of art, etc.; 2. personal meanings elicited by a *sign.

Illustration: The word *cat* is produced and comprehended in terms of three meaning dimensions: 1. a specific concrete meaning (denotation) as a 'mammal, with retractile claws, with whiskers, etc.'; 2. culturally appropriate connotations, such as 'household pet,' 'friendly animal,' etc.; 3. personal annotations, as shaped by an individual's previous experiences with cats.

anthropology
[< Greek ANTHROPOS 'man' + LOGOS 'word, reckoning']
Study of the physical and cultural characteristics, distribution, beliefs, customs, and social characteristics of humanity.

Note: The field of anthropology is generally

divided into two major areas: 1. *physical* *anthropology, which deals with the biological evolution and the physiological adaptations of humans; 2. *cultural* *anthropology, which deals with the ways in which people live in groups.

Anthropology emerged as a distinct field of study in the mid-19th century. In North America the founder of the discipline was Lewis Henry *Morgan, who conducted ground-breaking research on the Iroquois peoples. In Europe the founding figure was British scholar Edward B. *Tylor, who elaborated a theory of human culture based on *animism. Also in the mid-19th century, Danish archeologists at the Museum of Northern Antiquities in Copenhagen gave physical anthropology a firm empirical foundation by establishing the sequential development of tools from the Stone Age to the Bronze and Iron Ages.

anthropology, cultural
[< Greek ANTHROPOS 'man' + LOGOS 'word, reckoning']
Branch of *anthropology studying cultures comparatively.

Note: The goal of cultural anthropology is to develop broad generalizations about cultural systems and social behavior. Research describing food production, social organization, religion, clothing, material culture, language, and other aspects of communal life is referred to as *ethnographic*. In the 1970s, cultural anthropologists started adopting a comprehensive approach, called *ecological theory*, which requires a holistic, multivariable research strategy for explaining the patterns discovered in different cultures.

anthropology, physical
[< Greek ANTHROPOS 'man' + LOGOS 'word, reckoning']
Branch of *anthropology studying the interplay of biological and cultural factors in the evolution of human life and in the development of societies.

Note: Biological anthropologists hold that notions of 'pure' races are misleading and mistaken. All humans living today are descendants of *Homo sapiens*, and are thus cut from the same genetic fabric. Differences among peoples have arisen as a result of the complex interplay of genetic *adaptations with physiological and cultural (non-genetic) adaptations.

Fossil remains unearthed in the late 1970s and early 1980s have provided evidence that in the period from 1 million to 3 million years ago the genus *Homo* coexisted in East Africa with other advanced ape species known as *australopithecines*. Both of these appear to be descendants of an Ethiopian fossil, *Australopithecus afarensis*, 3 million to 3.7 million years old. This ancient ancestor of humans had the legs and body for walking bipedally, an event that freed the hands of *Homo*, allowing it to manipulate objects and, subsequently, to make tools.

anthropomorphism
[< Greek ANTHROPOS 'man' + MORPHĒ 'form']
Attribution of human characteristics to a god, an animal, or an inanimate thing.

Note: In the history of religions, anthropomorphism refers to the depiction of the divinities in terms of human bodily forms and emotions. Anthropomorphic concepts make it easier for human beings to understand and to think about metaphysical notions. In literature, anthropomorphism refers to the depiction of objects, animals, or plants as talking, reasoning, sentient, humanlike beings.

anthroposemiosis
[< Latin ANTHROPOS 'man' + SEMEION 'mark, sign']
[see also *biosemiosis; *zoosemiosis]
Human *semiosis (the production and comprehension of *signs) as both linked to, and

different from, animal semiosis (known as zoosemiosis).

anthroposemiotics

[< Latin ANTHROPOS 'man' + SEMEION 'mark, sign']
[see also *biosemiotics; *zoosemiotics]
Branch of semiotics dealing with human *semiosis (the capacity for producing and comprehending signs) as similar to, or different from, semiosis in other species.

anticlimax

[< Greek ANTI 'against' + KLIMAX 'ladder']
Sequencing of ideas in a phrase or sentence in abruptly diminishing importance, often for rhetorical or satirical effect.

Illustrations: 1. *First there is food for survival; then a beverage for satisfaction!* 2. *He is charming, delicate, nice, short.* 3. *A thousand people died when the Titanic sank; a great deal of jewelry was also lost.*

antihero

[< Greek ANTI 'against' + HEROS 'hero']
Main character in a dramatic or narrative work who lacks the traditional heroic qualities, such as idealism or courage.

Illustrations: 1. The character Holden Caulfield in J.D. Salinger's (1919–) novel *The Catcher in the Rye* (1951) is a well-known antihero of 20th-century fiction. 2. The character Yossarian in Joseph Heller's (1923–99) popular novel *Catch-22* (1961) is another example of a fictional antihero.

antinarrative

[see *antinovel]

antinomy

[< Greek ANTI 'against' + NOMOS 'law']
[see also *paradox]
Contradiction or inconsistency between two apparently reasonable principles, or between conclusions drawn from them.

Illustrations: 1. *In this case, what is good is really bad!* 2. *Whoever comes first in that race will end up last in how he or she is perceived!*

antinovel

[also called *antinarrative]
Fictional *narrative characterized by the absence of the traditional elements of the *novel, such as a coherent plot structure, a consistent point of view, realistic portrayals of character, etc.

Illustrations: 1. *The Voyeur* (1955) by Alain Robbe-Grillet (1922–); 2. *Molloy* (1951) by Samuel Beckett (1906–89).

antithesis

[< Greek ANTI 'against' + TITHENAI 'to place']
Two words, phrases, clauses, or sentences opposed to each other in meaning so that contrasting ideas can be emphasized.

Illustrations: 1. *You are going; I am staying.* 2. *My life is on the upswing; yours is in a downslide.*

antonomasia

[< Greek ANTI 'against' + ONOMA 'name']
1. use of an epithet or title in place of a name; 2. use of a well-known personage to describe someone.

Illustrations: 1. referring to a philanderer as a *Don Juan*; 2. calling a sovereign *Your Majesty*; 3. referring to a traitor as a *Benedict Arnold*; 4. calling a judge *Your Honor*.

antonym

[< Greek ANTI 'against' + ONOMA 'name']
[see also *synonym]
Word that is perceived to have an opposite meaning with respect to another word.

Illustrations: 1. *Night* is perceived as referring to the opposite of *day*. 2. *Good* is perceived as referring to the opposite of *evil*. 3. *Clean* is perceived as referring to the opposite of *dirty*. 4. *Rich* is perceived as referring to the opposite of *poor*.

antonymy

[< Greek ANTI 'against' + ONOMA 'name']
[see also *synonymy]
Relation by which different words, phrases, sentences, etc. stand in a discernible 'oppositeness' of meaning to each other.

Illustrations: 1. *sad* vs. *happy*; 2. *Go to hell!* vs. *Good luck!*

aphasia

[< Greek APHATOS 'unuttered']
Total or partial loss of the power to use or understand words, phrases, or sentences, usually caused by disease or injury to one of the brain's language centers.

Note: There are two main types of aphasia: 1. *motor* aphasia is the inability to carry out the movements necessary to form gestures, to articulate sounds, and to write graphic characters; 2. *sensory* aphasia is loss of the understanding of what symbols, gestures, etc. mean, leaving a person able to hear and see but not to understand words, characters, or gestures.

aphonia

[< Greek A- 'without' + PHONĒ 'voice']
Loss of the voice resulting from disease or injury to the vocal cords, or as a consequence of some psychological syndrome, such as hysteria.

aphorism

[< Greek APHORIZEIN 'to delimit']
[also called *adage]
Tersely phrased statement of a truism, forcing one to reflect upon its meaning.

Illustrations: 1. *Life is too short.* 2. *As soon as we are born, we start to die.* 3. *Night follows day.*

apologue

[< Greek APO 'from' + LOGOS 'speech']
Moral fable in which animals or inanimate objects are depicted as humanlike characters.

Illustrations: 1. Aesop's (6th century BC) *Fables* (e.g. 'The Tortoise and the Hare' and 'The Fox and the Grapes'). 2. The *Uncle Remus* tales by American writer Joel Chandler Harris (1848–1908).

a posteriori reasoning

[< Latin A 'from' + POSTERIORI 'later']
Reasoning from facts or particulars to general principles, or from effects to causes (= an 'after the fact' form of logical thinking).

Illustration: Upon seeing a rainbow, it can be concluded (a posteriori) that it either must have rained previously, or else that the spray of a waterfall must be nearby.

apostrophe

[< Greek APO 'from' + STREPHEIN 'to turn']
Rhetorical technique by which an actor turns from the audience, or a writer from his/her readers, to address a person who usually is absent or deceased, or to refer to an inanimate object or abstract idea.

Illustrations: 1. 'Why am I feeling thus, my long-departed friend?' 2. 'Oh Fate, why do you pursue me so relentlessly?'

apothegm

[< Greek APO 'from' + PHTHEGH 'to speak plainly']
[also called *maxim]
Terse, witty, instructive, but often sardonic, saying.

Illustrations: 1. *Humanity does not live by bread alone; sometimes it also needs drink!* 2. *Night follows day; but then day follows night!*

apperception

[see also *perception]
Conscious perception whereby a novel stimulus or idea is related to what is already known.

application software

Computer *software designed to assist in the performance of a specific task, such as word processing, accounting, inventory management, etc.

applied semiotics
[see *semiotics, applied]

apraxia
[< Greek A- 'without' + PRAXIS 'action']
Total or partial loss of the ability to carry out coordinated movements or to manipulate objects, caused by an impairment of a motor or sensory nature.

a priori reasoning
[< Latin A 'from' + PRIORI 'former']
1. reasoning from causes to effects (= a 'before the fact' form of logical thinking);
2. drawing a conclusion from a hypothesis or theory rather than from experimentation, experience, or observation.

Illustration: Upon seeing rain or the spray of a waterfall, it can be reasoned (a priori) that a rainbow could ensue (whether or not one actually does).

Aquinas, St Thomas
[1225–1274]
Italian theologian and philosopher who combined Aristotelian logic with Augustinian theology into a comprehensive system of thought that came to be *the* acclaimed philosophy of Roman Catholicism in the medieval period. In his *Summa theologiae,* Aquinas demonstrated convincingly how the truths of science and philosophy are discoverable by reason, whereas the tenets of religion, which are beyond rational comprehension, are understandable only on the basis of faith.

arbitrariness
[Latin < AD 'to' + BAETERE 'to come, to go']
View in semiotic theory that the relation between a *signifier and a *signified (e.g. a word and its meaning) is, in most cases, purely arbitrary and/or conventional.

Note: With arbitrariness theory, there is no evident reason for using, say, *tree* or *arbre* (French), to designate 'an arboreal plant.' Indeed, any well-formed word could have been coined in either language – so long as it was consistent with the orthographic, phonological, and morphological (word-structure) patterns of the language.

According to this view, there are some instances when a word may have been fashioned in imitation of some sound property. Onomatopoeic words (*drip, plop, whack,* etc.), for instance, do indeed attempt to reflect the sound properties that their referents are perceived to have. But arbitrariness theory maintains that this is a relatively isolated and infrequent phenomenon. Moreover, the highly variable nature of onomatopoeia across languages demonstrates that even this phenomenon is subject to arbitrary cultural conventions. For example, the word used to refer to the sounds made by a rooster is *cock-a-doodle-do* in English, but *chicchirichí* (pronounced 'keekkeereekee') in Italian; the word employed to refer to the barking of a dog is *bow-wow* in English, but *ouaoua* (pronounced wawa) in French; and so on. This suggests that such onomatopoeic creations are only approximate and more or less conventional imitations of perceived sounds.

archeology
[< Greek ARKHE 'chief' + LOGOS 'word, study']
Field studying the material remains of past human cultures, in order to reconstruct those cultures.

Note: The early history of archaeology begins in the Renaissance, when antiquaries collected ancient artifacts and speculated about their significance. In the 19th century, Danish geological studies led to the conception of the Stone, Bronze, and Iron Ages. In the same century, Egyptian hieroglyphic and Persian cuneiform writing were deciphered. In 1947, the development of the *radiocarbon* (carbon-14) dating method made it possible to make more accurate archaeological inferences. Archeologists now analyze layered deposits of artifacts, which allow them to establish a chronology of cultural activities during the period when humans occupied a site.

archetype

[< Greek ARCHE 'chief' + TYPOS 'model, stamp']
1. original pattern or model from which all other patterns of the same kind are made; 2. in psychology, any of several innate ideas or mental images that manifest themselves typically in conversations, dreams, myths, art forms, and performances across cultures.

Illustration: Term used by psychologist Carl *Jung to highlight the notion that there exist primordial figures in the evolution of the human species that are expressed by the different symbols made by cultures. The *trickster*, for instance, is an archetypal figure that shows up throughout the world: e.g. in Native American mythology tricksters are often depicted as solitary coyotes, hares, or ravens; in Western literature, the trickster has shown up as *Rumplestilskin*, as the *jester* in Shakespearean drama, and as the persona adopted by many modern-day comedians.

architecteme

[< Greek ARCHE 'chief' + TEKTON 'carpenter']
Minimal unit of an architectural style or code.

Illustrations: 1. a type of column; 2. a rood shape; 3. a type of portal; 4. a window design.

architectural code

[< Greek ARCHE 'chief' + TEKTON 'carpenter']
*code that underlies the design and construction of buildings.

Note: Buildings are 'read' as texts with various meanings. The height of a building in a city, for instance, conveys a specific kind of meaning. In medieval Europe the tallest building was built by the clergy. The churches were, literally and symbolically, places of power and wealth. But as the Church lost its clout and wealth after the Renaissance, cities were gradually redesigned architecturally to reflect the new cultural order. Today, the tallest buildings in sprawling urban centers are built by large corporations and banks. Wealth and power now reside in these institutions. Inside these monolithic structures hierarchical symbolism also follows an up-down architectural schema: the jobs and positions with the lowest value are at the bottom of the building; the ones with the most prestige are at the top. The company's executives reside, like the gods on Mount Olympus, on the top floor. This why we use such expression as *to work one's way up, to make it to the top, to climb the ladder of success, to set one's goals high*, etc.

The oldest designed environments stable enough to have left architectural traces date from the first development of cities. The Assyrian city of Khorsabad, built during the reign of Sargon II (722–705 BC) and excavated in 1842, became the basis for the study of the Mesopotamian world. The Egyptian pyramids – used for royal tombs – are examples of the power of buildings to convey a sense of majesty and power.

Many of the architectural trends in the West are modern-day versions of the building styles of ancient Greece and Rome. The best-known trends of Ancient Greece were (1) the Doric form exemplified by the Parthenon (448–432 BC), which crowns the Athenian Acropolis, (2) the Ionic form, which featured capitals with spiral volutes, slender shafts, and elaborate bases, and (3) the Corinthian form, a later development, which introduced Ionic capitals detailed with acanthus leaves. Roman architecture was noteworthy for its grandiose urban design, of which the most remarkable example is Hadrian's Villa (AD 125–32) near Tivoli. From the 4th century until the early Renaissance, Christianity came to dominate social systems, including architectural trends, prompting the building of many new churches. The Renaissance brought a revival of the principles and styles of ancient Greek and Roman architecture. In the 16th century the classical Roman elements were adopted in a way that came to be known as mannerist style, characterized by arches, columns, and entablatures that introduced perspective and depth into architecture. In the 18th century a new style arose, called rococo, reflecting a new affluence and elegance in society at large. Then, in the 19th century, with the advent of the Industrial Revolution, English architect Sir Joseph Paxton created the Crystal Palace (1850–1) in London, a vast exhibition hall that foreshadowed industrialized building and the widespread use of cast iron and steel.

At the beginning of the 20th century, some designers started a search for new organic architectural forms. The American architect Louis Sullivan (1856–1924) gave new expressive form to urban commercial buildings, inventing, in effect, the skyscraper. An apprentice of Sullivan's, Frank Lloyd Wright (1869–1959), became America's greatest architect. Wright is known above all else for breaking away from the 'box' style of modern architecture, introducing other geometrical forms (circular, elliptic, etc.) into building design. In Germany, the 'art of the modern skyscraper' came to be perfected by the so-called *Bauhaus School* (Weimar, 1919–25), which brought together architects, painters, and designers from several countries to formulate the goals for the visual arts in the modern age. Its first director was Walter Gropius (1883–1969). The Bauhaus style prevailed throughout the 1940s, 1950s, and most of the 1960s. Often referred to with the term modernism, its architectural approach can be seen in the chaste elegance and subtle proportions of the Seagram Building (1958) in New York.

The Bauhaus School envisioned a proletarian architectural landscape with no ornamental excesses (cornices, pillars, gables, etc.). Buildings were to be fashioned as box–like forms, so as to eliminate all the symbols of power. Office towers, housing projects, hotels, and other public buildings were built with the same basic cubic blueprint.

Between 1965 and 1980, architects started to reject modernism, which they found to be too monolithic and formulaic, and established a new style that came to be known as *postmodern* (see *architecture, postmodern). The postmodern architects valued individuality, intimacy, complexity, humor, and irony all mish-mashed into the design. By the early 1980s, postmodernism had become the dominant trend in American architecture and an important phenomenon in Europe as well. Its success in the United States owed much to the influence of Philip C. Johnson (1906–), whose AT&T Building (1984) in New York City became instantly a paragon of postmodern design. Today's new office buildings emphasize high-tech and glamorous professions. The diversity of Western society is reflected in the diversity of architectural styles.

architecture

[< Greek ARCHE 'chief' + TEKTON 'carpenter']
Art and science of designing and erecting buildings.

Note: The architectural forms of ancient Greece and Rome have directly determined the course of Western architecture to this day. In Greece, the *Doric style predominated on the mainland and in the western colonies. The acknowledged Doric masterpiece is the Parthenon (448–432 BC), which crowns the Athenian Acropolis. The other was the *Ionic style, which originated in the cities on the islands and coasts of Asia Minor. It featured capitals with spiral volutes, slender shafts, and elaborate bases. Roman architectural style was guided by great engineering feats – as can still be seen today in the complex system of roads, canals, bridges, and aqueducts the Romans left to posterity. Two Roman inventions introduced greater flexibility in architectural style: the *dome* and the *groin vault*, formed by the intersection of two identical barrel vaults over a square plan. The Romans also introduced the commemorative or triumphal *arch* and the *coliseum* or *stadium*

From the 4th century until the early Renaissance, Christianity came to influence and control architectural trends, prompting the building of many churches. Domed churches decorated with mosaics proliferated throughout the Byzantine era. By the 12th century, the Romanesque *basilica* became the basis for the development of Gothic architecture.

The Renaissance brought with it a revival of the principles and styles of ancient Greek and Roman architecture. The Italian architect Filippo Brunelleschi (1377–1446), with his dome design for the Florentine Cathedral (1420–36), stood at the threshold between Gothic and Renaissance styles. In the 16th century, Rome became the center for new architectural trends. Saint Peter's Basilica in Vatican City was the most important of many architectural projects in the century. Towards mid-century leading Italian architects began to use the classical Roman elements in ways that became known as *mannerist*. In the 17th century mannerist style was characterized by arches, columns, and entablatures that introduced perspective and depth into building designs. The best-known architect of the period was the sculptor Gianlorenzo Bernini (1598–1680), the designer of the great oval plaza (begun 1656) in front of St Peter's Basilica.

In the 18th century a style arose, called *rococo*, that reflected a new affluence and elegance in society at large. In the 19th century, English architect Sir Joseph Paxton created the Crystal Palace (1850–1) in London, a vast exhibition hall that set the tone for the advent of industrialized building design and the widespread use of cast iron and steel. At the beginning of the 20th century, the American architect Louis Sullivan (1856–1924) invented the modern skyscraper, developed by the Bauhaus school. The Bauhaus style, also known as *modernist* (see *modernism), prevailed throughout the 1940s, 1950s, and 1960s. By the early 1980s postmodern style (see below), emphasizing eclecticism and irony, had become the dominant trend in American architecture and an important phenomenon in Europe as well. Its success in the United States owed much to the influence of Philip C. Johnson (1906–), architect of the AT&T Building (1984) in New York City.

architecture, postmodern

[< Greek ARCHE 'chief' + TEKTON 'carpenter'] 20th-century movement in architectural style based on classical and other forms put together in a mish-mash, eclectic fashion.

Note: Postmodern architects call for individuality, complexity, and eccentricity in design, while also demanding acknowledgment of historical precedent – through an adaptation of traditional ornamental symbols and patterns. Shortly after its adoption in architecture in the 1970s, the notion of *postmodernism* started to catch on more broadly, becoming a general movement in philosophy and the arts.

Illustration: Perhaps the best-known example of a North American postmodern building is Philip C. Johnson's AT&T Building (1984) in New York City.

argot

[< French ARGOTER 'to beg']
1. type of secret language; 2. variety of a language typical of thieves, tramps, or special kinds of groups.

Illustrations: 1. pig for 'police officer'; 2. stool pigeon for 'a person acting as a police spy.'

argument

[< Latin ARGUMENTUM 'evidence, proof']
1. discussion in which disagreement is
expressed; 2. type of reasoning aimed at
demonstrating a truth or a falsehood;
3. summary of the plot or theme of a literary
work; 4. in computer science, a value used
to assess a procedure or subroutine; 5. in
*Peircean theory, a type of reasoning that
unfolds when propositions about something
are made.

Aristotle

[384–322 BC]
One of the greatest Western philosophers of
all time, Aristotle was a student of *Plato,
sharing his teacher's reverence for human
knowledge, but revising many of his men-
tor's ideas. Aristotle surveyed and systematized nearly all the extant branches of
knowledge in the Greece of his era, providing the first ordered accounts of biology,
psychology, physics, and literary theory. He
also invented the field known as formal or
syllogistic logic (see *syllogism).

Aristotle was among the first to take on
the task of investigating the nature of signs,
laying down a theory that has remained
basic to this day. He described words, for
example, as consisting of three dimensions:
1. the physical part of the word itself (e.g.
the sounds that make up the word *blue*);
2. the *referent* to which it calls attention (a
certain category of color); and 3. its evocation of a *meaning* (what the color *blue* evokes
psychologically and socially).

art

[< Latin ARS 'joining, fitting together']
[see also *aesthetics]
Disciplined expressive activity that provides
the people who produce it and those who
observe it with a range of aesthetic, emotional, and/or intellectual experiences.

Note: Among the earliest known visual art
works are the drawings executed deep
within caves of southern Europe during the
Paleolithic period, some 20,000 to 35,000
years ago. These portray humans, bison,
horses, deer, and other animals with remarkable fidelity. They may have been
painted as part of a ritual, although their
exact meaning is unclear. In a cave painting
at Lascaux, France, for example, a man is
depicted among the animals, and several
dark dots are included. But the purpose of
the design remains obscure.

More than 5000 years ago the Egyptians
began painting the walls of the pharaohs'
tombs with mythical representations and
with scenes of everyday activities such as
hunting, fishing, farming, and banqueting.
In the Hellenistic era, scenes and designs
represented in mosaics were probably imitations of lost monumental paintings. The
Romans decorated their villas with mosaic
floors and exquisite wall frescoes portraying
rituals, mythical scenes, landscapes, still-life
objects, and daily activities. The Romans
also introduced the technique known as
aerial perspective, in which colors and outlines of more distant objects are softened
and blurred in order to achieve a quasi-
three-dimensional effect.

Early Christian art dates from the 3rd and
4th centuries, consisting of fresco paintings
in the Roman catacombs and mosaics on the
walls of churches. Religious themes were
also typical of Byzantine art, associated with
the imperial Christian court of Constantinople, which survived from 330 to 1453. In the
Gothic period, from the latter part of the
12th century to the beginning of the Italian
Renaissance, artists established workshops
in Paris and other major centers, producing
elaborate works for aristocratic patrons.
Portraits of common subjects also survive
from this period, notably in Italy. A merging
of the artistic traditions of northern Europe
and Italy took place at the beginning of the
15th century, leading to a style of painting
that paid great attention to realistic detail.
The Italian painter Giotto (1267?–1337) was
among the first to depict human expression

and movement in a visually authentic way. The development of the principles of linear *perspective various architects and sculptors early in the 15th-century enabled painters to achieve the illusion of three-dimensional shapes. Innovations were also made in the depiction of human anatomy and in the use of new media, with oil painting competing with the general use of the fresco technique. The masters of the High Renaissance were Leonardo da Vinci (1452–1519), Raphael (1483–1520), Michelangelo (1475–1564), and Titian (1488?–1576). One of the most important 15th-century painters outside Italy was the Flemish Jan van Eyck (1390?–1441).

The late 16th and 17th centuries saw the emergence of *chiaroscuro techniques (contrasts of light and shadow). For instance, Peter Paul Rubens (1577–1640), the Flemish *baroque master, used chiaroscuro to dramatize his subjects. The greatest acclaimed painter of the era was the Dutchman Rembrandt (1606–69), whose works are, arguably, unmatched in how they portray subtle human emotions. In the 18th century, so-called *rococo style was, in many respects, a continuation of the baroque *chiaroscuro, particularly in its use of light and shadow. But rococo art was much more graceful in its subtle portraitures. In the latter part of the century, a classical revival in the arts, known as *neoclassicism*, emerged that stressed form and a clean classical approach to representation.

The 19th century saw romanticism imbue all forms of artistic expression. In painting Eugène Delacroix (1798–1863) introduced a divided-color technique (color applied in small strokes of pure pigment) that influenced the impressionists later in the century. Édouard Manet (1832–83), for instance, flattened his figures, thus neutralizing their emotional expressions. Edgar Degas (1834–1917) painted subjects in graceful movement, as though caught by a camera. Pierre Auguste Renoir (1841–1919) produced a

great number of portraits of female nudes. And Paul Cézanne (1839–1906) brought out the recurrent features of nature through suffused color images. Francisco Goya (1746–1828), Spain's foremost painter, went somewhat against the impressionist grain, producing works of great psychological acumen emphasizing the triteness of his subjects. The break from *impressionism, however, came in the work of the Dutch-born Vincent van Gogh (1853–90) and the French artists Paul Gauguin (1848–1903) and Henri de Toulouse-Lautrec (1864–1901). Van Gogh used pure color applied thickly in flickering strokes, conveying intense emotional expression; Gauguin used distortions of line and color to make symbolic allusions; Toulouse-Lautrec painted common folk – cabaret singers, dance-hall performers, and prostitutes – symbolizing the social decay of Paris.

The 20th century witnessed many artistic movements and styles. Early in the century, some visual artists became interested in aboriginal art. Henri Matisse (1869–1954), a leader of this movement, known as *fauvism, produced alluring images of indigenous dancers. Other painters, known as expressionists (see *expressionism), wanted art to record human emotions on canvas through the act of painting itself, rather than through the faithful representation of reality. Well-known expressionists include Wassily Kandinsky (1866–1944) and Paul Klee (1879–1940). A third movement, the cubist (see *cubism) style, developed by Pablo Picasso (1881–1973) and Georges Braque (1882–1963) between 1907 and 1914, rejected traditional perspective and representational fidelity even more than did expressionism. The cubists reduced natural forms to geometric structures, usually rendered as a set of cubes. During the First World War a group of war resisters in Zürich, disgusted with bourgeois values, chose a nonsense word, *dada (French for 'hobbyhorse'), to describe the art they created in defiance of traditional aesthetic forms and techniques. Marcel Duchamp (1887–1968), for instance, reproduced Leonardo da Vinci's famous portrait, La gioconda (Mona Lisa), adding a mustache and goatee to the female subject's face. Dada methods were adopted by their successors, the surrealists (see *surrealism), who emphasized the role of dreams in artistic creation. The most important surrealists were Salvador Dalí (1904–89) and René Magritte (1898–1967).

After the Second World War, the *pop art and *minimalist movements came to the forefront. Pop artists drew their subjects from advertising billboards, movies, comic strips, and ordinary, everyday objects. The major figure in this movement was Andy Warhol (1928?–87). Minimalists reduced painting to the use of simple geometric forms, patterns, and single colors. In the 1980s and 1990s a number of young European and American artists rebelled against such movements, returning to a more representational, realistic form of painting called neo-expressionism.

art, postmodern
[see also *architecture, postmodern]
Art movement that crystallized in the latter part of the 20th century, utilizing mainly parody to unmask the hidden assumptions and ideologies in traditional verbal and art forms.

Illustration: Godfrey Reggio's film Koyaanisqatsi is considered both a classic example of postmodern technique in cinema art and a scathing parody of industrialized, commercialized society. It is a film without words that unfolds through a series of discontinuous, narrativeless images, parodying documentary-style films and TV programs. Through a constantly changing camera angle, the industrialized world is captured in terms of contrasting images of cars on freeways, atomic bomb blasts, litter on urban streets, people shopping in malls, housing complexes, buildings being demolished, etc. To emphasize the insanity and absurdity of this world Reggio blends the mesmerizing music of Philip Glass (1937–) into his imagery. Indeed, the music acts as a guide to understanding the images, interpreting them totally. The senselessness of human actions in such a world is thus captured not only in jarring images but also in the contrasting melodies and rhythms of Glass's music, which assaults the senses.

art deco
[< Latin ARS 'joining, fitting together' + DECUS 'ornament']
Design style popular in the 1920s and 1930s (used primarily in furniture, jewelry, textiles, and interior design) whose streamlined forms conveyed a sense of elegance and sophistication.

Note: Although the art deco movement began about 1910, the term was not used until 1925, when it was coined from the title of a Paris design exhibition, Exposition Internationale des Arts Décoratifs et Industriels Modernes. Primary examples of art deco in the United States are the interior of Radio City Music Hall (1931) and the Chrysler Building (1930), with its sleek aluminum façades and pointed spire, both in New York City.

art film
[< Latin ARS 'joining, fitting together']
Film designed as a serious experimental artistic work, not for mass appeal.

article
[< Latin ARTICULUS 'part']
Part of speech used in association with a *noun, indicating that it refers either to something in general (indefinite article) or to something specific (definite article).

Illustrations: 1. a boy (= any boy in general); 2. the boy (= a specific boy).

articulation

[< Latin ARTICULARE 'to utter distinctly']
Moving and positioning of the vocal organs
(mouth, tongue, etc.) in order to produce
speech sounds.

articulatory phonetics

[< Latin ARTICULARE 'to utter distinctly';
PHONĒ 'sound']
[see also *acoustic phonetics]
Branch of *phonetics documenting, describing, and studying how language sounds are
produced by the vocal organs.

Illustration: Articulatory phonetics provides
a consistent system of symbols for representing speech sounds accurately and unambiguously, in contrast to *alphabet
characters, which do not always provide a
guide to actual pronunciation. For instance,
in English the [f] sound in *fish, philosophy,*
and *enough* is represented by three different
orthographic characters: by *f, ph,* and *gh*
respectively.

The [f] symbol used in phonetics (placed
between square brackets) stands for the
sound formed: 1. by the lower lip touching
the upper teeth; 2. as the airstream emanating from the lungs is expelled in a con-
stricted fashion through the mouth; 3. with
no vibration of the vocal cords (in the larynx). Phoneticians refer to articulatory feature 1. as *voiceless,* 2. as *interdental,* and 3. as
fricative. Thus, the [f]-sound is known more
precisely as a *voiceless interdental fricative.*

artifact

[< Latin ARS 'joining, fitting together' +
FACTUM 'thing made']
Object produced or shaped by human craft,
such as a weapon, a vase, a tool, a piece of
jewelry, etc.

Note: Artifacts provide valuable clues for
reconstructing extinct cultures or earlier
epochs in a culture's evolution. The artifacts found at a site are the *signifiers that
help archeologists recreate the cultural

*signifieds (patterns of meanings) of the
group. In a fundamental sense, a culture is a
'museum of the artifacts' it has produced
over time.

The Canadian communication theorist
Marshall *McLuhan viewed artifacts as
extensions of human limbs, organs, and
bodily processes. He saw bicycles and cars,
for instance, as extending the human foot,
weapons the hands, nails, and teeth, clocks
the body's internal rhythms, houses the
body's heat-control system, clothing the
skin, computers the central nervous system,
and so on.

artifactual medium

[see *medium, artifactual]

artificial intelligence

[< Latin ARTIFICIUM 'craft'; INTELLIGERE 'to
perceive, understand']
Branch of computer science concerned with
the development of *hardware and *software capable of imitating, or actually performing, human mental activities
(problem-solving, inferencing, speaking,
etc.).

Note: Artificial Intelligence (AI) research and
theories constitute attempts to explain how
the human brain functions. This has led to
some interesting ideas, but by and large AI
research has not produced any real findings
about what brains are capable of doing.
Work on developing programs that enable a
computer to understand written or spoken
language, for instance, has shown that
whereas the logic of language structure is
easily programmable, the problem of meaning may lie beyond the capacity of AI systems to encode. Nevertheless, some AI
researchers believe that *parallel processing –*
interlinked and concurrent computer operations – might some day lead to the development of true AI. Others believe that creating
networks of experimental computer chips,
called *silicon neurons,* will eventually allow

computers to mimic with a high degree of fidelity the data-processing functions of brain cells. Using analog technology, the transistors in these chips emulate nerve-cell membranes in order to operate at the speed of neurons.

art nouveau
[French for 'new art']
Style of painting of the late 19th and early 20th centuries, characterized primarily by the depiction of leaves and flowers in flowing, sinuous lines.

Note: The earliest examples of art nouveau are usually considered to be a chair designed in 1882 and an engraved frontispiece for an 1883 book (*Wren's Early Churches*) by English architect Arthur Mackmurdo. The illustrations of Aubrey Beardsley (1872–98) are considered to be the greatest examples of this style. In the 20th century, the art nouveau style became fashionable in interior decor and in magazine illustrations.

art therapy
[< Latin ARS 'joining, fitting together']
View of some psychoanalysts, including Sigmund *Freud, that drawing permits individuals with inner conflicts to resolve their unconscious conflicts by painting.

aspect
[< Latin AD 'to, at' + SPECERE 'to look']
Temporal modality of *verbs by which an action is conveyed as being either completed or uncompleted, repeated, or habitual.

Illustrations: 1. *I always used to watch cartoons when I was young* (= repeated action). 2. *I watched that cartoon only once in my life* (= completed action).

assembly language
[< Latin AD 'to' + SIMUL 'together']
Computer *programming language consisting of commands that have been made easy on purpose for programmers to understand and use with facility.

association
[< Latin AD 'to' + SOCIARE 'unite with]
1. connection made in the mind between two (or more) ideas, sensations, memories, etc.; 2. psychological theory positing that concepts are formed on the basis of one thought leading to another felt to be connected with it in some perceivable way.

Illustrations: 1. *Light* is associated with *clarity of mind*. 2. An *alarm sound* is associated with *danger*.

Note: The idea of associative thinking was first proposed by the English philosopher John *Locke and later expanded by David *Hume. This idea was accepted implicitly by the early psychoanalysts who saw, however, that unconscious associations can also be the result of repressions of various kinds. From the 1920s to the late 1960s, behaviorist psychologists used association theory as the primary framework for explaining how human beings acquire language, knowledge, and mental skills of various kinds.

assonance
[< Latin AD 'to' + SONARE ' to sound']
Resemblance of sound, especially of the vowels in words.

Illustrations: 1. 'gong-tormented sea' (William Butler Yeats); 2. 'tilting windmills'; 3. 'late-mate.'

atonality
[see *music]

auditory image
[see *image, mental]

auditory phonetics
[see also *acoustic phonetics; *articulatory phonetics]
Branch of *phonetics studying how speech sounds are perceived by the human ear.

Augustine, St

[AD 354–430]

Philosopher and religious thinker who was among the first to distinguish clearly between *natural* and *conventional* *signs and to espouse the view that there is a crucial interpretive component to the whole process of understanding what a sign means. A natural sign is one produced by natural sources (e.g., a bodily symptom); a conventional sign, by contrast, is one made by people and put into circulation by convention (e.g. a word).

Austin, John L.

[1911–60]

[see also *analytic philosophy]

British philosopher noted for his analysis of *speech acts. Austin viewed the fundamental task of philosophy to be that of analyzing and explicating the complexity of ordinary language.

Australopithecus afarensis

Genus of *Homo* discovered at a number of sites in eastern and southern Africa, dating from more than 4 million years ago.

auteur

[French for 'author']

Filmmaker or director who exercises complete creative control over the entire production of a film or play, and who usually has a strong personal style.

author

[< Latin AUCTOR 'creator']

[see also *reader]

Creator of a book, poem, play, etc.

Note: Traditional literary analysis attempts to figure out what the author of a work intended. More recently, however, the meaning of a work is seen to inhere in an interplay between authorial intent and the reader's interpretation.

authoring language

[< Latin AUCTOR 'creator']

Computer language or application system designed primarily for creating programs, databases, and materials for computer-aided instruction.

autobiography

[< Greek AUTOS 'self' + BIOS 'life' + GRAPHEIN 'to write']

[also called *memoirs; see also *biography]

Art or practice of writing one's own biography. British Romantic poet Robert Southey (1774–1843) is considered to be the one who coined this term in 1809.

automata theory

[< Greek AUTOMATOS 'self-thinking'; Greek THEORIA 'a looking at']

1. study of computing processes; 2. study of the relationship between psychological theories of the human mind and the operation of automated devices.

auxiliary verb

[< Latin AUXILIARIS 'helpful']

Verb, such as *have*, *can*, or *will*, accompanying the main verb in a clause, serving to signal distinctions in aspect, tense, etc.

Illustrations: 1. I have eaten already. 2. She may come tomorrow. 3. I will do it later.

axiom

[< Greek AXIOMA 'authority, authoritative sentence']

Statement, rule, notion universally accepted as necessarily true and, therefore, embraced without proof.

Illustrations: 1. Two straight lines meet at only one point (= axiom of geometry). 2. Two consecutive integers differ by 1 and only 1 (= axiom of arithmetic).

Note: Every scientific enterprise is constructed on the basis of axioms. This is the primary criterion for distinguishing a scientific enterprise from a nonscientific one, as established by the ancient Greeks, most probably during the 5th century BC. The axioms of any science must be consistent with one another and few in number.

B

Babbage, Charles
[1792–1871]
British mathematician who designed the *analytical engine, a machine capable of elementary logical operations, and whose principles of construction foreshadowed those of the modern computer. Babbage's book *Economy of Machines and Manufactures* (1832) initiated the field of study known today as *operational research*.

back formation
Word created by the removal of an *affix or some other part from an already existing word.

Illustrations: 1. *vacuum clean* from *vacuum cleaner*; 2. *pea* from the earlier English plural *pease*.

background
[see also *foreground]
1. part of a scene or picture that appears, to the eye, towards the back of the scene; 2. in grammatical theory, the mental image that appears, to the mental eye, towards the back of the scene.

Illustration: In the active sentence *Alexander ate the apple*, the subject (*Alexander*) is in the conceptual *foreground*, while the object (*apple*) is in the conceptual *background*. The action implied by the verb (*eating*) is imagined as an activity that occurs *from* the subject *towards* the apple. However, a change from active to passive, *The apple was eaten by Alexander*, changes the position of the foreground and the background to the mind's eye. The passive form brings the *apple* to the foreground, relegating the eater, *Alexander*, to the background. The action of eating is now seen to take place on the object, the 'receiver' of the action. In effect, passive sentences provide a different conceptual angle from which to view the same action.

Bacon, Francis
[1561–1626]
English philosopher who criticized classical *syllogistic reasoning as the basis for discovering physical laws. Bacon called for a scientific method based instead on observation, experimentation, and induction.

badge
*Emblem worn as an indication of rank, office, or membership in an organization.

Bakhtin, Mikhail
[1895–1975]
Russian philosopher and literary theorist who claimed that communication was not merely an exchange of information, but rather, an ongoing negotiation between interlocutors.

ballad
[< French BALLADE 'dancing song']
1. narrative poem, often of folk origin, consisting of simple *stanzas and usually having a recurrent *refrain; 2. popular song, especially of a romantic or sentimental nature.

ballet
[< Italian BALLETTO 'a little dance']
1. artistic dance form based on elaborate standardized techniques; 2. theatrical presentation of dancing based on a story, idea, or mood, usually with costumes, scenery, and musical accompaniment.

Note: The basis of ballet is a turned-out position of the legs and feet with certain juxtapositions of the arms, head, and torso producing a visually harmonious effect. A ballet may be choreographed either to music especially composed for it, or to already existing music. The plot of the ballet is called its *libretto* or *scenario*. Plotless ballets also exist. These are intended to create a mood, interpret a musical composition through bodily movement, or celebrate dancing for its own sake.

Early precursors of ballet were the lavish court dances of Renaissance Italy. The first ballet for which a complete score has survived was performed in Paris in 1581. Court ballet reached its peak during the reign of Louis XIV (1643–1715), whose nickname 'the Sun King' was derived from a role he danced in a ballet. Many ballets presented at his court were created by Italian-French composer Jean Baptiste Lully (1632–87) and French choreographer Pierre Beauchamp, who is said to have defined the basic positions of the feet in classical ballet. In 1661 Louis established the Académie Royale de Danse, a professional organization for dancing masters.

The ballet *La Sylphide*, to music by Frédéric Chopin (1810–49), and first performed in Paris in 1832, marked the beginning of romantic ballet, inspiring many changes in choreography, style, technique, and costume, which are in place to this day. In the 1920s and 1930s popular dance forms, such as jazz and folk, enriched ballet art. Two great American companies were founded in New York City in the 1940s, the American Ballet Theater and the New York City Ballet. Since the mid-20th century, ballet companies have been founded in many cities throughout North America. Beginning in 1956, famous Russian ballet companies, such as the Bolshoi Ballet and the Petersburg Kirov Ballet, began performing in the West.

balloon
[< French BALLON 'large ball']
In the art of *comics, the figure containing words which issue from the mouth or head of the character speaking; the figure is called a balloon because it resembles one.

baroque
[< Portuguese BARROCO 'imperfect pearl']
Art style that began in Europe around 1550 and lasted until around 1750, emphasizing refined ornamentation and an overall balance of disparate parts.

Note: Manifestations of baroque art appear in virtually every country in Europe, with other important centers in the Spanish and Portuguese settlements in the Americas. Perhaps the best-known baroque artist of all time is the German composer Johann Sebastian Bach (1685–1750), one of the greatest and most productive geniuses in the history of Western music. Bach was the supreme master of counterpoint, setting, moreover, the stage for the development of classical harmony in Western music.

Barthes, Roland
[1915–80]
French semiotician who claimed that systems of representation are largely based on concepts (see *myth) that manifest themselves in the content of everyday discourses, spectacles, performances, and commonsensical notions. Barthes studied popular culture extensively, demonstrating how common conversations, performances, and spectacles recall the ancient myths through *connotation. Recreational wrestling, for instance, is far from being just a sport, Barthes emphasized. Rather, it is a complex spectacle grafted from the mythic connotations associated with the bodily shapes, facial expressions, excessive gestures, and speech of the wrestlers. Taking his cue from *Hjelmslev, Barthes argued that connotation is the operative principle in all forms of cultural meaning-making.

Barthes is also associated with the so-called New Criticism, a literary movement in Europe and the United States, prominent after the Second World War, which emphasized interpreting the written text in itself, apart from considerations of a biographical, cultural, or historical nature.

BASIC
[acronym for 'Beginner's All-purpose Symbolic Instruction Code']
High-level programming language developed in the mid-1960s, becoming the first widely used programming language of microcomputers. BASIC is often taught to beginning programmers because it is easy to use and understand, while containing the same major concepts as many more complicated languages.

basic concept
[see *concept, basic]

bas-relief
[French 'low relief']
Sculptural relief that juts out only slightly from the background.

bathos
[< Greek BATHOS 'depth']
[see also *anticlimax]
Abrupt change from the lofty to the trivial in speech, producing a ludicrous effect.

Illustrations: 1. 'Life is sublime, living is the dumps.' 2. 'Today, I saw a red-and-yellow sunset and thought, How insignificant I am! Of course, I thought that yesterday, too, and it rained' (Woody Allen). 3. 'I don't know if there's an afterlife, but I'm taking a change of underwear' (ibid.).

Baudrillard, Jean
[1929–]
French sociologist well known for his studies of cultural image-making. Among Baudrillard's many interesting ideas, perhaps the one most discussed is that in consumerist societies a product is made not only to fulfill a need but, more often than not, to create it.

Bauhaus School
[< German BAUEN 'to build' + HAUS 'a house']
[see also *architecture; *modernism]
Architectural school, also known as *international style* or *modernism*, founded in Weimar, in 1919, by Walter Gropius (1883–1969), promoting a simple, unadorned style of building design.

Note: The Bauhaus School profoundly influenced 20th-century art and architecture by emphasizing that these must meet society's basic needs, and by insisting that there should be no distinction between the fine arts and the practical crafts. By 1933, its principles were known and discussed worldwide. Many of its followers immigrated to the United States, where the Bauhaus view dominated art and architecture for decades, and strongly contributed to the design of American skyscrapers.

Baumgarten, Alexander Gottlieb
[1714–62]
German philosopher who approached the question of beauty in art systematically, defining the *aesthetic experience of art as the recognition of perfection (an innate quality of the mind). Baumgartner coined the term *aesthetic theory* in his two-volume work *Esthetics* (1750, 1758). His other works include *Ethics* (1740), *Natural Law* (1765), and *General Philosophy* (1770).

beat generation
Term referring to certain American writers, including Jack Kerouac (1922–69), Allen Ginsberg (1926–97), William S. Burroughs (1914–), and Lawrence Ferlinghetti (1919–), whose unconventional work and lifestyle in the 1950s denounced the society of their era. Beat poetry in particular was characterized by a raw and improvisational quality, and dealt often with the themes of drugs, sex, and mysticism. The movement was centered in San Francisco and New York's Greenwich Village, and it revolved around poetry read-

ings and jazz performances, particularly in coffee shops.

beat gesture
[< Latin GERERE 'to bear, carry']
Hand gesture accompanying discourse, resembling the 'beating' of musical tempo.

Note: The execution of this type of gesture consists in the speaker's hand moving along with the rhythmic pulsation of speech, in the form of a simple flick of the hand or of the speaker's fingers moving up and down, or back and forth. Beat gestures are *indexes, marking the introduction of new themes, characters, etc., or summarizing the action during discourse.

beaux arts
[French for 'fine arts']
[see *fine arts]

behaviorism
[term coined in 1913 by John B. *Watson]
School of psychology based on the view that observable and quantifiable behavior provides the only valid data for psychologists to study.

Note: Behaviorism became the main school of psychology from 1913, when psychologists started investigating complex forms of behavior by measuring and analyzing the responses of human subjects to various stimuli. While the behaviorists did not deny the existence of inner experiences, such as feelings, they maintained that these could not be studied meaningfully, because they were not directly observable.

The key notion of behaviorism is that of the 'conditioned response,' which was developed initially by the Russian psychologist Ivan *Pavlov in 1904. When Pavlov presented a meat stimulus to a hungry dog, the animal would salivate spontaneously, as expected. This was the dog's 'unconditioned response.' Then, after Pavlov rang a

bell while presenting the meat stimulus a number of times, he found that the dog would eventually salivate only to the ringing bell, without the meat stimulus. Clearly, the ringing, which would not have triggered the salivation initially, had brought about a 'conditioned response' in the dog. Shortly thereafter, John B. Watson proposed that human conditioning could be studied with virtually the same type of laboratory procedure. In Watson's view, all complex forms of behavior – such as emotions and habits – were ultimately decomposable into simple muscular and glandular processes and could thus be observed and measured directly. In the mid-20th century American behaviorist B.F. *Skinner maintained that inner processes, such as feelings, should also be studied by the usual laboratory methods, with particular emphasis on controlled experimentation.

Starting in the late 1960s, behaviorism fell into disfavor among most psychologists. At best, today it is seen as explaining only certain types of behaviors and is thus viewed as part of a more comprehensive theory of human mentality.

Benedict, Ruth
[1887–1948]
American anthropologist, student of Franz *Boas, who pioneered research on Native American tribes during the 1920s and 1930s. On the basis of her research, Benedict maintained that every culture developed its own particular moral and lifestyle systems that largely determined the choices individuals reared in a specific culture made throughout their lives.

Benveniste, Emile
[1902–76]
French linguist who claimed that language cannot be studied apart from how it is put to use in daily life. Benveniste thus emphasized the study of *parole (language as it is

used) in order to understand how the system of *langue* (the grammar) is constructed in the native speaker's mind.

Bergson, Henri
[1859–1941]
French philosopher who was largely interested in the role of intuition as a means of attaining knowledge. Bergson rejected logical reasoning in favor of intuitive artistic expression – which he saw as the apprehension of reality unmediated by rational thought – as the primary means for coming to grips with the mysteries of life. *Laughter* (1900), an essay on the nature of comedy, is probably his most quoted work.

Berkeley, George
[1685–1753]
Irish prelate and philosopher who argued against the materialism of Thomas *Hobbes, casting doubts on Hobbes's claim the world could be known objectively through logical reasoning. Berkeley held that matter cannot exist independently of the mind and that sensory perception can be explained only by supposing a deity who continually evokes understanding in the human mind.

Bettelheim, Bruno
[1903–90]
Austrian-born American psychologist noted for his studies of children and education. Bettelheim contributed significantly to the study of the nature of autism in children. He also analyzed the human passion for fairy tales, arguing that this form of narrative was universal and, thus, that its categories (characters, plots, etc.) were archetypal in nature.

bibliography
[< Greek BIBLION 'book' + GRAPHEIN 'to write']
1. list of writings pertinent to a given subject; 2. description and identification of the editions, dates of issue, and authorship of books or other written texts.

Note: The British Library's *General Catalogue of Printed Books* and the catalogs of the Bibliothèque Nationale in Paris and the Library of Congress in Washington, DC, are widely used bibliographical sources. Information on the books put out by publishers is provided by trade bibliographies, which appear at regular intervals. In the United States these include *Publishers Weekly*, which first appeared in 1872, and *Books in Print*, which was first published in 1948. Standardization of bibliographical methods is promoted by such organizations as the International Federation for Documentation and the American Documentation Institute.

Bildungsroman
[< German BILDUNG 'formation' + French ROMAN 'a story in the vernacular']
Novel whose principal plot is the moral, psychological, and intellectual development of a youthful main character.

Illustrations: 1. *The Sorrows of Young Werther* (1774) by Johann Wolfgang von Goethe (1749–1832); 2. *Siddhartha* (1922) by Hermann Hesse (1877–1962).

binarism
[< Latin BINARIUS 'two by two']
View that two forms or *signs are kept recognizably distinct by the presence of a minimal difference between them.

Illustration: The forms *pin* and *bin* are recognizably distinct signs because of the difference between initial /p/ and /b/: the former is a *voiceless* consonant (produced without vibration of the vocal cords); the latter a corresponding *voiced* consonant (produced with the vibration of the vocal cords). This minimal, or *binary*, difference is what keeps the two words perceptibly distinct from one another.

binary feature
[< Latin BINARIUS 'two by two']
Feature that is marked as being present [+]

or absent [–] in the constitution of a sound, a word, etc.

Illustrations: 1. The difference between *boy* and *boys* is signaled by the binary feature [±singular]: *boy* is marked as [+singular] and *boys* as [–singular]. 2. The difference between *sip* and *zip* is signaled by the binary feature [±voice] (which refers to the vibration of the vocal cords in the articulation of a sound): *s* is marked as [–voice] and *z* as [+voice].

binit
[see *bit]

biography
[< Greek BIOS 'life' + GRAPHEIN 'to write']
1. written historical account of an individual's life, considered as a literary genre; 2. account of a person's life, as told by another.

Note: The penchant for writing biographies of famous historical personages is as old as recorded history. Rulers of the ancient world had their deeds recorded by biographers, so as to perpetuate their memory beyond the grave. Perhaps the best known ancient biographical work is the *Parallel Lives* by Plutarch (AD 46?–120?) – a collection of biographical sketches of legendary personages. Shakespeare drew from the Lives for his plays based on Roman history (*Coriolanus, Julius Caesar, Antony and Cleopatra*).

Until the middle of the 17th century, written biography was generally commemorative in Western society, condemning malefactors and tyrants, exalting heroes and heroines. In 1560 the Italian artist Giorgio Vasari (1511–74) published his *Lives of the Artists*, which reflected a new spirit of humanism and the idea that each individual life, not just the lives of heroes or public figures, had intrinsic worth. In 1640, Izaak Walton (1593–1683) published his *Life of Donne*, a biography of English poet John Donne. Over the next 25 years, it was revised and developed by its author, becoming a prototype for modern biographical writing.

The first modern biography is considered to be *The Life of Samuel Johnson* (1791) by James Boswell (1740–95). Since then, many significant biographies have appeared, becoming staples of literary tradition, such as the *Life of Sir Walter Scott* (7 volumes, 1837–8) by John Gibson Lockhart (1794–1854). In the 20th century biography retained its broad appeal as various literary fashions came and went. People's fascination with the lives of media personalities and historical figures alike was satisfied in the late 20th century by the television medium, as programs such as *Biography* on the Arts and Entertainment channel became a staple of television programming in the 1990s.

Among famous 20th-century biographical writers, the Frenchman André Maurois (1885–1967) and the Austrian Stefan Zweig (1881–1942) are perhaps the best known. Maurois's *Life of Shelley* (1923) made popular the romanticized biography, a form written in an engaging popular style, relying more on imaginative interpretation than on scholarly originality. Zweig's *Three Masters* (1920), a collection of biographical sketches of Honoré de Balzac, Charles Dickens, and Fyodor Dostoyevsky started the trend in literary criticism of evaluating the artist's work against the background of his/her life experiences.

biological anthropology
[see *anthropology, biological]

biosemiosis
[< Greek BIOS 'life' + SEMEION 'mark, sign']
[see also *anthroposemiosis; *zoosemiosis]
Term referring to *semiosis (the production and comprehension of *signs) in all living things.

biosemiotics

[< Greek BIOS 'life + SEMEION 'mark, sign']
Study of *semiosis (the capacity to produce
and comprehend *signs) in all living things,
from plants to human beings.

Note: Research in animal ethology has
shown how remarkably rich and varied
animal communication systems are. Scientists have recorded and identified, for instance, birdcalls for courting, mating,
hunger, food bearing, territoriality, warning,
and distress, and elaborate vocal signals
that whales and dolphins deploy to communicate over long distances underwater.
Biosemiotics aims to investigate such systems, seeking to understand how animals
are endowed by their nature with the capacity to use specific types of signals and signs
for survival (*zoosemiosis*), and thus how
human semiosis (*anthroposemiosis*) is both
linked to, and different from, animal
semiosis. As Thomas A. *Sebeok, a primary
figure in this movement, has emphasized,
the objective of biosemiotics is to distill
common elements of semiosis from its
manifestations across species, integrating
them into a taxonomy of notions, principles,
and procedures for understanding this phenomenon in its globality.

The study of animal communication
traces its roots to Darwinian evolutionary
biology, and especially to Darwin's contention that animal behavior constituted a
viable analogue for human mental functioning. So, by the end of the 19th century,
Darwinian-inspired work led to the establishment of comparative animal psychology.
Some of the early animal experiments in this
field led to the theory of classical conditioning in humans. The Russian psychologist
Ivan *Pavlov, for instance, rang a bell while
he presented meat to a dog. Initially, only
the meat stimulus evoked an instinctive
salivation response in the dog. However,
after repeated bell ringings, Pavlov found
that the bell alone would evoke salivation.

The dog had obviously been 'conditioned'
to associate the sound of the bell to the presence of meat. It was then claimed that humans too learned in a similar way. Work on
animal intelligence was pursued with great
fervor during the first quarter of the 20th
century. Robert Yerkes, for instance, succeeded in showing in 1916 that monkeys
and apes had the capacity to transfer their
conditioned responses to novel learning
tasks. And in 1925 Wolfgang Köhler showed
that apes could achieve spontaneous solutions to problems without previous training.

The goal of early comparative psychology
was not, however, to study animal behavior
in itself, but to generalize findings from the
animal experiments to human learning. The
assumption was that the same laws of learning applied across all species and, therefore,
that universal principles of learning and
problem solving could be deduced from
animal behavior. By the mid-20th century,
the use of animals as convenient substitutes
for people in the laboratory came under
attack and a new movement emerged,
known as *ethology*, which stressed that animals and people live in separate worlds,
and that animals should be studied within
their natural habitats.

Soon after, linguists and semioticians
came to regard the study of animal communication as particularly relevant to their
own fields of inquiry. In 1960 the linguist
Charles Hockett proposed a typology for
comparing animal and human communication systems that became widely used. Since
the 1960s, a slew of widely popularized,
and still ongoing, primate language experiments have caught the attention of scientists
and the general public alike. These have
been motivated by the proposition that
interspecies communication is a realizable
goal. Since gorillas and chimpanzees are
incapable of vocal speech because they lack
the requisite articulatory organs, the first
experimenters chose American Sign Lan-

guage as the code for teaching them human language. One of the first subjects was a female chimpanzee named Washoe, whose training by the Gardner husband and wife team began in 1966 when she was almost one year old. Remarkably, Washoe learned to use 132 signs in just over four years. What appeared to be even more remarkable was that Washoe began to put signs together to express a small set of relations.

Inspired by the results obtained by the Gardners, others embarked upon an intensive research program that is still ongoing. However, there really has emerged no solid evidence to suggest that chimpanzees and gorillas are capable of verbal behavior *in the same way* that humans are, nor of passing on to their offspring what they have learned from their human mentors. Like the comparative psychologists of a previous era, these experimenters have failed to accept the probable fact that human verbal semiosis is species-specific.

Biosemiotics takes its impetus from the work of the biologist Jakob von *Uexküll, who provided empirical evidence at the start of the 20th century to show that an organism does not perceive an object in itself, but according to its own particular kind of innate *modeling system. While the study of primate communication in itself remains a fascinating biosemiotic area of investigation, the question biosemioticians ask is not whether primates can speak like humans, but rather what modeling systems they share (if any) with humans. It is more likely that certain properties or features of semiosis cut across species, while others are specific to one or several species. Determining the universality or specificity of particular semiosic and modeling properties is a much more realizable goal.

biosphere

[< Greek BIOS 'life' + SPHAIRA 'sphere']
[see also *semiosphere]
Environment or habitat to which a species has become adapted. Large-scale divisions of the biosphere into regions of different growth patterns are called *biomes*.

bipedalism

[< Latin BI 'two' + PES 'foot']
Adaptation to a completely erect posture and a two-footed striding walk.

Note: Bipedalism is one of the earliest of the major hominid traits to have evolved, distinguishing the species *Homo* from its nearest primate relatives – gorillas, chimpanzees, and orangutans. Almost all other mammals stand, walk, and/or run on four limbs. Those standing on two have quite different postures and gaits from humans – kangaroos hop on their two feet; some monkeys may only on occasion walk bipedally, especially when carrying food; chimpanzees are capable of brief bipedal walks, but their usual means of locomotion is knuckle-walking, standing on their hind legs but stooping forward and resting their hands on the knuckles rather than on the palms or fingers. The uniquely S-shaped spinal column of humans places the center of gravity of the body directly over the area of support provided by the feet, thus giving stability and balance in the upright position.

birth and rebirth myth

[see *mythology]

bit

[abbreviation of binit = abbrev. of *binary digit*]
Unit of information content defined as the value n in the probability quotient $1/2^n$ specifying any outcome: an outcome with a probability of $1/2$ ($= 1/2^1$) carries *one bit* of information (because $n = 1$); an outcome with a probability of $1/4$ ($= 1/2^2$) carries *two bits* of information (because $n = 2$); an outcome with a probability of $1/8$ ($= 1/2^3$) carries *three bits* of information (because $n = 3$); and so on.

Illustration: If one were to toss a coin three times the possible eight outcomes would be (T = tail, H = head) 1. TTT, 2. THT, 3. THH, 4. TTH, 5. HHH, 6. HTH, 7. HTT, 8. HHT. The probability of one outcome, say TTT or HHH, is $1/8$ (= $1/2^3$, $n = 3$), and thus carries *three bits* of information.

Note: A bit is the smallest unit of information handled by a computer and is realized physically by a single pulse sent through a circuit or a small spot on a magnetic disk capable of storing either a 1 or a 0. Considered singly, bits convey little information a human would consider meaningful. In groups, however, bits become the familiar patterns used to represent all types of information.

BITNET
[acronym for 'Because It's Time Network']
Network connecting computers at universities, colleges, research institutions, secondary schools, and other institutions. BITNET was created in 1981 and is operated by the Corporation for Research and Educational Networking. It is used mainly as a news source of developments in academic research.

blazonry
[< French BLASON 'shield']
Heraldic practice, developed in tournaments during the Middle Ages, of blazoning ('blowing') a trumpet and then describing the *insignia of an unknown knight. From this practice the term blazonry came to designate the specific description of a coat of arms.

Bloomfield, Leonard
[1887–1949]
American linguist whose 1933 textbook, *Language*, bestowed systematicity and unity upon the study and practice of linguistics through its coherent synthesis of linguistic concepts and analytical techniques. Bloom-field was thus a key figure in providing a standard repertory of notions and procedures for carrying out detailed investigations and descriptive characterizations of specific languages.

Boas, Franz
[1858–1942]
American anthropologist who claimed that culture largely determined the ways in which individuals developed their personalities and their worldviews. Boas rejected the widely held 19th-century claim that cultures resulted from a natural evolutionary process, akin to *natural selection, arguing that the many differences found among peoples living in diverse cultures constitute solid evidence against a universal biological paradigm for culture. If anything, he retorted, the reverse was true – the emergence of culture as the distinguishing trait of the human species has become the primary 'reshaper' of human life.

body image
Subjective concept of one's physical appearance based on self-observation and the perceived reactions of others.

Note: Psychologists see body image as a key factor in imprinting one's personality. Having a 'poor body image' has been shown to lead to negative and injurious consequences. Anorexics, for instance, are thought to suffer distortions of body image, believing erroneously that their emaciated bodies are obese.

body language
[see also *kinesic code]
Bodily gestures, postures, and facial expressions by which a person communicates nonverbally with others.

book
Sheets bound together, containing verbal text, sometimes with illustrations.

Note: The forerunners of books were the *clay tablets* of ancient Mesopotamia and the *scrolls* of ancient Egypt, Greece, and Rome. Scrolls were strips of papyrus that were unrolled as they were read. Professional scribes reproduced works either by copying a work or by setting it down from dictation. Papyrus was brittle, and in damp climates it disintegrated in less than 100 years. By the 4th century AD, the rectangular *codex*, a ringed notebook consisting of two or more wooden tablets covered with wax, had replaced the scroll. In the early Middle Ages scribes in monasteries used quill pens to write out books. Books were thus few and costly, commissioned primarily by the literate aristocratic minority of the population.

The Chinese had invented printing from carved wood blocks in the 6th century AD. By the 11th century they had invented printing from movable type. In the 15th century Europeans learned about paper from the Islamic world, which had acquired it from China, inventing movable metal type independently – an invention usually credited to the German printer Johann Gutenberg (1400?-68?). The first major book printed was the Bible in 1456. Printing simplified book production, making it economically feasible. As a consequence, literacy among the general public increased greatly, especially since it was believed that every believer should read the Bible. From the Industrial Revolution onwards, book production has become highly mechanized and efficient.

Boole, George
[1815–64]
British mathematician and logician who developed an algebraic system, later known as *Boolean algebra*, after his name, that became central to the 20th-century study of pure mathematics and formal logic, and that contributed greatly to the design of modern computers. Boole believed that his system was capable of explaining human thought – a claim that has remained unsubstantiated.

borrowing
Process of taking a word or grammatical structure from another language for communicative purposes.

Illustrations: In English, abstract ideas expressed by nouns ending in *-tion* (*attention, education, nation*, etc.) have their roots in the Latin lexicon, as do most of the nouns ending in *-ty* (*morality, sobriety, triviality*, etc.). These were borrowed by speakers of English after the invasion and conquest of England by the Normans from northwestern France in 1066. Their French origin is no longer consciously recognized because they have become completely Anglicized in pronunciation and spelling. Among the words that English has borrowed from Italian in more recent times are *alarm, bandit, bankrupt, carnival, gazette, piano, sonnet, stucco, studio, umbrella, volcano, gusto* and *bravo*.

Borrowing is not limited to vocabulary. The English suffix *-er*, which is added to verbs to form nouns, as in the formation of *baker* from *bake*, is a borrowing of the Latin suffix *-arius*.

bound morpheme
[< Greek MORPHĒ 'form']
[see also *free morpheme]
*Morpheme (minimal meaningful unit in a language) that is attached to another morpheme.

Note: There are two main types of bound morphemes. 1. an *inflectional bound morpheme*, such as the verb form *learned*, which consists of the root *learn* plus the bound morpheme *-ed*, providing further information about the verb (namely that the action of learning has occurred in the past); 2. a *derivational bound morpheme*, such as the *-ly* in *cautiously* (= *cautious* + *-ly*), which changes the grammatical function of *cautious* from adjectival to adverbial.

bowdlerize

Process of eliminating from a novel, a poem, etc. whatever is deemed to be offensive.

Note: The word comes from the surname of Dr Thomas Bowdler (1754–1825), the English editor who, in 1818, published *The Family Shakespeare* from which he censored 'those words and expressions which cannot with propriety be read aloud in a family.'

brand image

[< Old English BRAND 'flame']
Creation of an 'image' or 'personality' for a product by giving it a catchy name, creating a specific logo for it, procuring a distinctive type of packaging for it (wherever applicable), and assigning it a particular kind of pricing (for a specific market segment).

brand name

[< Old English BRAND 'flame']
*Name given to a product in order to infuse it with a 'personality' with which certain consumers can identify.

Illustrations: 1. *Moondrops, Natural Wonder, Rainflower, Sunsilk, Skin Dew* (= names given to feminine cosmetic products designed to evoke connotations of natural beauty, cleanliness, sophistication); 2. *Eterna 27, Clinique, Endocil, Equalia* (= names given to feminine cosmetic products designed to given them an 'authoritative' personality); 3. *Brut, Cossak, Denim, Aramis, Devin* (= names given to men's cosmetic products designed to ascribe to them a 'virile' personality); 4. *Jaguar, Mustang, Triumph, Princess* (= names given to automobiles designed to give then a 'gendered' personality).

broadcasting

Transmission of a radio or television program for public use.

Note: After the First World War, the Westinghouse Electric Corporation established what many cultural historians consider to be the first commercially owned radio station to offer programming to the general public. Known as KDKA, it broadcast mainly variety and entertainment shows. Another early broadcaster was the American Telephone and Telegraph Company, which, in 1922, charged fees in return for airing commercial advertisements on its stations. Early radio broadcasting was dominated by adaptations of stage dramas redesigned for radio in the form of weekly action serials, situation comedies, and soap operas. Stage-based vaudeville routines provided the scripts for the comedy-variety programs, and daily newspapers provided the information for news coverage.

The earliest patent for an all-electronic television system in the United States was granted in 1927. As early as 1935, the BBC initiated experimental television broadcasts in London for several hours each day. The Radio Corporation of America (RCA) introduced television to the American public at the 1939 New York World's Fair, with live coverage of opening ceremonies. Immediately following the Second World War, the National Broadcasting Company (NBC), Columbia Broadcasting System (CBS), American Broadcasting Company (ABC), and DuMont Television Network (which went out of business in 1955) made extensive television broadcasting a reality. By the mid-1950s NBC, CBS, and ABC – collectively known as the Big Three – had successfully secured American network television as their exclusive domain. In the mid-1980s the Fox television network also went on the air. Before cable television ended channel scarcity in the 1980s, viewing choices were largely limited to the programming the networks provided.

Like radio broadcasting, most early television programming was based on material from other media, especially the stage and radio. The situation comedy, or sitcom, the series, the soap opera, and the news have proved to be the most durable and popular of American broadcasting genres.

The sitcom uses recurring characters and situations to explore life in the home and the workplace. The series genre has included the Western, the private-eye drama, and science-fiction. Soap opera was developed as a daytime serial genre aimed specifically at a female audience. Television news added images to the format used by radio newscasting.

In the United States *advertising agencies produce nearly all network shows. They use a ratings system to determine how many people they are reaching with their advertising. The Public Broadcasting Act of 1967 created a source of funding for noncommercial television stations and resulted in the formation of the Public Broadcasting Service (PBS). Public stations operate on contributions from viewers, corporate gifts, foundation grants, and support from the governmental agencies.

Canada has an elaborate and advanced physical structure for delivering radio and television programs comparable to that found in any other country in the world, and has been a pioneer in satellite communications. The national broadcasting service, the Canadian Broadcasting Corporation (CBC), distributes most of its programs nationally by satellites. The weak element in Canadian broadcasting lies not in the physical component but in the amount of original Canadian programming. The CBC produces a large number of radio and TV programs in English and French, but the private TV stations broadcasting in English have depended mostly on imported U.S. programs for prime time.

Broadcast systems continue to be developed. Direct Broadcast Satellite (DBS), for instance, now provides viewers with an antenna capable of bypassing closed-circuit systems to capture satellite signals. Most channels available from satellites require subscription fees and licenses.

Broca's area
[see also *wernicke's area]
Site in the left hemisphere of the brain responsible for the production and discrimination of vocal sounds.

Note: The discovery of this crucial linguistic neural area goes back to 1861 when the French anthropologist and surgeon Paul Broca (1824–80) noticed a destructive lesion in the left frontal lobe during the autopsy of a patient who had lost the ability to articulate words during his lifetime, even though he had not suffered any paralysis of his speech organs. Broca concluded that the capacity to articulate speech was traceable to that specific cerebral site – which shortly thereafter came to bear his name. Broca's discovery established a direct connection between a linguistic function and a specific area of the brain

Brunelleschi, Filippo
[1377–1446]
One of the inventors of perspective *painting, making him a key artistic figure in the transition of the visual arts from the Middle Ages to the modern era.

buffoonery
[< Italian BUFFONE 'jester']
Art of entertaining by means of jokes, funny antics, and ludicrous tricks.

bull's-eye model of communication
[see *information theory]

burlesque
[< Italian BURLA 'jest']
Comic performance characterized by ridiculous exaggeration.

Note: Burlesque first appeared in the plays of the Greek dramatists Aristophanes (448?–388? BC) and Euripides (480?–406 BC), and the Roman playwright Plautus (254?–184 BC). The playwright who made dramatic burlesque a high art form was the

17th-century Frenchman Molière (1622–73). There are two main forms of burlesque: 1. the *mock epic*, in which a trivial subject is treated majestically, and 2. the *travesty*, in which a serious subject is treated frivolously. In the United States, the word *burlesque* is applied to a form of theatrical production, especially popular in the 1920s and 1930s, characterized by ribald comedy and scantily clad women, and often including the striptease.

byte
[see also *computer memory]
Unit of computer information equal to 8 *bits.

Note: In computer processing and storage, it takes one byte of information to realize a single character, such as a letter, a numeral, or a punctuation mark. Measurements of computer memory and storage are usually given in *kilobytes* (= 2^{10} bytes) or *megabytes* (= 2^{20} bytes).

Byzantine style
Style of painting, architecture, and design that emerged in the 5th century AD in the Byzantine Empire, characterized by a high degree of formality, a frontal stylized presentation of figures, a rich use of color, and a focus on religious themes.

Note: Byzantine art originated in Constantinople (present-day Istanbul), which was previously the ancient Greek town of Byzantium, chosen as capital of the Eastern Roman Empire and renamed by the Roman emperor Constantine the Great. Byzantine art and architecture arose in response to the reverence that the Eastern Orthodox church had for religious icons. These were highly stylized and usually painted in a strictly frontal view on a small panel. Their abstract quality became the defining characteristic of the Byzantine style.

C

cacophony
[< Greek KAKOS 'bad, evil' + PHONĒ 'voice']
Use of harsh, jarring sounds to create a dissonant effect.

Illustrations: 1. *glitch* for *error*; 2. *cruddy* for *disgusting.*

cadence
[< Old Italian CADENZA 'a falling']
1. balanced, rhythmic flow in speech, poetry, or music; 2. falling inflection or modulation of the voice; 3. in music, the progression of chords moving to a harmonic close.

calligraphy
[< Greek KALLI 'beautiful' + GRAPHIA 'marks, writing']
Art of fine handwriting, in a specific type of script or alphabet.

calque
[< Italian CALCARE 'to press']
[also called loan translation]
Linguistic form literally translated into an equivalent form by a speaker of another language.

Illustration: 1. *superman* is a calque from German *Übermensch*: *Über* = 'super'; *mensch* = 'man'; 2. *masterpiece* is a calque from German *meisterstuck*: *meister* = 'master'; *stuck* = 'piece.'

cameo
[< Persian CHUMAHÄN 'agate']
1. medallion with a profile in it cut in raised relief; 2. brief, vivid portrayal or depiction (called a *literary cameo*); 3. brief but dramatic appearance of a prominent actor in a single scene (called a *cameo role*).

Campbell, Joseph
[1904–1987]
American writer and teacher, known for his

writings on *myth. Campbell was influenced by the ideas of psychoanalysts Sigmund *Freud and Carl *Jung, as well as by the novels of James Joyce (1882–1941) and Thomas Mann (1875–1955). He espoused the view that myths across the world are culture-specific manifestations of a universal need to explain cosmological and spiritual realities in metaphysical narrative form. Campbell's first original work, *The Hero with a Thousand Faces* (1949), became a classic. In that work he asserted that there is a single type of journey narrative that is shared by all cultures in their heroic myths. Campbell's other widely read work is the four-volume *Masks of God* (1959–67).

canon
[< Greek KANON 'measuring rod, rule']
1. established law or code of laws; 2. musical composition or passage in which the same melody is repeated by one or more overlapping voices (as in *Row, row, row your boat*); 3. text considered to be the foremost example of a field (e.g. Dante's *Divine Comedy* is the canon of Italian poetry).

cant
[< Latin CANTUS 'chant']
[< often used as a synonym for *argot]
1. variety of a *language or *dialect with a distinctive repertoire of stock words and phrases used by a particular sect, class, etc.; 2. monotonous talk filled with platitudes or undue piousness.

canto
[Italian, from Latin CANTUS 'song']
One of the principal divisions of a long poem.

caption
[< Latin CAPERE 'to seize']
Title, short commentary, or description accompanying an illustration, photograph, cartoon, etc.

caricature
[< Italian CARICATURA 'satirical picture'; literally 'an overloading']
Distorted visual representation of a person, exaggerating the particular physical or facial features, dress, or manners of the individual to produce a ludicrous effect.

Caricature of a Fifties Rock Star

Note: The art of caricature was known to the ancient Egyptians and Greeks. It was revived by Italian artists of the Renaissance and developed throughout Europe in the 18th century to ridicule political, social, or religious situations and institutions, or actions by various people, groups, or classes of society. At the end of the 18th century Spanish painter Francisco José de Goya (1746–1828) bitterly satirized the religious, political, and social injustices of his age in a series of 80 caricature etchings called *Caprichos* (1799). The English weekly magazine *Punch*, founded in 1841, became one of the best-known publications for caricature in the 19th century. In the 20th century caricaturists focused on political and social issues in popular magazines and daily newspapers. In the United States, the *New Yorker* magazine continues to be one of the best-known sources of caricature art.

Carnap, Rudolf
[1891–1970]
German philosopher who was a prominent figure in the philosophical movement known as *logical positivism*, the doctrine contending that sense perceptions are the only viable forms of information for con-

structing theories of knowledge. Carnap's work on the structure of scientific language, and his analyses of the verifiability of empirical statements, testify to his belief that the problems of science and philosophy are equivalent to problems of language.

Cartesian project

Term referring to the idea propounded by French philosopher and mathematician René *Descartes that a universal method can be devised whereby all human problems, whether of science, law, or politics, can, in theory, be worked out rationally and systematically by applying principles of mathematical logic to them.

cartography

[see *map]

cartoon

[< Italian CARTONE 'paper']
Drawing, often with a caption, caricaturing or symbolizing, often satirically, some event, situation, or person of topical interest.

Note: There are three main types of cartoons: 1. *editorial cartoons*, which serve as visual commentary, usually of a satirical nature, on current events, in magazines and newspapers; 2. *gag cartoons*, consisting of a single panel, which usually satirize causes, rather than lampooning individuals, in magazines and on greeting cards; 3. *illustrative cartoons*, which are used in conjunction with advertising or learning materials, serving to illuminate important points or highlight special aspects of a new product or educational topic.

In the 16th century the German *broadsheets* (single cartoons printed on large pieces of paper) were used for the first time to sway people's opinions. During the 18th century, the English painter and engraver William Hogarth (1697–1764) launched the idea of pictorial storytelling – similar to a comic strip. In England, this led to the art of satirical caricaturing. Later in the 19th century, as periodicals began including illustrations, the editorial cartoon became a staple of journalism. In the United States, too, cartoonists like Thomas Nast (1840–1902), began using cartoons to lobby for specific causes. Nast's best-known works include cartoons about the American Civil War in which he inveighed against slavery.

Editorial cartoons grew in popularity in the 20th century. The gag cartoon was popularized by the *New Yorker* magazine, which began publishing witty cartoons in 1925. The first daily comic strip appeared in the United States in 1904, and daily strips soon became a regular feature of most major newspapers, eventually filling a whole page each day. In 1933 advertisers began to produce books containing reprints of comic strips to give away with certain merchandise. Comic books with original stories were produced a little later. *Superman*, which was first published in 1938, is the most famous early comic book. Beginning in the 1960s, poster cartoons began to appear, usually as a vehicle for expressing political protest. The radical subculture of the period spawned a genre known as *underground comics* (or *comix*), which explored previously forbidden subjects (drugs, sexual freedom, and radical politics). In the 1980s and 1990s many mainstream comic strips began addressing controversial issues on a regular basis.

In the 20th century also, the comic strip genre was used as the basis for the *animated film* (or animated cartoon). Many of the first animated films used existing comic-strip stories and characters for their plot lines, but Walt Disney, William Hanna, Chuck Jones, and other American animators soon after created original characters of their own, such as Mickey Mouse and Bugs Bunny, which have since become integral figures of popular culture.

carving
Figurine or sculpture produced by cutting
material such as stone or wood.

case
[< Latin CASUS 'chance']
Syntactic relationship shown by changes in
the *form* of nouns, pronouns, and adjectives.

Illustrations: 1. *I* is in the nominative case; *me*
is in the accusative case; 2. *who* is in the
nominative case; *whom* is in the dative/
accusative case.

Cassirer, Ernst
[1874–1945]
German philosopher and educator whose
works dealt mainly with the theory of
knowledge and the philosophy of science.
Cassirer proposed that the themes, characters, events, etc. of the ancient myths still
guide the use of language, the creation of
symbols, and the unfolding of social actions.

catachresis
[< Greek KATAKHRĒSTHAI 'to misuse']
1. obscure use of a word or phrase for rhetorical effect; 2. improper use of a word or
phrase.

Illustration: The misuse of *blatant* to mean
flagrant is a typical example of catachresis.

cataphora
[< Greek KATA 'down' + PHEREIN 'to bear']
[see also *anaphora]
Reference to an entity that is about to occur
in discourse or a written text.

Illustrations: 1. *After he saw Sarah, Alexander
called her* (*he* = cataphoric pronoun anticipating *Alexander*). 2. *Seeing himself in the mirror,
Chris decided to shave* (*himself* = reflexive
cataphoric pronoun anticipating *Chris*).

category
[< Greek KATA 'down, against' + AGOREUEIN
'to declaim']

Class of ideas, terms, or things that mark
divisions or coordinations within a conceptual scheme.

Illustration: The word *blue*, which stands for
a *color gradation of approximately 630 to
750 nanometers on the long-wave end of the
visible spectrum, belongs to the conceptual
category that also contains *yellow, red, green,*
etc. This category allows speakers of English to talk and think about the physical
phenomenon of color.
   Now, this kind of categorical knowledge
is culture-specific. The very same referent to
which the word *blue* calls attention could be
divided or *encoded* differently: e.g. two or
more words could be used that, together,
would cover the same gradation encoded by
blue; or the gradation captured by *blue* could
be included within a larger unit of color.

catharsis
[< Greek KATHARSIS 'purification']
Purification of the emotions through the
experience of a work of art or a performance
of some kind (dramatic, musical, etc.).

Note: This concept was proposed by *Aristotle to explain the effect that tragic dramas
have on an audience. Aristotle perceived the
function of tragedy to be the release of pent-
up emotions. As a result of the audience
participating in the performance, its emotions are cleansed and purified, he claimed.
This same term is now also used by psy-
chiatrists to refer to the purging effect that
bringing fears and problems to conscious
awareness purportedly has.

catharsis hypothesis
[< Greek KATHARSIS 'purification']
Claim that the representation of violence
and aggression in media has a preventive
purging effect, since an involvement in
fantasy aggression may provide a release
from hostile impulses that otherwise might
be acted out in real life.

cave art

[also known as *Paleolithic art]
Earliest known art, dating back to between 10,000 and 40,000 BC, known as the late Paleolithic or Old Stone Age.

Note: The earliest sculpted objects were small carved pieces of wood, ivory, and bone, mainly of animals and human beings. The first drawings and paintings were handprints outlined in colored earth on cave walls, mainly of animals.

CD-ROM

[acronym for 'Compact Disc Read-Only Memory']
Compact disc storing computer-usable information, instead of magnetic discs or tapes, for reading data and instructions.

central processing unit

[abbreviated to CPU]
Microprocessor chip that translates commands and runs programs. The CPU coordinates computer functions, retrieves instructions from memory, executes instructions, and stores results in memory locations.

cerebral dominance

[< Latin CEREBRUM 'brain]
Neuroscientific theory positing that the left hemisphere of the brain is the dominant one controlling the higher mental functions, such as language and reasoning.

Note: The idea that the left hemisphere is the dominant one came to be widely held late in the 19th century and in the first half of the 20th. The origin of this term is obscure, and it took research in neuroscience most of the first half of the 20th century to dispel the notion that only the left hemisphere of the brain controlled higher forms of thinking. Today, the notion of dominance refers to the hemisphere (left or right) in which a specific function is located. In right-handed people the left hemisphere dominates mathemati-

cal, reasoning, and speech functions; the right hemisphere musical, spatial, and emotional functions. In left-handed people, however, this pattern of brain dominance is more variable.

channel

[< Latin CANALIS 'tube']
Physical system carrying a transmitted signal.

Illustrations: 1. speech is carried through the channel of air waves; 2. a television signal is carried instead through a specified frequency band.

chanson de geste

[French CHANSON 'song,' GESTE 'heroic exploit']
One of more than 80 Old French epic poems of the 11th to the 14th centuries celebrating the deeds of historical or legendary figures, especially the exploits of Charlemagne and his successors.

Note: The *Chanson de Roland* (c. 1100), attributed to the Norman poet Turold, is the most popular of the chansons. It recounts the Battle of Roncesvalles in 778 and the heroic feats of Roland, a knight of Charlemagne's court. Roland's death in a suicide-like defense of a mountain pass renders him a Christian martyr.

chaos theory

[< Greek CHAOS 'space']
Mathematical *theory portraying the behavior of natural systems as unpredictable, rather than as regular and predictable.

Note: Traditionally scientists trace the unpredictable behavior of systems to random influences that, if eliminated, would allow them to predict behavior. Chaos theorists argue, by contrast, that many systems exhibit long-term unpredictability without random influences. The French mathematician Henri Poincaré (1854–1912) was the first to argue, in the late 19th century, that the behavior of natural physical systems was not completely predictable. In the 1960s, computer models of weather showed, in fact, that accurate long-range forecasting was impossible. By the early 1980s experiments had shown that many physical and biological systems behave just as chaotically as the weather.

character
[< Greek CHARASSEIN 'to engrave']
1. role portrayed by an actor or actress; 2. personage depicted in a narrative, play, poem, etc.; 3. qualities that distinguish one person or group from another; 4. notable or well-known person (also called a *personage*); 5. mark or symbol used in a writing system, computer code, or *cipher.

Illustrations: 1. *Hamlet* is a well-known fictional *character*. 2. People are judged 'by their *character*.' 3. The letter *a* is a *character* in the English alphabet.

charade
[< Old Provençal CHARRAR 'to gossip']
Pantomime game in which the syllables of a word or an entire phrase are acted out so that they can be guessed; participants are generally divided into two competing groups, with each group acting out several items.

charge
Heraldic *insignia representing a familiar animal or mythical beast symbolizing the history or character of an individual or family.

Note: The most common charge is the lion, whose position is typically erect and facing right with only one foot on the ground. Other animals used as charges include bears, bulls, boars, deer, goats, dogs, foxes, horses, hedgehogs, eagles, and falcons. Mythical beasts such as the griffin, unicorn, and dragon are also used.

chiaroscuro
[Italian for 'light and dark']
Technique of using light and dark colors and/or shades in pictorial representation.

Illustrations: The indisputable masters of the chiaroscuro technique are Leonardo da Vinci (1452–1519), Raphael (1483–1520), Michelangelo Merisi da Caravaggio (1573–1610), Georges de La Tour (1593–1652), and Rembrandt (1606–69). The chiaroscuro technique is seldom found in pre-Renaissance or in non-Western art.

chiasmus
[< Greek CHIASMA 'a crosspiece']
Structural inversion of the second of two parallel phrases or clauses.

Illustrations: 1. *She went to London; to Rome went he.* 2. *Each throat was parched, and glazed each eye.*

Chicago School
American architectural movement, based in late-19th century Chicago, that produced the skyscraper, the first work of modernist architecture.

Note: In 1885 the architect-engineer William Le Baron Jenney (1832–1907) designed the ten-story Home Insurance Building (now demolished) in Chicago, employing an all-metal frame of cast-iron columns and steel beams to support the masonry shell of floors and walls. This became the model for all subsequent skyscraper design. The prime exponent of the Chicago School was Frank Lloyd Wright (1869–1959), who became one of the greatest architects of the 20th century.

Chinese room rebuttal
Counter-argument to the *Turing test formulated by American philosopher, John Searle, making it obvious that computers cannot 'think' in the way humans can.

Note: Searle argued that a computer does not 'know' what it is doing when it processes symbols, because it lacks conscious-ness. Just like an English-speaking human being who translates Chinese symbols in the form of little pieces of paper by using a set of rules for matching them with other sym-bols, or little pieces of paper, knows nothing about the 'story' contained in the Chinese pieces of paper, so too a computer does not have access to the 'story' inhering in human symbols.

Chomsky, Noam Avram
[1928–]
[see also *language; *language acquisition device; *linguistics]
American linguist who claims that the hu-man brain is especially constructed to detect and reproduce language. According to Chomsky, children instinctively apply gram-matical principles to process the verbal input to which they are exposed because they possess an innate language faculty that has information built into it about what languages must be like. Chomsky's theory of language is known generally as *genera-tive grammar.

choreography
[< Greek CHOREIA 'dance']
Art of composing dances, by specifying the movements and patterns that the dancers must follow.

chromaticism
[< Greek CHROMA 'color']
1. in painting, color perceived to have a saturation greater than zero; 2. in music, type of composition or style based on the chromatic (nonharmonic) scale.

chronemics
[< Greek CHRONOS 'time']
Study of how cultures 1. divide time into regular periods, 2. arrange events in the order of their occurrence, 3. assign dates to events.

chronicle
[< Greek CHRONOS 'time']
Extended narrative in prose or verse of historical events, sometimes including leg-endary material, presented in chronological order and without authorial interpretation or comment.

Cicero, Marcus Tullius
[106–43 BC]
Roman statesman, orator, and philosopher best known for his orations and for his mas-tery of Latin prose. In his writings Cicero created a rich prose style that has influenced all the literary styles of Europe.

cinema
[< Greek KINEMA 'motion']
Visual narrative art form developed from the technology of 'moving pictures,' i.e., of picture frames that follow each other with sufficient rapidity as to create the illusion of motion and continuity.

Note: Most historians trace the origin of cinema to the year 1896 when the French magician Georges Méliès made a series of films that explored the narrative potential on the new medium. Subsequently, in 1899, in a studio on the outskirts of Paris, Méliès reconstructed a ten-part film *Alfred Dreyfus* on the trial of the French army officer and filmed *Cinderella* (1900) in 20 scenes. He is chiefly remembered, however, for his clever fantasies, such as *A Trip to the Moon* (1902). His short films were an instant hit with the public and were shown across the world. Although considered little more than curi-osities today, they are significant precursors of an art form that was in its infancy at the time.

The theatrical fantasies of Méliès merged in the realistic fiction of American inventor Edwin S. Porter, who is often called the father of the silent film, producing in 1903 the first major American film, *The Great Train Robbery*, an eight-minute movie that greatly influenced the development of motion pictures because of its intercutting of scenes shot at different times and in different places to form a unified narrative, culminating in a suspenseful chase. With the production of D.W. Griffith's *The Birth of a Nation* (1915), small theaters sprang up throughout the United States, and cinema emerged as a de facto art form. Most films of the time were short comedies, adventure stories, or filmed records of performances by leading actors of the day.

The film industry moved gradually to Hollywood. Hundreds of films a year poured from the Hollywood studios to satisfy an ever-increasing craving from a fanatic movie-going public. The vast majority of them were Westerns, slapstick comedies, and elegant romantic melodramas such as Cecil B. DeMille's *Male and Female* (1919). In the 1920s, movies starring the comedian Charlie Chaplin ushered in the golden age of silent film. After the First World War, motion-picture production became a major American industry, generating millions of dollars in profit for successful studios. American films became international in character and dominated the world market. Artists responsible for the most successful European films were imported by American studios, and their techniques were adapted and assimilated by Hollywood.

The transition from silent to sound films was so rapid that many films released in 1928 and 1929 had begun production as silent films but were hastily turned into 'talkies,' as they were called, to meet the growing demand. Gangster films and musicals dominated the new 'talking screen' of the early 1930s. Filming popular novels became the vogue in the late 1930s, with expensively mounted productions of classic novels, including one that became one of the most popular films in motion-picture history, *Gone with the Wind* (1939). The trend towards escapism and fantasy in motion pictures was strong throughout the 1930s. A cycle of classic horror films, including *Dracula* (1931), *Frankenstein* (1931), and *The Mummy* (1932) spawned a series of sequels and spin-offs that lasted throughout the decade. One of the most enduring films of the decade was the musical fantasy *The Wizard of Oz* (1939), based on a book by L. Frank Baum – a children's movie with a frightful theme that reflected the emerging cynicism of society at large, namely, that all human aspirations are ultimately make-believe, that the 'Wizard' at the end of the 'road of life' is really a fraud, a charlatan.

One American filmmaker who came to Hollywood from radio in 1940 was the writer-director-actor Orson Welles (1915–85). His *Citizen Kane* (1941) and *The Magnificent Ambersons* (1942) influenced the subsequent work of virtually every major filmmaker in the world. From the late 1940s to the mid-1970s, Italian cinema achieved an intimacy and depth of emotion that radically transformed cinematic art. Classic Italian films of the period included Roberto Rossellini's *Open City* (1945), Vittorio De Sica's *The Bicycle Thief* (1949), Pier Paolo Pasolini's *The Gospel According to Saint Matthew* (1966), Federico Fellini's *La Strada* (1954), *La Dolce Vita* (1960), *8½* (1963), and *Juliet of the Spirits* (1965), Michelangelo Antonioni's *L'Avventura* (1959), and *Red Desert* (1964), Bernardo Bertolucci's *The Conformist* (1970), and *1900* (1977), and Lina Wertmuller's *Swept Away* (1975) and *Seven Beauties* (1976).

One of the most distinctive and original directors to emerge in the post–Second World War international cinema stage was Sweden's Ingmar Bergman (1918–), who brought an intense philosophical and intellectual depth to cinematic art. In *The Seventh Seal* (1956) he probed the mystery of life and spirituality through the trials of a medieval knight playing a game of chess with Death. In *Wild Strawberries* (1957) he created a series of poetic flashbacks reviewing the life of an elderly professor. He dissected the human condition starkly in a series of subsequent films – *Persona* (1966), *Cries and Whispers* (1972), *Scenes from a Marriage* (1973), and *Autumn Sonata* (1978) – in which he excoriated the absurd penchant in the human species to search for meaning in existence.

In the 1950s and 1960s color films virtually eclipsed black-and-white. But some filmmakers still preferred black and white, striving for quiet realism. Among these films *Psycho* (1960) by Alfred Hitchcock, *The Last Picture Show* (1971) by Peter Bogdanovich, *Raging Bull* (1980) by Martin Scorsese, *Zelig* (1983) and *Shadows and Fog* (1992) by Woody Allen, and *Schindler's List* (1994) by Steven Spielberg have become classics.

Of the many directors working in the last part of the 20th century, perhaps no one has been as successful at exploiting the film medium as a versatile art form as has Steven Spielberg (1947–). His *Jaws* (1975), about a killer shark that terrorizes a small beach community, became the model for a number of subsequent films in which fear-inspiring creatures threatened helpless victims. His *Close Encounters of the Third Kind* (1977) and *E.T.* (1982) capitalized on a widespread fascination with the possibility of extraterrestrial life. His other multimillion-dollar blockbusters have included *Raiders of the Lost Ark* (1981), *Indiana Jones and the Temple of Doom* (1984), and *Indiana Jones and the Last Crusade* (1989), all imitative of the serial cliffhangers of the 1930s. Most of Spielberg's films rely heavily on high-tech special effects, especially his *Jurassic Park* (1993), which features frighteningly realistic computer-generated dinosaurs. Within the first four weeks of its release, *Jurassic Park* became the highest-grossing film up to that time, only to be surpassed by *Titanic* (1998).

The 1980s and 1990s saw a revolution in the home-video market, with major releases being made available for home viewing.

This development, combined with the advent of cable television, which features relatively current films on special channels, seemed at first to threaten the long-term survival of movie theaters, creating a climate of apprehension similar to that of the early 1950s, when television began to challenge the popularity of motion pictures. As a result, film companies increasingly favored large spectacles with fantastic special effects in order to lure the public away from home videos and back to the big screen. But despite the challenge from video, the traditional movie theater has remained as popular as ever – a testament to the power of cinema as an art form for the modern imagination.

cinéma-vérité
[French 'cinema truth']
Style of filmmaking that stresses stark psychological realism in the portrayal of character.

Illustrations: 1. Carl-Theodor Dreyer's (1889–1968) *La passion de Jeanne d'Arc* (1928); 2. Luis Buñuel's (1900–83) and Salvador Dalí's (1904–89) *Un chien andalou* (1929).

cipher
[< Arabic sifr 'nothing']
Cryptographic message in which units of plain text of regular length, usually letters, are transposed or substituted according to a predetermined code.

Note: There are four main types of ciphers: 1. In *transposition ciphers* the message is usually written, without word divisions, in rows of letters arranged in a rectangular block. The letters are then transposed in a prearranged order such as by vertical columns, diagonals, or spirals, or by more complicated patterns. 2. In simple *substitution ciphers*, a specific letter or symbol is substituted for each letter. The letters are left in their normal order, usually with normal word divisions. 3. In *multiple substitution*

ciphers, a keyword is employed. The first message letter might be enciphered by adding to it the numerical value of the first letter of the keyword; the second message letter is enciphered similarly, using the second letter of the keyword, and so on.
4. In more complicated *polyalphabetic ciphers*, the letters of the keyword may indicate which of a series of mixed substitution alphabets is to be used to encipher each letter of the message.

circumfix
[< Latin CIRCUM 'around' + AFFIXUS 'fastened']
Two *affixes added simultaneously to a *morpheme (minimal unit of meaning).

Illustration: In Chickasaw, a Native language spoken in Oklahoma, the negative is formed by attaching both the prefix *ik-* and the suffix *-o* to the root of a word: e.g. *lakn* 'it is yellow,' *iklakno* 'it isn't yellow'; *palli* 'it is hot,' *ikpallo* 'it isn't hot.'

civilization
[< Latin CIVIS 'citizen']
Complex society, or group of societies, whose institutions are grounded in a mainstream culture, but which can encompass more than one culture.

Note: The term civilization implies essentially a society, or group of societies, with a distinctive recorded history and with common institutions (religious, political, legal, economic, educational, etc.). The first civilizations in the current-day Middle East came onto the scene between 5000 and 3000 BC. Sumer, Babylon, and Egypt were among the first large social groupings to encompass not only a mainstream form of culture, but also a complex diversity of peoples and languages, and to distinguish between civil and religious institutions. Other civilizations that history has recorded are the Andean one, which originated about 800 BC in South America; the Far Eastern, which started in China about 2200 BC; the Minoan, which originated in Crete about 2000 BC; the Byzantine, which arose in the 4th century AD; the Islamic, arising in the 8th century AD; and the Western, which arose in Western Europe in the early Middle Ages.

C-language
Computer programming language developed in 1972. Although **C** is considered by many to be more a machine-independent assembly language than a high-level language, it is used by many in the microcomputer world.

classical conditioning
[see *behaviorsm; *psychology]

classicism
[< Latin CLASSICUS 'relating to the highest classes']
Term describing the art and literature created by the ancient Greeks and Romans, as well as any style or period of creative work distinguished by qualities that suggest or are derived from classical aesthetics. The term has been applied especially to the Western art and music of the period that starts around 1750 and ends around 1820.

Clement of Alexandria
[AD 150?–215?]
Greek theologian and early Father of the Church who put the study and interpretation of ancient texts, especially religious or mythical ones, on a systematic grounding. Clement established the method of ascertaining, as far as possible, the meaning that a biblical writer intended on the basis of linguistic considerations, relevant sources, and historical background.

Clever Hans phenomenon
Term referring to the illusive belief that animals can understand human speech.

Note: Clever Hans was heralded the world over in 1904 as a German 'talking horse' who appeared to understand human language and communicate answers to questions by tapping the alphabet with his front hoof – one tap for A, two taps for B, three taps for C, and so on. A panel of scientists ruled out deception and unintentional communication by the horse's owner. The horse, it was claimed, could talk. Clever Hans was awarded honors and proclaimed an important scientific discovery.

Eventually, however, an astute member of the scientific committee that had examined the horse's purported abilities, the psychologist Oskar Pfungst, discovered that Clever Hans would not tap his hoof without *observing* his questioner. The horse had obviously figured out – as most horses can – what the *signals* that his owner was unwittingly transmitting meant. The horse tapped his hoof only in response to inadvertent cues from his human handler, who would visibly relax when the horse had tapped the proper number of times. To show this, Pfungst simply blindfolded Clever Hans who, as a consequence, ceased to be so clever. The *Clever Hans phenomenon*, as it has come to be known in the annals of psychology, has been demonstrated over and over with other animals as well (e.g. a dog will bark in response to certain signals unwittingly emitted by people).

cliché
[< French CLICHER 'to stereotype']
Trite or overused expression or idea.

Illustrations: 1. *All's well that ends well.* 2. *They lived happily ever after.*

climax
[< Greek KLIMAX 'ladder']
1. series of ideas, images, etc. arranged progressively so that the most forceful is last; 2. decisive turning point of the action in a drama, performance, or narrative.

Illustrations: 1. *First we criticize him, then we attack him, and finally we destroy him for what*

he did. 2. *Sarah starts by giggling, then she goes on to chuckle loudly, and ends up laughing raucously.*

closed work
[see also *open work]
Term coined by Umberto *Eco in reference to a type of text with a singular or fairly limited range of meanings.

Illustration: Most 'Whodunit?' mystery stories are closed works because only one solution to a crime eventually surfaces. An open work, by contrast, allows readers to make up their own minds as to what it means.

clothing
[see also *dress]
Any form of material body covering, developed by humans primarily as a protection against climate.

Note: Clothing is often contrasted with *dress* in semiotics. *Clothes* have a denotative meaning – they enhance human survivability considerably. They are human-made extensions of the body's protective resources; i.e. they are additions to protective bodily hair and skin. This is why clothing fabrics vary in relation to different climatic zones. But in social settings separate items of clothing cohere symbolically into the various *dress codes* that inform people how to present themselves in public.

clowning
[see *buffoonery]

coda
[< Latin CAUDA 'tail']
1. in linguistics, sound(s) that follow(s) the vowel in a syllable; 2. in music, passage at the end of a movement or composition that brings it to a formal close.

Note: A syllable is composed of an *onset* (the sound or sounds that precede the vowel *nucleus*) and a *rhyme*, made up of the *nucleus* and a *coda*. It is called *rhyme* because in rhyming words, the *nucleus + coda* of the final syllables must match: e.g. *sprint - flint*.

code

[< Latin CODEX 'wooden tablet for writing']
1. system of *signs given certain meanings;
2. system of signs and structural patterns for constructing and deciphering messages.

Note: A code can be compared to a computer program. The latter consists of a set of instructions that the computer can recognize and execute in converting information from one form into another. So too language, for instance, constitutes a set of phonetic, grammatical, and lexical instructions that the makers and interpreters of words and verbal texts can recognize and convert into messages. Language, dress, music, and gesture are examples of codes. These are systems of signs that are held together by specific relations.

coevolution

[see *sociobiology]

cognition

[< Latin COGNITIO 'knowledge']
Process of knowing in the broadest sense, including perceiving, remembering, and judging. The study of cognition began in earnest in the 1950s when psychologists started making parallels between the functions of the human brain and computer operations such as the *coding, storing, retrieving,* and *buffering* of information.

cognitive compression effect

[< Latin COGNITIO 'knowledge']
Compression effect of electronic media (especially TV) on the way information and ideas are perceived. By compacting ideas and information for time-constrained transmission, such media leave little opportunity for reflection on the content of messages.

Note: According to some psychologists this effect has led, in populations exposed to TV, to both shorter attention spans and a need for constant variety in information content. People habituated to large doses of *compressed* information – i.e. information cut up and packaged beforehand – tend to become psychologically dependent on information and visual stimulation for their own sake.

cognitive dissonance

[< Latin COGNITIO 'knowledge'; DIS 'apart'; SONUS 'sound']
Condition of conflict or anxiety resulting from an inconsistency between one's beliefs and one's actions, such as opposing the slaughter of animals while eating meat. People will seek out information that confirms their own attitudes and views of the world, or else reinforces aspects of conditioned behavior, avoiding information that is likely to be in conflict with their worldview and, thus, tending to cause cognitive dissonance.

cognitive grammar

[< Latin COGNITIO 'knowledge'; Greek GRAMMATIKE 'grammar, learning']
School of *linguistics based on the premise that language categories embody conventional imagery, which constitutes an essential aspect of their grammatical and semantic value.

Illustrations: 1. When we say that our *feelings* are *inside* us, we are construing the body as a *container*. 2. When we say that our *feelings* are *up*, we are construing our *feelings* in terms of an upward-looking sensation.

Note: Cognitive grammar is based on the idea that, in choosing a particular expression or construction, a speaker does so by construing the situation in a certain experiential way; i.e. the speaker selects one particular form or structure in forming a sentence in order to convey feeling, emotion, point of view, etc. These choices are called *cognitive routines,* and defined as mentally prepackaged assemblages that speakers can employ in essentially automatic fashion.

cognitive science
[< Latin COGNITIO 'knowledge'; SCIENTIA 'knowing']
Interdisciplinary field that emerged in the 1970s for studying human *cognition. Cognitive science extracts its notions from *artificial intelligence, *linguistics, *anthropology, *psychology, and other human sciences in order to formulate its own particular kind of theories about the mind.

Note: When Wilhelm Wundt (1832–1920) founded the first 'laboratory' of experimental psychology in 1879 in Leipzig, he laid the groundwork for establishing a new scientific discipline of the mind, separate from philosophy, which he claimed would have the capacity to discover the 'laws of mind' through a method of experimentation with human subjects. This became the basis for most of the experimental psychology of the first half of the 20th century. By the late 1960s, however, a new cadre of psychologists abandoned the experimental approach, finding it too anecdotal, and sought instead parallels between the functions of the human brain and those of computer programs. This led to the foundation of the cognitive science movement, based on the notion that there exists a level of mind wholly separate from the biological or neurological, on the one hand, and the sociological or cultural, on the other, that works like an electronic computer.

The basis for this view is the concept of *machine*, which is a mathematical abstraction tracing its roots to the work of the mathematician Alan *Turing (1912–54). Turing showed that four simple operations represented on a tape – *move to the right*, *move to the left*, *erase the slash*, *print the slash* – allowed a computer to execute any kind of program that could be expressed in a binary code (as for example a code of blanks and

slashes). So long as one could specify the steps involved in carrying out a task and translating them into the binary code, the *Turing machine* – now called a *computer program* – would be able to scan the tape containing the code and carry out the instructions.

Although Turing himself was well aware of the limitations of his notion, openly admitting that it could never come close to emulating the more spiritual aspects of human consciousness, to many psychologists his clever insight suggested not only that humans were, in effect, special kinds of protoplasmic *machines*, whose cognitive states, emotions, and social behaviors were therefore representable in the form of computer-like programs, but also that mechanical machines themselves could eventually be built to think, feel, and socialize like human beings.

The greatest criticism levelled against this view is that it is beyond the capacities of a machine to feel, imagine, invent, dream, construct rituals, art works, and the like. These are derivatives of bodily and psychic experiences. Computer-based theories and models of consciousness can perhaps give us precise information about the nature of the formal properties of mental states; but they tell us nothing about how these states are brought about in the first place.

cognitive style
[< Latin COGNITIO 'knowledge']
[see also *sense ratio]
Particular style by which information is processed: e.g. *auditory* cognitive style (= processing information by listening to it); *visual* cognitive style (= processing information by looking at it); etc.

cognitivism
[< Latin COGNITIO 'knowledge']
[see *cognition]
School of psychology originating in the 1950s based on the idea that mental func-

tions can be studied by seeking parallels between the brain and computer operations.

cognomen
[synonym for *surname]

cohesive gesture
[< Latin CUM 'together' + HAERERE 'to stick'; GERERE 'to bear, carry']
Gesture used during oral discourse that serves to show how the separate parts of an utterance are supposed to hold together.

Note: Cohesive gesturing unfolds through a repetition of the same gesture form, movement, or location in the gesture space. It is the repetition itself that is meant to convey cohesiveness.

collage
[French 'a pasting']
Artistic arrangement of materials and objects pasted on a surface, often with unifying lines and color. In painting the visual impression is built up by composition of color and line; in collage, bits of newspaper, labels, buttons, or chickenwire, etc., are attached to the surface.

collective unconscious
[see *unconscious, collective]

collocation
[< Latin CUM 'together' + LOCARE 'to place']
Meaning acquired by a word by virtue of its association with other words that tend to occur in linkage with it.

Illustration: The words *pretty* and *handsome* share the meaning of 'good-looking,' but *pretty* occurs in collocation with *girl, boy, woman, flower, garden, color,* etc. (*pretty girl, pretty boy,* etc.); whereas *handsome* occurs in collocation with *boy, man, car, vessel, overcoat, airliner,* etc. (*handsome boy, handsome man,* etc.). The collocation may overlap, but when it does, it entails different meanings: e.g. *pretty boy* vs. *handsome boy.*

color
[< Latin COLOR 'covering']
Sensation resulting from stimulation of the retina of the eye by light waves of certain lengths.

Note: The question of color is an intriguing one for psychology, linguistics, and semiotics. The light spectrum consists of a continuous gradation of hue from one end to the other. There are potentially 8 million gradations that the human eye is capable of distinguishing. If one were to put a finger at any point on the spectrum, there would be only a negligible difference in gradation in the colors immediately adjacent to the finger at either side. Yet, a speaker of English describing the spectrum will list the gradations as falling under the labels *red, orange, yellow, green, blue, indigo,* and *violet.* This is because the speaker has been conditioned by the specific lexical *categories the English language makes available for classifying the content of the spectrum.

There is nothing inherently 'natural' about the organizational scheme that English imposes on the spectrum. By contrast, speakers of other languages are predisposed to perceive the gradations on the spectrum in conceptually different ways. Speakers of Shona, an indigenous African language, for instance, divide it up into *cipswuka, citema, cicena,* and *cipswuka* (again), and speakers of Bassa, a language of Liberia, divide it into just two categories, *hui* and *ziza.* When an English speaker refers to, say, a ball as *blue,* a Shona speaker might refer to it as either *cipswuka* or *citema,* and a Bassa speaker as hui. The Bassa speaker would also refer to a *purple* and *green* ball as *hui.* But this does not stop a Bassa speaker from seeing differences in gradation expressed by the English terms. The specific color terms one has acquired in cultural context in no way preclude the ability to perceive the color categories of other cultures. This is, indeed, what a learner of another language ends up doing when studying the new color system: i.e. the student learns how to reclassify the content of the spectrum in terms of the new terms. Moreover, in all languages there exist lexical resources for referring to more specific gradations on the spectrum if the situation should require it. In English the words *crimson*, *scarlet*, and *vermilion*, for instance, make it possible to refer to gradations of *red*. But these are still felt by speakers to be *subcategories* of red, not distinct color categories on their own.

color, focal
[< Latin COLOR 'covering'; FOCUS 'hearth']
Color category that is purported by some psychologists and linguists to be universal.

Note: The term was introduced by psycholinguists Brent Berlin and Paul Kay in their classic 1969 study, *Basic Color Terms*. Berlin and Kay argued that differences in color terms are only superficial matters that conceal general underlying principles of color perception. Using the judgments of the native speakers of twenty widely divergent languages, Berlin and Kay came to the conclusion that there were 'focal points' in basic (single-term) color systems that clustered in certain predictable ways. They identified eleven focal colors, which correspond to the English words *red, pink, orange, yellow, brown, green, blue, purple, black, white,* and *gray.*
   Not all the languages they investigated had separate words for each of these colors, but there emerged a pattern that suggested to them the existence of a fixed way of perceiving color across cultures. If a language had two colors, then the focal points were equivalents of English *black* and *white*. If it had three color terms, then the third one corresponded to *red*. A four-term system had either *yellow* or *green*, while a five-term system had both of these. A six-term system included *blue*, a seven-term system *brown*. Finally, *purple, pink, orange,* and *gray* were found to occur in any combination in languages that had the previous focal points. Berlin and Kay found that languages with, say, a four-term system consisting of *black, white, red,* and *brown* did not exist.

color field painting
[< Latin COLOR 'covering']
Abstract expressionist painting technique in which color and shape are used for their own sake, without depicting anything in particular.

Note: Color field painting originated in the late 1940s, gaining popularity in the 1950s and 1960s. Like all forms of abstract *expressionism, it rejected the direct representation of recognizable forms, emphasizing instead the experience of pure color. Among the first examples of color field painting were Clyfford Still's (1904–80) large canvases splashed with thick color fields bounded by jagged contours. One of the best-known color field artists is Helen Frankenthaler (1928–), whose technique consists in pouring paint freely onto raw canvas, causing the paint to 'bleed' into the fabric in the form of pools.

comedy
[< Greek KOMOIDIA 'revel, carousal']
[see *drama]

comedy of manners novel
[see *novel]

comic relief
[< Greek KOMOS 'a reveling']
Humorous or farcical interlude in a serious literary work, designed to provide relief from dramatic tension.

comics
[< Greek KOMOS 'a reveling']
Visual narrative put together with *cartoon drawings arranged in horizontal lines, strips, or rectangles called *panels*, and read

from left to right; dialogue is represented by words encircled by *balloons, which issue from the mouth or head of characters.

Note: Most pop-culture historians trace the origin of the modern comic strip to Richard Felton Outcault's series *Hogan's Alley*, first published in 1895. Two other early cartoons were *The Katzenjammer Kids* (1897) by Rudolph Dirks and *Little Bears* (1892) by James Guilford Swinnerton. Shortly thereafter, comics became a staple feature of newspapers. The first successful daily comic strip, by Bud Fisher, began in 1907 under the title *Mr. A. Mutt*, later retitled *Mutt and Jeff*. Newspaper syndicates, which employed comic-strip artists, began the mass circulation of comics by selling strips to small-town newspapers.

One of the first comic books was a collection of the *Mutt and Jeff* strips reprinted from the *Chicago American* in 1911. The first comic book to sell on newsstands was *Famous Funnies*, which first appeared in 1934. The 1938 publication of the comic book *Action Comics* – of which the principal feature was the Superman comic strip – inspired hundreds of imitations. The adventure genre began with the publication in 1929 of *Tarzan* and *Buck Rogers*. *Flash Gordon* (1934) by Alex Raymond proved to be one of the most successful examples of comic-book fantasy. In the same year Al Capp began *Li'l Abner*, using it as a vehicle for satirizing American society.

In 1986 Jules Feiffer received a Pulitzer Prize for his literary cartoon critiques of radical politics. Gary Trudeau's *Doonesbury*, with its political satire and ironic sketches of counterculture lifestyles, had won a Pulitzer Prize in 1975, only five years after its inception. A satirical strip in a similar vein, *Bloom County* by Berkeley Breathed, won the Pulitzer in 1987. Gary Larson's single-panel daily feature, *The Far Side*, delighted many newspaper readers from the 1980s to the mid-1990s with its offbeat and sometimes macabre humor.

The most famous comic strip ever is, arguably, *Peanuts* by Charles M. Schulz (1922–2000), appearing in more than 2000 newspapers and translated into more than 20 languages. It ended a 50-year run at the end of 1999. Schulz has received many awards and honors, including the prestigious Reuben award given by the National Cartoonists Society. His clean drawing style and humor are dignified and intelligent. His characters, which include Charlie Brown, his sister Sally, his dog Snoopy, his friends Lucy, Linus, Schroeder, Peppermint Patty, Marcie, and the bird Woodstock have become cultural icons to whom people refer for insight and understanding in the same way they might refer to biblical figures, mythical personages, or Shakespearean characters.

commedia dell'arte

[< Italian COMMEDIA 'comedy' + DELL'ARTE 'of the guild']
[see also *drama]
Type of comedy developed in Italy in the 16th and 17th centuries, characterized by improvisation from standard plot outlines and stock characters, often in traditional masks and costumes. Although the governments of Spain and France attempted to censor and regulate *commedia* performances, the ribald humor and realistic character types of the *commedia* were eventually adopted by conventional theater.

Note: The *commedia dell'arte* originated in northern Italy in the 1550s and flourished for 200 years. In their improvised comedies, *commedia* troupes relied on stereotypical characters, masks, broad physical gestures, and clowning to entertain large, diverse crowds. Lecherous *Arlecchino* wore a black, snub-nosed mask, was extremely acrobatic, and possessed the slyness of an artful adolescent. *Pantalone*, a cheap and gullible merchant, attempted to disguise his old age and attract women by wearing tight-fitting Turkish clothes. The *Doctor* used meaningless

Latin phrases and prescribed dangerous remedies. Endlessly boasting of his victories in war and love, the *Captain* always proved to be a coward and an inane lover. *Pulcinella* was a pot-bellied rascal, who concocted outrageous schemes to satisfy his desires. *Columbine*, the wife of one of the *Old Men*, demonstrated intelligence and charm in a world of stupidity and misunderstanding.

commercial (radio and television)
[see *advertising]

commisurotomy experiments
[see *split-brain experiments]

communication
[< Latin COMMUNIS 'common']
1. production and exchange of messages by means of signals, facial expressions, talk, gestures, or writing; 2. art of expressing ideas, especially in speech and writing.

Note: In the human species, communication includes the following modes of delivery: 1. *gesture*, i.e. the use of the hands; 2. *vocal*, i.e. the use of the vocal organs; 3. *writing*, i.e. the use of pictures or graphic symbols; 4. *visual*, i.e. painting, sculpting, etc.; 5. *mechanical*, i.e. radio, computers, television, etc.; 6. *signaling*, i.e. body signal emission (natural or intentional).

communication, animal
[< Latin COMMUNIS 'common']
Scientific study of communication in animal species.

Note: Two theories guide the study of animal communication: 1. *nurture theory*, which postulates that animals learn everything they do from other animals; 2. *nature theory*, which asserts that they know what to do instinctively.

Nurture theory was given prominence after the Russian physiologist Ivan *Pavlov was able, at the threshold of the 20th century, to cause dogs to salivate at the sound

of a bell after he repeatedly sounded the bell just before feeding them. This 'nurtured behavior' was ascribed to *conditioning*. Later work showed that conditioning procedures that reward or punish behaviors, called *operant conditioning*, are highly effective. In contrast, *nature theory* holds that much of what animals know is instinctive, programmed into their genes at birth. Most animal communication systems are based on signaling behavior. Some species are known to have several signal repertoires, such as distinct signals for different varieties of predators, all producing diverse responses in the community. Certain primate groups, for example, use different signals for airborne and land predators; if the community hears the land predator call, they take cover in the tops of trees.

communication, verbal
[< Latin COMMUNIS 'common']
Communication by means of *language.

Note: Among the various models of verbal communication, the one by the Moscow-born linguist and semiotician who carried out most of his work in the United States, Roman Jakobson (1896–1982), is one of the most widely used ones today. Jakobson posited six 'constituents' that characterize all instances of verbal communication: 1. an *addresser* who initiates a communication; 2. a *message* that she/he recognizes must refer to something other than itself; 3. an *addressee* who is the intended receiver of the message; 3. a *context* that permits the addressee to recognize that the message is referring to something other than itself; 4. a mode of *contact* by which a message is delivered (the physical channel) and the primary social and psychological connections that exist or are established between the addresser and addressee; 5. a *code* providing the signs and structural patterns for constructing and deciphering messages.

Jakobson then pointed out that each of these constituents determines a different communicative function: 1. *emotive* = the influence of the addresser's emotions, attitudes, social status, etc. in the making of the message; 2. *conative* = the effect – physical, psychological, social, etc. – that the message has or is expected to have on the addressee; 3. *referential* = a message constructed to convey information unambiguously; 4. *poetic* = a message constructed to deliver meanings effectively, like poetry; 5. *phatic* = a message designed to establish social contact; 6. *metalingual* = a message designed to refer to the code being used.

Jakobson's analysis of verbal communication suggests that discourse goes well beyond a situation of simple information transfer. It involves determining *who* says *what* to *whom*; *where* and *when* it is said; and *how* and *why* it is said: i.e. human discourse is motivated and shaped by the setting, the message contents, and the participants, making an emotional claim on everyone in the communicative situation.

communication science

[< Latin COMMUNIS 'common'; SCIENTIA 'knowing']
Science studying all the technical aspects of *communication.

Note: Among the first to study the technical features of communication systems was the American electrical engineer Claude E. Shannon (1916–). In 1948, Shannon developed the mathematical laws governing the transmission, reception, and processing of information. In his model of communication, message transmission occurs between a *sender* (such as a person speaking) who *encodes* a message – i.e. uses a *code* such as *language* to construct it – and a *receiver* who has the capacity to *decode* the message – i.e. to use the same code to understand what the message means. To get the message across to the receiver, the sender must use some means or device to convert it into a physical signal in some *medium* – the voice,

writing, etc. A verbal message, for instance, can involve a *natural medium*, if it is articulated with the vocal organs; or else it can be transmitted by means of markings on a piece of paper through the *artifactual medium* of writing; and it can also be converted into radio or television signals for *mechanical* (electromagnetic) transmission.

*Semiotics is often confused with communication science. Although the two domains share much of the same theoretical and methodological territory, communication science focuses on the technical study of how messages are transmitted (vocally, electronically, etc.), and on the mathematical and/or psychological laws governing the transmission, reception, and processing of information, whereas semiotics pays more attention to *what* messages mean, and *how* they create meaning.

communication theory

[< Latin COMMUNIS 'common'; Greek THEORIA 'a looking at']
Theoretical study of how *communication unfolds, and of why it unfolds in that way.

Note: The areas that communication theorists investigate include verbal and nonverbal forms (gesture, body language, facial expression) of human communication, animal communication, symbolism, alphabets, and the effect of technological media on perception and cognition.

communicative competence

[< Latin COMMUNIS 'common']
Ability to use a language appropriately in social contexts for various functions.

Illustration: When a male adolescent high school student says good-bye to one of his teachers, to his mother, or to a peer, he will convey the same message typically in three different ways: 1. *Good-bye to Teacher*: 'Good-bye, sir/ma'am!' 2. *Good-bye to Mother*: 'See ya' later, ma!' 3. *Good-bye to a Peer*: 'I gotta' split, man!'

These are not interchangeable – i.e. the adolescent would not say 'I gotta' split, man!' to a teacher, nor would he say, 'Goodbye, sir!' to a peer. The choice of forms and structural patterns that are utilized in specific situations, such as these, will vary predictably. This kind of systematic knowledge is called *communicative competence*.

communicology
[< Latin COMMUNIS 'common']
[synonym of *communication theory]

commutation test
[< Latin COMMUTARE 'to change']
Technique for analyzing how meaningful differences in *signs unfold and are maintained, consisting of commuting structurally corresponding elements in a pair or set of forms in order to ascertain if such a commutation is meaning-bearing.

Illustrations: 1. In the word pair *pin* and *bin* one element of sound, namely the initial consonant, is commuted in order to see if it produces a difference in meaning between the two forms. 2. In the study of advertising, the commutation test consists in changing an image or word in an ad, removing it and replacing it with another one, in order to see what kind of reaction it generates.

comparative grammar
[see *grammar]

competence, linguistic
[< Latin COMPETENTIA 'meeting, agreement']
Abstract knowledge of language.
Note: This term was coined by the American linguist Noam *Chomsky, who defined it as the innate knowledge that people employ unconsciously to produce and understand grammatically well-formed sentences, most of which they have never heard before. Chomsky proposed a system of analysis, which he called transformational-generative *grammar, that would purportedly allow the linguist to identify and describe the general properties of this innate knowledge, sifting them out from those that apply only to particular languages. The former, called *universal principles*, are purported to be part of a species-specific language faculty that has genetic information built into it about what languages in general must be like; the latter, known as *parameters*, are said to constrain the universal principles to produce the specific language grammar to which the child is exposed. Although Chomsky assigns some role to cultural and experiential factors, he has always maintained that the primary role of linguistics must be to understand the universal principles that make up the speech faculty.

compiler
[< Latin COMPILARE 'to snatch together']
Computer program that translates another program written in a high-level language into a machine language so that it can be executed.

complementary distribution
[< Latin COMPLEMENTUM 'that which fills']
Process whereby one form does not occur in the same position or context that another form related to it does.

Illustration: The *phoneme represented by the letter *n* in English (/n/) has three variants. Each occurs in a different predictable phonetic position. The three sounds are said to *complement* each other in how they are *distributed* among the other sounds in the pronunciation of words. The /n/ is produced: 1. by letting the tongue touch the palate in a word such as *bench*; 2. by arching the tongue towards the back of the mouth in a word such as *bank*; 3. by letting the tongue touch the upper teeth in a word such as *bent*. The /n/ in (1) is conditioned by the following palatal consonant; the /n/ in (2) is conditioned by the following back (velar) consonant. In all other positions, (3), the

/n/ is realized as a dental. These articulations of /n/ are in *complementary distribution* – i.e. where one occurs, the other does not.

componential analysis

[< Latin COMPONERE 'to put together']
Study of the meaning of words or other meaningful forms on the basis of *binary features or *components* that keep them distinct.

Illustrations: 1. The difference in meaning between *man* and *woman* is encoded in part by the features [+male, –female] vs. [+female, –male]. 2. The difference between a *book* and a *cat* is encoded in part by the features [–animate] vs. [+animate].

computer

[< Latin COMPUTARE 'to reckon']
Machine that performs algorithmic tasks, such as mathematical calculations, under the control of instructions called a *program. There are four main types of computers: 1. *digital computers*, which manipulate numbers that represent switches turned on or off by electrical current; 2. *analog computers*, which use numerical values with a continuous range, including fractions; 3. *mainframe computers*, which have more memory, speed, and capabilities than workstations and are usually shared by multiple users; 4. *supercomputers*, which are powerful mainframe computers having the capacity to process complex calculations.

Note: In 1623, the German scientist Wilhelm Schikard invented a machine that could add, multiply, and divide. Shortly thereafter, in 1642, French philosopher and mathematician Blaise Pascal (1623–62) invented a machine that could perform addition and subtraction, automatically carrying and borrowing digits from column to column. The German mathematician Gottfried *Leibniz subsequently designed a special gearing system to enable multiplication on Pascal's machine. These three machines were early precursors of modern-day computing machines.

In the early 19th century French inventor Joseph-Marie Jacquard (1752–1834) devised a loom that used punched cards to program patterns of woven fabrics. In the 1820s British mathematician and scientist Charles *Babbage incorporated the loom's design into his *Difference Engine*, for solving mathematical problems. Babbage also made plans for the *Analytical Engine*, considered to be the direct forerunner of the modern computer. At the end of the century, Herman Hollerith (1860–1929), an American inventor, combined the use of punched cards with devices that electronically read the cards. The company Hollerith founded eventually merged with other companies in 1924 to become International Business Machines (IBM) Corporation.

In the 1930s American mathematician Howard Aiken (1900–73), developed the *Mark I* electronic calculating machine, built by IBM, probably inspired by the British mathematician Alan *Turing's idea of a machine that could process equations without human direction. Shortly thereafter, in 1945, the Hungarian-American mathematician John von Neumann (1903–57) developed the first electronic computer to use a program stored entirely within its memory. John Mauchley (1908–80) and J. Presper Eckert (1919–95), built the first successful, general digital computer in the same year. In 1948, a group of American physicists developed the *transistor*. In the late 1960s *integrated circuits*, electrical components arranged on a single chip of silicon, replaced individual transistors.

In the 1970s the *microprocessor* was developed. The number of transistors and the computational speed of microprocessors started doubling approximately every 18 months. Today the development of sophisticated operating systems such as Windows and Unix enables computer users to run programs and manipulate data in ways that were unthinkable 50 years ago. Communications between computer users and networks will benefit from new technologies that can carry significantly more data and carry it faster, to and from the vast interconnected databases that continue to grow in number and type.

computer art

[< Latin COMPUTARE 'to reckon'; Latin ARS 'art']
Broad term that can refer either to art created on a computer or to art generated by a computer, the difference being that the 'artist' is human in the former case and electronic in the latter.

computer graphics

[< Latin COMPUTARE 'to reckon'; Greek GRAPHEIN 'to write']
Display of 'pictures' (charts, drawings, etc.), as opposed to only alphabetic and numerical characters, on a computer screen.

computer memory

[< Latin COMPUTARE 'to reckon']
Data stored in a computer as binary digits, called BYTES.

Note: A byte is equivalent to eight *bits of information. A *kilobyte* is 1000 bytes, a *megabyte* is 1 million bytes, and a *gigabyte* is 1 billion bytes. The physical memory of a computer is either *random-access memory* (*RAM), which can be read or changed by the user, or *read-only memory* (*ROM), which can be read but not altered. Computer chips hold memory, as do floppy disks, hard disks, and *CD-ROMs (compact discs).

computer science

[< Latin COMPUTARE 'to reckon']
Study of *computers, including their design, operation, and use in processing information.

Note: Early work in the field of computer science during the late 1940s and early

1950s focused on automating the process of making calculations for use in science and engineering. Scientists and engineers developed theoretical models of computation that enabled them to analyze how efficient different approaches were in performing various calculations. Computer science overlapped considerably during that era with numerical analysis. As the use of computers expanded, the focus of computer science broadened to include the creation of artificial languages used to program computers, operating systems, and networks, exploring relationships between computation and human thought.

The major branches of computer science today include software development, computer architecture (hardware), human-computer interfacing (the design of the most efficient ways for humans to use computers), and artificial intelligence (the attempt to make computers behave intelligently).

conative function

[< Latin CONATIO 'attempt']
In Roman *Jakobson's model of communication, the intended effect – physical, psychological, social – that a message has or is expected to have on the target or receiver of the message.

conceit

[< Latin CONCIPERE 'to take in, receive']
1. fanciful or witty expression; 2. elaborate, often extravagant *metaphor or *simile that makes an association between things that are normally perceived to be totally dissimilar.

Illustrations: 1. *My life is a wart.* 2. *Her ideas are like thumb tacks.*

concept

[< Latin CONCIPERE 'to take in, receive']
General thought connection or pattern made by the human mind (within cultural

contexts) through *association, *induction, *deduction, and/or *abduction.

concept, abstract
[< Latin CONCIPERE 'to take in, receive'; ABSTRAHERE 'to draw from']
[see also *concept, concrete]
*Concept that cannot be demonstrated, understood, or observed directly.

Illustration: The word *love* refers to an abstract concept because, although love exists as an emotional phenomenon, it cannot be demonstrated or observed directly (i.e. the emotion itself cannot be demonstrated or observed apart from the behaviors, states of mind, etc. that it produces). In order to demonstrate what it is, something explanatory or descriptive is needed – a love poem, a courtship ritual, etc.

concept, basic
[< Latin CONCIPERE 'to take in, receive']
[also called a prototypical concept]
*Concept that has a typological (classificatory) function.

Illustrations: 1. The word *blue* entails a basic concept because it refers to a type of *color*.
2. The word *d*ime encodes a basic concept because it refers a type of *coin*.

concept, concrete
[< Latin CONCIPERE 'to take in, receive'; CUM 'together' + CRESCERE 'to grow']
[see also *concept, abstract]
*Concept that is demonstrable and observable in a direct way.

Illustration: The word *cat* refers to a concrete concept because one can always demonstrate or observe the existence of a cat in the physical world and can represent it in concrete ways (e.g. a drawing of a cat).

concept, subordinate
[< Latin CONCIPERE 'to take in, receive'; SUB 'under' + ORDINARE 'to arrange']
*Concept that has a detailing function.

Illustration: The shades of *blue – dark blue, navy blue, sky blue, celeste,* etc. – all encode subordinate color concepts that are needed for specialized purposes.

concept, superordinate
[< Latin CONCIPERE 'to take in, receive'; SUPER 'above' + ORDINARE 'to arrange']
*Concept that has a highly general classificatory function.

Illustration: The concept encoded by the word *color* is a superordinate concept, because it refers to the general phenomenon of chromaticism and encompasses all the colors (*red*, *blue*, etc.).

concept-formation
[< Latin CONCIPERE 'to take in, receive']
Process of acquiring a *concept.

Note: The formation of a specific concept can be characterized generally as a 'pattern-extracting' or 'pattern-inferencing' process that appears to serve some useful cognitive function. The main types of concept-formation processes are *induction, *deduction, *abduction, *association, *analogy, *metaphor, and *metonymy.

conceptual metaphor
[see *metaphor, conceptual]

conceptual metonym
[see *metonym, conceptual]

concrete concept
[see *concept, concrete]

concrete image
[see *image, mental]

concrete operational stage
[see *Jean Piaget]

Condillac, Étienne Bonnot de
[1715–1780]
18th-century French philosopher, whose theory, known as sensationalism, is re-

garded as a key contribution to the foundation of the science of *psychology. Condillac argued that human knowledge and conscious experiences are derived from sense perception alone.

conjecture

[< Latin CUM 'together' + JACERE 'to throw']
Inference or judgment based on inconclusive or incomplete evidence.

conjunction

[< Latin CUM 'together' + JUNGERE 'to join']
Part of speech serving to connect words, phrases, clauses, or sentences.

Illustrations: 1. I read <u>and</u> write English fairly well. 2. He understands English, <u>but</u> does not speak it well.

connectionism

[< Latin CUM 'together' + NECTERE 'to fasten']
[also called parallel processing theory]
Computer technique in which multiple operations are carried out simultaneously.

Note: In 1996 International Business Machine Corporation (IBM) challenged Garry Kasparov, the reigning world chess champion, to a chess match with a supercomputer called 'Deep Blue.' The computer utilized 256 microprocessors in a parallel architecture to compute more than 100 million chess positions per second. Kasparov won the match with three wins, two draws, and one loss. Deep Blue was the first computer to win a game against a world champion with regulation time controls. Deep Blue now serves as a prototype for developing computers with the capacity to solve complex problems.

connotation

[< Latin CUM 'together' + NOTARE 'to mark']
[see also *denotation]
Extended, secondary, or implied meaning of a *sign (word, symbol, etc.) or *text (conversation, story, etc.).

Illustration: The word *house* denotes 'any (free-standing) structure intended for human habitation.' This meaning can be seen in utterances such as *I bought a new house yesterday; House prices are continually going up in this city; We repainted our house the other day;* and so on. Now, the same word can be extended as follows: *The house is in session now* (= legislative assembly); *The house roared with laughter* (= theater audience); *He sleeps in one of the houses at Harvard* (= dormitory). In such connotative extensions, the *distinctive features of the word – [+structure], [+human], [+habitation] – remain implicitly; i.e. a legislative assembly, a theater audience, and a dormitory do indeed imply *structures* of special kinds that *humans* can be said to *inhabit* (occupy) in some specific way. Any connotative extension of the word *house* is thus constrained by its distinctive features: i.e. *house* can be applied to refer to anything that involves or implicates humans (or beings) coming together for some specific reason.

At a higher level, connotation is the operative mode in the production and decipherment of creative texts such as poems, novels, musical compositions, art works – in effect, of most of the non-mathematical and non-scientific texts that a culture produces. Mathematical and scientific texts, by contrast, are interpreted primarily in denotative ways. But this does not mean that meaning in science is encoded necessarily denotatively. On the contrary, many of the theories and models of science are born of connotative thinking, even though they end up being interpreted denotatively over time.

connotation, emotive

[< Latin CUM 'together' + NOTARE 'to mark'; Latin EX 'from' + MOVERE 'to move']
[sometimes called *annotation]
*Connotation that conveys personal perspective or emotion.

Illustration: The word *yes* can have various emotive connotations, depending on the tone of voice with which it is uttered. If one says it with a normal tone of voice, it will be understood as a sign of affirmation. If, however, one says it with a raised tone, as in a question, *yes?*, then it would imply doubt or incredulity. Such 'added meanings' to the word *yes* are examples of emotive connotation.

connotation, mythic
[< Latin CUM 'together' + NOTARE 'to mark']
[see also *myth]
*Connotation that alludes to, or evokes, a mythic theme.

Note: Mythic themes and personages are found frequently in advertising. For example, the myth of Persephone, daughter of Zeus, father of the gods, and of Demeter, goddess of the earth and of agriculture, is often implied in the advertisements of female lifestyle products, such as perfume, high heel shoes, etc. Hades, god of the underworld, fell in love with Persephone and wished to marry her. Although Zeus gave his consent, Demeter was unwilling. Hades, therefore, seized the maiden as she was gathering flowers and carried her off to his realm. As Demeter wandered in search of her lost daughter, the earth grew desolate. Finally Zeus sent Hermes, the messenger of the gods, to bring Persephone back to her mother. Before Hades would let her go, he asked her to eat a pomegranate seed, the food of the dead. She was thus compelled to return to the underworld for one-third of the year. As both the goddess of the dead and the goddess of the earth's fertility, Persephone is a personification of the revival of nature in spring. Her 'story' is thus often used to convey connotations of 'fertility,' 'sexuality,' 'coming of age,' etc.

connotative sequence (or chain)
[< Latin CUM 'together' + NOTARE 'to mark']
Sequence or chain of *connotations suggested by a *sign or *text.

Illustration: The use of dark colors in an advertising text can activate the following connotative sequence: *dark = night = mystery = fear = evil = forbidden desires =* etc.

connotatum
[Latin 'noted together']
Connotative referent of a sign.

Note: The word *lion* has a denotative (intended) meaning when it refers to the animal 'lion.' However, when it is used to refer to qualities of 'fierceness,' 'pride,' etc., as in *He's a real lion*, then these referents are called its *connotata* (plural of *connotatum*).

consciousness
[< Latin CUM 'with' + SCIRE 'to know']
Awareness of one's environment and one's own existence, sensations, and thoughts.

Note: Throughout history there have been many attempts to study and understand this truly unique phenomenon. The semiotic approach has traditionally viewed consciousness as a product of the body, mind, and culture nexus. Human consciousness starts out as a bodily-sensory phenomenon. Children come to know objects by experiencing them directly, through the senses (by tasting them, touching them, etc.). This form of 'sensory consciousness' is subsequently mediated and structured by the *signs learned in social context. These induce a reflective state of consciousness that is based on referentiality (i.e. on what signs call attention to). Finally, human consciousness entails access to a *culture-specific* way of knowing, i.e. a highly abstract state of consciousness that is based on a *signifying order.

In recent years, the phenomenon of consciousness has become the source of much interest among sociobiologists and cognitive scientists, who have tried to demystify it by explaining it as an outcome of genetic processes (see *sociobiology). To the sociobiologist the emergence and function of consciousness in the human species is, ipso facto, as explainable as is the evolution and function of taste, sight, or of any other organic system.

Although it seems like a radical proposal, the sociobiological perspective turns out, upon closer scrutiny, to be a contemporary descendant of a philosophical legacy that goes under the rubric of *physicalism. Although it has ancient roots, this doctrine gained widespread momentum in Western society after the establishment of Darwinian evolutionary biology in the 19th century. Sociobiologists view human consciousness and human cultural behaviors as products of evolution. So, human rituals such as kissing and flirting, for instance, are explained as modern-day reflexes of animal mechanisms.

The idea that there is a biological basis to conscious social behaviors is, of course, partially true; but it is not totally true. There is no evidence of a capacity for language, art, music, science, or any of the other characteristic attributes of humanity in other species. While culture may have certainly enhanced human survivability and reproductive success in some ways, in many others it has, curiously and incomprehensibly, put the human being's inbuilt instinctual survival systems at risk – humans undergo a long period of development before sexual maturity, they cannot run as fast on average as other primates, they commit suicide, and they do many other things that would seem indeed to put in jeopardy their very survival.

The psychoanalyst Sigmund *Freud (1856–1939) pointed out that consciousness was only the 'tip of the iceberg,' psychologically speaking. Below the 'tip' was the *unconscious*, the region of the human mind that he claimed contained wishes, memories, fears, feelings, and ideas that are prevented from expression in conscious awareness. They manifest themselves instead by their influence on conscious processes and, most

strikingly, through dreams, works of art, neuroses, and language forms. Like physicalists, however, Freud suggested that the unconscious had a biological origin and that culture was essentially a collective system that emerged to regulate and constrain sexual urges.

The Swiss psychologist Carl *Jung (1875–1961) saw Freud's interpretation of the unconscious as too narrow, preferring instead to explain consciousness in terms of a larger creative energy. He also made a distinction between the personal unconscious, or the specific feelings and thoughts developed by an individual during his/her life, and the *collective unconscious*, the universal feelings and thoughts of the species. Jung saw the latter as a kind of 'receptacle' of inherited primordial memories and images shared by all humanity that are too weak to become conscious. So, they gain expression in the symbols and forms that make their way into the myths, tales, fantasies, artistic expressions, and rituals that are found in cultures across the world. He called these universal symbols and forms *archetypes. For instance, the genital symbols and themes that cultures incorporate typically into their rites of passage, that surface commonly in their works of art, and that find their way into the stories that are communicated regularly in all kinds of cultural contexts are understandable in approximately the same ways by all humans because they evoke sexual images buried in the collective unconscious of the species. Archetypes are traces to these images that continue to influence patterns of perception and meaning-making in modern-day humans.

In effect, the study of consciousness is a study of the basic metaphysical questions that haunt humans everywhere: Why are we here? Who or what put us here? What, if anything, can be done about it? Who am I? and so on. The languages, myths, narratives, rituals, art works, etc. that human beings learn to employ early in life guide their search to discover answers to such questions.

consonant

[< Latin CUM 'together' + SONUS 'sound']
[see also *vowel]
Vocal sound produced with some obstruction to the airstream emanating from the lungs.

Illustrations: 1. In *coo* the *c* represents a consonant. 2. In *up* the *p* represents a consonant.

constructivism

[< Latin CUM 'together' + STRUERE 'to pile up']
1. movement in modern art originating in Moscow around 1920, characterized by the use of industrial materials to create abstract, geometric images, and art objects; 2. view in philosophy and semiotics that 'common sense' theories of the world are made by humans to suit their particular whims and needs and, thus, that *communal sense* is often mistaken for *common sense*.

consumer advertising

[see *advertising, consumer]

contact

[< Latin CONTINGERE 'to touch, seize']
In Roman *Jakobson's model of communication, the physical conditions (channel, situation, etc.) in which a message is delivered and the primary social and psychological connections that exist or are established between the participants.

contagion effect

[< Latin CONTAGIO 'a touching']
Term referring to the psychological power of the media to create a craze.

Note: A classic example of this effect can be seen in the 'Cabbage Patch doll craze' of 1983. Hordes of parents were prepared to pay almost anything to get one of these dolls for their daughters during that Christmas season. Scalpers offered the suddenly and unexplainably out-of-stock dolls for hundreds of dollars through classified ads. Grown adults fought each other in line-ups to get one of the few remaining dolls left in stock at certain mall toy outlets. Such mass hysteria was an extreme manifestation of the contagion effect, created by an effective media marketing campaign.

contagious magic

[see *magic]

content

[< Latin CUM 'together' + TENERE 'to hold']
[see *form]
Essential meaning of something.

Note: In a work of art the *content* is said to be what the work means, and the *form* how it has been put together. In semiotic theories, it is typically stressed that form and content are interconnected and not separable in the creation of a meaning.

content analysis

[< Latin CUM 'together' + TENERE 'to hold'; Greek ANA 'throughout' + LYSIS 'a loosing']
Research into *mass media that aims to identify, categorize, and analyze the content of messages.

Note: Content analysis involves counting the number of times a word or theme appears in a particular text. It has revealed, among other things, that people tend to find in a text the meanings that they are seeking at the time of decoding the text.

context

[< Latin CONTEXTUS 'a joining together']
1. parts of a sentence, paragraph, or discourse that impose a constraint on the composition of a form and/or on what a form means; 2. whole situation, background, or environment (physical, social, psychological) that determines the meaning of something.

Illustration: A discarded and damaged soup

can would be interpreted as rubbish if one were to come across this item on the sidewalk of a city street. But if the same person saw the same object on a pedestal, displayed in an art gallery, 'signed' by some artist, and given a title such as 'Waste,' then she/he would be inclined to interpret its meaning in a vastly different way. Clearly, the can's physical context of occurrence and social frame of reference – its location on a sidewalk vs. its display in an art gallery – will determine how one will interpret it.

contrast

[< Latin CONTRA 'against' + STARE 'to stand']
Minimal difference between two elements (two words, two symbols, etc.).

Illustration: The words *pat* and *pot* contrast with each other because of a minimal difference between their vowels. This contrast is said to be 'minimal' because it is sufficient to signal a difference in meaning.

conundrum

*Riddle whose answer relies on a *pun.

Illustrations: 1. *What's the difference between a jeweler and a jailer? One sells watches and the other watches cells.* 2. *What is black and white and red all over? A newspaper.*

conventional sign

[see *sign, conventional]

conversation

[< Latin CONVERSARI 'to live with, keep company with']
[see also *discourse]
Act of talking with someone to exchange ideas, opinions, etc.

Corinthian form

[see also *Doric form, *Ionic form]
Architectural column developed by the ancient Greeks, characterized by a slender shaft and a capital (top part) that is ornately decorated and carved in the shape of an inverted bell.

corollary

[< Latin COROLLARIUM 'a deduction']
Proposition that follows with little or no proof required from one already proved.

Illustration: If it is proved that in an isosceles triangle (a triangle with two equal sides) the angles opposite the two equal sides are equal, then, as a corollary, it follows that a triangle with two equal angles is isosceles.

cosmetics

[see *make-up]

cosmogonic myth

[see *mythology]

counterpoint

[< Italian CONTRAPPUNTO 'pointed against'; from the Latin PUNCTUS CONTRA PUNCTUS, 'point (or note) against point']
In music, style of composition whereby melodic material is added to an existing melody in such a way that the melodic strains establish a harmonic relationship while retaining their individuality.

Illustration: The song *Row, row, row your boat*, with its 'slightly off' progressive addition of voices, is in counterpoint style.

creole

[< Portuguese CRIOULO 'native to the region']
[see also *pidgin]
Language that arises through contact with another language, becoming the native language of its community.

Illustrations: In Guyanese creole, the French (1) *j'ai mangé* 'I have eaten' is rendered as *mo manje*, and (2) *Il est plus grand que vous* 'He is bigger than you' as *Li gros pas u*.

crest

Heraldic *insignia representing both a mark of rank and a conspicuous emblem in battle.

Note: The crest is attached to the top of the helmet; its base is surrounded by a wreath of twisted ribbons in the principal metal and color of the shield.

critical period hypothesis
[< Greek KRITIKOS 'a critic'; HYPO 'under' + TITHENAI 'to place']
Linguist Eric Lenneberg's hypothesis, formulated in his 1967 book *The Biological Foundations of Language*, that the critical period for language acquisition was from birth to about puberty, a period during which the brain organizes the distribution of the mental functions, especially the localization of language to the left hemisphere.

criticism
[< Greek KRITIKOS 'a critic']
Analysis of the qualities and value of a literary or artistic work.

Note: Literary criticism in the Western world began with *Plato, who asserted that poetry, while greatly inspirational, was no more than mere imitation of the transitory actual world. Plato's student *Aristotle, by contrast, argued that poetry embodied universal human feelings and experiences. The Roman poet Horace (65–8 BC) maintained that the function of poetry was simply to please and instruct. In the Middle Ages, the Italian poet *Dante showed, in his treatise *De Vulgari Eloquentia*, how language and the poet's intent were interrelated. Dante's view dominated Western literary criticism until the second half of the 19th century.

The movement that had the most resounding impact on early-20th-century criticism was the so-called New Criticism movement, which was greatly influenced by the American-born English poet and critic T.S. Eliot (1888–1965). The 'new critics' analyzed structure and imagery in order to determine a literary work's particular concrete meaning aside from historical context or authorship. By mid-century, criticism branched out in several directions. *Psychoanalytic* critics focused on the mythic images and themes in a literary work, as filtered through the collective unconscious of the human race; *semiotic* (or *structuralist*) critics investigated the literary work as a *code; *hermeneutic* critics examined the work in terms of its sources and linguistic characteristics; *Marxist* critics looked at a piece of writing as indicative of historical and ideological processes; *feminist* critics re-examined literary works in terms of women's roles and in reference to patriarchal systems of control; *deconstructivists* examined how texts referred more to other texts than to some central, fixed reality.

Croce, Benedetto
[1866–1952]
Italian philosopher and critic who viewed artistic expression as the intuitive apprehension of things without reflection. For Croce the reason why art exists in human life is to allow human beings to give expression to the forms of beauty and ugliness that are buried within the human spirit.

cryptogram
[< Greek KRIPTEIN 'to hide' + GRAMMA 'letter']
[also called cryptograph]
Piece of writing in *code or *cipher.

Illustration: 1-12-5-24 = *Alex:* each number stands for the number of a letter in the English alphabet (1 = first letter, *A*; 12 = twelfth letter *l*; 5 = fifth letter, *e*, 24 = twenty-fourth, letter *x*).

cryptography
[< Greek KRIPTEIN 'to hide' + GRAPHEIN 'to write']
[see also *cipher]
1. art of writing or deciphering messages in secret *code; 2. science of preparing messages using apparently incoherent text intended to be intelligible only to the person possessing the *key*, or method, of unlocking the hidden meaning.

cubism

[< Latin CUBUS 'cube']
Movement in 20th-century visual art characterized by a separation of the subject into cubes and other geometric forms in abstract arrangements, rather than by a realistic representation of the subject.

Note: Cubism began in Paris about 1908, reaching its height by 1914, and developed further in the 1920s. It drew inspiration from tribal art and marked the beginning of abstract art in Western visual representation. *Analytical cubism* emphasized the basic geometric solids or basic planes; *synthetic cubism* incorporated views of a subject from different angles into a unified composition. Cubist painters include Pablo Picasso (1881–1973), Georges Braque (1882–1963), and Marcel Duchamp (1887–1968). Cubist sculptors include Picasso, Raymond Duchamp-Villon (1876–1918), and Aleksandr Archipenko (1887–1964).

cuisine

[see *food vs. cuisine]

cultural anthropology

[see *anthropology, cultural]

cultural model

[< Latin COLERE 'to till' + MODUS 'mode']
[see also *metaphor, conceptual]
General abstract concept derived from the constant juxtaposition of conceptual metaphors.

Illustration: The abstract concept of *ideas* is commonly rendered as a combination of metaphorical concepts: e.g. in terms of build-ings, plants, commodities, geometry, persons, and substances: *That idea is on a solid foundation* (= ideas are buildings); *That idea has deep roots* (= ideas are plants); *I don't buy that idea* (= ideas are commodities); *Our ideas are parallel* (= ideas are geometrical figures); *Darwin is the father of evolutionary biology* (= ideas are persons); *You must weigh your ideas carefully* (= ideas are substances). The constant juxtaposition of such metaphorical concepts in common discourse produces, cumulatively, a cultural model of ideas:

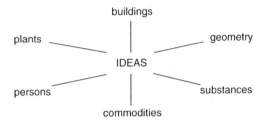

cultural semiotics

[see *semiotics, cultural]

culture

[< Latin COLERE 'to till']
System of socially transmitted group behavior patterns, arts, beliefs, institutions, and all other products of human work and thought.

[*Note*] In strictly semiotic terms, *culture* is defined as a synthetic system of different types of *signs that cohere into *codes which individuals and groups can utilize to construct *texts in order to make meanings or exchange messages in various *contexts. The system, called the *signifying order* (see figure below), *mediates* how people know

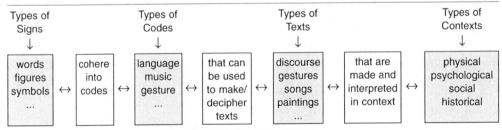

Types of Signs		Types of Codes		Types of Texts		Types of Contexts
↓		↓		↓		↓
words figures symbols ...	cohere into codes	language music gesture ...	that can be used to make/ decipher texts	discourse gestures songs paintings ...	that are made and interpreted in context	physical psychological social historical

THE SIGNIFYING ORDER

the world, and because representation is a selectional process – i.e. a sign, text, or code pre-selects what is to be known and memorized from the infinite variety of things that are in the world – it shapes worldview.

As an illustration of how culture mediates worldview, consider the concept of *health*. What is considered to be healthy in one culture may not coincide with views of health in another. Health cannot be defined ahistorically, aculturally, or in purely absolutist terms. This does not deny the existence of events and states in the body that will lead to disease or illness. All organisms have a species-specific bodily warning system that alerts them to dangerous changes in bodily states. But in the human species such states are also representable and thus interpretable in culture-specific ways. This is why in some cultures a 'healthy body' is considered to be one that is lean and muscular. Conversely, in others it is one that is more plump and rotund. A 'healthy lifestyle' might be seen by some cultures to inhere in rigorous physical activity, while in others it might be envisaged as inhering in a more leisurely and sedentary form of behavior.

culture hero myth
[see *mythology]

cultureme
[< Latin COLERE 'to till']
Unit of culturally based and culturally meaningful behavior (e.g. a taste in food, a type of pose on certain occasions, etc.).

cuneiform
[< Latin CUNEUS 'wedge']
Wedge-shaped writing system, partly pictographic and partly symbolic, used in ancient Akkadian, Assyrian, Babylonian, and Persian inscriptions.

Note: In the ancient civilization of Sumer around 3500 BC pictographic writing was used to record agricultural transactions and astronomical observations. Most of the Sumerian pictographs represented nouns for stars and animals, with a few for such qualifying adjectives as *small*, *big*, and *bright*. A few centuries later, this pictographic system was expanded to include verbs: *to sleep*, for example, was represented by a person in a supine position. To facilitate the speed of writing, the Sumerians eventually streamlined their pictographs and transformed them into symbols for the actual sounds of speech. These were written down on clay tablets with a stylus in a form of writing called *cuneiform* ('wedge-shaped').

cursor
[see *input hardware]

cybernetics
[< Greek KYBERNETES 'helmsman']
Interdisciplinary science dealing with communication and control systems in living organisms, machines, and organizations.

Note: The term was coined in 1948 by American mathematician Norbert Wiener (1894–1964). According to Wiener, control mechanisms for self-correction in machines serve the same purpose that the nervous system serves in coordinating information to determine which actions will be performed. This principle, known as *feedback*, is the fundamental concept of cybernetics. Another basic tenet is that information can be statistically measured in accordance with the laws of probability.

cyberspace
[< Greek KYBERNETES 'helmsman']
'Space' created by the 'computer culture' that has developed among users of computers.

Note: The term was coined by American writer William Gibson in his 1984 science fiction novel *Neuromancer*, in which he described cyberspace as a place of 'unthinkable complexity.' The term has given rise to a vocabulary of 'cyberterms,' such as *cybercafes* (cafes that sell coffee and computer time), *cybermalls* (online shopping services), and *cyberjunkies* (people addicted to being online).

cylindrical projection
[see *map]

D

---

dactylology
[< Greek DAKTULOS 'finger']
Use of the fingers and hands to communicate and convey ideas, as in the manual alphabets used by hearing- and speech-impaired people.

dada
[see *dadaism]

dadaism
[< DADA, French baby-talk for 'hobbyhorse'] [also called dada]
Movement in painting, sculpture, and literature, lasting from about 1916 to 1922, characterized by highly imaginative, abstract, or incongruous creations, and especially by the rejection of all accepted conventions of Western art.

Note: The term dada was selected randomly as the name of the movement by Romanian-born writer Tristan Tzara (1896–1963). In wanting to revoke all contemporary aesthetic and social values, dadaists frequently used artistic and literary methods that were deliberately incomprehensible, shocking, or bewildering, in order to provoke a reconsideration of accepted values.

dance
[< French DANSER 'to move back and forth'] [see also *ballet]

Art form based on bodily movements and gestures connected to each other through musical tempo and rhythm. The functions of dance include 1. aesthetic representation; 2. narration through bodily movement; 3. recreation; 4. ritual.

Note: Prehistoric cave paintings depicting figures in animal costumes that seem to be dancing, possibly in hunting or fertility rituals, or perhaps for education or entertainment, suggest that dancing is ancient. In Egypt, dancing was an intrinsic part of agricultural and religious festivals. Pyrrhic or warrior dances were part of military training in ancient Greece, and dancing during religious rites is believed to be the source of the inclusion of dance in Greek drama.

Variations of peasant dances originating in the Middle Ages continue today as folk dances. Ballet originated in the courts of Italy and France during the Renaissance, developing into a professional artistic discipline. In the late 19th and early 20th centuries, reaction against ballet's traditional forms led several influential American choreographers to develop other forms of art dancing. Popular and social dances, which are recreational dance forms, resemble folk dances in that they entail participation, are relatively easy to learn, and generally originate from the people rather than from a choreographer: for example, the swinging movements of African-American dance evolved into jazz dancing in the 1920s, 1930s, and 1940s, and rock-and-roll dances in the 1950s.

Dante Alighieri
[1265–1321]
Medieval Italian poet, and one of the greatest figures of world literature.

Note: Dante's epic masterpiece, *La divina commedia* ('The Divine Comedy'), was probably begun around 1307 and was completed shortly before his death. The work is an allegorical narrative in verse of Dante's imaginary journey through hell, purgatory, and heaven. In each of these realms the poet meets with mythological, historical, and characters of his era, each of whom symbolizes a particular fault or virtue. Dante is guided through hell and purgatory by the Roman poet Virgil, who is, to Dante, the symbol of reason. The woman Dante loved, Beatrice, whom he regards as an instrument of divine will, guides him through paradise. Dante intended the poem for his contemporaries. This is why he wrote it in Italian rather than Latin.

Darwin, Charles

[1809–1882]

British zoologist who formulated the theory of *natural selection, which holds that reproductive success in organisms tends to promote *adaptation that is necessary for survival. Darwin announced his theory in 1858, explaining it in his 1859 book, *On the Origin of Species*. Natural selection claims, in essence, that the young born to any species compete for survival. Those who survive pass on favorable natural variations through heredity. This gradual and continuous process is the source of the evolution of species. Darwin also introduced the concept that all related organisms are descended from common ancestors, and he pioneered the study of animal communication and intelligence, tracing many links between human and animal behaviors.

database

[< Latin DATUS 'given']

Any compilation of data organized for storage and access by computers. Databases became commercially available in the 1960s, but to a limited extent; on-line databases, available to anyone who could link to them, appeared in the 1970s.

decoding

[< Latin DE 'from' + CODEX 'wooden tablet for writing']

Process of deciphering a *sign or *text in terms of a specific *code.

Illustration: In order to decode the meaning of the numeral '10' one must know from which code it was made. If it was constructed from the code of decimal numbers, then it stands for the number 'ten'; if it was constructed from the code of binary numbers, then it stands for the number 'two.'

deconstruction

[< Latin DE 'down, from' + CUM 'together' + STRUERE 'to pile up']

Method of literary analysis originated by Jacques *Derrida in the mid-20th century, based on his view that, by the very nature of language and literary usage, no *text can have a fixed, central meaning.

Note: The deconstruction movement, also known as *poststructuralism, questioned traditional assumptions about certainty, identity, and truth, asserting that words can only refer to other words. Deconstructionist literary criticism was highly subjective, since it attempted to demonstrate how statements about any text subverted their own meanings.

deduction

[< Latin DE 'down, from' + DUCERE 'to lead']

[see also *abduction, *induction]

Reasoning and concept-formation that unfolds by the application of a *general* concept or line of reasoning to a *specific* occurrence.

Illustration: If A is greater than B, and B greater than C, then it can be *deduced* that A is (much) greater than C.

deep structure

[see also *surface structure]

Linguist Noam *Chomsky's notion that all sentences have an underlying level on which their meaning can be interpreted.

Illustration: The two sentences *John is eager to please* and *John is easy to please* have the same sequential, linear structure (known as *surface structure*). But the kinds of meanings the sentences implicate are rather different. In effect, the *surface structure* does not tell the whole story. A paraphrase of the two sentences reveals that they have different *deep structures: John is eager to please = John is eager to please someone; John is easy to please = It is easy for someone to please John.* The conflation of both these deep structures into a homologous surface structure is due to the operation of what Chomsky calls *transformational rules* which move around, delete, and add elements to deep structure forms.

default

[< Latin DE 'away' + FALLERE 'to fail']
Choice built into a computer program to which the computer resorts when the user does not specify an alternative.

Illustration: Unless otherwise altered, a computer program (e.g. *Microsoft Word*) will resort to a font, a letter case, etc. that is built into it as a default.

definition

[< Latin DEFINIRE 'to define']
Statement of the meaning of a word or phrase.

Illustration: The word *door* can be defined as 'a movable structure for opening or closing an entrance, as to a building or room, or giving access to a closet, cupboard, etc.'

deictic gesture

[< Greek DEIKTIKOS 'capable of proof'; Latin GERERE 'to bear, carry']
Gesture utilized during oral discourse that serves to indicate an abstract concept that had occurred earlier in the conversation.

Illustration: When someone says 'as I said earlier,' she/he typically flips the finger or hand in a backward motion, as if to imply that what she/he said had occurred in an area behind the head.

deixis

[< Greek DEIKTIKOS 'capable of proof']
[also called *indexicality]
Pointing out something by a gesture, word, or symbol, in order to locate it in time or space or in relation to something else.

Note: There are three types of deixis: 1. *Spatial deixis* is a form of reference by which the spatial locations of objects, beings, and events are either indicated or correlated by a manual sign like the pointing index finger, a demonstrative word like *this* or *that*, an adverb like *here* or *there*, etc. 2. *Temporal deixis* is a form of reference by which the temporal relations among things and events are either indicated or correlated by a manual gesture, an adverb like *before, after, now,* or *then,* a timeline graph representing points in time as located to the left and right, or on top and below, etc. 3. *Personal deixis* is a form of reference by which the relations among participants taking part in a situation are either indicated or correlated by a manual gesture, a personal pronoun like *I, you, he, she,* an indefinite pronoun like *the one, the other,* etc.

Deleuze, Gilles

[1925–1995]
French philosopher who claimed that biological life was not much different from the machines that humans build. Deleuze argued that the form given by humans to artifacts and machines mirrors the form of their physical and psychic life.

Democritus

[c. 460–c. 370 BC]
Greek philosopher who formulated the first atomic theory of matter. Democritus reduced the sensory qualities of things, such as warmth, cold, taste, and odor, to quantitative differences among their atomic properties. He claimed that even the mind could be explained in such purely physical terms. He thus formulated the first comprehensive statement of *physicalism* by which all aspects

of existence are purported to be explainable in terms of the operation of physical laws.

demonstrative
[< Latin DE 'from' + MONSTRARE 'to show']
Word specifying or singling out something relative to something else.

Illustrations: 1. *this* book; 2. *that* book; 3. *these* phones; 4. *those* phones; 5. *This* one is mine; *that* one is yours.

demotic
[< Greek DEMOTES 'one of the people']
Type of simplified script that replaced *hieroglyphic writing in ancient Egypt around 2755 BC.

denotation
[< Latin DE 'from' + NOTARE 'to mark']
[see also *connotation]
Initial meaning that a *sign is designed to capture.

Note: The denotative meaning of a word like *cat* is not something specific, but more precisely the quality of 'catness,' which is marked by specific *distinctive features such as [mammal], [retractile claws], [long tail], etc. This composite mental image allows us to determine if a specific real or imaginary animal under consideration will fall within the category of 'catness.' Similarly, the word *square* does not denote a specific 'square,' but rather a figure consisting of four equal straight lines that meet at right angles. It is irrelevant if the lines are thick, dotted, 2 meters long, 80 feet long, or whatever. So long as the figure can be seen to have the distinctive features [four equal straight lines] and [meeting at right angles], it is identifiable denotatively as a *square*.

denotatum
[< Latin DE 'from' + NOTARE 'to mark']
Denotative referent of a *sign.

Illustration: The *denotatum* of the word *square* does not imply a specific 'square,' but rather

a figure exemplifying 'squareness,' i.e. four equal straight lines meeting at right angles.

dénouement
[< Latin DE 'from, out' + NODUS 'knot']
Outcome, solution, or clarification of a plot in a drama or narrative.

dependency theory
[< Latin DE 'down' + PENDERE 'to hang'; Greek THEORIA 'a looking at']
View expressed commonly by media analysts that people can easily become 'dependent' upon mass media.

Note: It is claimed that people habituated to large doses of information and visual stimulation, especially by watching TV, tend to become psychologically dependent on the medium in ways that parallel substance dependency.

depth psychology
[infrequent synonym for *psychoanalysis]

derivational morpheme
[< Latin DERIVARE 'to divert'; Greek MORPHĒ 'form']
[see also *bound morpheme]
Bound morpheme that creates a word with a different grammatical function from the word to which it is bound.

Illustration: The word *cautiously* is an adverb consisting of the adjective root *cautious* plus the bound morpheme *-ly* (= *cautious* + *-ly*). The suffix *-ly* is known as a *derivational* morpheme because it creates a word with a different grammatical function than the word to which it is bound.

Derrida, Jacques
[1930–]
French philosopher whose work originated a method of analysis – known as *deconstruction – that has been applied to literature, linguistics, philosophy, law, and architecture. Central to Derrida's view is the

notion that in a text (a poem, a novel, etc.) there are layers of meaning that are constantly shifting and, therefore, that it is impossible to determine what a text means.

Descartes, René

[1596–1650]

French mathematician and philosopher, considered the founder of analytic geometry. Descartes refused to accept any belief, even the belief in his own existence, unless he could 'prove' it to be necessarily true. Descartes gave the Platonic mind-body problem its modern formulation, known as *dualism*. This is the notion that the mind's activities are independent of bodily states and processes. Descartes was, however, unable to explain the fact that two different entities, the mind and the body, can so affect each other.

descriptive grammar

[see *grammar]

desensitization

[< Latin DE 'down' + SENTIRE 'to feel']
Process by which audiences are considered to be made immune, or less sensitive, to human suffering or degradation as a result of relentless exposure to such suffering or degradation in media portrayals.

detective story

[< Latin DE 'from' + TEGERE 'to cover']
Narrative that features a private detective or a police officer as the hero, whose task it is to solve a crime.

Note: The detective story is told either as a first-person narration of the detective character or in the third person by the author. Typically, the detective interrogates suspects, ferrets out clues, and eventually tracks down the criminal. The detective shares all the clues with the reader but usually withholds their significance until the end.

The first fictional detective was Edgar Allan Poe's (1809–49) C. Auguste Dupin, who appeared in an 1841 story. Stories about detectives became very popular with the creation of Sherlock Holmes by British writer Sir Arthur Conan Doyle (1859–1930) shortly thereafter. In the 20th century, British writer G.K. Chesterton (1874–1936) introduced the character of Father Brown, a priest-detective, and British writer Agatha Christie (1890–1976) made Hercule Poirot famous. During the 1920s in the United States an action genre of detective story, featuring a tough private-eye or investigator, was developed. Authors of this genre include Erle Stanley Gardner (1889–1970), creator of lawyer-detective Perry Mason, Dashiell Hammett (1894–1961), creator of Sam Spade, and Raymond Chandler (1888–1959), creator of Philip Marlowe. In the early 1950s, stories about how real police detectives solve actual crimes became highly popular. Since then the detective story has become one of the most popular forms of narrative in novels, in cinema, and on TV.

determiner

[< Latin DE 'from' + TERMINARE 'to set bounds']
Word specifying a noun in some way.

Illustrations: 1. *the* boy; 2. *that* girl; 3. *which* book; 4. *both* parents.

determinism

[< Latin DE 'from' + TERMINARE 'to set bounds']
Philosophical doctrine holding that every event, mental as well as physical, has a cause, and that, the cause being given, the event follows invariably. This theory denies the element of chance and the concept of 'free will.'

Dewey, John

[1859–1952]
American educator and leader of the *pragmatic* movement in philosophy who rejected traditional methods of teaching by rote in

favor of a broad-based system of instruction emphasizing practical experience. Dewey also maintained that *truth* is a word that can be applied only to an idea that has worked in practical experience.

diachrony
[< Greek DIA 'through' + CHRONOS 'time']
[see also *synchrony]
Change in *signs, *texts, and *codes over time.

Note: The type of change can be either structural (i.e. as the result of tendencies within the code) or social (i.e. as a result of social forces). An example of the former is the loss of the pronunciation of /k/ before nasal consonants in English. Even though it is still written in words like *knife, knot*, etc., the /k/ is no longer pronounced, probably because in initial position the sequence /kn/ is exceptional in English syllable structure. An example of socially induced change is the elimination of the suffix *-man* in words such as *chairman, spokesman*, etc. (replaced by *chair, spokesperson*, etc.) as a result of the feminist critique of patriarchal forms in language starting in the 1960s.

diagram
[< Greek DIA 'through' + GRAPHEIN 'to write']
1. geometric figure, used to illustrate a mathematical statement, proof, etc.; 2. sketch, drawing, or plan that explains a thing by outlining its parts and their relationships; 3. chart or graph explaining or illustrating ideas, statistics, etc.

Note: Diagrams allow human beings to envision information and real-world phenomena. Because science often involves things that cannot be seen – atoms, waves, gravitational forces, magnetic fields, etc. – diagrams allow scientists to visualize something with the mental eye that is unseeable with the physical eye.

dialect
[< Greek DIA 'through' + LEGEIN 'to talk']

1. any form of speech considered as differing in specific ways from a real or imaginary standard form; 2. form or variety of a spoken language peculiar to a region, community, social group, occupational group, etc.

Note: A dialect restricted to a certain area or locale is called a *geographical dialect*; one spoken by a specific group of people of a similar level of education, social class, or occupation is called a *social dialect*. Some dialects are written; others are only spoken. Often the dividing line between dialects and between dialects and the standard language is difficult to establish.

dialect atlas
[< Greek DIA 'through' + LEGEIN 'to talk']
Atlas that shows how different dialectal forms are distributed geographically.

dialectic
[< Greek DIA 'through' + LEGEIN 'to talk']
Process of examining opinions or ideas logically, often by a method of question and answer, so as to determine their validity.

Illustrations: 1. In his *Dialogues*, Greek philosopher *Plato studied truth through discussions based on questions and answers. 2. Greek philosopher *Aristotle frequently used the term as a synonym for the science of logic. 3. German philosopher G.W.F. *Hegel believed that ideas are formed when a concept gives rise to its opposite and a third view arises. 4. German philosopher Karl *Marx applied the concept of dialectic to social and economic processes.

dialectology
[< Greek DIA 'through' + LEGEIN 'to talk' + LOGOS 'word, reasoning, study']
Branch of linguistics studying *dialects.

dialogue
[< Greek DIA 'through' + LOGOS 'word']
[see also *monologue]
1. type of *discourse in which the partici-

pants are involved in a give and take situation; 2. literary genre modeled on conversation.

dicent
[see *dicisign]

dicisign
[term of C.S. *Peirce; also called dicent]
In Peircean theory the term *dicisign* refers to the meanings elicited by such *indexical signs as words like *here*, *there*, etc.

dictionary
[< Latin DICERE 'to say']
[also called *lexicon]
1. book of alphabetically listed words in a language, with definitions, etymologies, pronunciations, and other information about them; 2. any alphabetically arranged list of words or terms relating to a special subject.

dictum
[< Latin DICERE 'to say']
Authoritative, often formal, pronouncement.

Illustration: 'If you understand it, it is not God' (St *Augustine).

didactic novel
[see *novel]

différence
[also called *opposition]
Ferdinand de *Saussure's notion that a *sign bears meaning by virtue of its perceptible difference in form from other signs.

Illustrations: 1. The difference between *cat* and *rat* is a phonological one: initial /k/ vs. /r/. 2. The difference between *night* and *day* is a conceptual one: daylight vs. lack of daylight. 3. The difference between *boy* and *boys* is a grammatical one: singular vs. plural.

digital computer
[see *computer]

dionysian
[< Greek DIONUSIOS 'Dionysus']
In the philosophy of German philosopher Friedrich *Nietzsche, a display of creative-intuitive power as opposed to critical-rational power.

directional reception
[< Latin DE 'from' + REGERE 'to keep straight']
Term referring to the ability of an organism to locate the source of a signal by using its hearing system's direction-finding capacity.

discourse
[< Latin DIS 'from, apart' + CURRERE 'to run']
1. communication of ideas, information, etc., by talking or writing; 2. long and formal treatment of a subject, in speech or writing; 3. system or style of communication (as in the 'discourse of postmodernity').

Note: Discourse participants must know how to start and end the discourse, how to make themselves understood, how to respond to certain statements, how to be sensitive to interlocutor concerns, how to take turns, etc. Discourse strategies vary not only among languages, but also within a language: e.g. the discourse of the child is different from that of the adult; the discourse of religious oratory is different from that of scientific exposition; etc.

discreteness
[< Latin DIS 'apart' + CERNERE 'to separate']
Term referring to the fact that *signs are fashioned from a small set of elements that form meaningful oppositions with each other.

Illustration: The sound /p/ is made up of three discrete phonic elements [+occlusive], [+bilabial], [−voice]: the first indicates that it is articulated by completely closing the air passage, the second by letting the lips touch, and the third by blocking the vocal cords (in the larynx) from vibrating.

discursive form

[< Latin DIS 'from, apart' + CURRERE 'to run']
Notion developed by philosopher Susanne *Langer, whereby the composition of an art work is governed by the linear, syntactic properties of language.

Note: Discursive forms have the property of detachment: e.g. one can focus on a word in a sentence or a phrase without impairing the overall understanding of the sentence or phrase. In contrast, *presentational forms cannot be broken up into their elements without impairing the meaning: e.g. one cannot focus on a note or phrase in a melody without destroying the sense of the melody.

disk drive

[see *storage hardware]

displacement

[< Latin DIS 'from, apart' + Greek PLATEIA 'street']
Feature of *signs whereby whatever they stand for can be evoked even if not present for the senses to perceive.

Illustration: To someone who does not speak English the word *chair* is perceived as a mumble of sounds with no meaning. But, once that person is told what it refers to, and once that person becomes familiar with its domain of applications to the real world, thenceforth that word will generate an image of one of its typical applications in the mind of that person, even when the object to which it refers is not physically present for him/her to see or touch. This displacement property of signs has endowed human beings with the remarkable capacity to think about the world beyond the stimulus-response realm, i.e. to think about it within mind-space.

distinctive feature

[< Latin DIS 'apart' + STINGUERE 'to prick']
Minimal trait that serves to keep forms perceptibly distinct.

Illustration: The distinctive features that make up /p/ in English words such as *pin, pop,* etc. are [+bilabial], [+occlusive], [−voice], and those that make up /b/ in words such as *bin, bop,* etc. are [+bilabial], [+occlusive], [+voice]: [+bilabial] refers to the touching of the lips, [+occlusive] to the expulsion of the airstream after it has been held momentarily by the two lips, and [±voice] to the vibration or lack of vibration of the vocal cords in the larynx. The distinctive feature that differentiates these two sounds can now be pinpointed as one of [−voice] vs. [+voice]. This is the feature that allows us to differentiate between *pin* and *bin* and between *pop* and *bop.*

Doctrine of Forms

[see *Platonic forms]

docudrama

[abbreviation of documentary drama]
Television or movie dramatization of events based on real life.

documentary

[< Latin DOCUMENTUM 'lesson']
Film or television program presenting political, social, or historical subject matter in a factual and informative manner, including actual news film footage and/or interviews accompanied by commentary.

Doric form

[see also *Corinthian form, *Ionic form]
In ancient Greek architecture, column with no base and a heavy shaft; the Doric column was basically an undecorated, square slab resting on a rounded disc that tapers down to the top of the shaft.

DOS

[acronym for disk operating system]
Generic term describing any operating system that is loaded from disk devices when the system is started or rebooted. The term originally differentiated between disk-based systems and primitive microcomputer operating systems that were memory-based or that supported only magnetic or paper tape.

drama

[< Greek DRAN 'to do']
[also called *play, *theater]
Literary composition that tells a story by means of dialogue and action, performed by actors on a stage or platform with the background support of setting and props.

Note: The earliest period in Western theatrical history is called *classical*, because it encompasses the theater of the classical civilizations of ancient Greece and Rome. Greek tragedy flourished in the 5th century BC. Of the more than 1000 tragedies written during that century, only 31 remain, all by Aeschylus (525–456 BC), Sophocles (496?–406 BC), and Euripides (480?–406 BC). These were written in verse and consisted of scenes with dialogue alternating with choral songs. The plays, mostly based on myth, dealt with the place of humanity in the world and the consequences of individual actions. The actors wore costumes of everyday dress and large masks, which aided visibility and indicated the nature of the character to the audience.

The great period of Roman playwriting began in the 2nd century BC and was dominated by the comedies of Plautus (254?–184 BC) and Terence (185?–159? BC). The plays generally dealt with the foolishness of domestic intrigue and were similar to contemporary TV sitcoms. The only tragedies to survive are by Seneca (4? BC–AD 65). These dealt with the nature of bloody violence and obsessive passion.

With the fall of the Roman Empire in 476, classical theater came to an end in the West. The theater genre lay in obscurity for 500 years until the 10th century, when it re-emerged in the form of the *liturgical dramas* designed to accompany church services. These enacted stories from the Bible played by the clergy or by choirboys. Liturgical dramas led in the 15th century to the *morality play*, which became a popular form of theater. Morality plays were self-contained dramas dealing with an individual's journey through life. Their allegorical characters included *Death, Gluttony, Good Deeds,* and other personified vices and virtues. Later in the century, Renaissance theater in Italy attempted to bring back the spirit of the Roman plays. A century later, the *commedia dell'arte introduced stock characters who were caricatures of personality types – comic servants, foolish old men, lovers, lawyers, doctors, etc. The greatest dramatic genius of the era was, undoubtedly, the English playwright William Shakespeare (1564–1616).

After the Renaissance, drama had to compete with fictional narratives (especially novels) for public interest. In the 18th century, theater in much of Europe was dominated by individual performers who had plays written for their particular talents; and in the romantic 19th century drama became imbued with passion. One of the best examples of romantic drama is *Faust* (part I, 1808; part II, 1832) by German playwright Johann Wolfgang von Goethe (1749–1832). Based on the classic legend of the man who sells his soul to the devil, the play depicted humankind's attempt to master all knowledge and power in its constant struggle with the universe. In the same century, *melodramas* emerged, dealing with the conflict between a virtuous protagonist and an evil villain. By the end of the century, dramatists began to focus on the destructive nature of society. The leading playwrights of this form were Norwegian dramatist Henrik Ibsen (1828–

1906) and Swedish author August Strindberg (1849–1912).

In the 20th century theatrical practices became highly varied. Many movements, generally categorized as avant-garde, attempted to introduce alternatives to realistic drama and production. In France the *symbolist movement, which started in the 1880s, called for the script and the acting, without props, to carry the meaning. The *expressionist movement, popular in the 1910s and 1920s, explored the darker corners of the human psyche, creating nightmarish situations on-stage. Other movements of the first half of the century, such as *dadaism and *surrealism sought to inject new artistic freedom into theater.

The most popular and influential dramatic genre of the 20th century was absurdism, which aimed to eliminate much of the cause-and-effect relationship among events on-stage, reduce language to a game, diminish characters to archetypes, and portray the world as alienating and incomprehensible. Absurdism reached a peak in the 1950s but remained influential throughout the 1960s and 1970s. In the second half of the 20th century, realist drama continued to dominate the commercial theater, especially in the United States. The plays of Arthur Miller (1915–) and Tennessee Williams (1911–83) introduced techniques such as memory scenes, dream sequences, and roles assigned to purely symbolic characters.

dramatic irony
[< Greek EIREIN 'to speak']
Dramatic effect achieved by informing an audience about an incongruity between a situation and the accompanying dialogue or action, while the characters in the play remain unaware of the incongruity.

dramatis personae
[Latin 'cast of characters']
The characters in a play or story.

dramaturgy
[< Greek DRAN 'to do']
[see *drama]
Art of the theater, especially the composition of plays.

dress
[< Old French DRECIER 'to set up, arrange']
[see also *clothing, *fashion]
System of clothing suitable for certain occasions or for a certain place or time (e.g. the appropriate dress for wedding ceremonies).

Note: In semiotics, *dress* is distinguished from *clothing*. At a biological level, *clothes* enhance survivability. But in social contexts, clothes invariably take on a whole range of connotations. These meanings cohere into the various *dress codes* that inform people how to clothe themselves in social situations.

Predictably, dress codes vary across cultures. To someone who knows nothing about Amish culture, the blue or charcoal *Mutze* of the Amish male is just a jacket. But to an Amish the blue *Mutze* signals that the wearer is between 16 and 35 years of age, the charcoal one that he is over 35.

Dress, like other representational activities, can be used to lie about oneself: e.g. con artists and criminals can dress in three-piece suits to look trustworthy; a crook can dress like a policeman to gain a victim's confidence; etc. To discourage people from deceiving others through clothing, some societies have even enacted laws that prohibit fake dressing and that define who can dress in a certain way. In Ancient Rome, for instance, only aristocrats were allowed to wear purple-colored clothes; in medieval Europe peasants were required to wear their hair short because long hair was the privilege of the aristocracy; in many religiously oriented cultures differentiated dress codes for males and females are strictly enforced.

For some semioticians and cultural historians, the history of clothing is the history of the culture. Up until the 18th century fashion was the privilege of the aristocracy. The Industrial Revolution made fashion for the masses an economic possibility. Indeed, throughout the 20th century fashion crazes for everyone became an intrinsic feature of social life. Today, clothing trends and styles are dictated by media personalities, fashion moguls, and other high-profile personages. Outside the Western world, however, clothing continues to be a code tied to religious and/or tribal traditions. Where non-Western cultures have come into conflict with Western ideas, traditional garments have often been displaced. Nevertheless, in Africa, the Middle East, and the Far East many aspects of traditional dress have survived.

dualism
[< Latin DUO 'two']
View that the mind and body function separately, and that human beings have two essential natures, the physical and the spiritual.

duality of patterning
[< Latin DUO 'two']
Feature of language whereby vocal sounds have no intrinsic meaning in themselves but combine in different ways to form elements (e.g. words) that do convey meanings.

Illustration: The sound /p/, articulated in isolation, has no meaning. However, when combined with other sounds in certain patterned ways, it becomes an ingredient in the make-up of meaningful words: *pin, ploy, print,* etc.

Durkheim, Émile
[1858–1917]
French sociologist and philosopher who discovered remarkable similarities among the world's myths that he explained as based in a 'collective consciousness' that evolved from specific functions of the brain. Durkheim also claimed that the *alienation* that modern people feel is due to the erosion of common values in industrialized cultures, which he believed to be the cohesive bonds that hold together a society.

DVD
[digital versatile disc]
Video, audio, and computer data that can be encoded on a compact disc (CD). Advocates of DVD technology intend to augment current digital storage formats, such as CD-ROM and audio CDs, with the single format of DVD, which offers greater storage capacity and speed of data retrieval, as well as better graphics and a sharper picture.

E

Ebbinghaus, Hermann
[1850–1909]
German psychologist who was a pioneer in the field of experimental psychology. He conducted key experiments on the value of repetition in memory, using nonsense syllables that he invented. He also devised the 'fill-in-the-blanks' tests for purportedly measuring the intelligence of children.

echoism
[< Greek ECHO 'sound']
Linguistic imitation of sounds heard in the environment.

Illustrations: 1. *chirp* = word that echoes bird sounds; 2. *rustle* = word that echoes the sound made by leaves; 3. *gush* = word that echoes the sudden flow of water.

Eco, Umberto
[1932–]
Italian semiotician and novelist who has provided various theoretical frameworks for the study of *signs and of *texts. One of Eco's widely discussed claims is that, while the interpretation of a text may indeed be influenced by cultural and reader variables, as many poststructuralists suggest, there is,

nevertheless, an authorial purpose that transcends these factors.

A large part of the increase in the popularity of *semiotics in the late 20th century was brought about by the publication in 1983 of his best-selling medieval detective novel, *The Name of the Rose*.

education

[< Latin EX 'out' + DUCERE 'to lead']
Knowledge or skill obtained or developed through a culturally based learning-instructional process.

Note: Educational practices are designed to ensure the continuity of a culture's *signifying order – i.e. of its system of *signs, *codes, and *texts – as well as its institutions. In early civilizations, education was controlled by religious leaders. In ancient Egypt, for instance, the priests of the society also taught writing, science, mathematics, and architecture in temple schools. In ancient Greece the practice of assigning the teaching of the liberal arts, mathematics, philosophy, aesthetics, and gymnastic training to secular teachers trained in each of these areas grew out of the notion of a 'well-rounded' education. After an initial period of intense loyalty to the old religious traditions, Roman society approved the appointment of Greek teachers, eventually training its own secular educators. According to the 1st-century educator Quintilian (c. AD 35–95), the proper training of the child was to be organized around the study of language, literature, philosophy, and the sciences, with particular attention paid to the development of character.

The early Fathers of the Church, especially St *Augustine (AD 354–430), emphasized the development of educational methods and curricula reflecting Christian ideas. Between the 8th and the 11th centuries the Moorish conquerors of Spain revived the secular idea of the Roman university in the capital city of Córdoba, which became a center for the study of philosophy, ancient civilizations, science, and mathematics. In the 12th century, education came under the influence of the ideas and doctrines of the scholastic theologians (see *scholasticism), who wanted to reconcile Christian theology with the classical ideas of *Aristotle and *Plato. The theologian Peter *Abelard (1079–1142?), and other renowned scholastic teachers, attracted many students, laying the intellectual foundations for the establishment of universities in northern Europe.

Of significance to the development of schooling systems during the Middle Ages were the views of Muslim and Jewish scholars. Not only did they promote innovative techniques in education within their own societies, but they also served as translators of ancient Greek writings, thus bringing the ideas of the classical world to the attention of European scholars. Many excellent teachers of the Greek language and literature who had migrated from Constantinople to Italy influenced the work of European educators, such as the Dutch humanist Desiderius Erasmus (1466–1536?) and the French essayist Michel de *Montaigne (1533–92).

During the 17th century, the emphasis shifted towards scientific disciplines. Influenced by the writings of Francis *Bacon, Christ's Hospital in London was probably the first secondary school to introduce a curriculum based on scientific subjects. In that same century the French philosopher and mathematician René *Descartes emphasized logical reasoning as a fundamental skill to be honed by teachers, while John *Locke, like Bacon before him, recommended a curriculum and method of education based on the direct apprehension of concrete facts before reaching conclusions. The greatest educator of the century was Jan Komensky, the Protestant bishop of Moravia, better known by his Latin name, Comenius (1592–1670). Comenius emphasized stimulating the pupil's interest and teaching with reference to concrete things rather than to verbal or logical descriptions of them.

The foremost educational theorist of the 18th century was Jean-Jacques *Rousseau, who insisted that educators should treat children as children, not as miniature adults, cultivating the personality of the individual child with great care and devotion. Motivated by Rousseau's persuasive arguments, governments in England, France, Germany, Italy, and other European countries established obligatory national school systems designed to actualize Rousseau's idea that true education should be based on the needs and potential of the child, rather than on the needs of society or the precepts of religion. This 'child-centered' view was entrenched further in the Western mindset by the ideas of the American philosopher and educator John *Dewey (1859–1952).

In the 20th century education came under the influence of psychology and its various schools of thought (behaviorism, cognitivism, etc.). Particularly influential were the ideas of the Swiss psychologist Jean *Piaget. Piaget identified four stages of a child's mental growth: 1. the *sensorimotor stage*, from birth to age 2, marked by the gaining of motor control and the sensory perception of physical objects; 2. the *preoperational stage*, from ages 2 to 7, marked by the rapid development of verbal skills; 3. the *concrete operational stage*, from ages 7 to 12, marked by the emergence of abstract concepts; and 4. the *formal operational stage*, from ages 12 to 15, marked by the crystallization of logical and systematic reasoning. Most school curricula, learning materials, and instructional systems have been tailored, by and large, to follow the Piagetian developmental sequence.

effigy
[< Latin EX 'from' + FINGERE 'to shape']
Unrefined figure or dummy made to resemble a hated person or group.

ego
[Latin FOR 'I']
[see also *id, *superego]
In *psychoanalysis, the central part of the personality that allows the individual to cope with reality. In classical psychoanalytic theory, the ego is said to begin forming as soon as the neonate starts to become aware of his/her encounters with the external world, learning to modify his/her behavior in socially expected ways.

egocentricism
[< Latin EGO 'I']
1. perception of oneself as the center of any interaction; 2. over-concern with the presentation of self to other people in social settings.

electronic mail
[see *e-mail]

elegy
[< Greek ELEGOS 'mournful song']
Poem or song composed especially as a lament for a deceased person.

Illustrations: 1. Ancient poets who used the elegiac form include Callimachus (3rd century BC) and Catullus (84?–54? BC). 2. The best-known elegies in English are *Lycidas* (1638), by John Milton (1608–74), and *Elegy Written in a Country Churchyard* (1751), by Thomas Gray (1716–71).

Eliade, Mircea
[1907–1986]
Romanian-born American historian of religions who saw *myth as the means by which humans come to a coherent understanding of existence. Eliade claimed that, although specific myths may over time become trivialized, people invariably have the ability to re-experience their true metaphysical nature and original functions.

ellipsis
[< Greek EN 'in' + LEIPEIN 'to leave']
1. omission of a word or words necessary

for making a complete grammatical construction, because the construction can be understood in the context in which it occurs; 2. series of dots used in writing or printing to indicate an omission.

Illustrations: 1. *if possible* = *if it is possible;* 2. *The colors are red, blue, ..., and yellow.*

e-mail
[abbreviation of *electronic mail*]
Messages sent via telecommunication links between microcomputers.

embedding
Process of joining phrases, clauses, and/or different sentences into one sentence.

Illustration: The two sentences *The boy is my brother* and *The boy is eating pizza,* in which *boy* refers to the same person, can be joined by embedding the second one into the first one. Syntactically, this entails 1. deleting the second occurrence of *The boy*; 2. replacing it with the relative pronoun *who*; and 3. inserting the resulting relative clause after the first occurrence of *The boy*. The result is the sentence *The boy, who is eating pizza, is my brother.*

emblem
[< Greek EMBLEMA 'insertion']
[see *symbol]
1. figure with a motto or verses, allegorically suggesting some moral truth; 2. visible symbol of a thing, idea, class of people, etc.; 3. object that stands symbolically for something else.

Illustrations: 1. The cross is an emblem of Christianity. 2. Symbols, logos, etc. that stand for a company, such as the golden arches of McDonald's, are emblems.

emic vs. etic
Distinction made in linguistics between units that are generic or representative of a category (= *emic* units), and those that are instantiations of the category (= *etic* units).

Note: These are derived from the suffixes in linguistic terms such as *phon<u>emic</u>* vs. *phon<u>etic</u>*. For example, the sounds represented by the letter *l* are representative of an *emic* category, namely the *phoneme /l/. Phonetically, however, /l/ is realized in two ways: 1. as a dental [l], and 2. as a back (velar) [l] (pronounced with the tongue arching towards the throat). The latter occurs at the end of a syllable or a word: *dull, filler, willing, bill,* etc.; the former occurs elsewhere: *lip, love, filter, pulp,* etc. These two realizations of /l/ are said to be its *etic* variants.

emotive connotation
[see *connotation, emotive]

emotive function
[< Latin EX 'from' + MOVERE 'to move']
In Roman *Jakobson's model of communication, the addresser's (sender's) emotions, attitudes, social status, etc. as they are worked into and shape the message-making process.

emotive image
[see *image, mental]

empiricism
[< Greek EMPEIRIA 'experience']
In philosophy, theory affirming that all knowledge is based on experience and denying the possibility of *a priori thought. The philosophy opposed to empiricism is *rationalism, which asserts that the mind is capable of recognizing reality by means of reason, a faculty that exists independently of experience.

enclitic
[< Greek ENKLINEIN 'to lean on']
Word or particle that has no independent status.

Illustrations: 1. In *Give 'em the works,* the form *'em* is an enclitic. 2. *In I'm here* the *'m* is an enclitic.

encoding
[< Latin IN 'in' + CODEX 'wooden tablet for writing']
[see also *decoding]
Process of constructing, selecting, or composing a *sign or *text in terms of a specific *code.

Illustration: The quantity 'two' can be encoded 1. with the symbol 2 in terms of the code of decimal numerals; 2. with the symbol 10 in terms of the code of binary numerals.

encyclopedia
[< Greek EN 'in' + KYKLOS 'circle' + PAIDEIA 'education']
Book or set of books giving information on all or many branches of knowledge.

Note: The oldest complete encyclopedia still in existence is the *Natural History* (c. AD 79), compiled by the Roman writer Pliny the Elder (AD 23–79). It is a compendium of natural-science facts that remained popular for almost 1500 years. The most important of all the medieval encyclopedias is the *Great Mirror*, compiled in the 13th century by the Dominican friar Vincent of Beauvais, containing the writings of 450 Greek, Hebrew, and Roman scholars.

The modern encyclopedia was largely a product of French Enlightenment scholars, who used alphabetical arrangement according to key words, names, or special topics in its construction. Denis Diderot (1713–84), for instance, compiled the famous *Encyclopedia of Sciences, Arts and Trades*, commonly called the *Encyclopédie*, between 1751 and 1772 in 28 volumes, including 11 volumes of illustration plates. In England this method was followed by John Harris, who compiled a *Lexicon Technicum*, published first in one volume (1704), then in a second edition of two volumes (1708–10). This is generally considered the first alphabetically arranged encyclopedia in the English language. The *Encyclopaedia Britannica* was first published in Edinburgh, Scotland, from 1768 to 1771.

The encyclopedic works published in the United States during the 19th and 20th centuries included many works of general reference in various formats. The 30-volume *Encyclopedia Americana* was originally put together in 1829, the *Funk & Wagnalls* in 1912, the *Columbia Encyclopedia* in 1935, and *Collier's Encyclopedia* in 1949. Notable children's encyclopedias included the *World Book Encyclopedia* of 1917 and Compton's Pictured Encyclopedia of 1922. In the 1980s encyclopedia publishing expanded to nonprint formats. The first compact-disc encyclopedia was produced by Grolier in 1985. *Compton's Multimedia Encyclopedia* was released in CD format in 1989, integrating sound, pictures, animation, and text in what came to be called a CD-ROM. In 1993 the Microsoft Corporation released *Encarta*, a multimedia encyclopedia on CD-ROM.

Encyclopedic works devoted to Canada have included *The Encyclopedia of Canada* (1935–7), the *Encyclopedia Canadiana* (1958), and *The Canadian Encyclopedia* (1985–). The latter now exists in both print and CD-ROM forms.

enigma
[< Greek AENIGMA 'speech in riddles']
Perplexing, usually ambiguous, statement or puzzle.

Illustration: What changes from dark to light regularly? (Answer: *night to day*).

Enlightenment
18th-century European philosophical movement that stressed reason over religious dogma and tradition for the meaningful pursuit of knowledge and social equality for all classes.

Note: Enlightenment philosophers saw religion – especially Roman Catholicism – as the principal force that had enslaved the human mind. However, most did not renounce it altogether, accepting the existence of God and of a spiritual hereafter, but rejecting most of the intricacies and rituals of

Christian theology. Human aspirations, they believed, should not be centered on the next life, but rather on the means of improving earthly life. Enlightenment intellectuals re-examined and questioned all received ideas and values, exploring new ways of thinking in many different domains of knowledge. The Enlightenment marked a pivotal stage in the decline of Church influence on Western society at large and in the growth of modern secularism.

entailment
Necessary consequence of some proof, event, argument, or proposition.

Illustration: The ability to walk upright *entails* the freeing of the hands from locomotion.

entropy
[< German ENTROPIE 'arbitrary use,' coined by German physicist R.J.E. Clausius, 1822–88]
Measure of the *information content of a message derived as a factor of its uncertainty or unexpectedness.

Illustration: In a building that has an alarm system, the state 'off' has virtually no information content, whereas the state 'on' (a sounding alarm) has a maximum information value for that system.

environmentalism vs. innatism
Two radically different views of human mental functioning and development: the former emphasizes the role of upbringing, the latter that of biology.

Note: From the environmentalist point of view, humans are born with their minds essentially a *tabula rasa*, assuming their character, personality, abilities, etc. in response to how and where they are reared. From the innatist perspective, humans are not born with an empty slate; rather, they are 'hard-wired' from birth to learn and behave in certain biologically programmed ways, no matter where or how they are reared.

epic
[< Greek EPOS 'word, song']
Extended narrative *poem in elevated or dignified language, celebrating the feats of a legendary or traditional hero.

Illustrations: Well-known examples of the folk epic are the Anglo-Saxon *Beowulf* (8th century) and the Indian epics the *Mahabharata* (300 BC–AD 300) and the *Ramayana* (3rd century BC). Well-known literary epics, which are the creation of known poets who consciously employ the epic form include the *Iliad* and *Odyssey* by Homer; the *Aeneid* by Virgil (70–19 BC); the *Book of Kings* (1010) by the Persian poet Abu al-Qasim Firdawsi (940?–1020?); the *Divine Comedy* (1307–21) by the Italian poet *Dante Alighieri; the *Lusiads* (1572) by the Portuguese writer Luís (Vaz) de Camões (1524–80?); *Jerusalem Delivered* (1581) by Italian poet Torquato Tasso (1544–95); the *Faerie Queene* (1590–1609) by English poet Edmund Spenser (1552?–99); *Paradise Lost* (1667) by English poet John Milton (1608–74); *The Prelude* (1850) by English poet William Wordsworth (1770–1850); *Song of Myself* by American poet Walt Whitman (1819–92); and *Four Quartets* (1943) by Anglo-American poet T.S. Eliot (1888–1965).

Epicureans
[c. 300 BC]
Members of a philosophical society in ancient Greece who emphasized the pursuit of pleasure, good food, comfort, and ease as the only meaningful goals of life.

epigram
[< Greek EPI 'upon' + GRAPHEIN 'to write']
1. short poem with a witty or satirical point;
2. any terse, witty, pointed statement, often with a clever twist in thought.

Illustration: Experience is the name everyone gives to one's mistakes.

Note: In ancient Greece epigrams were found inscribed on tombs and statues. Roman poets developed the epigram as a short satire in verse, with a twist or thrust at the end. English writers regarded as master epigrammatists are John Donne (1572–1631), Ben Jonson (1572–1637), John Dryden (1631–1700), Jonathan Swift (1667–1745), Alexander Pope (1688–1744), Samuel Taylor Coleridge (1772–1834), and Oscar Wilde (1854–1900). In France, Voltaire (1694–1778) wrote memorable epigrams, as did Gotthold Ephraim Lessing in Germany (1729–81). A literary form similar to the epigram occurs in Chinese and Japanese literature.

epilogue

[< Greek EPILOGOS 'conclusion of a speech']
1. short poem or speech spoken directly to the audience following the conclusion of a play; 2. short addition at the end of a literary work, often called an *afterword.*

episode

[< Greek EPI 'upon' + HODOS 'journey']
1. portion of a narrative or play that relates an event, forming a coherent subnarrative in itself; 2. separate part of a serialized novel or play; 3. section of a classic Greek tragedy that occurs between two choral songs; 4. in music, a passage between statements of a main subject or theme, as in a *rondo* or *fugue.*

episodic memory

[see *memory]

epistemology

[< Greek EPISTEME 'knowledge' + LOGOS 'word, reasoning, study']
Branch of philosophy studying the nature of knowledge.

Note: In the 5th century BC, the Greek *Sophists questioned the possibility of reliable and objective knowledge. *Plato rebutted the Sophists by proposing the existence of a world of unchanging, abstract forms about which it is possible to have exact and certain knowledge by reasoning. *Aristotle also regarded abstract knowledge as superior to any other, but he maintained that almost all knowledge is built from experience. The *Stoics and *Epicureans agreed that knowledge originates in sense perception, but they maintained that abstract thinking is a practical guide to life, rather than an end in itself.

In the Middle Ages, philosophers helped restore confidence in reason and experience by blending rational methods and faith into a unified system of beliefs. From the 17th to the late 19th century, the main issue in epistemology was reasoning versus sense perception in acquiring knowledge. British philosopher David *Hume argued that since most knowledge depends on cause and effect, one cannot hope to know the future with certainty. German philosopher Immanuel *Kant tried to solve this crisis by combining elements of rationalism with elements of empiricism. During the 19th century, German philosopher G.W.F. *Hegel revived the rationalist claim, while the American school of pragmatism at the turn of the 20th century carried empiricism further by defining knowledge as an instrument of action to be judged by its usefulness in predicting experiences.

In the early 20th century, German philosopher Edmund *Husserl outlined an elaborate procedure by which one is said to be able to distinguish the way things appear to be from the way one thinks they really are. Later in the century, the *analytic philosophers insisted that valid knowledge can be obtained by avoiding verbal confusion.

epithet

[< Greek EPITITHENAI 'to put on']
Adjective, noun, or phrase used to characterize some person or thing.

Illustrations: 1. *egghead* for 'an intellectual'; 2. *The Great Emancipator* for 'Abraham Lincoln.'

eponymy
[< Greek EPI 'on' + ONOMA 'name']
Name of a city, country, era, institution, or other place or thing derived from the name of a person.

Illustrations: 1. *Rome* was derived from the mythic name *Romulus*. 2. The city and the state of *Washington* are named after the first American president, *George Washington*. 3. *Broca's area* in the left hemisphere of the brain is named after its discoverer, the anthropologist and surgeon *Pierre-Paul Broca*.

epos
[variant of *epic]

eschatological myth
[see *mythology]

escutcheon
Heraldic *insignia usually in the shape of a conventional shield, with various charges, or figures, represented in different tinctures.

Note: The background of an escutcheon may comprise two or more tinctures (metals, colors, and furs) divided by one or more lines. The figures depicted on an escutcheon are classified as *honorable ordinaries*, which are simple geometrical figures delineated by straight lines or forms; *subordinaries*, which include the border of the shield; the *orle*, a narrower border that does not touch the edges of the shield; and the *lozenge*, a diamond-shaped figure with four equal sides.

esthetics
[variant spelling of *aesthetics]

ethnography
[< Greek ETHNOS 'people' + GRAPHEIN 'to write']
[also called participant observation]
In *cultural anthropology, type of research conducted by an anthropologist living in a community and observing what goes on.

Note: The anthropologist first becomes immersed in the life of the community and, through daily contacts, establishes rapport with the people. Through structured interviews (with samples of people), ethnographers investigate all aspects of a culture, presenting a perspective from which to understand modern society. In comparing the social organization of societies, ethnologists emphasize the interrelationship between the individual and the family, clan, tribe, and other groups that may exist within a society.

ethology
[< Greek ETHOLOGIA 'character portrayal']
[see also *communication, animal]
Scientific study of the characteristic behaviors and communication patterns of animals in their natural habitats.

etymology
[< Greek ETYMON 'literal sense of a word']
1. origin and development of a word, affix, phrase, etc.; 2. branch of linguistics tracing a word or other form back as far as possible in its own language and to its source in contemporary or earlier languages.

Illustrations: 1. The word *person* derives from the Greek *persona* 'mask.' 2. The word *idea* derives from the Greek verb *ideein* 'to see.'

euphemism
[< Greek EUPHEMOS 'of good sound or omen']
Use of a word or phrase that is less direct, but considered to be less distasteful, unpleasant, or offensive than another.

Illustrations: 1. *remains* for *corpse*; 2. *number two* for *defecation*.

evolutionary psychology
[see also *psychology, evolutionary]

evolutionism
[see *sociobiology]
View that cultures result from evolutionary tendencies that are built into the genetic structure of the human species.

exclamation
[< Latin EX 'out' + CLAMARE 'to call out']
Sudden outcry expressing strong emotion, such as fright, grief, or hatred.

Illustrations: 1. *Wow!* 2. *Yikes!* 3. *Damn!*

exegesis
[< Greek EX 'out' + HEGEISTHAI 'to lead']
Critical explanation or analysis of a *TEXT.

existentialism
[< Latin EX 'out' + SISTERE 'to cause to stand']
Philosophy that emphasizes the uniqueness and isolation of the individual's experience in a hostile or indifferent universe, stressing freedom of choice and responsibility for the consequences of one's acts. Existentialism has been a vital movement in literature, particularly in the works of Fyodor Dostoyevsky (1821–81), Franz Kafka (1883–1924), Albert Camus (1913–60), Samuel Beckett (1906–89), and Eugène Ionesco (1909–94).

expression
[< Latin EX 'from' + PREMERE 'to press']
1. putting into words or representing in language; 2. picturing, representing, or symbolizing in art, music, etc.; 3. symbol or set of symbols expressing some mathematical fact, such as a quantity or operation.

expressionism
[< Latin EX 'from' + PREMERE 'to press']
[also known as *abstract expressionism]
Art movement in the early part of the 20th century that emphasized the subjective expression of the artist's inner experiences.

extensional connotation
[see *connotation]

eye contact
Length of time involved in looking, and type of looking pattern, that people in social situations exhibit, conveying what kind of relationship they have with each other. Such looking may be bilateral (the common meaning of this term) or unilateral.

Note: Eye contact communicates specific meanings. Gazing, for instance, refers to prolonged looking that is often indicative of sexual wonder, fascination, awe, or admiration. To stare is to gaze fixedly, indicating sexual curiosity, boldness, insolence, or stupidity. Gaping suggests a prolonged open-mouthed look reflecting sexual amazement or awe. To glare is to fix another with a hard, piercing stare. To peer is to look narrowly, searchingly, and seemingly with difficulty. To ogle is to stare in an amorous, usually impertinent, manner.

eye-level line
[see *painting, perspective]

F

---

fable
[< Latin FABULA 'story']
Fictitious story meant to teach a moral lesson. In a fable the characters are usually talking animals, given the attributes of human beings; the moral is typically summed up at the end of the improbable story.

Note: Fables are *allegorical narratives. One of the earliest and most notable collections of animal fables is that of Aesop (6th century BC). Another famous collection of beast fables is the Sanskrit collection *Panchatantra*, probably written in the 3rd century AD. The writing of fables was revived in France during the 12th century. Between the 12th and 14th centuries a popular collection of animal fables entitled *Roman de Renart* appeared in France. One of the greatest of all French fabulists was Jean de La Fontaine (1621–95), whose verse fables were published between 1668 and 1694 and were extensively imitated by later writers. Other famous fabulists include 19th-century Danish writer Hans Christian Andersen (1805–75) and the 20th-century Italian novelist Italo Calvino (1923–85).

fabliau

[Old French 'fable']

Short, ribald tale, designed to parody human weaknesses and challenge authority, that became popular in France from the middle of the 12th to the middle of the 14th century.

Note: The fabliaux were composed and recited by wandering minstrels. Of the enormous number that they produced, about 150 have survived, and approximately 20 of the authors are known. The form was used subsequently by many English writers, including Geoffrey Chaucer (1343?–1400), whose masterpiece *The Canterbury Tales* contains six fabliaux. Because of its characteristic brevity and emphasis on plot and climax, the fabliau is considered a forerunner of the modern short story.

facial expression

Facial cast or look that conveys emotion.

Note: In 1963 psychologist Paul Ekman established the Human Interaction Laboratory in the Department of Psychiatry at the University of California, San Francisco, for the empirical study of facial expression. He was joined by Wallace V. Friesen in 1965 and Maureen O'Sullivan in 1974. Over the years, Ekman and his team have been able to link specific facial actions to different aspects of emotion. They have shown that a specific facial cast can be broken down into measurable components: eyebrow position, eye shape, mouth shape, nostril size, etc., which in various combinations determine the form and meaning of the expression. Ekman and his team have found very little variation across cultures in the composition and combinations of these components.

fairytale

Story about *fairies* – diminutive, supernatural creatures, generally in human form, dwelling in an imaginary region called *fairyland*, who intervene through magic in human affairs.

Illustrations: Fairy characters are present in ancient Greek literature, Sanskrit poetry, and in ancient Egyptian tradition. Traditional depictions of fairies can be seen in such works as *A Midsummer Night's Dream* (1595?) by playwright William Shakespeare (1564–1616), the *Tales of Mother Goose* (1697) by French writer Charles Perrault (1628–1703), and the *Fairy Tales* (2 volumes, 1812–15) by the Grimm brothers, Jacob (1785–1863) and Wilhelm Karl (1786–1859).

family name

[see *surname]

fantasia

[Italian for 'fantasy, imagination, creativity']

Italian term, made popular in philosophy by Giambattista *Vico, that embraces both the notions of 'imagination' and 'fantasy' in a holistic way.

Note: In Vico's philosophy, the *fantasia* is the faculty that has made possible the unique human ability to reflect on, and create, forms of meaning not dependent upon stimuli and response mechanisms. It inheres in the making at will of images and of creative arrangements of images in the mind.

farce

[< Latin FARCIRE 'to stuff']

Form of drama intended to evoke laughter through exaggeration and caricature.

Note: Farce differs from *comedy* chiefly in plot format: in farce characters are necessary only to act out the intricacies of the plot; whereas in comedy, plot is subordinated to characterization. The term farce seems to have been applied first in France, from the 15th century, to the plays produced by secular groups during annual festivals, in contrast to the morality plays produced by the religious orders. A characteristic of many of the early farces was the use of dialects and folk jargon. The French writer Molière (1622–73) later refined the farce form into the comedy of manners. Today, the term *farce* is freely applied to almost any performance in which comedic routines are carried out to ludicrous lengths.

fashion
[< Latin FACTIO 'a making']
[see also *dress]
Prevailing dress style or custom of an era, group of people, or entire society.

Note: Up until the 19th century, fashion was the exclusive privilege of royalty and the rich. The Industrial Revolution made possible the manufacturing of affordable fashionable clothes for the middle class, resulting in more rapid changes in the attire for men and women. Since the middle part of the 20th century, fashion has become part of lifestyle and personal statement.

Clothing fashion is also ideological statement. The hippies dressed to emphasize 'love' and 'freedom' in the 1960s. Motorcycle gang members wear leather jackets, boots, and various paraphernalia to convey toughness, group allegiance, and nonconformity with mainstream society. These are *uniforms* – literally 'unitary dress styles' – which, like military dress, connote loyalty and communal values. The wearing of military uniforms for fashion, on the other hand, can often be construed as a counterculture statement – a kind of dress parody of nationalistic tendencies – or as a statement of 'military toughness.' As with language, the history of clothing shows that it can be endearing, offensive, controversial, delightful, disgusting, foolish, charming.

fauvism
[< French FAUVE 'wild beast']
Movement in French painting, lasting from about 1898 to about 1908, rejecting the pale coloration features of *impressionism in favor of more intense colors.

Note: The leading figure in this movement was Henri Matisse (1869–1954), who used powerful colors to evoke strong emotional responses to his work.

feedback
In *information theory, the process of detecting signals or cues issuing from the *receiver of a message so that the performance or control of the communication system can be maintained or improved.

Note: In human communication, *feedback* refers to the fact that senders have the capacity to monitor the messages they transmit and to modify them to enhance their decodability. This includes, for instance, detecting physical reactions (facial expressions, bodily movements, etc.) in the receiver that signal the effect that the message is having on him/her.

feminist semiotics
Important movement within semiotics devoted to showing how *sign systems and social power structures coalesce to define gender categories.

fetish
[< Portuguese FEITIÇO 'charm' (< Latin FACTITIUS 'artificial')]
Object that is believed to have magical or spiritual powers, or to cause sexual arousal.

Illustrations: 1. In Western society, *high heel shoes*, worn be females, often constitute a sexual fetish. 2. Good luck charms are, frequently, perceived fetishistically.

fetishism
[< Portuguese FEITIÇO 'charm' (< Latin FACTITIUS 'artificial')]
[see also *animism]
Extreme devotion to objects.

Note: Although fetishism is found in primates and mammals, it is a term used generally to identify an extreme religious or sexual devotion to objects in humans. In some cultures, fetishism manifests itself as a form of belief and religious practice in which supernatural attributes are imputed to material, inanimate objects. The practice includes magic, often with many attendant ceremonies and rituals. The fetish is usually a figure modeled or carved from clay, stone, wood, or other material resembling a deified animal or other sacred object. Sometimes it is the animal itself, or a tree, river, rock, or place associated with it. In some cases the belief is so strong that the original association is obscured, and the belief becomes idolatry. In Western culture the term is used almost exclusively to refer to a sexual obsession with some object (shoe, underwear, etc.) or bodily part (feet, neck, etc.) that is perceived to be highly stimulative of desire.

fiction
[< Latin FINGERE 'to form, make, put together']
[see also *novel]
Literary work whose content is produced by the imagination and is not necessarily based on fact.

Note: Fiction emerged in the late Middle Ages, the era that invented *fabliaux, romances, novellas,* and, a little later, the *novel.* Before the Middle Ages, human cultures did indeed create stories – myths, legends, fables, etc. But these were not forged fictionally. The first myths and legends were descriptive accounts of metaphysical events and of divine or heroic figures.

fictitious image
[see *image, mental]

figurative meaning
[see *meaning, figurative]

figure
[< Latin FIGURARE 'to form']
1. likeness or simulative representation of a person or thing; 2. illustration, diagram, picture, or drawing; 3. word or phrase used with a nonliteral meaning (= a *figure of speech*).

figure of speech
[< Latin FIGURARE 'to form']
Expression using words in a nonliteral sense or unusual manner to add strength, vividness, beauty, etc. to what is said or written.

Illustrations: 1. *anticlimax*: sequence of ideas that abruptly diminish in importance at the end of a sentence or passage (*First there is life, then there's living!*); 2. *antithesis*: juxtaposition of two words, phrases, clauses, or sentences opposed in meaning in such a way as to emphasize contrasting ideas (*You are going; I am staying*); 3. *apostrophe*: addressing a person who usually is either absent or deceased, an inanimate object, or an abstract idea (*Oh Fate, why do you pursue me so relentlessly?*); 4. *climax*: arrangement of words, clauses, or sentences in the order of their importance, the least forcible coming first and the others rising in power until the last (*First we criticize him, then we attack him, and finally we destroy him for what he did*); 5. *conceit*: elaborate, often extravagant metaphor or simile making an analogy between totally dissimilar things (*His life has become a fungus*); 6. *euphemism*: substitution of a delicate or inoffensive term or phrase for one that has unpleasant associations (*She had to do number two*); 7. *hyperbole*: inordinate exaggeration according to which a person, thing, or condition is depicted as being better or worse, or larger or smaller, than is actually the case (*I could sleep for a year*); 8. *irony*: dryly humorous or lightly sarcastic mode of speech, in which words are used to convey a meaning contrary to their literal sense (*I love being tortured*); 9. *litotes*: understatement employed for the purpose of enhancing the effect of the ideas expressed (*This is no small problem*); 10. *metaphor*: use of a word or phrase for one kind of referent in place of another for the purpose of suggesting an association between the two (*Alexander is a fox*); 11. *metonymy*: use of a word or phrase for another to which it bears an important relation (*Washington has done nothing to intervene*); 12. *oxymoron*: combination of two seemingly contradictory or incongruous words (*There was a deafening silence in the room*); 13. *paradox*: statement that appears contradictory to common sense yet is true in fact (*Standing is more tiring than walking*); 14. *personification*: representation of inanimate objects or abstract ideas as living beings (*My cat speaks Spanish*); 15. *rhetorical question*: question asked not to receive an answer, but to assert more emphatically the obvious answer to what is asked (*You know what I mean, don't you?*); 16. *simile*: specific comparison by means of the words *like* or *as* between two kinds of referents (*He's as strong as an ox*); 17. *synecdoche*: use of the part to stand for the whole or the whole for a part (*The White House issued a press release yesterday*).

film
[see *cinema]

fine arts
Arts produced or intended primarily for aesthetic reasons (sculpture, painting, music, etc.) rather than utility (crafts).

firstness
[see also *secondness, *thirdness]
In Charles *Peirce's philosophy, the attempt to refer to something in a sensory way.

Note: Knowing the world directly involves the use of the senses. This can be seen when a child touches, tastes, and looks at objects. Attempts to capture the sensory properties of objects in signifying forms – e.g. referring to a round object by drawing a circular figure, imitating the sound of a falling object

onomatopoeically, etc. – is a 'once removed' form of knowing from direct sensory perception, or, in Peircean terms, a *firstness* representational process.

fixed-action pattern
Innate animal behavioral and/or signaling pattern that is adjustable automatically to unpredictable circumstances.

Note: Evolution has generated a nearly endless list of such patterns. Some species are known to have different signals for different varieties of predators, all producing different responses in the animal group.

flow chart
Sequential diagram employed in many fields, especially computer science, to show the stepwise procedures used in performing a task, such as solving a mathematical problem (see *algorithm).

focal color
[see *color, focal]

folklore
General term for the beliefs, traditions, narratives, sayings, and arts that are transmitted orally by the common people of a culture.

Illustrations: 1. *folk beliefs*: cures for diseases, superstitions, magic, divination, witchcraft, and apparitions; 2. *folk traditions*: festival customs, games, and dances; 3. *folk narratives*: based perhaps in part on real characters or historical events; 4. *folk sayings*: proverbs, nursery rhymes, verbal charms, and riddles; 5. *folk arts*: any form of art, generally created anonymously, shaped by community life.

folktale
Generic term for the various kinds of narrative prose literature found in the oral traditions of the world. Myths, legends, and fairytales are considered to be the three main types of folktale.

food
[see *food vs. cuisine]

food code
1. complex rules of how to prepare food and when to eat it; 2. meanings that specific dishes have vis-à-vis group membership; 3. set of rules governing eating events.

Note: Food codes dictate the 'performance' of eating events. The complex rules of how to prepare food and when to eat it, the symbolic meanings that specific dishes have, the subtle distinctions that are constantly made in the ways food items are cut and cleaned, etc. are all powerful signifiers. Devout Christians say grace before starting a meal together; Jews say special prayers before partaking of wine and bread.

Eating events are so crucial to the establishment and maintenance of social relations and harmony that there exists virtually no culture that does not assign an area of the domestic abode to them. All cultures, moreover, have a discrete set of table rituals and manners that are inculcated into the members of the culture from birth. If one does not know the *table-manner code* of a certain culture, then one will have to learn it in order to continue living in that culture without censure and disapprobation.

Cultures vary widely as to the degree of sociability associated with the eating event. At one extreme end of this continuum, some cultures see the act of eating as a private act similar to a sex act; at the other end, other cultures see it necessarily as a social act, never to be performed in private. Many cultures, as well, have a kind of 'pecking order' that is designed to indicate the social class or position of the eaters. In Western culture, eating in a high-class restaurant entails the activation and deployment of a whole set of complementary social codes and texts, from dress to language, that are meant to create a whole range of subtle and not-so-subtle messages about oneself.

Many of the symbolic meanings of certain foods derive from mythic and religious accounts of human origins. The story of Adam and Eve in the Western Bible, for instance, revolves around the eating of an apple. In actual fact, the Hebrew account of the Genesis story tells of a 'forbidden' fruit, not an apple. The representation of this fruit as an apple came in medieval depictions of the Eden scene, when painters and sculptors became interested in the Genesis story artistically. In the Koran, by contrast, the forbidden fruit is a banana. Now, the biblical symbolism of the apple as 'forbidden knowledge' continues to resonate in Western culture. This is why the apple tree symbolizes the 'tree of knowledge'; why the 'Apple' computer company has chosen the logo of this fruit to symbolize its quest for 'forbidden' knowledge; and so on. Foods like bread and lamb also evoke latent religious symbolism in Western culture.

food vs. cuisine
Distinction meant to emphasize the difference between the biological and cultural spheres in human life in the area of eating.

Note: At a biological level, survival without food is impossible. But food and eating invariably take on a whole range of connotations in social settings. The term that is often used to designate these is *cuisine.* This refers to *what* people eat, *how* they make it, and *what* it reveals about the makers and eaters.

The anthropologist Claude *Lévi-Strauss traced the origin of food as a signifying system to the evolutionary distinction that he termed 'the raw' vs. 'the cooked.' Cooked food is food that has been transformed by culture into something more than a survival substance. According to Lévi-Strauss this transformation was accomplished by two processes – roasting and boiling – both of which were among the first significant technological advances made by humans. Roasting is more primitive than boiling because it implies a direct contact between the food and a fire. So, it is slightly above 'the raw' in evolutionary terms. But boiling reveals an advanced form of techno-logical thinking, since the cooking process in this case is mediated by both a pot and a fire.

foreground
[see also *background]
1. in painting, part of a scene, landscape, etc. represented in perspective as nearest to the viewer; 2. in linguistic theory, the concep-tual domain that has more salience.

Illustration: In the active sentence *Sarah ate the candy*, the subject (*Sarah*) is in the fore-ground of the mind's eye, while the object (*candy*) is in its background. The action implied by the verb (*eating*) is spotlighted as an activity of the subject. The overall mental view that such an active sentence conveys is one of the subject as an agent, a 'perpetra-tor' or 'executor' of the action. However, a change from passive to active, *The candy was eaten by Sarah*, changes the position of the foreground and the background in the cognitive processing of the sentence. The passive form brings the candy to the fore-ground, relegating the eater *Sarah* to the background. The action of eating is now spotlighted on the object, the 'receiver' of the action. In effect, passive sentences pro-vide a different mental angle from which to view the same action in mind-space.

form
[< Latin FORMA 'shape, figure, image']
1. shape, outline, or configuration of any-thing; 2. in linguistics, any of the different variations in which a word may appear owing to changes of inflection, spelling, or pronunciation; 3. in philosophy, the ideal nature or essential character of a thing as distinguished from its material manifesta-tion.

Note: In a work of art the *content* is said to be what the work means, and the *form* how it has been put together. In recent theories, it is stressed that form and content are intercon-nected and not separable.

formal operational stage
[see Jean *Piaget]

format
[< Latin FORMA 'shape, figure, image']
Structure or appearance of data in a file, database, spreadsheet, document, or other computer program or system. To format a disk means to prepare it for use, so that data can be systematically stored on it and/or retrieved from it.

formation
[< Latin FORMA 'shape, figure, image']
Process by which communication systems are *formed* in the organism by exposure to appropriate input in context and become subject to change or even dissolution over time. In all species, other than the human one, communication systems are formed primarily through the biological program of the species; only human beings acquire their ability to communicate from both biology and culture.

formulas in advertising
[see *advertising, use of formulas in]

FORTRAN
[FOR(mula) + TRAN(slation).]
High-level programming language for prob-lems that can be expressed algebraically, used mainly in mathematics, science, and engineering. FORTRAN uses a compiler program to convert its statements, com-mands, and subroutines into the machine code that a computer actually uses.

Foucault, Michel
[1926–1984]
French semiotician and philosopher who argued that the basic ideas which people normally take to be permanent truths about

human nature and society are instead no more than the products of historical processes. Foucault studied how everyday practices impel people to define their identities and systematize knowledge. In *Madness and Civilization* (1960), for instance, he traced the shifts in Western thought on the idea of madness.

foundation myth
[see *mythology]

frame
[< Old English FRAMIAN 'to be helpful']
1. anything made of parts fitted together according to a design; 2. in linguistics, a syntactic construction with a blank left in it for testing which kinds of words are permissible there; 3. in cinema, the rectangular image on a movie screen.

free morpheme
[< Greek MORPHĒ 'form']
[see also *bound morpheme]
*Morpheme that can exist on its own in a phrase.

Illustration: In the word *irregular* only the part *regular* can exist on its own, whereas *ir-* cannot. The former is a *free* morpheme, the latter a *bound* morpheme.

free variation
Alternation of forms in a language, without changing their meaning, according to use, geographical area, etc.

Illustration: The pronunciation of the *e* in *economics* is both /i/ ('ee') and /ɛ/ ('eh'). Since these different pronunciations do not change the meaning of the word, the two sounds are said to be in free variation in that word.

Frege, Gottlob
[1848–1925]
German philosopher and mathematician who synthesized Boolean algebra with *Aristotelian logic, thus completing the edifice of modern mathematical logic initiated by George *Boole. Frege also introduced the distinction between *sense* and *referent*. The referent is the object named, whereas the sense is a mode of representation. In an idiomatic phrase such as *Venus is the Morning Star*, there are two terms with different senses, *Venus* and *Morning Star*, but with the same referent (the planet). This is an ornamental version of *Venus is Venus*, involving a reference to an astronomical discovery.

Freud, Sigmund
[1856–1939]
German psychologist and founder of psychoanalysis who claimed that the moral behavioral patterns that have ensured the survival of the human species are built into human genetic structure. Freud also formulated the theory of the *unconscious as a region of the mind that contains wishes, memories, fears, feelings, and ideas that are prevented from expression in conscious awareness. These manifest themselves instead in symbolic and unusual ways, especially in dreams, neurotic syndromes, and artistic texts. Freud pointed out that *consciousness* was only the 'tip of the iceberg,' psychologically speaking. Below the 'tip' was the *unconscious*.

Freud also introduced terms such as *ego*, *id*, and *Oedipus complex*, among others, that have become staples of psychological discourse in Western society. He was also the first to emphasize the formative influence that childhood experiences have on the individual during his/her mature years.

Frye, Northrop
[1912–1991]
Canadian literary critic who showed that literary trends and movements fell, following Giambattista *Vico, into three general evolutionary stages: the metaphorical, the metonymic, and the ironic. This is why

poetry dominates a culture's early literary productivity (= metaphorical stage), fables, stories, and legends the culture's middle literary forms (= metonymic stage), and irony, satire, and parody its contemporary forms (= ironic stage).

functional grammar
[see *grammar]

functionalism
[< Latin FUNCTIO 'performance']
1. in architecture, 20th-century movement stressing functional design of a building;
2. in psychology, school of thought that stresses the study of the mind as a functioning component of the entire physiological individual.

Note: American psychologist William James (1842–1910) was one of the earliest proponents of functionalism, followed by American philosopher John *Dewey (1859–1952), who was the first to teach it formally.

G

Galen of Pergamum
[c. AD 130–c. 200]
Greek physician and writer on medicine and philosophy who entrenched *Hippocrates' view of medical diagnosis as a semiotic process, i.e. a process of decoding bodily signs, known as symptoms. Galen's anatomical studies on animals and his observations of how the human body functions dominated medical theory and practice for 1400 years. He produced about 500 treatises on medicine, philosophy, and ethics, many of which have survived in translations.

gambit
[< Italian GAMBETTO 'act of tripping someone']
Verbal strategy used for initiating discourse or for maintaining discourse flow.

Illustrations: 1. A muttering such as *uh...huh* in a conversation is a gambit acknowledging that one is listening to an interlocutor. 2. A phrase such as *May I ask you ...?* is an invitation to initiate discourse.

gaze
[< Scandinavian GASA 'to stare']
Looking at someone intently and steadily.

Note: The gaze is seen as relevant in semiotics because it reveals information about social relations. The gazer and the one gazed at form a social power relation. In Western society, the gazers have typically been considered to be the males; the ones gazed at, the females. With few exceptions, this pattern has surfaced in the artistic and erotic portrayals that have characterized the history of Western visual representation until recently.

gender
[< Latin GENUS 'origin']
[see also *sex]
Sexual identity and role established in cultural terms.

Note: In each individual culture, certain behaviors are perceived as constituting differential male and female gender qualities. These are the result of *gender codes* that define 'masculinity' and 'femininity' within a tribe or society. This is why gender behaviors vary considerably: e.g. in Western society, men are often expected to be the 'sex-seekers,' to initiate courtship, and to show an aggressive interest in sex; but among the Zuñi peoples of New Mexico, in contrast, these very same actions and passions are expected of the women.

general Turing machine
[see *Turing machine]

generative grammar
[< Latin GENERARE 'to beget']
Analysis of language initiated in 1957 by

Noam *Chomsky in his book *Syntactic Structures* by which sentences are viewed as hierarchically organized structures generated by rules that are said to make up the native speaker's *linguistic competence.

genetic classification
[< Latin GENESIS 'birth']
Classification of languages by relating them to a source language.

Illustration: Italian, French, Spanish, Portuguese, Romanian, Friulian, Sardinian, Rumansh, and a few other languages are all modern-day descendants of the same parent language, Latin. In effect, they are all *genetic* descendants of Latin spoken in territories that achieved nationhood at some point after the demise of the Roman Empire. Their status rose to that of *national languages*, not because they were forged as such, but because they assumed autonomy from the parent language as a result of political, social, and other *nonlinguistic* factors. The source language, Latin, is called the *mother* tongue and the descendants are called *sister* languages.

genotype
[< Greek GENOS 'race, kind']
[see also *phenotype]
1. fundamental constitution of an organism in terms of its hereditary factors; 2. type/species of a genus.

genre
[< Greek GENOS 'race, kind']
Works of literature, art, etc. classified together according to subject, theme, or style.

Illustrations: 1. Examples of literary genres are *poetry, prose, drama, fiction, science fiction, mystery novel*, etc. 2. Examples of musical genres are *symphony, concerto, opera, string quartet, sonata*, etc.

geologic map
[see *map]

Gestalt psychology
[German for 'form']
School of psychology studying the effects of forms (*Gestalten*) on perceptual and cognitive processes. Gestalten are integrated patterns of thought that make up experience. These have specific properties that can neither be derived from the elements of the whole, nor considered simply as the sum of these elements.

Note: Gestalt psychology traces its roots to the early work on the relationship between form and content in representational processes by Max Wertheimer (1880–1943), Wolfgang Köhler (1887–1967), and Kurt Koffka (1886–1941), as well as to the work on metaphor conducted in the early part of the 20th century. The two primary objectives of Gestalt psychology are 1. to unravel how the perception of forms is shaped by the specific contexts in which the forms occur; and 2. to investigate how forms interrelate with meanings. One of the more widely used techniques in semiotics, known as the *semantic differential, was developed by the Gestalt psychologists.

gesticulant
[< Latin GESTICULARI 'to make mimic gestures']
Movement with the hand(s) intended to add nuances or force to one's oral speech.

Note: The research by linguist David McNeill, reported in his 1992 book *Hand and Mind: What Gestures Reveal about Thought*, has shown precisely how gesticulants reinforce and complement oral discourse. Speech is linear through time, gesture is simultaneous and global. Gesticulants exhibit images that cannot be shown overtly in speech, as well as images of what the speaker is thinking about. Speech and gesture thus constitute a single integrated referential/communication system in which both cooperate to express the person's meanings.

On the basis of his findings, McNeill was able to classify gesticulants into five main categories: 1. *iconic gesticulants*, which bear a close resemblance to the referent or referential domain of an utterance (e.g. when describing a scene from a story in which a character bends a tree back, a speaker observed by McNeill appeared to grip something and pull it back); 2. *metaphoric gesticulants*, which have an abstract content (e.g. McNeill observed a speaker announcing that what he had just seen was a cartoon, simultaneously raising up his hands as if offering his listener the cartoon itself); 3. *beat gesticulants*, which resemble the beating of musical tempo, marking the introduction of new characters, summarizing the action, introducing new themes, etc. during the utterance; 4. *cohesive gesticulants*, which serve to show how separate parts of an utterance are supposed to hold together, unfolding through a repetition of the same gesticulant form in the gesture space; 5. *deictic gesticulants*, which are aimed not at an existing physical place, but at an abstract concept that had occurred earlier in the conversation (e.g. when someone says 'as I said earlier,' she/he typically flips the finger or hand in a backward motion, as if to imply that what she/he said had occurred in a place behind the head).

gesticulation

[< Latin GESTICULARI 'to make mimic gestures']
Use of hand(s) and arm(s) to accompany speech.

Illustrations: 1. Gesticulation is employed commonly to represent the shape of objects: e.g. to refer to a round object people tend to use both hands together moving in opposite – clockwise (the right hand) and counter-clockwise (the left hand) – directions.
2. Gesticulation involving the fingers is used commonly to represent symbols (by portraying the outline of the symbol); the most typical uses of this kind of 'finger gesturing' can be found in the sign languages for the hearing-impaired.

gestural code

[< Latin GERERE 'to bear, carry']
System of communication based on *gesture.

Illustrations: 1. the many sign languages used in communities of the hearing-impaired; 2. the alternative sign languages used by religious groups during periods of imposed silence or for various ritualistic practices; 3. the hand signals used to control traffic; 4. the hand and arm movements used by conductors to lead an orchestra.

gesture

[< Latin GERERE 'to bear, carry']
Movement, or movements collectively, of the body, especially the hands, to express or emphasize ideas and emotions.

Note: Although there are cross-cultural similarities, substantial differences also exist both in the extent to which gesture is used and in the interpretations given to particular gestures. For example, the head gestures for *yes* and *no* used in the Balkans seem inverted to other Europeans. In 1979, anthropologist Desmond Morris, together with several of his associates at Oxford University, examined 20 gestures in 40 different areas of Europe. The research team found that many of the gestures had several meanings, depending on culture: e.g. a tap on the side of the head can indicate completely opposite things – 'stupidity' or 'intelligence' – according to cultural context.

Theories connecting gesture to vocal language abound. These posit that the use of gesture to refer to objects and beings in the environment was the proto-form of communication and language. The transfer of this form of representation to the subsequently dominant vocal channel is explained by gestural theorists in terms of an imitation and substitution process by which gestural signs were transferred osmotically to the vocal apparatus. The version of gesture theory that has become a point of departure for all subsequent ones was formulated by the philosopher Jean Jacques Rousseau (1712–78) in the middle part of the 18th century. He became intrigued by the question of the origins of language while seeking to understand what he called the 'noble savage.' He proposed that the cries of nature that early humans must have shared with the animals, and the gestures that they must have used simultaneously, led to the invention of vocal language. He explained the evolutionary transition in this way: When the accompanying gestures proved to be too cumbersome, their corresponding cries were used to replace them completely. However, he did not provide any scientific explanation linking the two.

In the early 20th century, various linguists attempted to fill in the obvious evolutionary gap that Rousseau had left by relating gestural signs to vocal ones in terms of simulation, whereby manual gestures were purportedly copied unconsciously by positions and movements of the lips and tongue. The continual apposition of gestures and vocal movements led eventually to the replacement of the former by the latter.

The most suggestive evidence that gesture may have been the evolutionary antecedent of vocal language is the fact that it is a universal mode of representation that can satisfy all basic communicative needs. The child developmental literature has documented, moreover, that children invariably pass through an initial stage of pointing and gesturing before they develop vocal language. Gestural communication is used by children for practical purposes (e.g. pointing to something desired). Although vocal speech eventually becomes the dominant form of communication, the gestural modality does not vanish completely. It remains a functional subsystem of human communication that can always be utilized as a more generic form when an interaction is otherwise impossible. This happens typically when two interlocutors speak different languages. And, of course, in individuals with impaired vocal organs or hearing, gesture constitutes a primary mode of communication.

gigabyte
[see also *computer memory]
Term referring to 1 billion (or 2^{30}) *bytes. In reference to computers bytes are often expressed in multiples of powers of two. Therefore, a gigabyte can also be expressed as 1000 megabytes, where a megabyte is considered to be 2^{20} bytes.

global village
Marshall *McLuhan's term designating a world that depends upon electronic media for information and is thus united, electronically, as if in a village.

Note: In the 1960s McLuhan predicted that electronic media would have an impact far greater than that of the material they communicate. He argued that this is so because the medium in which information is recorded and transmitted is decisive in determining the cognitive character of a culture. e.g. an oral tribal culture is vastly different in organization and outlook than an alphabetic one; so too an electronic one is vastly different than either a purely oral or alphabetic culture. Because people the world over can now see themselves as participants in events going on in some other part of the world by simply switching on their television sets, they tend to feel interconnected, as if living in a 'global village.'

gloss
[< Latin GLOSSA (< Greek GLOSSA 'tongue') 'foreign word requiring explanation']
Brief explanatory note or translation of a

difficult or technical expression, usually inserted in the margin or between lines of a text or manuscript.

glossary
[< Latin GLOSSA (< Greek GLOSSA 'tongue') 'foreign word requiring explanation']
List of difficult or specialized words with their definitions, often placed at the back of a work.

glossematics
Approach in semiotics and linguistics initiated by Louis *Hjelmslev (1899–1965) and Hans Jørgen Uldall (1907–57) that formalizes the basic binary notions of *structuralism: e.g. *denotation vs. *connotation, *paradigm vs. *syntagm, etc.

glottogenetics
[< Greek GLOSSA 'tongue']
Branch of linguistics studying language origins.

glyph
Symbol or figure on a public sign that imparts information nonverbally (i.e. through *iconic representational features).

Illustrations:

1. *No Smoking!*   2. *This Way!*

Gödel, Kurt
[1906–1978]
Austrian-American logician, known primarily for his paper, published in 1931, setting forth what has become known as *Gödel's proof* (or incompleteness theorem). This states that the propositions on which a mathematical system is in part based are unprovable, because it is possible, in any logical system using symbols, to construct an axiom that is neither provable nor unprovable within the same system.

Goffman, Erving
[1922–1982]
Canadian-born sociologist who introduced the notion of *presentation of self*, i.e. of the self-image that people present to a social audience, into semiotics and communication theory. He also argued that individuals took on the characteristics of their social roles. Goffman provided both the models and a theoretical rationale for the study of how people adapt themselves to the situation. He insisted that everyday life was the foundation of social reality, underlying all statistical and conceptual abstractions. Goffman's views have spurred intensive sociological investigations using tape recorders and video cameras in natural rather than artificially contrived social situations.

Gothic
Architectural and artistic style prevalent in western Europe from the 12th through the 15th century.

Note: Gothic style represents a union of two of the major influences in the development of European culture, the Roman Empire and the Germanic tribes that invaded it. The word *Gothic* was first recorded in 1611 in a reference to the language of the Goths. It was extended in sense in several ways, meaning 'Germanic' and 'medieval, not classical.'

Gothic novel
[see *novel]

graffiti
[< Italian GRAFFIO 'a scratch']
Inscription or drawing scratched, incised, or drawn on a wall or other public surface. Graffiti have been used by linguists to reconstruct an earlier form of a language, and by social scientists to penetrate the mindset of a particular social group or subculture.

graph   103

grammar

[< Greek GRAMMATIKE 'grammar, learning']
1. in Latin and Greek, term referring to the whole apparatus of language and literary study; 2. in the medieval period it referred to the study of Latin, and hence to all learning as recorded in Latin; 3. in linguistics, it refers to the study of the form and structure of words, with their customary arrangement in phrases and sentences.

Note: There are various types of grammars: 1. *Normative*, or *prescriptive*, *grammar* defines the role of the various parts of speech and purports to tell what is the norm, or rule, of so-called correct usage. 2. *Historical grammar* is concerned with the changes in word and sentence construction in a language over time. 3. *Comparative grammar* studies sound and meaning correspondences among languages to determine their relationship to one another. 4. *Functional grammar* involves the investigation of how words and word order are used in social contexts to transmit information. 5. *Descriptive grammar* is concerned with determining how the meaningful arrangement of the basic word-building units and sentence-building units can best be described. 6. *Transformational-generative grammar* attempts to formalize the knowledge that human beings have about language.

The earliest surviving grammar is that of the Sanskrit language of India, compiled by Indian grammarian *Panini, who lived c. 400 BC. His sophisticated analysis showed how words are formed and what parts of words carry meaning. The study of grammar in the West began with the ancient Greeks, who engaged in philosophical speculation about languages and described language structure. By the Middle Ages, European scholars began to speculate about how languages might be compared. Later, in the 18th century, German philosopher Gottfried Wilhelm *Leibniz proposed that most languages of Europe, Asia, and Egypt came from the same original Indo-European language. Comparative grammar developed, subsequently, as the dominant approach to linguistic science in the 19th century, as scholars developed systematic analyses of parts of speech.

Not until the early 20th century did grammarians begin to describe languages on their own terms. German-American anthropologist Franz *Boas challenged the application of conventional comparative methods of language study to those non-Indo-European languages with no written records. He saw grammar as a description of how human speech in a language is organized within cultural contexts. Descriptive linguistics became dominant in the United States during the first half of the 20th century, whence it became the norm that grammar should be studied by examining living speech rather than by analyzing written documents. The approach to grammar that developed with this view is known as structural. In the latter part of the century, linguists such as Noam *Chomsky started viewing grammar as a theory of the innate capacity for language.

grammatology

[< Greek GRAMMA 'letter, character']
Study of language from the perspective developed by Jacques *Derrida whereby oral speech is seen as a derivative of writing, and not the other way around, as linguists have traditionally maintained. Derrida formulated grammatological theory on the basis of archeological evidence, which suggested to him that pictographic language preceded vocalized language.

graph

[< Greek GRAPHEIN 'to write']
1. type of *diagram (curve, broken line, series of bars, etc.) representing the successive changes in a variable quantity or quantities in mathematics; 2. unit in a writing-system representing a phoneme, a syllable, etc.

Note: The use of graphs in mathematics shows how practical this form of visual representation is. A graph shows relationships, often making it possible to see the presence of patterns or trends in a compilation of random facts.

grapheme
[< Greek GRAPHEIN 'to write']
Letter or set of letters of an alphabet that represent a *phoneme.

Illustration: The phoneme /f/ is represented by three types of characters: 1. *f* in a word like *fish*; 2. *ph* in a word like *graph*; and 3. *gh* in a word like *enough*.

graphic art
[< Greek GRAPHEIN 'to write']
Pictorial art in two-dimensional form. Graphic art refers to the types of illustrations found in advertisements, book designs, posters, and the like.

graphics
[< Greek GRAPHEIN 'to write']
1. pictorial representation and manipulation of data, as used in computer-aided design, in typesetting, the graphic arts, and in educational and recreational programs; 2. term used to refer to the process by which a computer displays data pictorially.

graphology
[< Greek GRAPHEIN 'to write' + LOGOS 'word, study']
Study of handwriting, especially when employed as a means of analyzing character.

Greimas, Algirdas Julien
[1917–1992]
French semiotician who developed the branch of semiotics known as *narratology, i.e. the study of how human beings in different cultures invent remarkably similar stories (myths, tales, etc.) with virtually the same stock of characters, motifs, themes, and actions. Greimas's most significant contribution to semiotic theory is the semiotic square, which is his description of the structure of meaning: e.g. the word *rich* takes on meaning only in contrast to *not rich*, *poor*, and *not poor*. Thus, the meaning of *rich* is extractable from a 'semiotic square' of oppositions, whose four 'vertices' are *rich–not rich–poor–not poor*.

ground
1. in *metaphor theory, the meaning of the metaphor; 2. in *painting, the entire or connecting surface of a scene.

Illustration: In the metaphor *John is a gorilla* the ground is the meaning 'John is belligerent, aggressive, etc.' The ground is an open-ended system that can never be fixed, as can literal meaning.

Group f/64
[see *photographic art]

gustatory icon
[see *iconicity]

gustatory image
[see *image, mental]

Gutenberg Galaxy
[after German printer Johann Gutenberg (c. 1400–68), reputedly the first European to print with movable type]
Marshall *McLuhan's term describing the radical new social order that ensued from the invention of print technology.

Note: The event that started the globalization of culture was, according to McLuhan, the invention of print technology and the subsequent widespread use of the book to codify knowledge. Literacy introduces a level of abstraction in human interaction that forces people to separate the maker of knowledge from the knowledge made. And this in turn leads to the perception that knowledge can exist on its own, spanning time and distance. Before literacy became widespread, humans lived primarily in oral-auditory cultures, based on the spoken word. The human voice cannot help but convey emotion, overtly or implicitly. So, the kind of consciousness that develops in people living in oral cultures is shaped by the emotionality of the voice. In such cultures, the knower and the thing known are seen typically as inseparable. By contrast, in literate cultures, the kind of consciousness that develops is shaped by the written page, with its edges, margins, and sharply defined characters organized in neatly-layered rows or columns, inducing a linear-rational way of thinking in people. In such cultures, the knowledge contained in writing is perceived as separable from the maker of that knowledge primarily because the maker of the written text is not present during the reading and understanding of his/her text, as he/she is in oral communicative situations. The spread of literacy through the technology of print since the Renaissance has been the determining factor in the objectification of knowledge in the modern world and thus the main factor in the process of globalization.

H

Habermas, Jürgen
[1929–]
German philosopher who claimed that social systems are self-corrective, because the systems of meaning in a culture as expressed in art, literature, etc. are constantly undergoing change from within the culture to meet people's changing needs and aspirations. Running through his work is a critique of Western industrial democracies for their reduction of the human world to some form of economic efficiency, which has promoted a distorted mind-set disfigured by a destructive impulse towards domination:

e.g. the domination of Nature by science and technology. Habermas's major works include *Theory and Practice* (1973), *Knowledge and Human Interests* (1971), *A Theory of Communicative Action* (1984), and *The Philosophical Discourse of Modernity* (1985).

hagiography
[< Greek HAGIOS 'holy']
[also called hagiology]
Literature dealing with the lives of saints.

Hall, Edward T.
[1914–]
American anthropologist who studied how people interact nonverbally. Hall coined the term *proxemics, defining it as the study of interpersonal *zones. He was among the first to see the relevant implications, and thus to investigate the patterns and dimensions, of the zones people establish and maintain between each other when interacting, noting that these could be measured very accurately, allowing for predictable statistical variation. In North American culture, Hall found that a distance of under six inches between two people was perceived as an 'intimate' distance; while a distance at from 1.5 to 4 feet was the minimum one perceived to be a 'safe' distance.

Halliday, M.A.K.
[1925–]
British linguist who is responsible for the movement known as *social semiotics*. For Halliday language is generated by the social contexts in which it occurs; i.e. speech is not an application of language; rather language categories are derived from speech situations.

handshaking
Common form of bodily communication involving hand contact.

Note: Handshaking is an intrinsic component of formal greeting rituals. Intimate friends do not shake hands, unless they haven't seen each other for a protracted period of time or unless they want to congratulate one another. Cross-culturally, the form that handshaking assumes varies considerably. People can give a handshake by squeezing the other's hand, shaking the other's hand with both hands, shaking the other's hand and then patting the other's back or hugging him/her, leaning forward or standing straight while shaking, and so on. But handshaking is not universal. Southeast Asians, for instance, press their palms together in a praying motion, without making contact.

haptics
[< Greek HAPTEIN 'to touch']
1. having to do with the sense of touch;
2. branch of semiotics studying touching patterns during social interaction.

Illustrations: 1. handshaking to make social contact; 2. patting the arm, shoulder, or back to indicate agreement or to compliment; 3. linking arms to indicate companionship; 4. putting arms around the shoulders to indicate friendship or intimacy; 5. holding hands to indicate affection; 6. hugging to convey happiness; 7. kissing on the cheeks to exchange greetings.

hardware
[see *software]
Mechanical, magnetic, and electronic design, structure, and devices of a computer for the realization of its three main functions: input, output, and storage.

harmony
[< Greek HARMOS 'a fitting']
1. in music, the simultaneous sounding of two or more tones perceived as pleasant to the ear; 2. structure of chords and how they relate to each other in a piece of music (distinguished from *melody* and *rhythm*).

Note: Most Western music written between the 17th century and the 19th century is referred to as *tonal* because it is based on a central tone, called the *tonic*, towards which all other tones gravitate. *Intervals*, or pairs of notes, are the building blocks of tonal harmony. Some are *consonant* (the two notes blend with each other), whereas others are *dissonant* (the two notes clash). The fundamental unit of harmony in tonal music is a three-note chord called a *triad*. The three notes of a triad are called the *root*, *third*, and *fifth*. In order for a pitch to be a tonic, it must be the focal point of a group of pitches that fall into either of two scale patterns: the *major scale* or the *minor scale*. A *key* consists of a tonic *note* together with its *scale* and the *triads* built on the notes of that scale. Thus, a composition in the key of C major has the note C as its tonic and is constructed around the C-major scale.

In the Middle Ages, Western composers began to add parts to plainchant, which had developed as a single-part musical form. Over the centuries composers explored different combinations of intervals and different ways of connecting them. By the 16th century, the movement from one triad to another was so arranged in the parts that a complete triad was sounding almost all the time. In the second half of the 17th century, 'the laws of harmony' were established. By the 19th century functional harmonic progressions had been in use for so long that composers considered them too commonplace for many of their expressive needs. So, they explored new forms of harmony, including connecting chords previously considered only distantly related to one another, adding non-harmonic tones that lasted for most of the duration of a chord, and employing dissonant chords more often.

As a result of these trends, the laws of classical Western harmony had ceased to be a potent force in new music by the early 20th century. While some composers continued to write music based on a tonal center, others abandoned tonality altogether and began writing *atonal* music. In this music, the earlier distinction between consonance and dissonance no longer holds.

hedonism
[Greek HEDONĒ 'pleasure']
In ancient Greek philosophy, the doctrine that pleasure is the sole or chief good in life and that the pursuit of it is the ideal aim of conduct.

Note: The *Epicureans were the ones who best articulated the philosophy of hedonism, contending that true pleasure is attainable only by reason. They stressed the virtues of self-control and prudence. In the 18th and 19th centuries such British philosophers as Jeremy Bentham (1748–1832), James Mill (1773–1836), and his son, John Stuart Mill (1806–73) propounded the doctrine of universalistic hedonism, better known as *utilitarianism*. According to this doctrine, the ultimate objective of human existence is the good of society, and the guiding principle of individual moral conduct should be devotion to that which promotes the well-being of the greatest number of people.

Hegel, Georg Wilhelm Friedrich
[1770–1831]
German philosopher who argued that the individual's sense of reality was filtered largely by his/her acquired systems of representation, although he also believed that there existed a rational logic that governed these systems. Hegel argued that art allows people to grasp religious concepts by means of images and symbols; philosophical concepts, by contrast, are acquired through rational thinking.

Heidegger, Martin
[1889–1976]
German philosopher widely regarded as one of the most original and influential of 20th-century thinkers. Heidegger posited that the individual is always in danger of being submerged in the world of objects, everyday routines, and the conventional crowd. He felt that modern technological society had deprived human life of meaning. He called the psychic state that such a social order has induced *nihilism* – a term that has become widely used. His most influential work, *Being and Time* (1927), dealt with the philosophical question 'What is it to be?' His work had a crucial influence on French philosophers Michel *Foucault and Jacques *Derrida.

Heisenberg's principle
[also called the uncertainty principle or the indeterminacy principle]
Principle elaborated by 20th-century physicist Werner Heisenberg (1901–76), debunking the notion of an objective physical reality independent of culture and of the scientist's personal perspective.

Note: An anecdotal illustration of Heisenberg's principle is the following one. Suppose that a scientist reared and trained in North America sees a physical event that she has never seen before. Curious about what it is, she takes out a notebook and writes down her observations in English. At the instant that the North American scientist observes the event, another scientist, reared and trained in the Philippines and speaking only the indigenous Tagalog language, also sees the *same* event. He similarly takes out a notebook and writes down his observations in Tagalog. Now, to what extent will the *contents* of the observations, as written in the two notebooks, coincide? The answer of course is that the two sets of observations will not be identical. The reason for this discrepancy is not, clearly, due to the nature of the event, but rather to the fact that the observers were different, psychologically and culturally. So, as Heisenberg's principle aptly suggests, the true nature of the event is indeterminable, although it can be investigated further, paradoxically, on the basis of the notes taken by the two scientists.

Heisenberg's uncertainty principle was important in the development of quantum mechanics and also contributed to modern philosophical thinking. He was awarded the 1932 Nobel Prize in physics.

helm
Heraldic type of *insignia representing helmets of knights, princes, peers, and gentlemen.

Helmholtz, Hermann
[1821–1894]
German scientist, whose contributions in physiology, optics, acoustics, and electrodynamics greatly advanced 19th-century scientific thought. Helmholtz believed that physiological forces as well as the forces of Nature could be perceived by the senses, mechanically measured, and thus explained. He also researched thoroughly the physiology and physics of vision and hearing.

helper
[see *actant]

hemisphericity
[< Greek HEMI 'half' + SPHAIRA 'sphere']
Neuroscientific notion referring to the fact that the human brain is functionally bilateral, i.e. that it carries out its tasks through an inbuilt 'cooperation' of the functions associated with both its left and right hemispheres.

heraldry
[< Germanic HARIWALD 'army chief']
System of coats of arms, genealogies, armorial bearings, ornamental figures, and/or insignia used as tribal, family, or national emblems.

Note: The practice of using insignias on shields and banners began during feudal times when a knight needed to be recognized from a distance. In the 14th century, the family insignias were embroidered on surcoats, giving rise to the term *coat of arms.* The use of insignia developed subsequently into a complex system for identifying social status. The design of a coat of arms includes the *escutcheon*, or shield, the *helm* or *helmet*, the *crest*, the *motto*, the *mantle*, the *supporters*, and the *torse* or *wreath*.

Herder, Johann Gottfried von
[1744–1803]
German philosopher who emphasized the profound differences that existed among individuals who lived in different cultures. His work laid the foundation for the comparative study of civilizations. Herder developed the idea that national character is expressed by a people's language and literature. He attempted to demonstrate that Nature and human history obey the same laws, and that in time contending human forces will be reconciled.

hermeneutics
[< Greek HERMENEUEIN 'to interpret']
1. in semiotics, the study and interpretation of *texts; 2. in psychology, the study of the meanings derived from social behavior and experience.

hero
[see also *actant]
1. in mythology and legend, a personage, often of divine ancestry, who is endowed with great courage and strength, celebrated for his bold exploits, and favored by the gods; 2. principal character in a novel, poem, or dramatic representation.

Herodotus
[c. 484–425 BC]
Greek thinker and first historian who spent a large part of his life traveling in Asia, Egypt, and Greece, noting and recording for posterity differences in the dress, food, etiquette, and rituals of the people he encountered. His annotations have come to constitute some of the first analyses of cul-

tural differences, chronicling the language, dress, food, etiquette, legends, history, and rituals of the people he came across. The comparative observations Herodotus made in his great work *History* – the Greek word for 'inquiry' – constitute the first significant accounts of the cultures of virtually the entire ancient Middle East, including those of the Scythians, Medes, Persians, Assyrians, and Egyptians. Inspired by the *History*, other ancient historians, like the Roman Tacitus (c. AD 55–117), also made it a point to describe the languages, character, manners, and geographical distribution of the peoples they visited.

heuristic
[< Greek HEURISKEIN 'to find']
1. something designed for helping someone understand or learn (e.g. an educational method, a *flow chart, etc.); 2. in computer science, a problem-solving technique in which the most appropriate solution to a problem (among several alternatives) is selected at successive stages of a program's operation.

hieratic
[< Greek HIEROS 'sacred']
Type of cursive script developed by the Egyptians around 2700 BC, which replaced *hieroglyphic writing for most purposes; hieratic writing was executed with blunt reed pens and ink on papyrus.

hieroglyphic writing
[< Greek HIEROS 'sacred' + GLYPHEIN 'to carve, hollow out']
Ancient Egyptian system of writing, developed around 3000 BC, in which pictorial symbols were used to represent *referents or consonants, or a combination of referents and consonants.

Note: Hieroglyphic writing was used to record hymns and prayers, to register the names and titles of individuals and deities, and to annotate various community activi-

ties. Hieroglyphic inscriptions were composed of two basic types of signs: *ideograms* and *phonograms*. Ideograms represented visually either the specific object drawn or something closely related to it; phonograms were used purely for their phonetic value. Phonograms could represent one consonant or the combination of two or three consonants in a specific order; vowels were not written. A specific hieroglyphic *sign might serve as an ideogram in one word and as a phonogram in another. Most words were written with a combination of these two types of signs.

Hieroglyphic inscriptions could be written either vertically or horizontally, usually from right to left. The latest hieroglyphic inscription dates from AD 394. Around 2700 BC, the Egyptians developed a more cursive script that replaced hieroglyphs called *hieratic. An even more cursive and ligatured script called *demotic was also employed a little later. After the 1799 discovery of the Rosetta Stone, a slab inscribed in Greek and in hieroglyphic and demotic Egyptian, French Egyptologist Jean François Champollion (1790–1832) deciphered hieroglyphic writing.

high-level language
Computer *programming language whose commands resemble categories of natural human language; a compiler program turns a high-level into a machine language.

Hippocrates
[460?–377? BC]
Greek founder of Western medical science who established the practice of diagnosis based on the decipherment of symptoms, which he called *semeiotics*. Hippocrates defined a symptom as a *semeion* 'mark, sign,' and he asserted that the physician's primary task was to unravel what a symptom stands for. At the time, his idea that, by observing enough cases, a physician could predict the course of a disease, was a revolutionary one.

historical grammar
[see *grammar]

historical linguistics
[see *linguistics, historical]

historicism
[< Latin HISTORIA 'a learning by inquiry, narrative']
1. theory that events are determined or influenced by phenomena beyond the control of human beings; 2. theory that stresses the significant influence of history on human life, on art, etc.

historiography
[< Latin HISTORIA 'a learning by inquiry, narrative' + GRAPHEIN 'to write']
Systematic study and documentation of history in general, or of the history of some nation, event, movement, discipline, etc. in particular.

Note: Western historiography originated with the ancient Greeks. In the 5th century BC *Herodotus and Thucydides (460?–400? BC) recorded contemporary or near-contemporary events relying in part on eyewitnesses or other reliable sources. Roman historian Sallust (86?–34? BC) introduced the practice of political commentary in the historical account. During the 4th century AD, secular and religious themes were interspersed in historiographical accounts. With the fall of the Western Roman Empire in the 5th century, many monasteries kept annals that recorded events year by year, annotated with religious commentary. The renewal of classical education in 15th-century Renaissance Italy encouraged a new secular approach to historical commentary. From the 16th century onward writers of histories started collecting factual sources for their accounts.

In the 19th century historiography achieved its status as an autonomous academic discipline. By the 20th century, it had developed into a method based on the use of archival collections and new sources of evidence. In recent years, historiography has been affected by the view that history-writing can never be objective.

history
[< Latin HISTORIA 'a learning by inquiry, narrative']
1. account of what has or might have happened, in the form of a narrative, play, story, or tale; 2. recorded events of the past.

history fabrication effect
[< Latin HISTORIA 'a learning by inquiry, narrative']
View that TV both documents and fabricates historical events.

Note: TV induces the impression in viewers that some ordinary event – an election campaign, an actor's love affair, a fashion trend, etc. – is a momentous happening. People's opinion of someone's guilt or innocence is shaped by watching news and interview programs. In effect, the events that receive airtime are perceived as more significant and historically meaningful to society than those that do not. TV imbues events and people with historical status and, therefore, with significance.

The horrific scenes coming out of the Vietnam War that were transmitted into people's homes daily in the late 1960s and early 1970s brought about an end to the war, mobilizing social protest. Political and social protesters frequently inform the news media of their intentions, and then dramatically stage their demonstrations for the cameras. Sports events like the *World Series*, the *Super Bowl*, or the *Stanley Cup Playoffs* are transformed by television into Herculean struggles of mythic heroes. Events such as the John Kennedy and Lee Harvey Oswald assassinations, the Vietnam War, the Watergate hearings, the Rodney King beating, the O.J. Simpson trial, the Bill Clinton sex scandal are transformed into portentous and prophetic historical events by TV images. In a phrase, TV has become the *maker* of history and its *documenter* at the same time.

Hjelmslev, Louis
[1899–1965]

Danish linguist who elaborated *Saussurean theory into a framework known as *glossematics, in which he formalized the Saussurean notions in a synthetic way. Hjelmslev also emphasized that *signs encompass not only internal denotative meaning, but a mass of information coming from outside the sign itself: namely, the historical meanings and connotations associated with the sign.

Hobbes, Thomas
[1588–1679]

English philosopher who saw the mind as the sum of the internal activities of the body. For Hobbes, sensation, reason, value, and justice could be explained simply in terms of matter and motion. He defined ratiocination bluntly as arithmetical computation: i.e. as a process akin to the addition and subtraction of numbers. Hobbes claimed that thinking was essentially a rule-governed mechanical process and that, in principle, machines capable of thought could be built. For Hobbes, causes entailed effects as rigorously as Euclid's propositions entailed one another. The human brain, he claimed, is a logical machine that has allowed humans literally 'to follow' consequences entailed by causes. In his best-known work, *Leviathan* (1651), Hobbes held that people are fearful and predatory and must submit to the absolute supremacy of the state, in both secular and religious matters, in order to live sanely and rationally.

hologram
[see *holograph]

holograph
[< Greek HOLO 'whole' + GRAPHEIN 'to write']
Pattern produced on a photosensitive me-dium that has been exposed by *holography and then photographically developed.

holography
[< Greek HOLO 'whole' + GRAPHEIN 'to write']
Method of making three-dimensional photographs without a camera, by splitting a laser beam into two beams and projecting on a photographic plate the tiny interference patterns made by one beam going from the laser to the plate and the other beam going from the laser to the object to the plate.

holophrases
[< Greek HOLO 'whole' + PHRASTIKOS 'suited for expressing']
Monosyllabic forms that children start uttering starting around 6–12 months (*mu, ma, da, di,* etc.); these are imitations of what the child has heard in social context.

Note: Holophrastic utterances have been shown to serve three basic functions: 1. naming an object and event; 2. expressing an action or a desire for some action; 3. conveying emotional states. Holophrases are typically monosyllabic reductions of adult words – *da* for *dog*, *ca* for *cat*, etc. Over 60% will develop into nouns; and 20% will become verbs in the child's second year. During the second year children typically double their holophrases – *wowo* 'water,' *bubu* 'bottle,' *mama* 'mother,' etc. These early efforts are, clearly, imitative *signs, as are the various words and sounds children make when they play to accompany their rhythmic movements, to simulate the sounds of their toys, and to generate emotional responses in those around them.

homeopathic magic
[see *magic]

Homo
[Latin 'man']
General term for the human species.

Homo erectus

Genus of *Homo* that lived 700,000 to 1.75 million years ago and that emigrated, at the close of its evolution, into the temperate parts of Asia and Europe. *Homo erectus* had a fairly large brain and a skeletal structure similar to that of modern humans. It knew how to control fire and probably had primitive language skills.

homograph

[< Greek HOMOS 'same' + GRAPHEIN 'to write']
Word that is spelled the same as another but with a different meaning.

Illustration: bow = the front part of a ship; *bow* = to bend; *bow* = a decorative knot.

Homo habilis

Genus of *Homo* that lived between 1 and 2.5 million years ago, possessing many traits that linked it both with the earlier australopithecines and with later members of the genus *Homo*. *Homo habilis* had a large brain, walked upright, and had a dexterous hand. *Homo habilis* lived in semi-permanent camps, and had a food-gathering and -sharing culture.

homonym

[< Greek HOMOS 'same' + ONOMA 'name']
Word with the same pronunciation as another but with a different meaning, origin and, usually, spelling.

Illustrations: If the homonymy is purely phonetic, then the words are known as homophones (e.g. *bore* vs. *boar* are homophones, but not homographs). If the homonymy is graphic, then the words are known as *homographs (*play* as in Shakespeare's *play* vs. *play* as in *He likes to play*). It is not the case that all homographs are homophones: e.g. the form *learned* has two pronunciations as in: *He learned to play the violin* vs. *He is a learned man*.

homonymy

[< Greek HOMOS 'same' + ONOMA 'name']
Verbal coincidence by which two or more words with distinct meanings are pronounced and/or spelled in the same way.

Illustrations: 1. The words *meet* and *meat* are pronounced in the same way but they mean different things. 2. In *He can come* and *This is a Coca Cola can*, the word *can* has two meanings.

homophone

[see *homonym]

homophony

[< Greek HOMOS 'same' + PHONĒ 'sound']
Musical style characterized by a single melodic line with accompaniment.

Illustration: A perfect example of homophonic composition is the familiar song *Twinkle, twinkle little star* in which a simple melody is heard over a constant accompaniment.

Homo sapiens

Genus of *Homo* that originated between 200,000 and 300,000 years ago, characterized by a proportionately larger brain than any of its hominid ancestors. *Homo sapiens* had complete manual dexterity, stereoscopic vision, culture, and an early form of language.

Homo sapiens sapiens

Term used to refer to modern humans, appearing around 30,000 to 40,000 years ago, possessing language and full symbolism, and living in a tribal culture.

honeybee dancing

Movement patterns performed by worker honeybees returning to the hive from foraging trips informing other bees in the hive about the direction, distance, and quality of a food source.

Note: Several kinds of dance patterns have

been documented by entomologists. When the cache of food is nearby, the bee moves in circles alternately to the left and to the right; when the food source is further away, the bee moves in a straight line while wagging its abdomen from side to side and then returning to its starting point. The straight line in the wagging dance points in the direction of the food source, the energy level of the dance indicates how rich the food source is, and the tempo provides information about its distance. In one experimental study, a feeding dish was placed 330 meters from the hive, and the bees represented it with 15 complete rounds in 30 seconds, whereas a dish located 700 meters away was communicated by only 11 runs carried out in the same period of time.

Humboldt, Wilhelm von
[1767–1835]
Prussian statesman, educational reformer, and philologist who claimed that language reflects the culture and character of its speakers and that the study of language cannot be extricated from a consideration of the cultural system to which it belongs.

Hume, David
[1711–1776]
Scottish philosopher who claimed that all knowledge arises from sensory perception. For Hume, even physical theories could not really explain causes and effects, since these depended largely upon the disposition of human beings to form associations between events that are regularly linked in sensory experience. For Hume, reason and rational judgments were merely the results of making habitual associations between distinct sensations or experiences. He called into question the fundamental laws of science, and even denied the existence of the individual self, maintaining that people 'are nothing but a bundle or collection of different perceptions.'

humor
[< Latin HUMOR 'moisture']
Ability to perceive, enjoy, or express something as amusing, comical, incongruous, or absurd.

Note: Theories of humor have existed since ancient times. But there still is no true understanding of why people laugh and find certain phenomena 'humorous.' The most widely held theory is, essentially, that human beings react to incongruity and absurdity by laughing because these violate their sense of order and pattern. Humor is thus a form of 'circumvention' or 'surprise' reaction to such violations.

Husserl, Edmund
[1859–1938]
German philosopher who claimed that cognition had a sensory basis. Husserl is considered the founder of *phenomenology*, the view that only that which is present to the senses is real. Husserl contended that the philosopher's task is to understand how the meaning of an object can be arrived at by systematically varying that object in the imagination. In his *Ideas: A General Introduction to Pure Phenomenology* (1913), he introduced the term 'phenomenological reduction' to explain his belief that consciousness contains unchanging structures called 'meanings' that determine what object the mind is directed towards at any given time. Phenomenology has, since Husserl, become a very influential movement dedicated to describing the structures of experience as they present themselves to consciousness, without recourse to any theoretical or explanatory framework.

hydrographic map
[see *map]

hymn
[< Latin HYMNUS 'song of praise']
Song or poem of praise or thanksgiving to a deity.

Note: The earliest hymns for which the music has been preserved are two Greek hymns to Apollo, discovered at Delphi, dating from the 2nd century BC. Hymn singing within Judaism dates from at least the time of the biblical Book of Psalms, which means 'Praise Songs.' The first collection of Christian hymn texts was the Gnostic Psalter; its success led Syrian monk Saint Ephrem of Edessa to write hymns in Syriac in order to spread the Christian faith.

hyperbole
[< Greek HYPER 'above, beyond' + BALEIN 'to throw']
Rhetorical exaggeration for effect.

Illustrations: 1. *He's as strong as an ox.* 2. *She's smarter than Einstein.* 3. *I could sleep for a year.* 4. *This book weighs a ton.*

hypercard
[< Greek HYPER 'above, beyond']
In computer science, software designed for the Apple Macintosh that provides users with an information-management tool consisting of a series of cards collected together in a stack; each card can contain text, graphical images, and sound.

hypermedia
[< Greek HYPER 'above, beyond']
Computer-based information retrieval system that enables a user to gain or provide access to texts, audio and video recordings, photographs, and computer graphics related to a particular subject. A hypermedia 'navigation' might include links to such topics as *language, semantics, communication, semiotics,* and *media.*

hyperonomy
[see *hyponomy]

hypertext
[< Greek HYPER 'above, beyond' + Latin TEXTUS 'fabric']
Electronic *text that provides links between key elements, allowing the user to move through information non-sequentially.

Note: The term *hypertext* was coined in 1965 to describe computer textuality as opposed to the linear textuality of books, film, and speech. The former permits the user to browse through related topics, regardless of the presented order of the topics. These links are often established both by the author of a hypertext document and by the user, depending on the intent of the hypertext document. For example, 'navigating' among the links to the word *language* in an article might lead the user to the *International Phonetic Alphabet*, the science of *linguistics*, samples of the world's languages, etc.

hypoicon
[< Greek HYPO 'under' + EIKON 'image']
Charles *Peirce's term for an *icon that is shaped by cultural convention but that can nonetheless be figured out by those who are not members of the culture (with prompting).

Illustration: The V-sign made with the index and middle fingers can stand for a series of meanings. It is difficult to figure out what it means unless one is a member of the same culture as the sign-user. But if told that it stands for *victory*, then it can easily be deduced that it has been made to reproduce the shape of the initial letter of the word *victory.*

hyponym
[< Greek HYPO 'under' + ONOMA 'name']
Concept, expressed by a word, that is inclusive of another.

Illustrations: 1. *flower* is a hyponym of *rose*; 2. *insect* is a hyponym of *ant.*

hyponymy
[< Greek HYPO 'under' + ONOMA 'name']
[also called hyperonymy]
Semantic relation whereby one concept embraces another.

Illustrations: 1. *Scarlet* is a type of *red*. 2. *Tulip* is a type of *flower*.

hypothesis

[< Greek HYPO 'under' + THESIS 'a position']
1. tentative explanation that has been fashioned to account for a set of facts so that it can be tested by further investigation; 2. something assumed to be true for the purpose of argument or investigation.

I

---

icon

[< Greek EIKON 'image']
1. *sign that is made to resemble its *referent through some form of replication, resemblance, or simulation; 2. a visual image of some kind; 3. picture of a sacred or sanctified Christian personage; 4. one who is the object of great attention and devotion (an idol); 5. in computer science, picture on a screen that represents a program or a specific command.

Illustrations: 1. Onomatopoeic words such as *drip, plop, bang, screech* are *vocal icons* simulating the sounds that certain things, actions, or movements are perceived to make. 2. Portraits of people are *visual icons* reproducing faces from the perspective of the artist. 3. Perfumes are *olfactory icons* simulating natural scents. 4. Chemical food additives are *gustatory icons* simulating natural food flavors. 5. A block with a letter of the alphabet carved into it is a *tactile icon* reproducing the letter's shape in relief.

iconicity

[< Greek EIKON 'image']
Process of representing things with *iconic signs (onomatopoeic words, photographs, etc.).

Note: Iconicity entails that the human representational capacity is, at its roots, attentive to the recurrent patterns of color, shape,

dimension, movement, sound, taste, etc. Archeological evidence attests to the ancientness of iconicity. In fact, the first inscriptions, cave drawings, small sculptures, and relief carvings of animals and female figures found in caves throughout Europe, such as those at Lascaux in France and Altamira in Spain, were created some 30,000 to 40,000 years ago. But even in the verbal domain iconicity was probably the primordial semiosic force in word creation. Only at a later stage, after the utilization of iconically forged words in daily communication, did people start to forget how their words originated. Indeed, as Charles *Peirce so often remarked, the verbal symbols and abstractions that seem so remote from the sensorial realm were nonetheless born of sensory representation that has become unconscious as a result of protracted usage in social contexts.

iconic gesture

[< Greek EIKON 'image'; Latin GERERE 'to bear, carry']
Gesture used while speaking that bears a close resemblance to what is being talked about.

Illustration: When talking about bending something back, like a tree branch, a speaker might execute a gripping action with his/her hands, appearing to grab something and pull it back.

iconography

[< Greek EIKON 'image' + GRAPHEIN 'to write']
Study of art focusing on visual images and symbols.

Note: Iconography has traditionally dealt with religious and allegorical symbols in painting and sculpture. The use of iconographic symbols began as early as 3000 BC, when the civilizations of the Middle East represented their gods symbolically in artwork. In ancient Greece and Rome, gods were represented in terms of specific objects. The Romans also used secular allegorical symbols. For example, a woman surrounded by grapes and sheaves of wheat represented earth's bounties. Christian art has utilized iconographic symbols to represent people as well as ideas.

id

In psychoanalytic theory, the element of personality that undergirds instinctual drives.

Note: The *id* is one of the three basic elements of personality, according to psychoanalysis, the other two being the *ego and the *superego. It is equated with the *unconscious, which is the reservoir of the instinctual drives and accumulated memories of the individual.

idealism

[< Greek IDEIN 'to see']
Theory of reality and of knowledge positing that physical objects are mind-dependent and can have no existence apart from a mind that is conscious of them. This view is in opposition to *materialism, which maintains that consciousness itself is purely physical, and to *realism, the view that mind-independent physical objects exist and can be known through the senses.

Note: The ancient Greek philosopher *Plato postulated the existence of a realm of ideas that is imperfectly reflected in the objects of common experience. In the 18th century Irish philosopher George *Berkeley extended Plato's concept, by claiming, essentially, that everything of which one is conscious is reducible to innate ideas. German philosopher Immanuel *Kant refined this view, maintaining that all that can be known of things is the way they manifest themselves to perception. G.W.F. *Hegel disagreed with Kant's theory, arguing instead for the ultimate intelligibility of all existence.

ideogram

[< Greek IDEIN 'to see' + GRAPHEIN 'to write']
[also called ideograph]
Graphic sign representing an object or idea

without indicating the pronunciation of the word or words that stand for the object or idea.

Illustration: 1. @ (= 'at'); 2. $ (= 'dollars'); 3. & (= 'and'); 4. ☞ (= 'in that direction').

ideograph

[see *ideogram]

idiom

[< Greek IDIOS 'personal, private']
Speech form or expression that is peculiar grammatically or cannot be understood from the individual meanings of its elements.

Illustrations: 1. *to kick the bucket* (= 'to die'); 2. *to cut someone off* (= 'to interrupt').

illocution

[< Latin LOCUTIO 'a speaking']
Utterance that relates to the speaker's intention as distinct from what is actually said or the effect on an auditor.

Illustrations: 1. *I wish you would open the window.* 2. *I promise to come as well.*

illocutionary act

[< Latin LOCUTIO 'a speaking']
[synonymous expression for *illocution]
Type of speech act that specifies a call to action, expresses a promise or wish, etc.

Illustrations: 1. *It is time to leave.* 2. *Why don't you come along too?*

illusion

[< Latin ILLUSIO 'a mocking']
Erroneous perception of reality or of some referent.

Illustration:

People reared in Western cultures are typically fooled by these lines. Lines AB and CD are actually *equal* in length, but the *orienta-*

tion of the arrowheads fools the Western eye into seeing AB as longer than CD. As psychologists have found, many people living in non-Western cultures do not experience the same illusion, called the Müller-Lyer illusion. The reason why people from Western cultures see one line as longer than the other is because they have become conditioned by their upbringing to view drawings in *perspective*. This refers to the ability to create an illusion of depth or length on a two-dimensional surface. Perspective artists have learned how to manipulate and guide perspective by means of line, shape, color, value, and texture so as to induce a specific range of interpretations to their visual texts. Their craft dates back to the Renaissance (from the 14th to the 16th centuries) when the Italian artist Filippo Brunelleschi (1377–1446) popularized the technique of perspective. Since then, the Western eye has become accustomed to reading pictures in terms of Brunelleschi's technique.

image
[< Latin IMAGO 'imitation, copy, image']
1. mental picture of something; 2. concept of a person, product, institution, etc. held by the general public, often one deliberately created or modified by publicity, advertising, propaganda, etc. 3. in *psychoanalysis, a picture or likeness of a person, buried in the unconscious.

image, mental
[< Latin IMAGO 'imitation, copy, image']
[also called simply *image]
Mental imprint of something (a shape, a sound, etc.). The mental image is not a 'replica'. It is a form based on cultural norms and on personal experiences. There are four basic types of images, *concrete, abstract, fictitious, narrative*; each of these can be elicited mentally in *visual, auditory, olfactory, gustatory, kinesic,* or *emotive* ways.

Illustrations: 1. A *concrete image* is one that evokes a specific kind of mental picture or form: e.g. *a square, a cat, a table.* 2. An *abstract image* is one that does not evoke a specific type of mental form: e.g. *love, hope, justice.* 3. A *fictitious image* is one elicited by imaginary referents: e.g. *a winged table.* 4. A *narrative image* is one that unfolds within mind-space like a story: e.g. the recollection of an encounter with someone from start to finish.

The image of *cat* is a *visual* image because it entails a 'picturing' of something. Images can be nonvisual: e.g. 1. the sound of thunder, 2. the feel of wet grass, 3. the smell of fish, 4. the taste of toothpaste, 5. the sensation of being uncomfortably cold, 6. the sensation of extreme happiness. Image (1) has an *auditory* form, (2) a *tactile* one, (3) an *olfactory* one, (4) a *gustatory* one, (5) a *kinesic* one, (6) an *emotive* one.

imagery
[< Latin IMAGO 'imitation, copy, image']
1. ability of the mind to evoke some referent; 2. use of figurative language to represent objects, actions, or ideas; 3. use of expressive or evocative images in art, literature, or music.

Note: In modern humans, the brain is structured to carry out a symmetrical 'division of labor'. Its two hemispheres work cooperatively to produce the mental functions. The left hemisphere is the neural substrate that underlies rational analytical thinking, speech, and self-awareness. The right one balances out these functions. It is the locus where intuitive thinking, imagery, and emotional states originate. According to some psychologists, the imagistic right hemispheric chamber once controlled most of human thinking; the left hemispheric chamber assumed more of the thinking load as the mind became more and more capable of abstraction, and thus more bilateral (capable of coordinating thought processes according to hemisphere).

The topic of imagery has a long history in psychology. Individual differences in the ability to experience imagery were recorded already in the previous century. People can picture faces and voices accurately and quickly, rotate objects in their heads, locate imaginary places in their mind-space, scan game boards (like a checker board) in their minds, and so on with no difficulty whatsoever. While researchers might disagree on exactly what it is that their subjects 'see' or 'experience' in their minds, there is general agreement that something is 'going on' in the mind.

image schema

[< Latin IMAGO 'imitation, copy, image'; Greek SCHEMA 'form']
Term introduced by American linguist George Lakoff and American philosopher Mark Johnson referring to largely unconscious mental *images of sensory experiences that underlie the understanding and/or genesis of most abstract concepts.

Illustrations: Image schemas reduce a large quantity of sensory information into general patterns. Lakoff and Johnson identified three such patterns. The first one involves mental *orientation*. This underlies concepts that are derived from physical experiences of orientation – *up vs. down, back vs. front, near vs. far*, etc. This image schema can be detected in such expressions as *I'm feeling up today*. The second type involves *ontological* thinking. This underlies the understanding of emotions, ideas, etc. in terms of entities and substances: e.g. *I'm full of memories*. The third type of schema is an elaboration of the other two. It is called a *structural schema*: e.g. *My time is money*, which shows that we perceive time as both a *resource* and a *quantity*.

Each one of these general image schemas produces specific types of image schemas, according to culture. These are all operative in concept-formation: e.g. *Put this into your head* (= container schema); *To get what we wanted, we had to get around his opposition* (= impediment schema); *My life is going some-*

where finally (= journey schema); *Love is sweet* (= taste schema). The *container* and *taste* schemas are types of *ontological* schemas; the *impediment* and *journey* schemas are types of *orientational* schemas.

imagination

[< Latin IMAGO 'imitation, copy, image']
Conscious mental process involved in producing ideas or images of objects, events, relations, qualities, or processes either experienced or perceived in the past or not experienced. Psychologists occasionally distinguish between 'passive imagination,' by which images originally perceived by the senses are produced mentally, and 'active imagination,' by which the mind produces images of events or objects that are either little related or unrelated to past and present reality.

imperative form in advertising

[see *advertising, use of the imperative form in]

impressionism

[see also *art]
Style of painting developed in France during the 1870s, characterized by representations of the immediate visual impression produced by a scene and by the use of unmixed primary colors simulating actual reflected light.

Note: Impressionism in painting arose out of dissatisfaction with traditional painting techniques. Impressionists painted landscapes, street scenes, and figures from everyday life, being concerned more with the effects of light on an object than with exact depiction of form. Édouard Manet (1832–83) is sometimes called the first impressionist, since he was the first to paint by juxtaposing bright, contrasting colors, rather than by shading with intermediary tones. Other well-known impressionists include Camille Pissarro (1830–1903), Edgar Degas (1834–

1917), Claude Monet (1840–1926), Berthe Morisot (1841–95), and Pierre Auguste Renoir (1841–1919).

incompleteness theorem
[see Kurt *Gödel]

indeterminacy principle
[see *Heisenberg's principle]

index
[< Latin INDICARE 'to point out']
*Sign whose function is pointing out something real or imaginary in temporal, spatial, or relational terms.

Illustrations: 1. The pointing index finger is an index that allows people to refer to the spatial locations of objects, beings, and events. 2. Demonstrative words such as *this* or *that* are indexes that also allow people to refer to the relative spatial location of objects. 3. Adverbs such as *here* or *there* are, similarly, indexes that allow people to indicate the relative location of things. 4. Adverbs such as *before, after, now,* or *then* are indexes allowing people to indicate the relative temporal occurrences of things and events. 5. Pronouns such as *I, you, he,* or *she* are indexes that allow people to refer to the participants taking part in a situation in relation to one another.

indexicality
[< Latin INDICARE 'to point out']
Process of representing something with *indexes. The presence of *indexicality* in representational systems across the world is evidence that human consciousness is attentive to recurrent cause-and-effect patterns and to the fact that referents occur in time, space, and in relation to one another: *this* or *that, here* or *there, before* or *after, now,* or *then, the one* or *the other,* etc.

induction
[< Latin IN 'in' + DUCERE 'to lead']
[see also *abduction, *deduction]

Reasoning and concept-formation that unfolds by the extraction of a *general* pattern from *specific* facts or instances.

Illustration: If one were to measure the three angles of, say, 100 *specific* triangles (of varying shapes and sizes), one would get the same total (180°) each time. This would then lead one to *induce* that the sum of the three angles of *any* triangle is the same.

inference
[< Latin INFERRE 'to bring or carry in']
Reasoning that unfolds by observing something known or assumed.

Illustrations: 1. From your smile, I infer that you're pleased. 2. I gather from your remark that you don't care.

infix
[< Latin IN 'in' + FIXUS 'fastened']
*Affix added internally to a *morpheme or word.

Illustrations: In the Bantoc language (spoken in the Philippines): 1. the word *fumikas* 'to be strong' consists of the basic form *fukas* 'strong' and the infix *–mi-* 'to be'; 2. the word *sinulat* 'written' consists of the form *sulat* 'write' and the infix *–in-* 'passive.'

inflection
[< Latin IN 'in' + FLECTERE 'to bend']
1. change in the form of a word; 2. change in tone of voice.

Illustrations: In English, inflection characterizes the conjugation of verbs (*plays, played*), the declension of some nouns and adjectives (*man, men*), and comparison (*big, bigger, biggest*).

information
[< Latin INFORMATIO 'representation, outline, sketch']
1. in *information theory and computer science, precise measure of the *information content of a message; 2. any fact or datum that can be stored and retrieved by humans or machines.

information content

[< Latin INFORMATIO 'representation, outline, sketch']

Amount of information in a message, represented as I, measured as an inverse function of its probability.

Note: The highest value of I, $I = 1$, is assigned to the message that is the least probable. On the other hand, if a message is expected with 100% certainty, its information content is $I = 0$. For example, if a coin is tossed, its information content is $I = 0$, because we already know its result 100% of the time – i.e. we know that it will have a 100% probability of ending up as *either heads or tails*. There is no other possible outcome. So, the information carried by a coin toss is nil. However, the two separate outcomes *heads* and *tails* are equally probable.

In order to relate information content to probability, information theorist Claude *Shannon devised a simple formula, $I = \log_2 1/p$, in which p is the probability of a message being transmitted and $\log_2$ is the logarithm of $1/p$ to the base 2. $\log_2$ of a given number is the exponent that must be assigned to the number 2 in order to obtain the given number: e.g. $\log_2$ of 8 = 3, because $2^3 = 8$; $\log_2$ of 16 = 4, because $2^4 = 16$; and so on. Using Shannon's formula to calculate the information content of the outcome of a *single coin toss* will, as expected, yield the value of 0, because $2^0 = 1$. Shannon used binary digits, 0 and 1, to carry out his calculations because the mechanical communications systems he was concerned with worked in binary ways – e.g. *open* vs. *closed* or *on* vs. *off* circuits. So, if *heads* is represented by 0 and *tails* by 1, the outcome of a coin flip can be represented as either 0 or 1. For instance, if a coin is tossed three times in a row, the eight equally possible outcomes (= messages) that could ensue can be represented with *binary digits* as follows: 000 (= three heads) 001 (= two heads in a row, a tail) 010 (= a head, a tail, a head) 011 (= a head, two tails) 100 (= a tail, two heads)

101 (= a tail, a head, a tail) 110 (= two tails in a row, a head) 111 (= three tails).

information science

[< Latin INFORMATIO 'representation, outline, sketch']

Discipline that deals with the generation, collection, organization, storage, retrieval, and dissemination of recorded knowledge. The field brings together ideas and techniques from the social sciences, computer science, cybernetics, linguistics, management, neuroscience, and systems theory.

Note: Information science grew from the field of documentation, which emerged when digital computers were developed during the 1940s and early 1950s. In the 1960s massive collections of documents were transferred to databases, enabling various searches to be done by computer. By 1980 information science had become a thoroughly interdisciplinary field, and in the mid-1980s *artificial intelligence (AI) was very quickly becoming the center of its research activity. Artificial intelligence refers to the machine's capacity to mimic intelligent human behavior.

information theory

[< Latin INFORMATIO 'representation, outline, sketch']

Theoretical framework developed by Claude *Shannon in the late 1940s for improving the efficiency of telecommunication systems. Shannon's model has come to be known as the *bull's-eye* model of communication, because it essentially depicts a *sender aiming a message at a *receiver as in a bull's-eye target.

Note: Because this model came forward to provide a comprehensive framework for representing *information, independently of its specific content or meaning, and of the devices that carried it, it was appropriated in the 1950s and 1960s by linguists and psychologists as a general framework for investigating human information and communication systems. Although many semioticians have been openly critical of the view that human communication works according to the same basic mathematical laws as mechanical information systems, the general outline and notions of the bull's-eye model have proved to be highly convenient for relating how communication unfolds between human beings.

ingegno
[Italian for 'ingenuity, creativity, express-ivity']
[see also *fantasia, *memoria]
Term introduced into philosophy by Giambattista *Vico to refer to the innate capacity of humans to invent at will.

Innenwelt
[German for 'inside world']
[see also *Umwelt]
Specific perceptual and cognitive apparatus of a species that allows it to make sense of the input it receives from the outside world. This term is often used in *biosemiotics for referring to the fact that all organisms pos-sess species-specific modeling capacities that allow them to respond in kind to their outer experiences.

input
[see also *output]
Something put into a computer system or expended in its operation so as to achieve an output, i.e. a result of some kind.

input hardware
*hardware that provides information and instructions to the computer.

Note: Types of input hardware include the following: 1. a mouse, i.e. a one-handed pointing device (or ball) that allows the user to control an on-screen cursor; 2. a keyboard, which allows the user to type in text and commands; 3. an optical scanner, which con-verts images into electronic signals; 4. a voice-recognition module, which converts

speech into signals; 5. a modem, which con-nects a computer to a telephone line.

insignia
[< Latin IN 'in' + SIGNUM 'sign']
1. badge of office, rank, membership, or nationality; 2. a distinguishing sign.

instrumental learning
[see *psychology]

intaglio
[Italian for 'engraving']
Figure or design carved into or beneath the surface of some material or surface.

integrated circuit
[< Latin INTEGRARE 'to make whole']
Tiny slice or chip of material on which is etched or imprinted a complex of electronic components and their interconnections.

interface
Point of interaction or communication be-tween a computer and any other entity, such as a printer or human operator.

Note: User interfaces consist of the graphical design, the commands, prompts, and other devices that allow a user to interact with a program. In hardware, interfaces include cards, plugs, and other devices that connect pieces of hardware with the computer so that information can be moved from place to place.

interjection
[< Latin INTER 'between' + JACERE 'to throw']
1. sudden, short utterance; 2. an ejaculation.

Illustrations: 1. Ugh! 2. Wow! 3. Hey! 4. Well!

International Phonetic Alphabet
[abbreviated to IPA]
Set of standard phonetic symbols, originally devised in the late 19th century by the Inter-national Phonetic Association.

Note: Each symbol in the IPA represents a single sound or type of articulation, whether the sound or articulation occurs in only one language or in more than one. For example, [k] stands for the same sound written vicariously by *k*, *ch*, and *q* in English: *kit*, *chemistry*, *quick*.

Internet
Matrix of networks that connects computers around the world, via telephone lines, optical fibers, and radio links.

Note: Internet features include operating a computer from a remote location, transferring files between computers, and reading and interpreting files on remote computers. The Internet was initially developed in 1973 for linking computer networks at universities and laboratories in the United States. The *World Wide Web* was developed in 1989. This consists of a collection of files, called *web sites* or *web pages*, identified by *uniform resource locators* (URLs). Computer programs called *browsers* retrieve these files.

interpersonal zone
[see *zone, interpersonal]

interpretant
[< Latin INTERPRES 'negotiator, explainer']
Charles *Peirce's term for the meaning that one gets from a *sign, whereby the sign-user evaluates or responds to what the sign means socially, contextually, personally, etc.

Note: The *interpretant* is itself a sign created in the mind of a person. There are three phases of interpretants: 1. the *immediate interpretant*, which manifests itself in the correct understanding of the sign (e.g. looking at the *cat* pointed out by someone's index finger); 2. the *dynamic interpretant*, which is the direct result of the sign (i.e. of looking at things generally in response to pointing fingers); 3. the *final interpretant*, which is the result of a specific sign (e.g. realizing that the finger is pointing to a specific type of cat, say, a tabby).

Peirce suggested, moreover, that there were three types of *interpretants* (what the

sign-user or sign-interpreter intends with the sign): 1. a *rheme* is an interpretant of a *qualisign; 2. a *dicisign* is an interpretant of a *sinsign; 3. an *argument* is an interpretant of a *legisign.

interpretation
[< Latin INTERPRES 'negotiator, explainer']
1. process of deciphering what a *sign or *text means; 2. act or result of deriving the meaning of something; 3. realization of a person's conception of a work of art, subject, etc. through acting, playing, writing, criticizing, etc. (e.g. a pianist's interpretation of the Beethoven sonatas).

intertext
[< Latin INTER 'between' + TEXTUS 'a weaving together']
Culture-specific *text alluded to within a main text. The text can be cited, rewritten, prolonged, or transformed by the main text.

Illustrations: 1. Homer's *Odyssey* is an intertext of novelist James Joyce's *Ulysses*; 2. The *Bible* is an intertext of playwright Samuel Beckett's *Waiting for Godot*.

intertextuality
[< Latin INTER 'between' + TEXTUS 'a weaving together']
Allusion within a text to some other text or texts of which the reader would normally have knowledge.

Illustrations: 1. The *Bible* is cited, transformed, or alluded to in many Western narratives. 2. Classical mythical themes and stories often appear in various forms in fairytales, legends, and other kinds of narratives.

intimate zone
[see *zone, intimate]

intonation
[< Latin IN 'in' + TONUS 'a sound']
1. significant levels and variations in pitch

sequences within an utterance; 2. type of pitch used at the end of a spoken sentence or phrase (as, for instance, in a question).

Ionic form
[see also *Corinthian form, *Doric form] Ancient Greek tapered column that rose from a richly molded circular base, and was topped with a capital decorated by spiral forms. It functioned either as a pillar to support a building or, occasionally, as a freestanding monument.

irony
[< Greek EIREIN 'to speak']
1. humorous or subtly sarcastic expression in which the intended meaning of the words stands in direct opposition to their usual sense; 2. cool, detached attitude of mind, characterized by recognition of the incongruities and complexities of experience.

Illustrations: 1. *I love being tortured* (= uttered through tears). 2. *Beautiful day today, isn't it?* (= uttered when the temperature is well below freezing and a frigid snowstorm is taking place).

Note: Irony allows someone to make a comment on a situation without any personal stake or involvement in it. As such, it is both a protective strategy, deflecting attention away from the self towards others, by which one can make value judgments of others without commitment, and a verbal weapon that can be used to show aggression towards others.

isomorphism
[< Greek ISO 'equal' + MORPHĒ 'form']
Similarity in appearance or structure of *signs belonging to different *codes.

Illustrations: 1. Binary and decimal numerals can be put into an isomorphic relation easily: e.g. the decimal numeral 2 = the binary numeral 10. 2. Roman numerals can be put into an isomorphic relation with Hindu-Arabic numerals: e.g. the Roman numeral IV = the Hindu-Arabic numeral 4.

J

Jakobson, Roman
[1896–1982]
Moscow-born linguist and semiotician who carried out most of his work in the United States. Among his contributions to semiotics, linguistics, and communication theory is his widely used model that identifies the main functions and components of human communication (see *communication, verbal). He also put forward the notion of linguistic structure as constantly adaptive to human needs and whims, rather than innate and hard-wired into human behavior.

jargon
Version of a language with specialized vocabulary and idioms used typically by those in the same profession or line of work: sportswriters, bureaucrats, lawyers, doctors, bankers, educators, musicians, psychologists, etc.

Illustrations: 1. *perorbital hematoma* (= 'black eye'), in medicine; 2. *licorice stick* (= 'clarinet'), among jazz musicians.

jingles in advertising
[see *advertising, use of jingles in]

Jung, Carl Gustav
[1875–1961]
Swiss psychiatrist who argued that the *unconscious mind consisted of two interacting dimensions: the *personal unconscious*, the repressed feelings and thoughts developed during an individual's life, and the *collective unconscious*, those feelings, thoughts, and memories shared by all humanity. Jung used the term *archetype* to refer to the latter. Jung saw archetypes as primor-

dial memories that are too weak to become conscious. So, they gain expression in the symbols and forms that find their way into the myths, tales, fantasies, artistic expressions, and rituals displayed in cultures across the world.

K

Kant, Immanuel
[1724–1804]
German idealist philosopher who argued that reason is the means by which the phenomena of experience are translated into understanding. Kant was, however, wary of ascribing all mental representations to converted experiences, positing instead that the two – reason and experience – are interdependent.

The cornerstone of Kant's philosophy is contained in his *Critique of Pure Reason* (1781), in which he differentiated knowledge into *analytic* and *synthetic* propositions. In analytic thinking, the truth of something can be discovered by analysis of the phenomenon itself; in synthetic thinking, experience, not analysis, must be used to determine its truthfulness. Kant's philosophy is usually known as *transcendentalism*, because he regarded the objects of the material world as fundamentally unknowable, serving merely as the raw material from which sensations are formed.

keyboard
[see *input hardware]

Khaldun, Ibn
[1332–1406]
Medieval Algerian scholar who wrote a fascinating treatise on the difference between nomadic and city-dwelling Bedouins, in which he suggested that the environment where the two types of Bedouins lived determined their differential behaviors and dissimilar personalities. His work, therefore, is not only a valuable guide to the history of 14th-century North African cultures, but also an early blueprint for relativistic theories of culture, which hold that culture and habitat mold the individual's character and worldview. A society, he observed, was held together by the unifying force of religion, and it arose and fell according to 'cultural laws' that could be empirically discovered by an observer, since they reflected both a group's pattern of adaptation to habitat and the kinds of representational systems (language, rituals, etc.) it had developed over time.

kilobyte
1. one thousand *bytes; 2. unit of measurement of the memory capacity of a computer, equal to 2^{10} bytes.

kinesic code
[< Greek KINESIS 'motion']
[also spelled kinetic]
*Code based on properties of the body.

Illustrations: Gender and grooming codes are examples of kinesic codes. These condition how people behave in courtship and other sexual situations. They are products of cultural history and convention, being quite specific as to what facial and eye-contact patterns, and which bodily postures, are appropriate in specific contexts. Their primary function is to regulate physical interaction and behavior. The ways in which people present and represent the body are conveyors of social persona.

kinesic image
[see *image, mental]

kinesics
[< Greek KINESIS 'motion']
[also spelled kinetics]
1. science or study of human muscular movements, especially as applied in physical education; 2. study of bodily *semiosis.

kinestheme
[< Greek KINESIS 'motion']
Minimal unit of significant bodily movement: e.g. a posture, a pose, a look, etc.

kinetic code
[variant spelling of *kinesic code]

Köhler, Wolfgang
[1887–1967]
German *Gestalt psychologist who demonstrated experimentally that apes could solve problems spontaneously without the benefit of previous training.

Kress, Gunther
[1940–]
Semiotician who is well known for having shown that the patterns that children exhibit in learning representational behavior in social context is the clue to understanding *semiosis in general.

Kristeva, Julia
[1941–]
Contemporary semiotician whose work draws heavily upon psychoanalytic theory. Kristeva originated the idea of *intertextuality in the analysis of narrative.

L

---

labyrinth
[< Greek LABURINTHOS 'double-headed ax']
1. in Greek mythology, intricate structure of interconnecting passages through which the Minotaur was confined; 2. something highly intricate or convoluted in character.

Note: Of the many labyrinths built in the ancient world, perhaps the most celebrated was a funeral temple built by Amenemhet III in Egypt, which contained 3000 chambers. The term *labyrinth* is also applied to maze-like patterns on the floors of some medieval churches, and to garden mazes walled by clipped hedges.

Lacan, Jacques
[1901–1981]
French psychoanalyst who claimed that the human *unconscious is shaped by the language one learns. Lacan also divided human experience into the *imaginary*, the *symbolic*, and the *real*. These three correspond, more or less respectively, to *signification, *signifier, and *signified.

lament
[< Latin LAMENTUM 'lament']
Song or *poem expressing deep grief or mourning.

lampoon
[< French LAMPER 'to gulp down']
1. broad satirical piece that ridicules a person, group, or institution; 2. a light satire.

Langer, Susanne
[1895–1985]
American educator and philosopher who introduced the distinction between the discursive symbols used in conventional language and the nondiscursive ones (presentational) used in various art forms. Discursive forms have the property of detachment: e.g. one can focus on a word in a sentence or a phrase without impairing the overall understanding of the sentence or phrase. In contrast, *presentational forms cannot be broken up into their elements without impairing the meaning: e.g. one cannot focus on a note or phrase in a melody without destroying the sense of the melody.

language
[< Latin LINGUA 'tongue']
1. ability to communicate by means of a system of vocal sounds and combinations of such sounds to which meaning is attributed; 2. code that permits vocal *semiosis and *representation.

Note: The essential feature of language is called the *phonemic principle*, which refers to the fact that the *signifiers of a language are constructed with phonemes linked together in structurally predictable ways. Consider the word *green*. It is made up with legitimate English sounds (known as *phonemes), connected in an appropriate fashion (according to English *syllable structure). The signifier *çeñ*, by contrast, would not be an acceptable word because it contains two phonemes, represented by the alphabet characters *ç* and *ñ*, that do not exist in English. Nor is *gpeen* a legitimate word, even though each of its sounds are acceptable phonemes, because it violates syllable structure (the sequence *gp* does not occur in English to start a syllable). This is how words are formed in all languages. But language is not just a collection of words. When words are used in verbal representation and communication they allow people to deliver messages in the form of *sentences and *discourses.

Phonemes are perceived by the hearing center of the brain and produced through its motor pathways via a complex system of coordination between brain and vocal organs. There are twelve cranial nerves. Seven of these link the brain with the vocal organs. Some perform a motor function, controlling the movement of muscles; while others perform a sensory function, sending signals to the brain. The larynx controls the flow of air to and from the lungs, so as to prevent food, foreign objects, or other substances from entering the trachea on their way to the stomach. The ability to control the vocal folds makes it possible to build up pressure within the lungs and to emit air not only for expiration purposes, but also for the production of sound.

The *recognition* of phonemes, along with the *discrimination* of phonic differences, has its physiological locus in the left hemisphere (LH) of the brain. This discovery goes back to 1861, when the French anthropologist and surgeon Paul Broca (1824–80) noticed a destructive lesion in the left frontal lobe during the autopsy of a patient who had lost the ability to articulate words during his lifetime, even though he had not suffered any paralysis of his speech organs. Broca concluded that the capacity to articulate speech was traceable to that specific cerebral site – which shortly thereafter came to bear his name (*Broca's area). This discovery established a direct connection between a semiosic capacity and a specific area of the brain. Then, in 1874 the work of the German neurologist Carl Wernicke (1848–1905) brought to the attention of the medical community further evidence linking the LH with language. Wernicke documented cases in which damage to another area of the LH – which came to bear his name (*Wernicke's area) – consistently produced a recognizable pattern of impairment to the faculty of speech comprehension. Then, in 1892 Jules Déjerine showed that problems in reading and writing resulted primarily from damage to the LH alone. So, by the end of the 19th century the accumulating research evidence provided an empirical base to the emerging consensus in neuroscience that the LH was the cerebral locus for language. Unfortunately, it also contributed to the unfounded idea that the RH (right hemisphere) was without special functions and subject to the control of the 'dominant' LH.

In the 1970s research in neuroscience brought seriously into question the idea that the LH alone was responsible for language. The brain research suggested, in fact, that for any new verbal input to be comprehensible, it must occur in contexts that allow the synthetic functions of the RH to do their interpretive work. In effect, it showed that the brain is structured to interpret verbal input primarily in terms of its contextual characteristics.

At birth, the position of the larynx in human infants is high in the neck, like it is in that of other primates. Infants breathe, swallow, and vocalize in ways physiologically similar to gorillas and chimps. But, some time around the first six months of life, the infant's larynx starts to descend gradually into the neck, dramatically altering the ways in which the child will carry out such physiological functions from then on. Nobody knows why this descent occurs. It is an anatomical phenomenon unique to humans. This new low position means that the respiratory and digestive tracts now cross above the larynx. This entails a few risks: food can easily lodge in the entrance of the larynx; and humans cannot drink and breathe simultaneously without choking. But in compensation, it produces a pharyngeal chamber above the vocal folds that can modify sound. This is the key to the ability to articulate sounds.

Interestingly, research on the casts of human skulls has established that the lowered larynx did not occur earlier than 100,000 years ago. This suggests that there may have been language without speech in pre–*Homo sapiens* groups. The most probable mode of delivery of language was gesture. When speech became physiologically possible, it is likely that it was used in tandem with the previous gestural signs, not replacing them completely. This is the most conceivable reason why we still use gesture as a default mode of communication (when vocal speech is impossible), and why we gesticulate when we speak.

language acquisition
[< Latin LINGUA 'tongue']
Process by which languages are learned.

Note: In childhood, language acquisition is a complex and largely spontaneous and unconscious process. Children are equipped by Nature with certain cognitive abilities and physical structures that predispose them to learn any language to which they are exposed from birth to about the age of 2.

For the linguist Noam *Chomsky, this is strong evidence that there exists a universal grammar (UG) present in the brain at birth that is subjected to culture-specific 'parameters' during infancy. The UG is a species-specific neurological generator of language structures in human beings; culture is the external force that determines which of these are relevant to the language spoken in social context. This implies that all natural languages are built on the same basic neural plan and that differences are explainable as choices of rule types from a fairly small inventory of possibilities – made available to the child through environmental input. Hence the universality and rapidity of language acquisition – when the child learns one fact about a language, she/he can easily infer other facts without having to learn them one by one.

According to many other language researchers, the problem with UG theory is that it is restricted to accounting for the development of *grammar* in the child. As such, it ignores a much more fundamental creative force in early infancy – *iconicity, or the ability to make imitative models of the world. The application of vocal sound to model the world imitatively can already be seen when the child reaches six months and starts to emit monosyllabic utterances (*mu, ma, da, di*, etc.), which are imitations of what the child has heard in social context. These are called *holophrastic* (one-word) utterances, and have been shown to serve three basic functions: 1. naming an object and event; 2. expressing an action or a desire for some action; 3. conveying emotional states.

language acquisition device
[abbreviated to LAD]
Linguist Noam *Chomsky's term for an inbuilt neurological generator of language structures in the human species that allows children to develop their native language with no effort whatsoever.

langue
[French for 'language']
[see *langue* vs. *parole*]
Term used by Ferdinand de *Saussure to

refer to the largely unconscious knowledge that speakers of a language share about what forms and grammatical structures are appropriate in that language.

langue vs. *parole*
[French for 'language' and 'word']
Distinction made by Ferdinand de *Saussure in his *Cours de linguistique générale* of 1916 between language as system (*langue*) and language in usage (*parole*).

Note: Saussure made an analogy to the game of chess to clarify the crucial difference between these two terms. The ability to play chess, he observed, is dependent upon knowledge of its *langue*, i.e. of the rules of movement of the pieces – no matter how brilliantly or poorly someone plays, what the chess board or pieces are made of, what the color and size of the pieces are. *Langue* is a mental code that is independent of such variables. Now, the actual ways in which a person plays a specific game – why he/she made the moves that he/she did, how he/she used his/her past knowledge of the game to plan his/her strategies and tactics, etc. – are dependent instead on the person's particular execution abilities, i.e. on his/her control of *parole*. In an analogous fashion, Saussure suggested, the ability to speak and understand a language is dependent upon knowing the rules of the language game (*langue*); whereas the actual use of the rules in certain situations is dependent instead upon execution (psychological, social, and communicative) factors (*parole*).

larynx, lowering of the
Phenomenon that starts virtually right after birth whereby the larynx, which is high in the human neck at birth, begins to descend in the neck, so that by the age of 18 months to 2 years it alters the ways in which the child will thenceforth carry out certain physiological functions.

Note: Nobody knows why this descent occurs. It is an anatomical phenomenon unique to humans. The new low position of the larynx means that the respiratory and digestive tracts cross above it. This entails a few risks: food can easily lodge in the entrance of the larynx; and humans cannot drink and breathe simultaneously without choking. But in compensation, this new position produces a pharyngeal chamber above the vocal folds that can modify sound. This is the key to the human ability to articulate sounds.

legal semiotics
[< Latin LEGALIS 'of the law'; Greek SEMEION 'mark, sign']
Branch of *semiotics aiming to study the representational system underlying law-making.

Note: Rudimentary types of legal systems existed in early tribal cultures. They were built from a blend of custom, religion, and magic, grounded in consensus about what was appropriate and right for the tribe as a whole. The visible authority was the powerful clan member and/or the religious ruler; the ultimate authorities were the gods, whose will was thought to be revealed in the forces of Nature and in the revelations of the religious leader. Wrongs against the tribe, such as acts of sacrilege or breaches of custom, were met with group sanctions, ridicule, and hostility. The wrath of the gods, on the other hand, was appeased typically through ritualistic ceremonies ending in sacrifice or in the expulsion of the wrongdoer. Wrongs against individuals, such as murder, theft, adultery, or failure to repay a debt, were avenged by the family of the victim, often in the form of actions against the family of the wrongdoer.

In early civilizations, legal practices grew in tandem with political systems. The establishment of 'courts' and 'written laws' came about to replace religious principles or rules and the advice-giving practices of tribal chieftains, elders, or shamans. One of the first set of written laws dates from

Hammurabi, king of Babylon, who united the diverse tribes in Mesopotamia by strategically conquering territories in the region from approximately 1792 to 1750 BC. The first significant example of a written legal code is the ancient Roman one, which has influenced most of the legal systems of the modern world. In the 8th century BC Rome's legal system was characterized largely by a blend of custom and the control of magistrates, who were thought to interpret the will of the gods. But the magistrates eventually lost their legitimacy as the plebeian classes threatened to revolt against their discriminatory practices. This crisis led to one of the most consequential developments in the history of law – the *Twelve Tables of Rome*, which consisted of laws engraved on bronze tablets in the 5th century BC. Concerned with matters of property, payment of debts, and appropriate compensation for damage to persons, these tables are the source for the widespread modern belief that fairness in human affairs demands that laws regulating human conduct be expressed in writing.

Awareness of the role of *civil law* in human affairs can already be seen in *Plato, who attempted to reconcile the religious and political spheres of society by proposing a model of a community that would be governed by an aristocracy of 'philosopher-kings.' But it was *Aristotle who recognized the ever-increasing power of the political, legal, and economic spheres in city-state societies. In his *Politics*, he suggested that these were often in conflict with the religious sphere because of the tension created by their overlapping moral jurisdictions.

This tension extended well into the Middle Ages, an era in Western history characterized by a protracted struggle for supremacy between the Roman Catholic church and the Holy Roman Empire. This conflict was reflected in the scholarly writing of the era. The philosopher St Thomas *Aquinas, for instance, defended the traditional role of the Church in his *Summa Theologiae* (1265–73), while the great Italian poet *Dante Alighieri argued, in his *De Monarchia* (c. 1313), for a united Christendom under one emperor and pope, each supreme in his appropriate sphere.

By the time of the Renaissance, intellectuals such as Niccolò Machiavelli (1459–1527) transcended the traditional church-state debate by evaluating the problems and possibilities of governments seeking to maintain power in non-religious, non-moralistic ways. Some years later, the English philosopher Thomas *Hobbes argued that the power of the political sphere in regulating the affairs of a culture should be unlimited, since he believed culture to be primarily a 'social contract' that individuals living in a society agreed to accept so that they could protect themselves from their own brutish instincts and make possible the satisfaction of desires. As the philosopher John *Locke observed, political and legal systems, unlike religious ones, can legitimately be overthrown if they fail to discharge their functions to the people, since these systems are perceived as being totally the brainchildren of human minds.

legend
[< Latin LEGERE 'to read']
1. story handed down for generations and popularly believed to have a historical basis, although not verifiable; 2. story of the exploits of a heroic figure (e.g. the *legend of King Arthur and the Knights of the Round Table*); 3. title, brief description, or key accompanying an illustration or map story.

legisign
[< Latin LEGALIS 'of the law']
Term coined by Charles *Peirce referring to a *sign that designates something by convention (and instituted 'by law'). Peirce viewed all legisigns as provisional.

Illustrations: 1. The sound of the referee's whistle indicating stoppage of play is a legisign that everyone understands, and obeys, by convention. 2. The siren sound emitted by a police cruiser is understood by motorists as a legisign of an emergency and must be obeyed by force of law.

Leibniz, Gottfried Wilhelm

[1646–1716]
German philosopher and mathematician who discovered the mathematical principles of calculus, independently from the earlier discoveries of English scientist Sir Isaac Newton (1642–1727). Leibniz also invented a calculating machine that is considered a pioneering effort in the development of computers. Leibniz's philosophical works *Monadology* (1714) and *New Essays Concerning Human Understanding* (1703) influenced 18th-century German philosopher Immanuel *Kant.

leitmotif

[German for LEIT 'to lead' + MOTIV 'motive']
Clearly defined musical melody or rhythmic motif recurring throughout a composition that represents or symbolizes an object, a living being, an idea, an emotion, or a supernatural force. Although the German composer Richard Wagner (1813–83) did not use this term, it is most often associated with his music dramas (see *opera), in which he used such recurring motifs to identify characters and to provide musical commentary through the orchestra on the dramatic action.

Lévi-Strauss, Claude

[1908–]
Belgian-born anthropologist based in Paris whose theory of culture as an external manifestation of *sign systems has received considerable attention. Also widely discussed is his idea that myth is the basis of the language spoken by a particular group, and that behaviors, language patterns, and myths demonstrate a common framework underlying all human life.

lexeme

[< Greek LEXIS 'word']
Fundamental meaningful unit in the lexicon of a language.

Illustrations: 1. *Find, found,* and *finding* are different forms of the English lexeme *find.* 2. *big, bigger, biggest,* and *big-ness* are different forms of the lexeme *big.*

lexical field

[< Greek LEXIKOS 'of words']
Set of lexical items (words) related to each other by topic, category, or theme.

Illustrations: 1. color terms = *red, blue, green, yellow,* etc.; 2. kinship terms = *mother, father, son, daughter,* etc.

lexicography

[< Greek LEXIKOS 'of words' + GRAPHEIN 'to write']
[see also *dictionary]
1. study of the structure, content, and style of dictionaries; 2. craft of making dictionaries.

Note: The *Storehouse for Children or Clerics,* compiled in 1440 by the Dominican monk Galfridus Grammaticus, is considered to be the first English dictionary. It consisted of Latin equivalents of 10,000 English words and remained a leading reference tool for several generations. At the start of the 18th century, the *New English Dictionary* (1702) by John Kersey included ordinary English words as well as unfamiliar terms. This was followed by *A Dictionary of the English Language* (1755) by Samuel Johnson (1709–84), which remained the model of English lexicography for more than a century. In 1857, the English Philological Society began the most comprehensive lexicographical work in the English language, *A New English Dictionary on Historical Principles,* popularly known as the *Oxford English Dictionary* (OED). The first ten volumes were published between 1884 and 1928.

The first historically significant contribution to American lexicography was the *New and Accurate Standard of Pronunciation* (1783), popularly known as *Webster's Spelling Book*, compiled by Noah Webster (1758–1843) as the first part of his *Grammatical Institute of the English Language* (1783–5). Its unexpected success led Webster to compile his first American lexicon, *A Compendious Dictionary of the English Language* (1806). His major contribution, *An American Dictionary of the English Language*, was published in 1828. In 1894 another line of dictionaries began with *A Standard Dictionary of the English Language*, edited by Isaac Kauffman Funk (1839–1912). Funk introduced a new format for definitions, beginning with the current meaning of the word and ending with the older meanings in reverse historical order. Ever since the publication of *Webster's Third New International Dictionary of the English Language* in 1961, American lexicographers have increasingly attempted to reflect contemporary usage. Many slang words and technical terms are now included in dictionaries.

lexicon
[< Greek LEXIS 'word']
[also called *dictionary]
1. compilation of special words or terms of a particular author, field of study, etc.; 2. record or inventory of all words and terms collected in a volume; 3. total stock of *morphemes in a language.

libido
[Latin for 'pleasure']
In psychoanalysis, the psychic and emotional energy associated with instinctual sexual drives. According to the theories of Austrian psychoanalyst Sigmund *Freud, the libido is the sex instinct, which can be rechanneled as artistic creation. Swiss psychiatrist Carl *Jung rejected the sexual basis, believing that the general will to live is the force that drives creativity.

linguistic competence
[< Latin LINGUA 'tongue'; COMPETENTIA 'a meeting']
Term used by Noam *Chomsky to designate the innate, unconscious knowledge of general linguistic properties that allows people to produce and understand sentences, many of which they have never heard before.

linguistic performance
[< Latin LINGUA 'tongue']
Term used by Noam *Chomsky to designate the ability to use a language in actual situations.

linguistic relativity hypothesis
[< Latin LINGUA 'tongue']
Claim that language, cognition, and culture are interdependent.

Note: This hypothesis was formulated explicitly for the first time by the philosopher Johann von *Herder, who saw an intimate connection between language and ethnic character, and the philologist Wilhelm von *Humboldt, who gave Herder's hypothesis a more specific articulation by claiming that the categories of a specific language were formative of the thought and behavior of the people using it for routine daily communication. The hypothesis was given its modern-day formulation in the 1920s and 1930s by anthropologist Edward *Sapir and his student Benjamin Lee *Whorf, both of whom produced research that purported to show how a language shapes the specific ways in which people think and act. The question of whether or not the *Sapir-Whorf hypothesis*, as it is also called, is tenable continues to be debated to this day. If the categories of a particular language constitute a set of strategies for classifying, abstracting, and storing information in culture-specific ways, do these categories predispose its users to attend to certain specific events and ignore others? If so, do speakers of different languages perceive the world in different ways? These are the kinds of intriguing questions that this hypothesis raises.

linguistics
[< Latin LINGUA 'tongue']
Science studying *language, including its uses in *cultures.

Note: The modern science of linguistics is the twin sister of *semiotics, since both trace their modern parentage to Ferdinand de *Saussure's *Cours de linguistique générale* of 1916. Linguistics proper focuses on studying the forms and functions of sounds, words, and grammatical categories of specific languages, as well as the formal relationships that exist among different languages.

Linguists divide language into various levels. *Phonetics* is concerned with the physical properties of sounds; how sounds are produced, the characteristics of sound waves, and how sounds are perceived. *Morphology* is the study of *morphemes (grammatical elements smaller than words) and the ways in which they combine into words. For example, the word *cats* has two morphemes, *cat*, meaning 'feline animal,' and *-s* meaning 'more than one.' The former morpheme is often referred to as a *lexeme, because it has lexical rather than pure grammatical meaning. *Syntax* is the study of how words are organized to make sentences. A general characteristic of language is that words are not directly combined into sentences but rather into intermediate units, called *phrases*, which then are joined into sentences. *Semantics* is the study of the meaning of words, phrases, syntactic constructions, etc. *Pragmatics* deals with how language is used in discourse, and how it varies in socially determined ways.

The first attempts to study a language scientifically can be traced as far back as the 5th century BC, when the Indian scholar Panini compiled a grammar of the Sanskrit language of India. His sophisticated analysis showed how words are formed systematically and what parts of words carry meaning. He wrote his grammatical analysis to help in the interpretation of Hindu religious literature written in Sanskrit.

The Greek grammarian Dionysius Thrax, who lived between 170 and 90 BC, wrote what became one of the first influential models for writing grammars in Europe – the *Art of Grammar.* Indeed, many later Greek, Latin, and other European grammars were based on his model. With the spread of Christianity and the translation of the Scriptures into the languages of the new Christians, written literatures began to develop among previously nonliterate peoples. This led to an interest in *grammar as a formal approach to the study of languages. The Arabs are believed to have initiated the grammatical study of their language before medieval times. In the 10th century the Jews completed a Hebrew lexicon and grammar. By the late Middle Ages, European scholars generally knew, in addition to their own vernaculars and Latin, the languages of their nearest neighbors. The access to several languages set scholars to thinking about how languages might be compared. The revival of classical learning in the Renaissance laid the foundation, however, for a misguided attempt by grammarians to describe all language grammars as derivatives of Greek and Latin grammar.

It was in 16th and 17th centuries that scholars took it upon themselves to conduct in-depth surveys of all the then-known languages in an attempt to determine which language might be the oldest. In the 18th century the comparisons were becoming increasingly precise, culminating in the assumption by the German philosopher Gottfried Wilhelm *Leibniz that most languages of Europe, Asia, and Egypt came from the same original one – a language referred to as *Indo-European.*

In the 19th century scholars developed systematic analyses of the parts of speech, mostly built on the earlier analyses of Sanskrit by Panini. This allowed them to compare and relate the forms of speech in numerous languages methodically. Sir William Jones (1746–94), an English scholar, observed that Sanskrit bore similarities to Greek and Latin, and proposed that the three languages might have developed from a common source. Inspired by Jones, language scholars in the 19th century started in earnest to compare languages systematically. The German philologist Jacob Grimm (1785–1863) and the Danish philologist Rasmus Christian Rask (1787–1832) studied how the sounds of one language corresponded in a regular way to similar sounds in related words in another language. For example, the initial sounds of Latin *pater* (father) and *ped-* (*foot*) correspond to the English *father* and *foot*.

By the late 19th century much research had been conducted on sound correspondences. A group of European language scholars known as the *neogrammarians* put forward the view that not only were sound correspondences between related languages regular, but any exceptions to these could develop only from borrowings from another language (or from additional sound changes). For example, Latin /d/ should correspond to English /t/ as in *dentalis* = *tooth*. The English word *dental*, however, has a /d/ sound. The neogrammarian conclusion was that English borrowed *dental* from Latin, whereas *tooth* (which has the expected /t/) was a native English word.

It was the Swiss linguist Ferdinand de *Saussure who founded modern linguistic analysis in the same century when he made the first distinction between *diachronic and *synchronic aspects of language study. Saussure also advanced the view of language as a system or as structures serving as links between thought and vocal expression. His view came to be known as *structuralism*. In America, the structuralist approach was expanded through the efforts of anthropologist Franz *Boas and his stu-

dent Edward *Sapir, who worked primarily with Native American languages, and also by Leonard *Bloomfield, whose book *Language* (1933) established the basic notions and procedures for carrying out a systematic structural analysis of any language.

Boas was especially influential in establishing linguistics as a science. He saw grammar as a description of how human speech in a language is organized. A descriptive grammar, he claimed, should describe the relationships of speech elements in words and sentences. At about the same time, the Danish linguist Otto Jespersen (1860–1943) stressed that grammar should be studied by examining living speech rather than by analyzing written documents. Jespersen also wanted to ascertain what properties were common to the grammars of all languages.

In 1957, the American linguist Noam *Chomsky published a book entitled *Syntactic Structures*, in which he attempted to analyze the syntax of English from a different perspective than the structuralist one. This effort led him to see grammar as a theory of language rather than as a description of actual sentences. Since the early 1970s various schools of linguistics have come forward to challenge the Chomskyan perspective. As a consequence, modern-day linguistic methodology is more eclectic and less partisan to one school of thought or the other than it ever was in the early 20th century.

Today, languages are being described and analyzed from several points of view. Moreover, the field of linguistics has become a vast one. Currently, linguistic studies are divided into *theoretical* and *applied*. *Theoretical* linguistics is concerned with devising models or theories to describe languages or to explain their patterns. *Applied* linguistics, by contrast, applies the findings of theoretical linguistics to language teaching, dictionary preparation, speech therapy, computerized machine translation, and automatic speech recognition. A number of hybrid fields study the relations between language and the subject matter of related academic disciplines, such as *sociolinguistics* (sociology and language), *psycholinguistics* (psychology and language), and *neurolinguistics* (neuroscience and language).

linguistics, cognitive

[< Latin LINGUA 'tongue'; COGNITIO 'knowledge']
Field of linguistics studying the connection between concepts and grammar. The view in mainstream linguistic theory has generally been that grammatical rules are arbitrary and that meaning is objectively determinable in the syntactic structure of language. Cognitive linguists have provided data and reasons to show why this view is no longer tenable.

linguistics, historical

[< Latin LINGUA 'tongue'; COGNITIO 'knowledge']
Study of how languages change over time.

literacy

[< Latin LITTERA 'letter']
1. acquired ability to read and write a language at some level of proficiency; 2. acquired technical knowledge of how to decode written *signs and *texts of any kind (*media literacy*, *TV literacy*, etc.)

Note: Although today we have electronic means of recording knowledge, the use of the writing medium is still prevalent. Indeed, in Western culture, to be an alphabet-user is to be *literate* and thus *educated*. The first schools were a logical outgrowth of the invention of writing. So close has the link between the two been forged that today we can scarcely think of knowledge unless it is recorded in some alphabetic form and preserved in some library for posterity.

literal meaning

[see *meaning, litera]

literature

[< Latin LITTERA 'letter']
[see also *fiction, *novel, *poetry, *drama]
Writing of imaginative prose, verse, etc., often distinguished from scientific writing, news reporting, etc.

litotes

[< Greek LITOS 'smooth, simple, plain']
[also called meiosis]
Understatement for effect, especially by negation of the contrary.

Illustrations: 1. *I received not a few regrets.*
2. *This is no small problem.*

loan translation

[see *calque]

localization theory

In neuroscience and linguistics, view that specific mental functions have precise locations in specific areas of the brain.

Locke, John

[1632–1704]
English philosopher who introduced the formal study of *signs into philosophy in his *Essay Concerning Human Understanding* (1690), anticipating that it would allow philosophers to understand the interconnection between representation and knowledge. Locke attacked the prevailing belief of his times that knowledge was independent of experience, although, paradoxically, he accepted the mechanistic approach of the physical sciences to study the mind. Locke defined *semiotics* as the 'doctrine of signs.'

locution

[synonym for *locutionary act]

locutionary act

[< Latin LOCUTIO 'a speaking']

Speech act that entails reference to something specific.

Illustrations: 1. *The washroom is over there.*
2. *I live four blocks from here.*

logic

[< Greek LOGOS 'word, reckoning, thought']
1. science of reasoning; 2. system of principles underlying any art or science; 3. necessary connection or outcome; 4. in computers, systematized interconnection of switching functions, circuits, or devices.

logo

[see *logotype]

logocentrism

[< Greek LOGOS 'word, reckoning, thought']
[literally 'word-centered']
Notion that language shapes worldview and personal attitudes; logocentric cultures are those that depend on the written word for gaining knowledge.

logogram

[< Greek LOGOS 'word']
[also called logograph]
Symbol representing an entire spoken word without expressing its pronunciation.

Illustration: 1. 4 = *four* in English, *quattro* in Italian; 2. + = *plus* in English, *più* in Italian.

logograph

[see *logogram]

logos

[< Greek LOGOS 'word, reckoning, thought']
1. in philosophy, synonym for *reason* as manifested by the speech faculty; 2. in Christian theology, the eternal thought or word of God, made incarnate in Jesus Christ

logotype

[< Greek LOGOS 'word, reckoning, thought']
[abbreviated to logo]
Distinctive company insignia or trademark.

Illustrations: In advertising logos are often designed to evoke *mythic themes or symbols. For instance, the logo of the apple suggests the story of Adam and Eve in the Western Bible. Its biblical symbolism as 'forbidden knowledge' resonates latently, for example, in the 'Apple' computer company's logo. The 'golden arches' of McDonald's also resonate with biblical paradisiacal symbolism.

long-term memory

[see *memory]

Lorenz, Konrad

[1903–1989]
Austrian zoologist who was instrumental in the founding of *ethology, the scientific study of animals in their natural habitats. Lorenz is perhaps best known for his discovery that auditory and visual stimuli from an animal's parents are needed to induce the young to follow the parents, but that any object or human being could elicit the same response by presenting the same stimuli. He called this phenomenon *imprinting.*

Lotman, Jurij M.

[1922–1993]
Estonian semiotician whose writings have become instrumental for the study of the semiotic basis of culture. His central contribution to semiotics is the idea that culture is a derivative of *semiosis, and is thus subject to the same kind of dynamism that characterizes physical and psychological systems.

lovemap

Term used by some psychologists to designate a mental image developed by an individual around puberty of what his/her ideal mate's physical features are like.

Note: Psychologists have found that specific individuals are responsive sexually to certain particular kinds of faces and not to others from puberty onwards. One explanation as to why such preferences surface at puberty is the presence of 'lovemaps' in the mind. These are fixed mental images that determine the specific kinds of features of the face that will evoke sexual arousal and love moods (such as infatuation) in an individual. Lovemaps are developed during childhood in response to various psychosocial experiences and influences. At adolescence, they unconsciously generate an image of what the ideal 'sweetheart' should be like, becoming quite specific as to details of the physiognomy, build, race, and color of the ideal lover, as well as to his/her general demeanor.

lyric poetry

[< Greek LYRA 'lyre']

*Poetry that conveys subjective thoughts and feelings, often in a song-like style or form.

Note: In ancient Greece, lyrics were sung or recited to the accompaniment of the lyre. In medieval times French lyricists were *troubadours* and *trouvères*, and in Germany they were the *minnesingers*. Most medieval lyrics were written anonymously. In the 16th century, sung lyrics are found in songs of English musicians Thomas Campion (1567–1620) and John Dowland (1562–1626), as well as in songs in plays by English playwright William Shakespeare (1564–1616). By the Renaissance the term *lyric* also applied to verse that was not sung. Italian poets such as Petrarch (1304–74) developed the sonnet, a lyric form that became popular in the late Renaissance and in early 17th-century Europe. Well-known lyric poets of the 18th and 19th centuries include Johann Wolfgang von Goethe (1749–1832) and Heinrich Heine (1797–1856) of Germany, Thomas Gray (1716–71), Elizabeth Barrett Browning (1806–61), and A.E. Housman (1859–1936) of England, Robert Burns (1759–96) of Scotland, Charles Baudelaire (1821–67) of France, and Walt Whitman (1819–92) and Emily Dickinson (1830–86) of the United States.

Some 20th-century poets who have written lyrics are American poet Robert Frost (1874–1963), Irish poet William Butler Yeats (1865–1939), Anglo-American poet W.H. Auden (1907–73), Welsh poet Dylan Thomas (1914–53), German poet Rainer Maria Rilke (1875–1926), Austrian poet Hugo von Hofmannsthal (1874–1929), French poet Guillaume Apollinaire (1880–1918), Spanish poet Federico García Lorca (1898–1936), and Greek poet Constantine Cavafy (1863–1933).

M

magic

[< Greek MAGIKE 'magic (art), sorcery']

Use of charms, spells, and rituals in the hope that they will cause or control events, or else influence certain natural or supernatural forces.

Note: Anthropologists distinguish among three types of magic: 1. *homeopathic magic,* which consists in the use of small portions of a thing in order to affect the whole; 2. *sympathetic magic,* by which a symbolic action is purported to affect an object; 3. *contagious magic,* which attempts to influence one thing through contact with another that is believed to be magically charged.

Magical practices are based on a belief in hidden relationships among entities within the universe. Magic is widely practiced in tribal and traditional societies. In such cultures, it is often associated with religion. Western traditions of magic can be traced back to ancient Egypt, Mesopotamia, Greece, and Rome. During the Middle Ages, science, religion, and magic often were not clearly distinguished. From the 15th century to the 18th century, i.e. during the periods of the Renaissance, the Reformation, and the Age of Enlightenment, the relationship between science and magic underwent a fundamental readjustment as Western society entered the scientific era. The Roman Catholic church and Protestantism, as well as scientists, undermined belief in magic. By the end of the 18th century, magic had lost many of its believers.

mainframe computers
[see *computer]

make-up
Decoration of the face in order to present oneself in social situations.

Note: The cosmetic make-up that we use today has a long and unbroken connection with ritualistic fertility and courtship behaviors. In semiotics, the colors applied, jewelry added, and alterations made to the face during courtship are viewed as *signifiers in the facial *text. Making up the face to present the self reveals that humans perceive the face as a sign of self. Facial make-up, hairstyling, and the wearing of facial jewelry (earrings, nose rings, etc.) are human *representational* strategies for enhancing physical attractiveness or for making messages about one's social status.

Malinowski, Bronislaw
[1884–1942]
Polish-born British anthropologist who argued that cultures came about so that the human species could solve similar basic physical and moral problems the world over. Malinowski claimed that the *signs, *codes, rituals, and institutions that humans create, no matter how strange they might at first seem, have universal psychic properties that allow people everywhere to solve similar life problems. Marriage, for instance, was instituted to regulate sexual urges that could otherwise lead to overpopulation; economic institutions were founded to ensure the provision of sustenance; and so on.

mannerism
[< Latin MANUARIUS 'of the hand']
In art, a style that developed in Italy in the 16th century, characterized by thin, elongated figures in exaggerated postures.

Note: Mannerism resulted from a deliberate systematization of the way the human figure was treated by Renaissance masters Raphael (1483–1520) and Michelangelo (1475–1564). The first examples of the style appeared after around 1520 in Rome, lasting until around 1580, when it began to give way to a more realistic style. A well-known mannerist painter is the Spaniard El Greco (1541–1614).

mantle
[< Latin MANTELLUM 'a cloth']
Heraldic insignia representing originally the cloth that protected the helmet from the sun.

Note: The mantle was usually shown in the principal colors of the shield. The supporters were figures, usually people or animals, placed on each side of the shield.

manualism
[< Latin MANUS 'hand']
Ability to use hands to do things as a consequence of *bipedalism.

Note: Fossils discovered in Africa provide evidence that hominids walked erect and had bipedal stride even before the great increase in their brain size. Complete bipedalism freed the human hand, allowing it to become a supremely sensitive limb for precise manipulation and grasping. The most important structural detail in this refinement was the elongated human thumb, which developed the ability to rotate freely for the first time and, thus, become fully opposable to the other fingers. No doubt, this evolutionary development made tool making and tool-use possible. Moreover, many linguists claim that manualism made *gesture, a precursor of vocal speech, possible, and then gave rise to the subsequent evolution of the physiological apparatus for speech, since it brought about the lowering of the *larynx and its positioning for controlled breathing.

map

[< Latin MAPPA 'napkin, cloth']

1. drawing or other representation, usually on a flat surface, of all or part of the earth's surface, ordinarily showing countries, bodies of water, cities, mountains, etc.; 2. similar representation of part of the sky, showing the relative position of the stars and planets.

Illustrations: 1. A *topographic map* shows the natural features of an area as well as certain artificial features; political boundaries may also be shown. 2. A *hydrographic map* represents the surface and shores of large bodies of water. 3. A *political map* shows only political divisions without topographic features. 4. A *geologic map* shows the geologic structure of an area. 5. A *statistical map* shows social and scientific data.

Note: Maps are textual representations of culturally significant territories or spaces drawn with a combination of *iconic, *indexical, and *symbolic elements: i.e. they are made with indexical (indicating where places are), iconic (representing places in topographical relation to each other), and symbolic (notational system) *signifiers. Remarkably, maps have enabled the human species to travel and explore the world with ease, not to mention classify the *terra firma.*

The earliest existing maps were made by the Babylonians about 2300 BC and consisted largely of land surveys for the purposes of taxation. The first map to represent the known world is believed to have been made in the 6th century BC by Greek philosopher Anaximander (611–547 BC). One of the most famous maps of classical times was drawn by Greek geographer Eratosthenes (3rd century BC) around 200. It represented the known world from England to Africa to India and was the first to have transverse parallel lines to show equal latitudes. Following the fall of the Roman Empire, European mapmaking all but ceased. Arab sailors, however, made highly accurate charts during this same period.

In the 15th century, editions of the maps of Greek mathematician and astronomer Ptolemy were printed in Europe; for the next several hundred years these maps exerted great influence on European cartographers. In 1568 Flemish geographer Gerardus Mercator (1512–94) devised the system of map projection that bears his name. In 1570 Flemish mapmaker Abraham Ortelius published the first modern *atlas.* It contained 70 maps. By the 18th century, the scientific principles of mapmaking were well established and the most notable inaccuracies in maps involved unexplored parts of the world. In the late 18th century a number of European countries began to undertake detailed national topographic surveys. During the 20th century mapmaking underwent a series of major technical innovations. Aerial photography was developed and, later, satellite surveying was introduced. Satellite photographs can furnish a wealth of accurate information about various features on the earth's surface, including the location of mineral deposits, the extent of urban sprawl, vegetation infestations, and soil types.

For the representation of the entire surface of the earth without any kind of distortion, a map must have a spherical surface; a map of this kind is known as a *globe.* A flat map cannot accurately represent the rounded surface of the earth except for very small areas where the curvature is negligible. To show large areas with accuracy, the map must be drawn in such a way as to compromise among distortions of areas, distances, and direction.

The various methods of preparing a flat map of the earth's surface are known as *projections.* In making a *cylindrical projection,* the cartographer regards the surface of the map as a cylinder that encircles the globe, touching it at the equator. The parallels of latitude extend outward from the globe, parallel to the equator. The resulting map represents the world's surface as a rectangle. Although the shapes of areas on the cylindrical projection are increasingly distorted towards the poles, the size relationship of areas on the map is equivalent to their size relationship on the globe. The *Mercator projection* is related to the cylindrical projection, with certain modifications. It portrays equatorial regions accurately but greatly distorts areas in the high latitudes. Directions are represented faithfully, and this is valuable in navigation.

marked category
[see *markedness]

markedness
Relation whereby some members in a category or system, referred to as *marked*, are specific and thus not representative of the entire category, while others, referred to as *unmarked*, are typical and thus representative of the category or system.

Illustration: In the indefinite article system of English, the form *a* is said to be *unmarked* because it is the general, or typical, form (*a boy, a girl, a man, a woman,* etc.); whereas *an* is the *marked* form because it is constrained to occurring before vowels (*an egg, an apple,* etc.).

market test
[< Latin MERCATUS 'marketplace']
Technique designed to study the reactions of human individuals and/or groups to promotional and persuasion techniques used to sell a product, including advertising, packaging, brand naming, etc.

Note: Marketing agencies conduct surveys to determine the potential acceptance of products or services before they are advertised. If the survey (or market test) convinces the manufacturer that one of the versions of, say, an ad will attract enough purchasers, a research crew then pretests various provisional draft advertisements to consumers, asking them to indicate their preference. After the one or two best-liked advertisements are identified, the manufacturer produces a limited quantity of the new ad and introduces it in a test market. On the basis of this *market test* the advertiser-manufacturer can make a decision as to whether a national campaign should be launched. In effect, marketing science envisions consumers as 'recurrent units' that can be classified into 'taste groups,' 'lifestyle groups,' 'market segments,' etc. and who can, therefore, be understood, managed, and manipulated in specific ways.

Marx, Karl
[1818–1883]
German social theorist who claimed that new forms of a society emerged as a consequence of individuals struggling to gain control over the production, use, and ownership of material goods. In every historical epoch, the prevailing economic system determines the form of social and political organization, as well as the intellectual history of the epoch. Thus, the history of society is a history of the struggles between ruling and oppressed social classes. In Marx's conception of utopia, there is no capitalism and no state, just a working society in which all citizens give according to their means and take according to their needs.

mask
[< Italian MASCHERA 'a mask']
[see also *persona]
1. material covering for the face or part of the face, to conceal the identity of the wearer; 2. figure of a head worn on the stage by an ancient Greek or Roman actor to identify a character and amplify the voice.

Note: In tribal societies, a performer who wears a mask in a ceremony is frequently believed to be transformed into, or possessed by, the spirit represented by the mask. Ritual masks generally depict deities, mythological creatures, and spirits; or else they are worn for entertainment, storytelling, social satire, or curative rites, or to protect the wearer against diseases. Traditions carried on today in Western culture that involve the wearing of masks for ritualistic reasons include Halloween, Carnival, and masked balls.

Masks are also used in the theater. Masks worn by actors in ancient Greek plays were large, with conventionalized features and exaggerated expressions. The masks were divided into *tragic* and *comic*. In the mystery plays of medieval Europe, masks were used to portray dragons, monsters, allegorical characters, and the Devil. During the Renaissance, half-masks covering the eyes and nose were used in courtly entertainment. In modern Western theater, masks are used mainly to represent animal characters. In the traditional pageants and religious plays of China masks are used typically to represent royalty and grotesque characters.

mass media
[< Latin MEDIUS 'middle']
Means of public communication reaching a large audience through radio, television, newspapers, periodicals, etc.

materialism
[< Latin MATERIA 'matter']
In philosophy, theory of reality and of knowledge that posits consciousness as being the result of purely physical (evolutionary) processes.

Note: There are many schools of materialistic thought. *Extreme* materialism explains matter and mind as merely aspects of each other. *Antireligious* materialism is motivated by hostility towards organized religions. *Historical* materialism proposes that in every historical era the prevailing economic system that produces the necessities of life determines the form of social organization and the political, religious, ethical, intellectual, and artistic institutions of the epoch.

maxim
[< Latin MAXIMUS 'greatest']
[also called *apothegm]
Succinct formulation of a principle, perceived truth, or rule of conduct.

Illustrations: 1. *Moderation is the greatest virtue.* 2. *Genius is 1% native ability, 99% hard work.*

McLuhan, Marshall
[1911–1980]
Canadian communication theorist who argued that electronic technology has transformed the world into a *global village, and that technological innovations have become the primary factors in directing the course of human evolution. McLuhan is best known for coining the phrase 'the *medium is the message,' which became popular in the 1960s. He argued that in each cultural era the medium in which information is recorded and transmitted is decisive in determining the character of that culture. McLuhan's fascinating works include *The Mechanical Bride: Folklore of Industrial Man* (1951), *The Gutenberg Galaxy: The Making of Typographic Man* (1962), *Understanding Media: The Extensions of Man* (1964), *The Medium Is the Massage: An Inventory of Effects* (1967), and *War and Peace in the Global Village* (1968).

Mead, George Herbert
[1863–1931]
American philosopher who emphasized the influence of the social milieu in shaping the experience and behavior of the individual. He claimed that even that the type of self-awareness an individual develops is dependent upon the social order in which she/he is reared.

Mead, Margaret
[1901–1978]
American anthropologist, student of Franz *Boas, widely known for her studies of primitive societies and her contributions to

cultural anthropology. Mead spent many years studying how culture influences individual personality, maintaining that the specific child-rearing practices of a culture shape the behavior and temperament of the maturing individual. She also analyzed many problems in contemporary American society, particularly those related to young people.

meaning

What is referred to or understood by a *sign, *concept, *text, etc.

Note: Determining the absolute meaning of something is an impossible task. The dictionary definition of *cat*, for instance, as 'a small carnivorous mammal domesticated since early times as a catcher of rats and mice' is said to be the *meaning* of the word. The problem that emerges with this definition, however, is the use of *mammal* to define *cat*. Indeed, the definition makes the unwarranted assumption that *mammal* somehow explains what a *cat* is. Looking up this term in a dictionary is also of little use because *mammal* is defined as 'any of various warm-blooded vertebrate animals of the class Mammalia' – a definition which begs yet another question: What is an *animal*? The dictionary defines an *animal* as an *organism*, which it defines in another listing as 'an individual form of *life*,' which it defines further as 'the property that distinguishes living *organisms*.'

At that point the dictionary has gone into a loop, since we have come across an already used word, *organism*, in our effort to derive a meaning for the word *cat*. Moreover, it would seem that there is no way out of this loop. Given such problems associated with determining the absolute meaning of something, semioticians prefer the technique of binary opposition (see *binary feature) to flesh out what a sign means in relation to other signs. This approach assumes that the meaning of sign is something that cannot be determined in the absolute,

but only in relation to other signs: e.g. *cat* vs. *dog*, *cat* vs. *bird*, etc. From such oppositions we can see what differentiates a *cat* from a *dog*, from a *bird*, and so on. Such oppositions cumulatively allow us to pinpoint what *cat* means by virtue of how it is different from other signs.

This extraction of the sign's meaning through oppositions is called *signification*. Signification is not an open-ended or looping process; it is constrained by a series of factors, including conventional agreements as to what oppositions entail in specific contexts, the nature of the code to which the signs belong, and so on. Without such in-built constraints, determining what a sign means would be virtually impossible.

meaning, figurative

[< Latin FIGURARE 'to form']
Extended meaning of a word or expression.

Illustrations: 1. *screaming headlines* (= *screaming* is used figuratively, since *scream* refers to a kind of vocal cry); 2. *cool ideas* (= *cool* is used figuratively, since *cool* refers to a temperature condition); 3. *hot book* (= *hot* is used figuratively, since *hot* also refers to a temperature condition).

meaning, literal

[< Latin LITTERA 'letter']
[see also *meaning, figurative]
Primary meaning of a word or phrase.

Illustrations: 1. *She <u>screamed</u> when she saw that horror film* (= literal meaning); vs. *She read the <u>screaming</u> headlines* (= figurative meaning). 2. *She felt the <u>cool</u> breeze against her cheeks* (= literal meaning); vs. *Her friend has many <u>cool</u> ideas* (= figurative meaning).

mechanical medium

[see *medium, mechanical]

medium

[< Latin MEDIUS 'middle']
1. any means, agency, or instrument of communication; 2. the physical means by which

a *sign or *text is *encoded (put together) and through which it is transmitted (delivered, actualized).

Note: Before the advent of alphabets the primary media for communicating were the oral-auditory and the pictographic ones. With the advent of the *alphabet, there occurred a 'paradigm shift,' as the philosopher Thomas Kuhn (1922–96) called a radical change in social cognitive style, whereby the alphabetic medium became the primary form of encoding and disseminating knowledge. Marshall *McLuhan appropriately called the social world in which the use of printed texts became widespread the *Gutenberg Galaxy*, after the German printer Johan Gutenberg (1400?–68?), who is traditionally considered the inventor of movable type in the West.

McLuhan pointed out that human beings are endowed by Nature to process information with all the senses. Our *sense ratios*, as he called them, are equally calibrated at birth to receive meaningful information. However, in social settings, it is unlikely that all senses will operate at the same ratio. One sense or the other increases according to the representational modes and media employed. In an oral culture, the *auditory sense ratio* dominates information processing and message interpretation; in an alphabetic one, the *visual sense ratio* dominates. This raising or lowering of a sense ratio is not preclusive. Indeed, in our own culture, we can have various sense ratios activated in tandem. The ebb of ratios, up and down, in tandem, in opposition, is what defines one's *cognitive style* of information processing. For example, if one were to hear the word *cat* uttered by someone, the auditory sense ratio would be the more operational one in processing the meaning of the word. If, however, one were to see the word written on a sheet of paper, then the person's visual sense ratio would be the operational one. A visual depiction of the *cat* together with the utterance of the word *cat* on TV (as in children's learning programs) would activate the auditory and visual sense ratios in tandem.

Now, each medium implicates knowledge of specific kinds of *codes – if the sign or text is transmitted through an auditory medium, then the *phonemic code of a language must be known, otherwise interpretation is impossible; if it is written on a piece of paper, then the *alphabetic code of the language must be known; and so on. In effect, the medium determines which code is to be deployed. It can even be said that the physical characteristics of the medium will determine how one interprets the sign or text. This is probably what McLuhan meant when he said 'the *medium is the message.'

medium, artifactual
[< Latin MEDIUS 'middle']
Artifactual means or mode of encoding and decoding a message.

Illustrations: 1. books; 2. paintings; 3. sculptures; 4. letters.

medium, mechanical
[< Latin MEDIUS 'middle']
Mechanical means or mode of transmitting a message.

Illustrations: 1. telephones; 2. radios; 3. television sets; 4. computers; 5. videos.

medium, natural
[< Latin MEDIUS 'middle']
Natural means or mode of encoding and decoding a message.

Illustrations: 1. the voice (speech); 2. the face (expressions); 3. the body (gesture, posture, etc.).

medium is the message
[< Latin MEDIUS 'middle']
Marshall *McLuhan's famous statement

referring to the fact that each *medium implicates knowledge of specific kinds of *codes.

Illustration: If the word *cat* is to be transmitted vocally, then the *phonemic code of a language must be known; if it is transmitted on a piece of paper, then the language's *alphabetic code must be known. In effect, the medium determines which code is to be deployed, and thus the medium's physical characteristics will determine how one encodes and decodes a sign or text.

Note: A conversation, narrative, play, etc. can be *encoded* in more than one medium – in an auditory medium (e.g. an oral story), in an alphabetic medium (e.g. a written novel), in a multisensory medium (e.g. a movie), etc. It will thus be *decoded* according to the characteristics of the medium (or media) deployed. So, for instance, the story of Romeo and Juliet can be transmitted to someone orally, activating the auditory sense ratio; it can be encoded as a novel, activating the visual sense ratio; it can be portrayed through cinema, activating several sensory ratios in tandem; and so on. In this model, *encoding* can be defined simply as the use of a *code* or *codes* to select or create a sign or text according to the medium through which the sign or text will be transmitted; *decoding* is the process of deciphering the sign or text on the basis of the code or codes used.

megabyte

1. unit of computer storage capacity equal to 2^{20} *bytes; 2. one million bytes.

meiosis

[see *litotes]

melodrama

[< Greek MELOS 'song' + DRAN 'to do']
1. play, film, or television program, characterized by exaggerated emotions, stereotypical characters, and interpersonal conflicts;

2. in music, work in which a spoken text is integrated with music.

Note: The melodrama traces its origins to the ancient Greek theater, but became popular in the West only in the 18th century. By extension, the term melodrama has come to be applied to any play with a romantic plot in which the author manipulates events to act on the emotions of the audience without regard for character development or logic. Also known as 'tearjerkers,' melodramas today include television soap operas and some made-for-TV movies.

melody

[< Greek MELOIDIA 'singing choral song']
In music, pleasing sounds that in combination make a continuous phrase.

Note: Melodies are distinguished from one another by such traits as melodic contour, range, and scale. For example, the opening of the song *Twinkle, twinkle, little star* rises and falls in pitch (melodic contour), spans the interval of a major sixth (range), and consists of three tones based on a scale. Melodies can be built by combining and varying motives (short recognizable groups of notes). Several motives can be combined in a melodic fragment, used as part of a larger composition. In European music since the 1600s, *harmony created through chord successions has provided the main scaffolding for melody making.

meme

[see also *sociobiology]
Term coined by sociobiologist Richard Dawkins (1941–) in imitation of *gene* to refer to the units of information and conceptualization (fashions, tunes, ideas, etc.) that are acquired and transmitted in cultural settings.

memoirs

[see *autobiography, *biography]

memoria

[Latin/Italian for 'memory']

[see **fantasia*, **ingegno*]

Notion of memory as a source for the imagination, introduced into philosophy by Giambattista *Vico.

Note: The Vichian *memoria* is the repository of images of the *fantasia* and the invented forms of the *ingegno*. It is *memoria* that allows us to conjure up the past and to make new images and new inventions.

memory

[< Latin MEMORIA 'memory']

Capacity of the brain to encode information, ideas, feelings, etc.

Note: Memory is subdivided into 1. *recollection*, the reconstruction of events or facts on the basis of partial cues; 2. *recall*, the active and unaided remembering of something from the past; 3. *recognition*, the ability to identify previously encountered information as familiar; 4. *relearning*, the ability to learn once-familiar material more easily than unfamiliar material. Psychologists also talk of *short-term* and *long-term* memory. The former refers to the temporary retention of information, the latter to the storage of the information on a long-term basis.

Recently memory forms have also been divided in *episodic* and *semantic:* 1. Episodic memory unfolds as a recall of past events, as if they were imagistic episodes in a sequence (as in a comic strip). 2. Semantic memory unfolds as a recall of meanings through words, phrases, etc.

Mercator projection

[see *map]

Merleau-Ponty, Maurice

[1908–61]

French philosopher, whose studies of the body's role in perception and society opened a new field of philosophical investigation. His major work, *Phenomenology of Perception* (1945), is a detailed study of perception and a critique of *cognitivism and *existentialism. Merleau-Ponty argued that traditional psychology presupposes an original and unique perceptual relation to the world that cannot, however, be explained or even described in scientific terms.

mesmerism

[After Franz Mesmer (1734–1815)]

1. strong or spellbinding appeal; 2. hypnotic induction believed to involve animal magnetism.

Note: Franz Mesmer, a visionary 18th-century Austrian physician, sought to treat disease through animal magnetism, an early therapeutic application of hypnotism. He believed cures could be effected by having patients do things such as sit with their feet in a fountain of magnetized water while holding cables attached to magnetized trees. Mesmer then came to believe that magnetic powers resided in himself, and during highly attended curative sessions in Paris he caused his patients to have reactions ranging from sleeping or dancing to convulsions. It is now thought that these reactions were probably brought about by hypnotic powers that Mesmer was unaware he possessed.

message

[< Latin MITTERE 'to send']

1. communication (information, feelings, ideas, etc.) passed on or transmitted by talking, writing, etc.; 2. in software, a piece of information passed from the application or operating system to the user.

metacognition

[< Greek META 'over'; Latin COGNITIO 'knowledge']

Theory or statement about *cognition, whose purpose it is to examine the nature of cognition.

metacommunication

[< Greek META 'over'; Latin COMMUNIS 'common']
Theory or statement about *communication, whose purpose it is to examine the nature of communication.

metafiction

[< Greek META 'over'; Latin FINGERE 'to form, make, put together']
[also called metanarrative]
Fiction about *fiction, whose purpose it is to examine the nature of fiction and narrative.

metalanguage

[< Greek META 'over'; Latin LINGUA 'tongue']
Theory or statement about *language, whose purpose it is to examine the nature of language.

metalingual function

[< Greek META 'over'; Latin LINGUA 'tongue']
In Roman *Jakobson's model of communication, message referring to the code used.

Illustrations: 1. *The word noun is a noun.* 2. *Is green an adjective?*

metanarrative

[also called *metafiction]

metaphor

[< Greek META 'over' + PHEREIN 'to bear']
Application of a word or phrase with one meaning to another that has a different meaning, thus creating a new meaning by association.

Note: In the metaphor *The professor is a snake*, for instance, the two words are analyzed as follows: 1. the primary referent, *professor*, which is known as the *topic* of the metaphor, is the domain which is to be described or explained (the A-domain); 2. the referent, *snake*, which is known as the *vehicle* of the metaphor, is the domain that does the describing or explaining (the B-domain). Their association creates a new meaning, [A is B],

called the *ground*, which is not the simple sum of the two meanings, A and B – for it is not the *denotative meaning of the vehicle that is applied to the topic, but rather its *connotations. So, the meanings of *snake* that are applied to describe the *professor* are the characteristics perceived in snakes, namely 'slyness,' 'danger,' 'slipperiness,' etc.

Metaphor was discovered and named by *Aristotle, who noticed that it revealed how people attempt to understand things. However, Aristotle also affirmed that, as useful as it was in facilitating thought, the most common function of metaphor was to spruce up literal ways of speaking. Today, the study of metaphor pursues Aristotle's original conception of metaphor, namely, as a process revealing how the mind forms many concepts.

Metaphor reveals a basic tendency of the human mind to think of certain referents (the topic of the metaphor) in terms of others (the vehicle). The question now becomes, Is there any psychological motivation for this? In the case of *The professor is a snake*, the probable reason for correlating two semantically unrelated referents seems to be the de facto perception that humans and animals are interconnected in the natural scheme of things.

metaphor, conceptual

[< Greek META 'over' + PHEREIN 'to bear']
Generalized metaphorical formula that underlies how a specific *abstract concept is understood.

Illustrations: The metaphorical expression *The professor is a snake* (see *metaphor) is really a token of something more general, namely, *people are animals*. This same formula underlies similar expressions such as *John is a gorilla, Mary is a puppy, That man is a pig, She's a hedge-hog*, and so on. Each specific metaphor is not an isolated example of metaphorical creativity; each one is really a particular manifestation of the same metaphorical idea – *people are animals*. Such formulas are what George Lakoff and Mark Johnson call *conceptual metaphors* in their 1980 book *Metaphors We Live By*.

Each of the two parts of the conceptual metaphor is called a *domain: people* is called the *target domain* because it is the abstract topic itself (the 'target' of the conceptual metaphor); and *animals* is called the *source domain* because it is the class of vehicles that deliver the metaphor (the 'source' of the metaphorical concept). This suggests that many abstract concepts are formed systematically as conceptual metaphors and that specific metaphors (as they occur in conversations) are traces to the target and source domains. For example, in sentences such as *Those ideas are circular, I don't see the point of your idea, Her ideas are central to the discussion, Their ideas are diametrically opposite*, etc., the target domain can be seen to be *ideas* and the source domain *geometrical figures*. The conceptual metaphor in this case is *ideas are geometrical figures*.

Lakoff and Johnson showed meticulously and persuasively how conceptual metaphors coalesce to form the backbone of everyday thought and discourse. They trace the psychological source of conceptual metaphors to *image schemas (mental impressions of sensory experiences of locations, movements, shapes, etc.). These schemas permit us not only to recognize patterns within certain bodily sensations, but also to anticipate certain consequences and to make inferences and deductions. Image-schema theory thus suggests that the source domains enlisted in delivering an abstract topic were not chosen originally in an arbitrary fashion, but derived from the experience of events related to the concept. The formation of a conceptual metaphor, therefore, is the result of an experiential *abduction.

Work on conceptual metaphors since the early 1980s has shown that cultural groupthink is built on layers of conceptual meta-

phors, which fuse into a system of abstract thinking that holds together the entire network of associated meanings in the culture. This is accomplished by a kind of 'higher-order' metaphorizing – that is, as target domains are associated with many kinds of source domains, they become increasingly complex, leading to what Lakoff and Johnson call *cultural* or *cognitive models*. For example, the target domain of *ideas* is conceptualized as food *(It is hard to digest those ideas all at once)*, geometrical figures *(That is a central idea in philosophy)*, and fashion *(That idea went out of style a while ago)*. There are, of course, many other ways of conceptualizing ideas. Now, the relevant point to be made here is that the constant juxtaposition of such conceptual metaphors in common discourse produces, cumulatively, a *cultural model* of ideas: *ideas = food, geometrical figures, fashion, …*

metaphoric gesture

[< Greek META 'over' + PHEREIN 'to bear']
Gesture accompanying discourse that depicts the vehicle (concrete part) of a metaphor being utilized in the discourse.

Illustration: This type of gesture typically accompanies expressions such as *presenting an idea, putting forth an idea, offering advice*, whereby the speaker tends to raise up his/her hands as if offering his/her listener a kind of object.

metaphorology

[< Greek META 'over' + PHEREIN 'to bear' + LOGOS 'word, reckoning']
Branch of *semiotics studying *metaphor and figurative language generally.

metaphysics

[< Greek META 'over' + PHUSIS 'nature']
Branch of philosophy dealing with the nature of reality, including the relationship between mind and matter. Metaphysics is customarily divided into *ontology*, which examines the question of how many entities

compose the universe, and *metaphysics proper*, which is concerned with describing the most general traits of reality.

Note: The subjects treated by Greek philosopher *Aristotle fixed the content of metaphysical speculation for centuries. In the 13th century, the scholastic philosopher St Thomas *Aquinas declared that knowledge of God was the aim of metaphysics. The central figure in metaphysics, however, was 18th-century German philosopher Immanuel *Kant. Before Kant, metaphysics was characterized by a rationalistic method of inquiry. The most famous rationalist was French philosopher René *Descartes, who maintained that the body and the mind were fundamentally different entities. Kant combined several metaphysical viewpoints, developing a distinctive philosophy called *transcendentalism*. He denied the possibility of an accurate knowledge of ultimate reality, because he saw all knowledge as limited by individual experiences. He maintained that God, freedom, and human immortality are understood through moral faith rather than scientific knowledge. Some of Kant's most distinguished followers included German philosopher G.W.F. *Hegel and American philosopher John *Dewey.

In the 20th century the validity of metaphysical thinking has been disputed by *analytic philosophers, who asserted that expressions that cannot be tested empirically have no factual meaning, and by *Marxist dialectical materialists, who asserted that the mind is conditioned by and reflects material reality. Existentialist philosophers, in contrast, contended that the questions raised by metaphysics are too important to ignore, whether or not the responses to them can be verified objectively.

metatheory
[< Greek META 'over'; Greek THEORIA 'a looking at']

Theory or statement about *theories, whose purpose it is to examine the nature of theories and theorizing.

meter
[< Greek METRON 'measure']
Measured arrangement of words in poetry, by accentual rhythm, syllabic quantity, or the number of syllables in a line.

metonym, conceptual
[< Greek META 'over' + ONOMA 'name']
Generalized metonymic formula that underlies a specific type of abstraction.

Note: Sentences such as *He's just another pretty face*, *There are an awful lot of faces in the audience*, and *We need some new faces around here* are, clearly, not isolated examples of *metonymy. Each one is really a particular manifestation of the same metonymic idea – *the face is the person*.

Such general formulas are conceptual metonyms that, like conceptual metaphors, are interconnected to other domains of signification in a culture. The formula *the face is the person* is the reason why portraits, in painting and photography, focus on the face. The face is, in effect, a metonym for personality.

metonymy
[< Greek META 'over' + ONOMA 'name']
[see also *synecdoche]
Use of an entity to refer to another that is related to it.

Illustrations: 1. the *White House* for the *American presidency*; 2. the brand *Scotch tape* for all *adhesive tape*; 3. *strong bodies* for *strong people*; 4. *set of wheels* for *automobile*.

Metz, Christian
[1931–1993]
French cinema semiotician who applied the notions of *structuralism to the study of cinema. Metz's meticulous work showed that a movie is really no more than a set of

distinct units that, like the *phonemes of a language, combine to create meaning not in an absolute way, but through the relations they have to each other.

mime

[< Greek MIMOS 'imitator, actor']
[see also *pantomime]
1. ancient Greek or Roman farce, in which people and events were mimicked and burlesqued; 2. representation of an action, character, mood, etc. by means of gestures and actions rather than words.

mimesis

[< Greek MIMESIS 'imitation']
[also called mimicry]
1. imitation in art, literature, or representation; 2. in biology, physical or behavioral resemblance of one species to another that benefits the mimicking species or sometimes both.

Note: The species being mimicked is usually one with traits that discourage predators. Mimicry was explained in 1862 by British naturalist Henry Walter Bates, who found two similarly marked but unrelated families of Brazilian butterflies, one of which was poisonous to birds. Bates explained that the non-poisonous butterflies had survived by evolving similar warning markings. This is known as 'Batesian mimicry.'

minimal pair

[< Latin MINIMUS 'least']
Two items that are the same except for one element in the same position.

Illustrations: In linguistics, the minimal pair is used to determine if a sound is *phonemic, i.e. capable of distinguishing meaning in a language. For example, the two words *pin* and *bin* constitute a minimal pair because they are constructed with the same sounds except in initial position. The difference in meaning that these two initial sounds generate is said to be phonemic.

Similarly, in music a major and minor triad in the same key constitute a minimal pair because they are constructed with the same tones except in the middle position.

minimalism

[< Latin MINIMUS 'least']
Movement in art, dance, music, etc., beginning in the 1960s, in which only the simplest design, structure, and forms are used, often repetitiously.

Illustration: Perhaps no other artist best exemplifies minimalism than American composer Philip Glass (1937–). Glass's musical works emphasize continual repetition of rhythm with slight alterations in melodic and harmonic pattern. His operas include *Einstein on the Beach* (1976), *Satyagraha* (1980), *Akhnaten* (1984), *The Voyage* (1992), and *La Belle et la Bête* (1994).

modality

[< Latin MODUS 'measure, manner, mode']
In *logic the qualification in a proposition which indicates that what is affirmed or denied is possible, impossible, necessary, or contingent.

mode

[< Latin MODUS 'measure, manner, mode']
1. manner or way of acting, doing, or being; 2. customary usage, or current fashion or style, as in manners or dress; 3. in philosophy the form, or way of being, of something, as distinct from its substance.

model

[< Latin MODUS 'measure, manner, mode']
1. small copy or imitation of an existing object; 2. preliminary *representation of something; 3. archetype.

modeling system

[< Latin MODUS 'measure, manner, mode'; Greek SYSTEMA 'a placing together']
Species-specific system that allows a species to make models of things in the world.

Note: The American semiotician Thomas A. *Sebeok argues that there are three types of modeling systems in the human species that make human representation highly advanced with respect to that of other species: 1. the *Primary Modeling System* (PMS) = the neural system that predisposes the human infant to engage in simulative forms of semiosis, which in turn permit imitative and indicational representational activities; 2. the *Secondary Modeling System* (SMS) = the more complex neural system that predisposes the human infant to engage in verbal forms of semiosis, which in turn permit linguistic representational activities; 3. the *Tertiary Modeling System* (TMS) = the highly complex neural system that predisposes the maturing child to engage in highly abstract forms of semiosis, which in turn permit symbolic representational activities (narration, art, etc.).

The two crucial insights of modeling systems theory can be summarized as follows: 1. representation is tied to three semiosic phases; and 2. these phases are evolutionary – i.e. the development of complex symbolic activity (= a TMS endowment) is dependent upon a prior emergence of verbal representational activities (= a SMS endowment), which is itself dependent upon the development of early imitative and indicational semiosis (= a PMS endowment).

modem
[mo(dulator) + dem(odulator)]
Device that converts data to a form that can be transmitted, as by telephone, to data-processing equipment, where a similar device reconverts it.

modernism
[< Latin MODUS 'measure, manner, mode']
1. any of several movements variously attempting to redefine biblical and Christian dogma and traditional teachings in the light of modern science, historical research, etc.;

2. movement in architecture, also known as the *Bauhaus School, emphasizing simplicity of design; 3. any movement in art, science, philosophy that came after the Renaissance.

monologue
[< Greek MONO 'single' + LEGEIN 'to speak']
[also called *soliloquy]
1. long speech by one speaker, especially one monopolizing the discourse on stage; 2. passage or composition, in verse or prose, presenting the words or thoughts of a single character; 3. part of a play in which one character speaks alone; 4. play, skit, or recitation for one actor only.

montage
[French for 'a mounting, setting together']
1. art of making a composite picture by bringing together into a single composition a number of different pictures or parts of pictures and arranging these, by superimposing one on another, so that they form a blended whole while remaining distinct; 2. in cinema, sequence of abruptly alternating or superimposed scenes or images shown whirling about, flashing into focus, etc.

Montaigne, Michel de
[1533–1592]
French essayist who tried to dispel the pejorative view that had arisen in the 16th century vis-à-vis 'primitive' cultures, arguing that it was crucial above all else to understand the morality of other peoples on its own terms, not in terms of one's own cultural predispositions and system of ethics.

Morgan, Lewis Henry
[1818–1881]
American philosopher and anthropologist who claimed that all cultures, no matter how diverse, developed according to a regular series of predictable stages – from savagery, to barbarism, to civilization.

morpheme
[< Greek MORPHĒ 'form']
Smallest meaning-bearing unit or form in a language.

Note: A morpheme is not the equivalent of a *word*. People sometimes erroneously assume that a *word* is something that represents a 'single piece of meaning.' But this is not necessarily so. For instance, the form *illogical* is one word, but it is 'segmentable' into smaller bits that also have meaning: namely, the basic form, *logic*, which has a 'dictionary meaning,' the negative prefix *il-*, which has a recurring functional meaning ('opposite of'), and the suffix *-al*, which also has a functional meaning ('the act or process of being something'). These three bits are called *morphemes.*

Morphemes may be word roots (as the *rasp-*, in *raspberry*) or individual words (as in *logic, play, boy*); word endings (as the *-s* in *boys, -ed* in *played, -ing* in *playing*); affixes (as *il-* and *-al*, in *illogical*); and internal alterations indicating such grammatical categories as tense (*sing–sang*), number (*mouse-mice*), etc.

Morphemes are sometimes categorized as *lexical* if their meaning is lexical (dictionary) or *grammatical* if it is purely grammatical (e.g. the *-s* in *cats*). The process of identifying morphemes is known as *segmentation*, since it entails segmenting a form into units that cannot be split any further. The form *il-* in *illogical* cannot be segmented any further, nor can *logic* or *-al*. To make an analogy, a word such as *illogical* can be considered to be a *molecule* of meaning, namely, a verbal 'compound' that can exist in a free state and still retain the characteristics of one or more morphemic *atoms* of which it consists, namely, *il-, logic*, and *-al*.

morphology
[< Greek MORPHĒ 'form' + LOGOS 'word, study']
1. formal structure of words and other forms; 2. branch of *linguistics that deals with the internal structure of *morphemes.

Morris, Charles
[1901–1979]
American semiotician who divided semiotics into the study of 1. relations between a sign and other signs, which he called *syntactics*; 2. relations between signs and their denotative meanings, which he called *semantics*; 3. relations between signs and interpreters, which he called *pragmatics*.

motion picture
[see *cinema]

motto
[< Latin MUTTUM 'a grunt']
In *heraldry, a phrase or sentence alluding to the family, the arms, or the *crest, placed above the crest or below the shield.

movies
[see *cinema]

MS-DOS
[acronym for Microsoft Disk Operating System]
Computer operating system controlling such operations as disk input and output, video support, keyboard control, and many internal functions related to program execution and file maintenance.

museum
[< Greek MOUSEION 'shrine of the Muses']
Building, place, or institution devoted to the acquisition, conservation, study, exhibition, and educational interpretation of objects having scientific, historical, or artistic value.

Note: Not until the Renaissance was the term *museum* applied to a collection of objects of beauty and worth. The first *museum*, however, was founded about 290 BC in Alexandria, Egypt, by Ptolemy I. Ancient Greek and Roman temples and other public spaces contained art objects dedicated to the gods. Before the year AD 1000 royal collections of art objects were preserved in palaces and temples in China and Japan.

During the Middle Ages, European churches and monasteries became repositories for art works and other valuable objects. In the 16th century it became customary to display sculpture and paintings in the long halls, or galleries, of palaces and the residences of the wealthy. Thus originated the use of the term *gallery* for a place where works of art are hung or arranged for viewing. Museums as they are known today were first established in Europe in the 18th century. During the French Revolution, the Louvre became the first great public art museum. Since then, museums have been built to collect, preserve, study, and interpret various objects

music, classical

[< Greek MOUSIKĒ 'musical (art)']
Western art form based on vocal or instrumental tones put together on the basis of a system of melody, harmony, rhythm, and timbre.

Note: The earliest European music known is that of the ancient Greeks and Romans, dating from about 500 BC to AD 300. The rhythm of Greek music was closely associated with language. In a song, the music duplicated the rhythms of the text. In an instrumental piece, it followed the rhythmic patterns of the verse. The Romans carried on the Greek musical traditions. In the Middle Ages, the Christian church did not encourage performances of secular music, developing its own religious chant, known as Gregorian chant, after Pope Gregory I. By the 9th century, musicians added an extra voice part to be sung simultaneously with sections of the chant. This was the first step toward the development of *polyphony (multipart music). During the early 14th century a new polyphonic style called *ars*

nova developed. Composers used rhythmic patterns of a dozen or more notes, which they repeated over and over in one or more voice parts of a composition. The technique was known as *counterpoint.

In the 15th century composers preferred a simple style of music with smoothly flowing melodies, smooth-sounding harmonies, and less emphasis on contrapuntal composition. Late in the 16th century developments in Italy changed the sound and structure of music. Many Italian musicians favored less-intricate compositions marked by frequent emotional contrasts, a readily understandable text, and an interplay of various voices and instruments. Such elements became especially prominent in *opera. Instrumental music became increasingly prominent during the 17th century, often in the form of a continuous contrapuntal composition. An important 17th-century innovation, called the *concerto*, changed the style of much late Renaissance music into one marked by numerous contrasting elements. By the 17th and early 18th centuries composers started integrating counterpoint with harmonic relationships into a new system called *tonality*. This system was used masterfully by the great baroque composers, Henry Purcell (1659?–95), Antonio Vivaldi (1675?–1741), Johann Sebastian Bach (1685–1750), and George Frideric Handel (1685–1759). Beginning around 1720, some musicians found baroque counterpoint too rigid and intellectual. They developed a more *homophonic* style based on a dominant melody with accompaniment. The height of 18th-century homophonic composition came in the works of the Viennese classical school, which was dominated by Joseph Haydn (1732–1809), Wolfgang Amadeus Mozart (1756–91), and Ludwig van Beethoven (1770–1827).

At the beginning of the romantic 19th century musicians, inspired by the innovations of Beethoven, began to explore new ways of composing. The romantic composers made increasing use of *chromaticism, a harmonic style with a high proportion of tones outside the prevailing key. Prominent romantic composers include Hector Berlioz (1803–69) Franz Liszt (1811–86), Franz Schubert (1797–1828), Robert Schumann (1810–56), Johannes Brahms (1833–97), Giuseppe Verdi (1813–1901), Peter Ilich Tchaikovsky (1840–93), and Frédéric Chopin (1810–49).

Individuality and personal expression in music grew more pronounced in the 20th century. Chromaticism continued to be a prominent feature of harmony, and in the first decade of the century, *atonality*, or the complete absence of tonality, was introduced into the music by a few composers, notably Austria's Arnold Schoenberg (1874–1951). The other innovative harmonic styles in 20th-century music include *polytonality*, or the simultaneous use of more than one tonality, and *minimalism*, the reduction of melody to its basic harmonic elements. Prominent 20th-century classical composers include Richard Strauss (1864–1949), Sergei Rachmaninoff (1873–1943), Sergei Prokofiev (1891–1953), Dmitri Shostakovich (1906–75), Igor Stravinsky (1882–1971), and Phillip Glass (1937–).

myth
[< Greek MYTHOS 'word,' 'speech,' 'tale of the gods']
1. ancient story dealing with supernatural beings, ancestors, or heroes; 2. any story or narrative that aims to explain the origin of something in metaphysical ways.

Note: The original myths were metaphorical narratives in which the characters were gods, heroes, and mystical beings, the plot was about the origin of things or about dramatic human events, and the setting was a metaphysical world juxtaposed against the real world. The divine characters in myths do not represent beings as such, but are attempts to seek a reason for the occurrence of natural phenomena (thunder, lightning, etc.). The plot of myths involves a sequencing of events to explain such phenomena in metaphysical terms. For example, to explain climatological events, the ancient Romans invented *Neptune*, the god of the sea, and brother of *Jupiter*, the supreme god of the skies. Originally a god of springs and streams, Neptune became identified with the Greek god of the sea, *Poseidon*. The myth of *Neptune* is a story created to explain the interconnectedness of natural phenomena, thus giving a metaphysical coherence to the world.

The study of myth has attracted great interest over the centuries. Italian philosopher Giambattista *Vico, for instance, claimed that myths are the founding stories of a society. The gradual increase of control humans had over their environment and the increasing complexity of human institutions was reflected by the functions that new gods assumed. For Vico, myth was constructed not on the basis of a rational logic but of what he called a *poetic logic*, a form of thinking based upon, and guided by, conscious bodily experiences that were transformed into generalized ideas. The course that humanity runs, according to Vico, goes from an early mythical age, through a heroic one, to a rationalistic one. Each age has its own kind of culture, art, language, and social institutions. The poetic mentality, for instance, generated myths; the heroic one, legends; and the rational one, narrative history.

Because myth is a narrative, many attempts to understand it have focused on its linguistic structure. German scholar Friedrich Max Müller (1823–1900) viewed myth as an example of the historical development of language. He believed that in the texts of ancient India the gods did not represent beings but, rather, were figurative embodiments of natural phenomena. French anthropologist Claude *Lévi-Strauss saw myth as a special case of linguistic usage. In myth, he claimed, there are certain clusters of relationships that, although expressed in the narrative and dramatic content, obey the systematic order of the language's structure. British anthropologist Edward Burnett *Tylor believed that myth in archaic cultures was based on a confusion of the real with the ideal. French philosopher Lucien Lévy-Bruhl (1857–1939) held that people in archaic cultures experience the world without benefit of logical categories, gaining their knowledge of the world through mystical participation in reality, and that this knowledge is expressed through myths. Romanian-born philosopher Mircea *Eliade argued that myths are primitive linguistic explanations of the nature of being.

Myth has also been explained as the expression of psychic and moral tendencies in humanity. French sociologist Émile *Durkheim claimed that myths constitute a moral system and a cosmology as well as a history. This conception of myth was shared by British anthropologist Bronislaw *Malinowski, who argued that myths can express and codify belief while enforcing morality. German philosopher Ernst *Cassirer argued that myth arises from the emotions but is not identical with them. Instead, it is the expression of the emotions. Austrian psychoanalyst Sigmund *Freud used themes from older mythological structures to exemplify the conflicts and dynamics of the unconscious psychic life. For example, Freud resorted to the myth of *Oedipus* to explain a subconscious sexual desire in a child for the parent of the opposite sex, usually accompanied by hostility to the parent of the same sex. In Greek mythology, Oedipus the king, abandoned at birth, unwittingly killed his father and then married his mother. Swiss psychiatrist Carl *Jung saw, in the mythic themes, evidence for the existence of a collective unconscious shared by all humanity. In a comprehensive study of myths, American writer Joseph *Campbell formulated a general theory of the origin, development, and unity of all human cultures. Campbell pointed out that many myths encode fear

and awe of the world of Nature itself. During the primitive stages of cultural life myth stands out as the primary mode by which communal sense making is established. Not possessing the knowledge to understand or explain environmental events in scientific terms, the first humans ascribed them to awesome and frightful 'gods' or 'divine' creatures, thus producing humanity's first archetypes (literally, an original model of something). Out of these emerged the first 'human dramas' with the first 'heroes.'

mytheme
[< Greek MYTHOS 'word,' 'speech,' 'tale of the gods']
Anthropologist Claude *Lévi-Strauss's term referring to a basic event, role, or theme that goes into the make-up of a mythical story.

Illustration: Cadmos kills the dragon and *Oedipus kills the sphinx* are instantiations of the same mytheme [X *kills* Y].

mythologie
[French for 'mythology']
Term used by semiotician Roland *Barthes referring to the fact that the original mythic themes continue to reverberate residually in modern-day societies, especially in discourse, rituals, and performances.

Note: To distinguish between the original *myths* and their modern-day versions, the semiotician Roland Barthes (1915–80) designated the latter as *mythologies*. In early Hollywood westerns, for instance, the mythic theme of good vs. evil manifested itself in various symbolic and expressive ways: e.g. heroes wore white hats and villains black ones. Sports events, too, are mythological dramas juxtaposing the good (the home team, who often wear white uniforms) vs. the bad (the visiting team). The fanfare associated with preparing for the 'big event' has a ritualistic quality to it similar to the pomp and circumstance that ancient armies engaged in before going out to battle. Indeed, the whole event is perceived to be a mythic battle. The symbolism of the home team's (army) uniform, the valor and strength of the players (the heroic warriors), and the skill and tactics of the coach (the army general) has a powerful effect on the home fans (one of the two warring nations). The game (the battle) is perceived to unfold in moral terms, i.e. as a struggle of Herculean proportions between the forces of good and evil in the universe. Sports figures are exalted as heroes or condemned as villains.

A *mythologie* often takes the form of a concept or social trend. Childhood, for instance, emerged as a *mythologie* during the Industrial Revolution of the 19th century, when for the first time children were considered to be human beings at a stage of life as yet uncorrupted and untainted by civilization. The concept of such a period of life did not exist in previous eras, nor is it a universal one today. The images of children as pure and innocent is part of a *mythologie*, not of a psychology or sociology of childhood.

mythologizing effect

[< Greek MYTHOS 'word,' 'speech,' 'tale of the gods']
Effect of television on perception by which TV and movie personages are viewed as mythic figures, larger than life.

Note: Like any type of privileged space – a platform, a pulpit, etc. designed to impart focus and significance to someone – television and cinema create mythic heroes by simply showing them on a screen, where they are seen as suspended in time and space, in a mythic world of their own. This is why meeting actors, musical stars, etc. causes great enthusiasm and excitement in many people.

mythology

[< Greek MYTHOS 'word,' 'speech,' 'tale of the gods' + LOGOS 'word, study']

Branch of *semiotics and *anthropology studying *myths.

Note: In Europe, interest in myth grew during the *Age of Enlightenment (18th century), as scholars tried to make sense of mythic stories and developed disciplines devoted to the study of myths. Thinkers of the romantic movement turned to the older Indo-European myths as intellectual and cultural resources, viewing myth as a form of human expression and perception as important as the rational grasp of reality.

Usually the most important myth in a culture is the *cosmogonic* myth, which explains how the world came into being. In some cosmogonic accounts, the creation of the world proceeds from nothing; in others it emerges from the lower worlds. *Eschatological* myths, by contrast, have been created by many cultures to describe the end of the world. These usually predict the destruction of the world by a divine being who will send humans to a paradisiacal existence or to one of eternal torment, depending on how people have lived their lives. An apocalypse, i.e. universal upheaval and destruction, are parts of eschatological mythology. Many cultures tell myths of *birth and rebirth* that inform people how life can be renewed or tell them about the coming of an ideal society or of a savior. Myths of the *culture hero* are also common. These describe beings who discover a cultural artifact or technological process that radically changes the course of history.

Rarely do we realize how much of the representational fabric of our modern cultures is cut from myth. From the original myths we have inherited, for instance, the names of the days of the week and months of the year: e.g. *Tuesday* is the day dedicated to the Germanic war god Tir, *Wednesday* to the Germanic chief god Wotan, *Thursday* to Thor, *Friday* to the goddess of beauty Frigga, *Saturday* to the god Saturn, *January* to the Roman god Janus, and so on. Our planets bear a similar pattern of nomenclature: *Mars* is named after the Roman god of war, *Venus* after the Greek god of beauty, etc. The residues of mythic thinking can also be seen in the fact that we continue to read horoscopes or *Fortune* magazine, implore the gods to help us, and so on.

N

---

name

[< Greek ONOMA 'name']
Word that identifies a person, object, or place.

Note: Name-giving is a product of historical traditions. Across cultures, a neonate is not considered a full-fledged member of the culture until she/he is given a name. The act of naming a newborn infant marks his/her first rite of passage in society, becoming identified as a separate individual with a unique personality. If a person is not given a name by his/her family, then society will step in to do so. A person taken into a family, by marriage, adoption, or for some other reason, is also typically assigned the family's name. In Inuit cultures an individual is perceived to have a body, a soul, and a name; a person is not seen as complete without all three. The use of numerical identification for prisoners and slaves is, in effect, a negation of their humanity.

In some countries, like Brazil, a child must be given an appropriate Christian name before she/he can be issued a birth certificate. By and large, however, in Western culture, name giving is an unregulated process. But even in the West, it is shaped by several customs and trends – e.g. modern names often are derived from sources such as the names of the months (*May*), precious stones (*Ruby*), popular contemporary personalities (*Elvis, Marilyn*), flowers (*Blossom*), places (*Georgia*), or figures in classical myth (*Diana, Jason*). New names are frequently coined from variant spellings (*JoEtta, Beverleigh*), or even completely invented. The late rock musician and composer Frank

Zappa (1940-93), for instance, named his daughter *Moon Unit* and his son *Dweezil*.

A *name* has both *indexical and *symbolic properties because, like a pronoun, it identifies the person and, usually, his/her ethnic origin, and because, like any word, it is a product of historical forces and thus tied to conventional systems of signification. Less often, names are coined iconically (see *icon): trivial but instructive examples of this can be seen in the names given to household animals – *Ruff, Purry*, etc.

Until the late Middle Ages, one personal name was generally sufficient as an identifier. Duplications, however, began to occur so often that additional differentiations became a necessity. Hence, *surnames were given to individuals (literally 'names on top of names'). These were at first either indexical, in that they identified the individual in terms of place or parentage (descendancy), or descriptive, in that they referred to some personal or social feature (e.g. occupation) of the individual. [See *surname* article for illustrations.]

Name giving is extended across cultures to inanimate referents. When this is done, the objects somehow take on, as if by 'word magic,' an animate quality of their own. So, when a name is given to a brand product or a tropical storm, for instance, these seem to take on an identity, a personality.

narrative

[< Latin NARRARE 'to tell']
[see also *novel]
Something told or written, such as an account, story, tale.

Note: A *narrative* is a *text that is constructed to reflect a perceived causal and interconnected sequence of events involving characters. Actually, by their very nature, narratives may be said to establish a causality between people and their actions. The narrative sequence may be purely fact-based, as in a newspaper report, a psychoanalytic session, etc., or fictional, as in a novel, a comic strip, a film, etc. Needless to say, it is often difficult, if not impossible, to determine the boundary line between narrative fact and fiction.

Narrative texts are characterized by four basic elements: *plot*, *character*, *setting*, and a *narrator*. The *plot* is basically what the narrative is all about, encompassing the sequence of events to which the narrative draws attention. *Character* is an account of the people who are the perpetrators and/or participants in the plot. The *setting* is the location where, and the time when, the plot unfolds. The teller of the story is called the *narrator*. The narrator can be a character of the narrative, the author of the narrative, or some other person or medium. Each type of narrator provides a different *perspective* of the story for the reader. The reader can thus feel a part of the narrative, looking at the action as if she/he were in it (*looking from within*); or aloof from it, looking at the action as if from the outside (*looking from without*).

There is evidence that fictional narrativity has ancient roots. In papyri from the 4th Egyptian Dynasty, we read about how King Cheops (2590–2567 BC) delighted in hearing fictional stories that his sons told him. The Greek statesman and general Aristides (530?–468? BC), moreover, wrote a collection of what we would now call *short stories* about his hometown, Miletus, to celebrate the victory over the Persians at Salamis. The *Golden Ass* of Apuleius (AD 125?–200?) in Latin, too, constituted a fictional narration aimed at providing social and moral commentary. But, by and large, the ancient world told tales of the gods, or of the foibles of human personages. These were hardly perceived as fictional. Fiction became a standard narrative craft only after the medieval ages, after the Italian Giovanni Boccaccio (1313–75) wrote the *Decameron* (1351–3), a collection of 100 fictional tales set against the gloomy background of the Black Death – as the bubonic plague that swept through Europe in the 14th century was called. The *Decameron* is the first real

example of fiction in the modern sense of the word – the telling of stories just for the sake of the telling. To escape an outbreak of the plague, ten friends decide to take refuge in a country villa outside Florence. There they entertain one another over a period of ten days with a series of stories told by each member of the party in turn. Each day's storytelling ends with a *canzone*, a short lyric poem. The *Decameron* is thus crafted from fictional stories, unfolding as a penetrating analysis of human character. Boccaccio gathered material from many sources for his book, including the French fables of his time, the Greek and Latin classics, folklore, and contemporary Italian life.

Narrative is *textual* representation, involving a main text, subtexts, and intertexts. The term *subtext* designates any implicit narrative within the text that is not immediately accessible to interpretation. A subtext is, in other words, *a text within the main text*. An *intertext* is a narrative to which a text alludes by implication. It is *a text from without the main text*. Subtextuality and intertextuality render narratives interconnected with other codes of the signifying order and with the entire system of culture. Understanding of the narrative, therefore, is dependent upon the reader's knowledge of the culture's textual repository and network.

narrative grammar

[< Latin NARRARE 'to tell'; GRAMMA 'letter']
[also called narrative structure]
Theory that the categories of *narrative correspond to the categories of linguistic *grammar.

Note: The serious study of narrative grammar was initiated in semiotics after the Russian scholar Vladimir Propp argued persuasively in 1928 that ordinary discourse was built upon this structure. According to Propp, there exists a relatively small number of 'narrative units,' or plot themes, which go into the make-up of all conversations and which, consequently, shape grammatical categories. These are innate features of human understanding.

The theory of narrative grammar has been used to explain why narrative is the medium through which children learn about the world. Stories of imaginary beings and events allow children to make sense of the real world and, furthermore, provide the intelligible formats that mobilize the child's natural ability to learn grammatical structure from context. Narrative imparts the sense that there is a *plot* to life, that the *characters* in it subserve some meaningful purpose, and that the *setting* of life is part of the human condition. Each one of these elements is transformed into syntactic categories such as verb, subject, and object. Narrative also impels the child to think of a master *Narrator* – thus leading to metaphysical concepts of God and of a dimension beyond the physical.

After Propp, the semiotician who most influenced the study of narrative grammar was Algirdas Julien *Greimas. Greimas's main contention was that human beings in different cultures invent remarkably similar stories with virtually the same types of plot lines, characters, and settings. These constitute what he called an '*actantial grammar.' The 'parts of speech' of this grammar are called *actants, or 'minimal narrative units.' In order to explain the passage from these to actual narration, Greimas posited a 'generative trajectory' that maps the units onto other constituents of language to produce the narration.

narrative image
[see *image, mental]

narrativity
[< Latin NARRARE 'to tell']
[also called *narrative grammar]
Innate human capacity to produce and comprehend *narratives.

narratology
[< Latin NARRARE 'to tell' + Greek LOGOS 'word, study']
Branch of *semiotics that studies narrativity, narrative structure, and narratives (see *narrative).

narrator
[< Latin NARRARE 'to tell']
The teller of the *narrative.

Note: The narrator can be a character in the narrative telling the story directly to the reader ('first-person narration'), or it can be some other person ('third-person narration')

national public radio
national noncommercial radio network established in 1970 in the United States. Public radio stations are financed in much the same way as public television stations and usually offer a wider variety of programming than do commercial radio stations.

natural medium
[see *medium, natural]

natural selection
[< Latin NATURALIS 'by birth']
Theory formulated by biologist Charles *Darwin according to which the young of a species that survive to produce the next generation tend to embody favorable natural variations (however slight the advantage may be), passing these variations on genetically.

Note: Natural selection was only part of Darwin's radical theory; he also introduced the idea that all related organisms are descended from common ancestors. The most publicized and scathing attacks on Darwin's ideas came at first not from academia but, understandably, from the religious community. The very thought that human beings could have evolved through natural processes denied, to the shocked minds of the religious people of the late 19th and early 20th century, the special creation of humankind by God and seemed to place humanity on a plane with brute animals. But the potency of the early religious opposition to evolutionary theory was weakened by a discovery made, ironically, by an Augustinian monk, Gregor Johann Mendel (1822–84). Mendel cultivated and tested more than 28,000 pea plants. His tedious experiments showed, for instance, that by crossing tall and dwarf parents of peas, hybrid offspring would result that resembled the tall parent rather than being a medium-height blend. To explain this he conceived of hereditary units, now called *genes*, which he claimed were responsible for passing on dominant or recessive characteristics.

natural sign
[see *sign, natural]

naturalism
[< Latin NATURALIS 'by birth']
1. system of thought holding that all phenomena can be explained in terms of natural causes without attributing spiritual or metaphysical significance to them; 2. in art, practice of reproducing subjects as precisely as possible.

Nature vs. Culture debate
[also called *environmentalism vs. innatism] Debate centering on the role of Nature in determining the development of character and behavior vs. the role of upbringing and social environment.

Neanderthal
Genus of *Homo*, named after the Neander Valley in Germany where one of the earliest skulls was found, that occupied parts of Europe and the Middle East from 100,000 to about 35,000 to 40,000 years ago, after which it disappeared from the fossil record.

neologism
[< Greek NEOS 'young'; LOGOS 'word']
New word, expression, or usage.

Illustrations: 1. *channel surfing*, the act of scanning through television programs by use of a remote control; 2. *gender bender*, a person who dresses and behaves like a member of the opposite sex; 3. *infomercial*, a television program that is an extended advertisement, often including a discussion or demonstration; 4. *wuss*, a weak, cowardly, or ineffective person.

neomania
[< Greek NEOS 'young'; MANIA 'madness']
Term coined by semiotician Roland *Barthes in reference to the abnormal craving for new objects of consumption engendered by consumerist lifestyle and media advertising.

neoteny
[< Greek NEOS 'young' + TEINEIN 'to stretch']
Prolonged juvenile stage of brain and skull development in relation to the time required to reach sexual maturity that is uniquely characteristic of the human species.

network
1. chain of radio or television broadcasting stations linked by wire or microwave relay; 2. company that produces the programs for these stations; 3. in computer science, system of computers interconnected by telephone wires or other means.

neurolinguistics
[< Greek NEURON 'nerve' + Latin LINGUA 'tongue']
Branch of *linguistics studying the relation of language to the brain.

neuron
[< Greek NEURON 'nerve']
[also called nerve cell]
Nerve cell that is the fundamental unit of the nervous system. A neuron is an impulse-

conducting cell found in the brain, consisting of a nucleated cell body with one or more dendrites and a single axon.

neuroscience

[< Greek NEURON 'nerve' + Latin SCIENTIA 'knowing']
Field studying how the brain processes information, generates mental processes, and underlies all aspects of behavior.

news

Popular form of radio or television program that reports events in the world. The early years of television offered little news coverage. In 1956, the NBC network introduced *The Huntley-Brinkley Report*, a half-hour national telecast presented in the early evening and featuring filmed reports of the day's events. The other networks soon followed with their own news programming.

nickname

Descriptive *name added to or replacing the actual name of a person.

Illustrations: 1. *Lefty* (= nickname for someone who is left-handed). 2. *Shorty* (= nickname for someone who is short in height).

Nietzsche, Friedrich

[1844–1900]
German philosopher who led the romantic revolt against the emphasis on reason and logically planned social organization initiated by *Enlightenment philosophers, stressing natural instinct, self-assertion, and passion instead. Nietzsche's contention that traditional values had lost their influence over individuals was expressed in his proclamation 'God is dead.' His claim that new values could be created to replace traditional ones led to his concept of the *superman*. According to Nietzsche, the masses conform to tradition, whereas the superman is secure, independent, and individualistic.

nihilism

[< Latin NIHILUN 'a trifle']
Term applied to various radical philosophies, usually by their opponents, implying that adherents reject all positive values and believe in nothing. The term was first used to describe Christian heretics during the Middle Ages. It was applied in Russia in the 1850s and 1860s in reference to young intellectuals who repudiated Christianity, considered Russian society backward, and advocated revolutionary change. The best-known fictional nihilist is Bazarov in the Russian novel *Fathers and Sons* (1862) by Ivan Turgenev (1818–83).

noise

In communication theory, anything that interferes with the reception and successful decipherment of a message. In radio and telephone transmissions, *noise* is electronic static; in voice transmissions, it can vary from any interfering exterior sound (physical noise) to the speaker's lapses of memory (psychological noise).

nominalism

[< Greek ONOMA 'name']
Doctrine of the late Middle Ages that all universal or abstract terms are mere necessities of thought or conveniences of language and therefore exist as names only.

Note: Nominalism grew up in opposition to the philosophical theory called extreme *realism, according to which mental universals have a real and independent existence prior to and apart from particular objects. Nominalism evolved from the view of Greek philosopher *Aristotle that all reality consists of individual things; extreme realism was first enunciated by Greek philosopher *Plato in his doctrine of universal mental forms. The nominalist-realist controversy became prominent in the late 11th and 12th centuries. The nominalist position was debated persuasively by the scholastic thinker Roscelin. The most effective defense of nominalism was undertaken by 14th-century English scholastic philosopher William of Ockham (1285?–1349?). This prepared the way for various modern nominalistic theories, such as *pragmatism and *analytic philosophy.

nonverbal semiotics
[see *semiotics, nonverbal]

normative grammar
[see *grammar]

Nostratic
[< Latin NOSTER 'ours']
Term used by linguists referring to the original language spoken by humans.

noun
[< Greek ONOMA 'name']
Word referring to a person, place, thing, quality, or action that can function as the subject or object of a verb, the object of a preposition, or as an appositive.

Illustrations: 1. The <u>cat</u> purred profusely. 2. He called the <u>professor</u> yesterday.

novel
[< Italian NOVELLA 'new thing']
[see also *fiction]
Fictional prose *narrative of considerable length, typically having a *plot that unfolds through the actions, speech, and thoughts of *characters.

Note: The British writer and literary critic Edmund Gosse (1849-1928) traced the novel as far back as Aristides (530?–468? BC), who wrote a story about his hometown, Miletus, called the *Milesiaka*. Fictional narratives in prose were composed throughout the ancient world, but the novel as such is a medieval invention, even though in Japan the Baroness Murasaki Shikibu (978?–1031?) wrote what many scholars regard as the first real novel, *The Tale of Genji*, in the 11th century.

Fiction can be said to start in the West with the long verse tale, the prose romance, and the Old French **fabliau* in the medieval period, culminating with Giovanni Boccaccio's (1313–75) *Decameron*. Advances were made in Spain during the 16th century with the so-called *picaresque* novel, in which the protagonist is typically a vagabond who goes through a series of exciting adventures. The classic example is the novel by Spanish writer Miguel de Cervantes Saavedra (1547–1616), *Don Quixote de la Mancha* (part I, 1605; part II, 1615), which is considered the first truly great novel of the Western world. The novel became the dominant and most popular form of narrative art in the 18th and 19th centuries, as more and more writers were devoting their lives to it. Novels became more psychologically real, depicting and often satirizing contemporary life and morals. During this same era, the novel spawned its own genres, including the *didactic novel*, in which theories of education and politics were expressed, and the *Gothic novel*, in which the element of horror is created by making supernatural phenomena the main elements of plot, character, and setting. The first Gothic novel was *The Castle of Otranto* (1764) by Horace Walpole (1717–97), but perhaps the most well-known example is *Frankenstein* (1818) by Mary Wollstonecraft Shelley (1797–1851). One of the most enduring genres of the period is the *comedy of manners*, which is concerned with the clash between characters from different social backgrounds. The novels of Jane Austen (1775–1817) are considered by many to be the unchallenged epidome of the genre. French novelists Stendhal (1783–1842) and Honoré de Balzac (1799–1850) used the novel form to attack hypocrisy. In America, Herman Melville (1819–91) wrote *Moby Dick* (1851), a great poetic narrative of pursuit and obsession in the guise of a whaling story. And in his comic masterpiece *The Adventures of Huckleberry Finn* (1884), Mark Twain (1835–1910) showed how ex-

pressive native American style could be. In
the same era, the Russians Fyodor Dostoyevsky (1821–81) and Leo Tolstoy (1828–1910)
wrote some of the greatest epic novels of all
time.

For most of the first part of the 20th century, the novel remained a powerful medium for probing human nature and human
society. Novelists were as popular and well
known as media personalities are today.
Their critiques of society led to social
change; their portrayal of human actions
gave the early psychologists insights on
how to investigate human character. The
French writer Marcel Proust (1871–1922), for
instance, explored the nature of memory;
the German author Thomas Mann (1875–
1955) searched for the roots of psychic angst
in social systems; and English authors Virginia Woolf (1882–1941) and James Joyce
(1882–1941) plumbed the emotional source
of human thoughts and motivations. Since
the end of the Second World War the novels
of an increasing number of writers in developing or socially troubled countries have
come to the forefront. Many of these portray
with vivid realism the clash between classes
and races, the search for meaning in a world
where materialism reigns supreme, and the
desire to reform the world. A significant
contemporary American novelist is Toni
Morrison (1931–), who writes of African-
American life. In Canada, the novels of
Robertson Davies (1913–95) and Margaret
Atwood (1939–) have achieved international
fame.

Cinema has taken over from the novel as
the main narrative art form of the contemporary world. But often a novel is the inspiration for a movie script. The conversion of
novel to cinematic form is an envisionable
task because the two tap the same narrative
structure. In many ways the movie is a
'visual novel,' with the role of the narrator
taken over by the camera, and that of narrative perspective by the camera's angle.

novella
[< Italian NOVELLA 'new thing']
Short prose tale, often ending in a moral;
considered the precursor of the *short story
and the *novel.

Illustration: The first and still most famous
collection of novellas is Giovanni Boccaccio's (1313–75) *Decameron*, begun in 1348
and completed in 1353. This is a collection
of 100 stories, told by a group of friends
who had escaped Florence during an outbreak of the plague in order to entertain one
another over a period of ten days. Each
day's storytelling ends with a *canzone*, a
short lyric poem. The stories are notable for
their penetrating character analysis.

nudity
[< Latin NUDUS 'naked']
In semiotic analysis, nudity is seen as the
counterpart of *dress.

Note: Nudity is defined culturally. We are all
born nude, but we learn in childhood that
nudity has special connotations. That part
of the body which is considered acceptable
to expose will vary widely from culture to
culture, even though the covering of genita-
lia seems, for the most part, to cross cultural
boundaries.

Visual artists have depicted the nude
figure for various reasons. The ancient
Greek and Roman nude statues of male
warriors, Michelangelo's powerful *David*
sculpture (1501–4), and Rodin's *The Thinker*
(c. 1886) are all suggestive of the brutal
power of male sexuality. On the other side
of this paradigm, the female body has historically been portrayed as soft, sumptuous,
and submissive, although this has changed
in tandem with changing definitions of
gender in the West.

nursery rhyme
Short, rhymed, traditional poem for children.

Note: The oldest nursery rhymes are those

related to telling time, counting, or the alphabet. The rhyme beginning *Thirty days hath September*, for example, has its origins in a medieval French poem. Like popular songs or ballads, some nursery rhymes have an appeal owing to their musical quality as well as their words: e.g. *London bridge is falling down* probably comes from an old English dance tune. Collections of nursery rhymes began to appear in the 18th century.

O

object
[< Latin OBJECTUS 'a casting before']
1. in grammar, noun or other substantive that directly or indirectly receives the action of a verb, or is governed by a preposition; 2. in philosophy, anything that can be known or perceived by the mind; 3. in semiotics, a synonym for *signified or *referent.

objectification
[< Latin OBIECTUS 'a casting before']
Perception that objects are *signifiers forming an integrated system of meanings.

Note: From the dawn of civilization, objects have been assigned great personal and cultural significance for no apparent reason other than they appeal to people. Gold, for instance, is considered a 'precious metal,' from which all kinds of valuable artifacts continue to be made, from money to wedding rings. Some objects are felt to have magical qualities. If some people find a 'lucky object,' like a penny, they somehow feel that the gods are looking favorably upon them. If, however, they lose some valued object, then they feel that their fate is insecure. The assigning of meanings to objects of all kinds is called *objectification*, which refers to the fact that the connotations objects have are intertwined with the broader system of meanings that constitute the level of culture.

ode
[< Greek OIDĒ 'song']
Poem of some length, usually of a serious or meditative nature and having an elevated style and formal structure.

Note: Among the ancient Greeks, odes were songs performed to the accompaniment of a musical instrument. Pindar (518–438 BC) is considered the greatest lyric poet of Greece and the best-known writer of odes. Roman poets such as Horace (65–8 BC) and Catullus (84?–54? BC) imitated the Greeks' single-voice odes, but they wrote them to be spoken rather than sung. The modern form of the ode dates from the Renaissance; like the Latin ode, it was not intended to have musical accompaniment. Since then, many of the world's great poets have written odes, although its popularity has waned in recent years. Perhaps the best-known ode, worldwide, is the 'Ode to Joy' (1785) by the German poet Friedrich von Schiller (1759–1805), for the reason that it was set to music by the composer Ludwig van Beethoven in his Ninth Symphony.

Ogden, C.K.
[1889–1957]
British psychologist and educator who investigated the effects of particular kinds of *signs and sign systems on perception and cognition. His main contribution in this area is the notion that the meanings of signs are interconnected to each other by association.

olfactory icon
[see *icon]

olfactory image
[see *image, mental]

onomastics
[< Greek ONOMA 'name']
Branch of semiotics and linguistics studying *names.

onomatopoeia

[< Greek ONOMA 'name' + POIEIN 'to make']
Coining of a word in imitation of the natural sound associated with the object or action to which it refers.

Illustrations: 1. *tinkle*; 2. *buzz*; 3. *bang*; 4. *boom*; 5. *swoosh*; 6. *flop.*

ontogenesis

[also called *ontogeny]

ontogeny

[< Greek ONT- 'being' + -GENY 'generation, development']
[see *phylogeny]
1. life cycle of a single organism; 2. biological development of the individual during childhood.

ontological schema

[see *image schema]

ontology

[< Greek ONTOS 'of being' + LOGOS 'word, study']
[see also *metaphysics]
Branch of metaphysics dealing with the nature of being, reality, or ultimate substance.

op art

school of abstract art characterized by the use of geometric shapes and brilliant colors to create optical illusions.

open work

Semiotician Umberto *Eco's notion of a *text with (in theory) an unlimited range of meanings.

Note: The open work, Eco claimed, requires a particular kind of reader, as distinct from the *closed work, which often presupposes an average reader. For instance, reading James Joyce's (1882–1941) *Finnegans Wake*, which is an open work, requires the type of reader who can make up his/her own mind as to its meaning.

opera

[< Latin OPUS 'a work, labor']
Theatrical play having all or most of its *text set to *music and usually characterized by elaborate costuming, scenery, and choreography.

Note: Opera was developed in Italy in the late 16th and early 17th centuries by a group of musicians and scholars who called themselves the *Camerata* (Italian for 'salon'). The Camerata had two chief goals: to revive the musical style used in ancient Greek drama and to develop an alternative to the highly contrapuntal music of the late Renaissance. Specifically, the Camerata musicians wanted composers to pay close attention to the texts on which their music was based, and to make the music reflect, phrase by phrase, the meaning of the text. The Camerata developed a style of vocal music called *monody* (Greek for 'solo song'), consisting of simple melodic lines with contours and rhythms that followed the spoken inflections and rhythms of the language. Two members of the Camerata, Giulio Caccini and Jacopo Peri, realized that monody could be used for soliloquies and dialogues in a staged drama. In 1597, Peri made use of this insight by writing the first true opera, *Dafne*.

The first composer of genius to apply himself to opera was the Italian Claudio Monteverdi (1567–1643). His operas made use not only of the word-centered monodic style but also of songs, duets, choruses, and instrumental sections. Monteverdi thus demonstrated that a wide variety of musical procedures and styles could be used in opera to enhance the drama.

Shortly thereafter, opera spread quickly throughout Italy. The principal Italian opera center up to and including the 17th century was Venice. The next most important were Rome and Naples. In this period a clear differentiation was made between the *aria* (used for emotional reflection) and the *recitativo* (used for plot information and dialogue). Baroque opera was characterized, above all else, by spectacle. The Venetian and Roman audiences loved lavish stage productions and spectacular visual effects, such as storms and descents of the gods from the heavens. Ballet was introduced into the spectacle, not as an intrinsic component of the opera but, typically, as simple diversion between acts or parts.

Perhaps the most important Italian composer of the baroque period was the Sicilian Alessandro Scarlatti (1660–1725), who made virtuosic solo singing a key ingredient of the 'whole show.' The *recitativo-aria* form become standard throughout Italy. In order to advance the story line baroque composers differentiated between two kinds of recitative: *recitativo secco* ('dry recitative'), which was accompanied only by *basso continuo* – a bass line played on chordal instruments (harpsichord, organ, or lute), and sometimes supported by a bass string instrument (cello or viola da gamba) – and *recitativo accompagnato* ('accompanied recitative'), which was used for tense situations and accompanied by the entire orchestra. Baroque composers also introduced the *arioso*, a form that combined aria-like melodic snippets with the conversational rhythms of a recitative.

Throughout the 17th century, the Italian style, with its emphasis on tuneful, entertaining music, had been established in most parts of Europe. The only country where this did not happen was France. There, an Italian-born composer, Jean-Baptiste Lully (1632–87), founded a French school of opera. His patron was Louis XIV. Lully designed his operas to convey the pomp and splendor of the French court. He accomplished this primarily through massive, slow-moving choral and instrumental episodes. Lully also used ballet more prominently than did Italian composers. His texts, known as *libretti* – literally 'little books' – were based on classical French tragedies. But perhaps Lully's greatest contribution was the establishment of a standardized *overture* – the opening orchestral piece that announces the principal melodic themes of the opera, setting the mood for the entire performance.

Italian opera was, however, extremely popular in England. But various English composers of the era became well known for their own brand of opera, the most famous example being *Dido and Aeneas* by Henry Purcell (1659–95). By and large, the operas of English composers were an outgrowth of the English courtly stage spectacles, incorporating French and Italian elements, particularly the instrumental writing of Lully and the emotional arias of the Italian composers.

By the 18th century, opera had become a major art form throughout the world. But, as a consequence, the bulk of operas became rigidly formalized, consisting of little more than a series of spectacular arias based on a *da capo* ('from the beginning') form. Singers were valued more for their beautiful voices and virtuoso singing abilities than for their acting and musicality. Several composers in the 18th century tried to change matters, the most notable being George Frideric Handel (1685–1759), a German-born, Italian-trained musician who did his major work in England. He gave the *da capo* aria form greater flexibility and expressiveness, allowing for sharper delineation of character and more cogent dramatic development. In addition, his orchestral skills enhanced the instrumental texture of this ever-changing musical genre.

Other composers of the time helped develop different forms of the aria, making greater use of choral and instrumental music, and introducing a new type of opera, which came to be known under various names – in England it was called *ballad opera*, in France *opéra comique*, in Germany *Singspiel*, and in Italy *opera buffa*. This was lighter in style than the traditional *opera seria* ('serious opera'). Some of the dialogue was spoken rather than sung, and the plots concerned ordinary people and places rather than mythological characters and settings. Comic operas emphasized naturalness and acting skills, leading to a new *realism* in opera generally.

In Italy it was Giovanni Battista Pergolesi (1710–36), born near Ancona, who excelled at *opera buffa* style. His *Serva padrona* (1733), now considered his masterpiece, gained him universal fame and became a model for comic operas generally. But the composer who transformed Italian *opera buffa* into a 'serious' art form Wolfgang Amadeus Mozart (1756–91), who wrote his first opera, *La finta semplice* (1768), at the age of twelve. His three Italian-language masterpieces – *Le nozze di Figaro* (1786), *Don Giovanni* (1787), and *Così fan tutte* (1790) – display a genius for musical characterization, and in *Don Giovanni* he created one of the first great romantic roles – the Don himself. Mozart's German-language *Singspiels* range from the purely comical, in *The Abduction from the Seraglio* (1782), to the highly spiritual, in *The Magic Flute* (1791).

France, Germany, and Italy developed characteristic operatic styles during the 19th century. In that century, Paris became the center of *grand opera* – a lavish combination of stage spectacle, action, ballet, and music, much of which was written by foreign composers who settled in France. The style reached its climax in the works of such composers as Giacomo Meyerbeer (1791–1864), Hector Berlioz (1803–69), and Charles Gounod (1818–93). German opera's first great 19th-century work was *Fidelio* (1805) by Ludwig van Beethoven (1770–1827), a dramatic *Singspiel* whose theme was the rescue of an unjustly held captive, a plot that became popular during the French Revolution. This was followed by Carl Maria von Weber's (1786–1826) *Der Freischütz* (1821), with its famous supernatural 'Wolf's Glen' scene. The summit of German romantic opera was reached, however, by Richard Wagner (1813–83), who devised a new form called *music drama*, in which the text (written by himself), score, and staging were all blended together. Wagner also perfected the technique of the *leitmotif* (he used the term 'motif of memory'), a musical theme that identifies a particular personage or idea and that recurs throughout the opera in the orchestra, often illuminating the action psychologically. Both this technique and the music-drama form are epitomized in his four-part *Ring* cycle of operas. With his innovations, both in composition and staging, Wagner exerted enormous influence on musicians of all countries for many years.

In Italy, romantic composers continued to place primary emphasis on the voice. Gioacchino Rossini (1792–1868), who composed mainly comic operas such as *Il Barbiere di Siviglia* (1816) and *La Cenerentola* (1817), entrenched the *bel canto* ('beautiful singing') style – characterized by smooth, expressive, and often spectacular singing – into opera. This style also flowered in the works of Vincenzo Bellini (1801–35), especially in *Norma* (1831), *La Sonnambula* (1831), and *I Puritani* (1835), and in Gaetano Donizetti's (1797–1848) works, especially *Lucia di Lammermoor* (1835), *L'Elisir d'amore* (1832), and *Don Pasquale* (1843). However, the composer who embodied romantic Italian opera more than anyone else was Giuseppe Verdi (1813–1901), born near Parma. Verdi infused Italian opera with dramatic emotionalism. His early masterpieces – *Nabucco* (1842), *Ernani* (1844), *Rigoletto* (1851), *Il Trovatore* (1853), *La Traviata* (1853), *Un Ballo in maschera* (1859), and *La Forza del destino* (1862) – have become staples of the repertoire. His *Aida* (1871), with its visual splendor and musical grandiosity, epitomizes what opera is in the mind of most people today. In his last two operas, *Otello* (1887) and *Falstaff* (1893), Verdi adapted the two Shakespearean plays to the operatic stage, emphasizing human passions in a way that has rarely been surpassed.

With the staging of *Carmen* (1875), by the

French composer Georges Bizet (1838–75), opera took on an even stronger realistic thrust towards the late 19th century. Realism in Italian opera became known by the name *verismo*, from the Italian word for 'truth.' The two foremost examples of operatic *verismo* were *Cavalleria rusticana* (1890) by Pietro Mascagni (1863–1945) and *Pagliacci* (1892) by Ruggero Leoncavallo (1858–1919). These are short, searing melodramas about passion and murder in sunbaked southern Italian villages; hence they are often put together on the same operatic bill. But the most important *verista*, the true successor to Verdi, was Giacomo Puccini (1858–1924), who composed such widely known and eminently singable operas as *Manon Lescaut* (1893), *La Bohème* (1896), *Tosca* (1900), *Madama Butterfly* (1904), and the unfinished *Turandot* (produced posthumously, 1926). The works of the German Richard Strauss (1864–1949), which grew out of the lush expressiveness of late romanticism, display rich tonalities, melodious vocal textures, and brilliant orchestral scoring. *Salome* (1905) and *Der Rosenkavalier* (1911) are among his most celebrated works.

Throughout the 20th century, operatic styles reflected national approaches. The Russian Sergei Prokofiev (1891–1953) wrote the piquant *Love for Three Oranges* (1921) while traveling through the American West. Dimitri Shostakovich (1906–75), who frequently fell out of favor with the Soviet government of the day for his musical innovations, composed the well-known *Lady Macbeth of Mtsensk* (1934), which was later revised with the title *Katerina Ismailova* (1963).

Most 20th-century Italian opera remained relatively conservative, although some composers followed radical 'atonal' approaches – as did, for example, Luigi Dallapiccola (1904–75) in *Il prigionero* (1950) and Luigi Nono (1924–90) in *Intolleranza* (1960). But atonal opera reached its peak in German composer Alban Berg's (1885–1935) stark masterpiece,

Wozzeck (1925). In the United States, the influence of jazz and popular American music also asserted itself in masterpieces like *Porgy and Bess* (1935) by George Gershwin (1898–1937), *Four Saints in Three Acts* (1934) and *The Mother of Us All* (1947) by Virgil Thompson (1896–1989), and *Regina* (1949) by Marc Blitzstein (1905–64). The most popular American operas in the 20th century, however, were penned by the Italian-born Gian-Carlo Menotti (1911–), who in 1958 founded the Festival of Two Worlds in Spoleto, Italy; and in 1977 inaugurated an American counterpart of the festival in Charleston, South Carolina, which, beginning in 1994, became a separate festival. Menotti's main operatic works, for which he also wrote the libretti were *Amelia Goes to the Ball* (1936), *The Telephone* (1947), *Amahl and the Night Visitors* (1951) – the first opera written specifically to be performed on television – and *La Loca* (1979).

Today, opera continues to thrive, attracting large audiences. While there are certainly not as many opera composers as in previous eras, the operatic genre still provides an outlet for those who seek to express their musical creativity through the poetry of the human voice.

operating system
[< Latin OPUS 'a work, labor'; Greek SISTEMA 'a placing together']
*Software program designed to control the hardware of a computer in order to allow users to employ it easily.

opponent
[see *actant]

opposition
[< Latin OB 'toward' + PONERE 'to place']
Process by which signs are differentiated through a minimal change in their form.

Illustrations: 1. The two words *sip* and *rip* show a minimal opposition in their first sound, which is enough to differentiate them. 2. The visual signs → and ← show a minimal opposition in their orientation, which is enough to differentiate them.

orientation
[< Latin ORIENS 'rising']
Body posture or position that conveys personal and social meanings.

Illustrations: 1. Standing up at the front of an audience is an orientation that is perceived as more important than sitting down – speeches, lectures, classes, musical performances, etc. are oriented in this way. 2. Sitting behind a desk is an orientation that conveys importance and superiority.

orientation schema
[see *image schema]

orthography
[< Greek ORTHO 'straight' + GRAPHEIN 'to write']
1. spelling of words in accordance with accepted usage; 2. study of writing systems.

otherness
[see *alterity]

output hardware
Hardware that transfers information to the user, such as video displays and printers.

oxymoron
[< Greek OXYMOROS 'acutely silly']
Figure of speech in which opposite or contradictory ideas or terms are combined.

Illustrations: 1. *thunderous silence*; 2. *sweet sorrow*; 3. *jumbo shrimp*.

P

---

painting
[see also *art]
1. art of applying paints to canvases, paper, etc. in order to produce visual representations (scenes, portraits, etc.); 2. picture or composition so produced.

Note: Paintings have been traced back some 30,000 years: e.g. the vivid carvings of animals that covered the roofs and walls of caves like those at Lascaux in France and Altamira in Spain. The human knack for visual representation is innate. Research on children's drawings has shown that at about the same time that children utter their first words they also start scribbling and doodling. The act of drawing in childhood appears to be pleasurable in itself; usually identification of the drawn figures is provided, if at all, only after the child finishes drawing. Of course, shapes eventually suggest 'things' to the child as his/her ability to use language develops, but in the beginning, pleasure and satisfaction occur without larger or more explicit associations of meaning. This form of representational activity in childhood is truly an example of 'art for art's sake.'

painting, perspective
[< Latin PER 'through' + SPECERE 'to look']
Technique of representing three-dimensional objects and depth relationships on a two-dimensional surface.

Illustration: The following figure has been drawn with straight lines drawn on a two-dimensional surface (the page). Yet, our eyes have been conditioned to see it as a three-dimensional box. This is because our eyes have become accustomed to *perspective* representation, the technique by which three-dimensional space can be simulated on a two-dimensional surface:

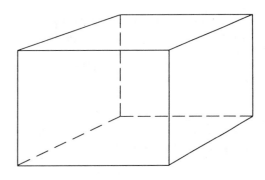

This technique is based on the fact that in visual perception distant objects appear smaller and less distinct than near objects. The flat surface of the painted picture is known as the *picture plane*; the horizon line is the *eye-level line* that divides a scene in the distance; and the *vanishing point* is located on the horizon line, where parallel lines in the scene appear to converge. The person who systematized the technique of perspective drawing was the Italian architect Filippo Brunelleschi (1377–1446), through a series of experimental paintings he made between 1417 and 1420.

Paleolithic art
[see *cave art]

paleontology
[< Greek PALEOS 'ancient' + LOGOS 'word, study']
Field that documents and interprets prehistoric life forms through the study of fossils.

Note: Paleontologists have divided the last 570 million years into the following eras: 1. the *Paleozoic*, lasting about 345 million years (characterized by the appearance of invertebrates, various plants and animals, and, by the end of the period, all the phyla of the animal kingdom, except for vertebrates); 2. the *Mesozoic* era, also known as the *Age of Reptiles*, which lasted about 160 million years (characterized by the appearance of extinct cephalopods called ammonites, dinosaurs, various insects, marsupials, the first placental mammals, and deciduous plants); 3. the *Cenozoic*, which began about 65 million years ago and includes the present (characterized primarily by the appearance of insectivores, primates, rodents, aquatic mammals, modern birds, and humans).

palindrome
[< Greek PALINDROMOS 'running back']
Word, phrase, or sentence that reads the same forward or backward.

Illustrations: 1. *madam* 2. *pop*.

Panini
[c. 400 BC]
Indian grammarian whose *Ashtadhyayi* foreshadows the science of *linguistics. In it, Panini analyzed word-formation in Sanskrit in a precise systematic way, not much differently from how morphologists (word-structure analysts) analyze words today.

pantomime
[< Greek PANTOMIMOS 'a mimic, actor']
1. in ancient Rome, an actor who played a part by gestures and action without words; 2. any theatrical presentation without words, involving only action and gestures.

Note: In the open-air theaters of ancient Greece and Rome, where the audience could see more easily than it could hear, pantomime was an important element of acting. Pantomime was also essential to the *commedia dell'arte*, an improvised comedy style that began in 16th-century Italy. In the 17th and 18th century, the *harlequinade*, an offshoot of the *commedia dell'arte*, which depicted the adventures of Harlequin, his sweetheart, Columbine, and her father, Pantaleone, incorporated pantomime into its style. Actors in early 20th-century silent motion pictures relied mainly on pantomime to convey the story.

parable
[< Greek PARA 'beside' + BALLEIN 'to throw']
1. name given originally by Greek rhetoricians to a literary illustration; 2. in the New Testament a short, fictitious narrative, designed to illuminate a spiritual truth.

Illustration: In the 'Parable of the Sower,' Jesus tells a story about seeds scattered on the ground and left to grow. He later reveals that the scattered seeds represent the people who hear God's word.

paradigm
[< Greek PARA 'beside' + DEIGMA 'example']
In semiotics, structural relation between *signs that keeps them distinct and therefore recognizable.

Note: Signs bear meanings in *structured* ways. In pairs such as *pin-bin, fun-run,* and *duck-luck,* the initial consonant of each word is sufficient to keep them distinct. This differentiation feature of signs is known as *paradigmatic* structure, which is the relation whereby some minimal feature in a sign is sufficient to keep it differentiated from all other signs of the same kind. These words are legitimate signs, not only because they reveal paradigmatic structure, but also because the combination of sounds with which they are constructed is consistent with English syllable structure. The latter is an example of *syntagmatic* structure – the relation whereby signs are assembled in some definable sequence or combination.

In essence, something is a sign or text if it has both a discernible (repeatable and predictable) shape or form (= paradigmatic structure) and if it is constructed in a definable (patterned) way (= syntagmatic structure).

paradox
[< Greek PARA 'beside' + DOXA 'opinion']
1. statement that seems contradictory, unbelievable, or absurd but that may be true in fact; 2. statement that is self-contradictory and, hence, false; 3. circular statement.

Illustration: A classic example of a logical paradox is the liar paradox, formulated by the ancient Greek poet Epimenides in the 6th century BC. It has come down to us more or less in the following form. A Cretan philosopher once said: 'All Cretans are liars.' Did the philosopher speak the truth? Because the philosopher is himself a Cretan, his statement leads to a circularity. Here's why. The philosopher is a Cretan. Therefore he is a liar. So, his statement is false. What is his statement? All Cretans are liars. But, then, the statement is true. Cretans are indeed all liars. So, the philosopher is not a liar after all. He told the truth. But, then, his statement leads us to conclude that the philosopher is both a liar and not a liar, which is logically impossible.

parallelism
[< Greek PARA 'beside' + ALLELOS 'other']
Use of a parallel structure in speech and writing.

Illustrations: 1. *I am the king, I am the monarch.* 2. *Ted is the champion, he is the victor.*

parallel processing theory
[see *connectionism]

parameter
[< Greek PARA 'beside' + METRON 'measure']
1. quantity or constant whose value varies with the circumstances of its application; 2. term used by linguists to designate a constraint on the development of grammar imposed by culture.

paraphrase
[< Greek PARAPHRAZEIN 'to say in other words']
Rewording of something spoken or written.

Illustrations: 1. *He is a snake*: paraphrase: *He is a dangerous, slippery, disgusting person.* 2. *She's feeling up today*: paraphrase: *She's in a good mood and is feeling happy today.*

parody
[< Greek PARA 'beside' + OIDE 'song']
Work imitating the characteristic style of someone or some other work in a satirical or humorous way.

Note: For the ancient Greeks, parody was a comic imitation of a serious poem. The essence of parody is the treatment of a light theme in the style that is imitative of a serious work 'The Nun's Priest's Tale' from *The Canterbury Tales* by the 14th-century English writer Geoffrey Chaucer (1340?–1400) is a classic example. In this tale the hubbub caused by Master Reynard the fox in the widow's barnyard is described in language suggestive of the fall of Troy. In parody, the theme and the characters are greatly modified or completely changed, but the style of the original is closely followed in those peculiarities that easily lend themselves to ridicule.

parole
[French for 'word']
[see also *langue* vs. *parole*]
Term used by Ferdinand de *Saussure to refer to the use of a language for various purposes, such as communication.

participant observation
[see *ethnography]

PASCAL
[after French mathematician and philosopher Blaise Pascal (1623–62)]
Concise procedural computer programming language, designed 1967–71 by Niklaus Wirth, used widely during the 1970s and the early 1980s. PASCAL now is losing ground to C (see *C-language) as a standard development language for microcomputers.

pathetic fallacy
[< Greek PATHOS 'suffering, disease, feeling'; Latin FALLACIA 'deception']
Attribution of human feelings and characteristics to inanimate things.

Illustrations: 1. *the angry sea;* 2. *a stubborn door.*

pathos
[< Greek PATHOS 'suffering, disease, feeling']
Aspect of a real situation or in a literary or artistic work that evokes sympathy, sorrow, or pity.

Pavlov, Ivan
[1849–1936]
Russian physiologist who developed the first contemporary theory of human learning – the theory of *classical conditioning* – from experiments with dogs. Pavlov presented a meat stimulus to a hungry dog, causing the animal to salivate spontaneously. This was the dog's 'unconditioned response.' Then, after Pavlov rang a bell while presenting the meat stimulus a number of times, he found that the dog would eventually salivate to the ringing bell alone,

without the meat stimulus. Clearly, the ringing, which did not trigger the salivation initially, had brought about a 'conditioned response' in the dog. Pavlov's experiments thus led, shortly thereafter, to the first true psychological theory of learning, known as 'conditioning theory' and, a little later, as 'association theory.'

Peirce, Charles Sanders
[1839–1914]
American philosopher, logician, and mathematician who, along with Ferdinand de *Saussure, is considered one of the founders of modern-day *semiotic method. Born in Cambridge, Massachusetts, Peirce was educated at Harvard University, and lectured on logic and philosophy at Johns Hopkins and Harvard Universities. He expanded the system of logic created by the British mathematician George *Boole, but is best known for his philosophical system, later called *pragmatism*, which maintains that the significance of any theory or model lies in the practical effects of its application, and for his typology of *signs. Peirce defined semiotics as the 'doctrine' of signs. The word *doctrine* was not used by Peirce in its religious sense, but rather in its basic meaning of 'system of principles.'

Peircean theory of the sign
American philosopher Charles *Peirce's theory of the *sign as consisting of a *representamen* (= literally 'something that does the representing'), referring to some *object* (= whatever the representamen calls attention to), eliciting a meaning, called the *interpretant* (= whatever it means to someone in some context).

Note: Peirce described three kinds of *representamina* in human representational systems. He called these *qualisigns, sinsigns,* and *legisigns*. A *qualisign* is a representamen that draws attention to, or singles out, some *quality* of its referent. In language, an adjective is a qualisign since it draws attention to the qualities (color, shape, size, etc.) of referents. In other codes, qualisigns include the colors used by painters, the harmonies and tones used by composers, etc. A *sinsign* is a representamen that draws attention to, or singles out, a particular object in time-space: e.g. a pointing finger, the words *here* and *there*, etc. A *legisign* is a representamen that designates something by convention: e.g. words referring to abstract concepts, mathematical symbols, etc.

Peirce then pointed out that there were three kinds of *objects* (or *referents*). A referent that has been represented through some form of replication, simulation, or resemblance is an *icon:* e.g. a photo resembles its referent visually, a word such as *bang* resembles its referent phonically, and so on. A referent that has been represented through some form of indication is an *index:* e.g. a pointing index finger is an indication of where an object is in space, smoke is an indication of a fire source, and so on. A referent that has been represented conventionally is a *symbol:* e.g. a *rose* is a symbol of love in some cultures, words such as *love* and *hope* refer by convention to various emotions or concepts, and so on.

Peirce suggested, moreover, that there were three types of *interpretants* (= what the sign-user or sign-interpreter intends with, or gets from, a specific kind of sign): a *rheme* is an interpretant of a qualisign (i.e. the kind of meaning that is extractable from a qualisign); a *dicisign* is an interpretant of a sinsign; and an *argument* is an interpretant of a legisign.

pen name
[see *pseudonym]

percept
[< Latin PER 'through' + CAPERE 'to seize']
Recognizable sensation or impression received by the mind through the senses; namely, a unit of perception.

perception
[< Latin PER 'through' + CAPERE 'to seize']
Discernment of objects, qualities, etc. by means of the senses.

Note: According to classical perception theory, most *percepts* (= units of perception) result from a person's ability to synthesize past experience, relating it to current sensory cues. As a newborn explores its world, it soon learns to organize what it sees into a three-dimensional pattern. Using sensory cues (visual, tactile, auditory, etc.), the infant quickly learns to perceive that there exist specific percepts that correspond to the properties of objects in the physical world. Proponents of the classical theory of perception believe that most percepts are derived by an unconscious inferencing process.

performance
[< Old French PARFOURNIR 'complete thoroughly']
1. formal exhibition or presentation before an audience, of a play, a musical program, etc.; 2. representation and communication of some text, framed in a special way and put on display for an audience; 3. in linguistics, the actual use of language in concrete situations.

perlocutionary act
[< Latin PER 'through' + LOCUTIO 'a speaking']
Speech act that involves a request for some action.

Illustrations: 1. *Come here!* 2. *Don't say that!*

persona
[< Greek PERSONA 'mask']
1. voice or character representing the speaker in a literary work; 2. character in a dramatic or literary work; 3. in psychoanalysis, role that one assumes or displays in society as distinguished from the inner self.

Note: Personality usually refers to what is unique about a person, *persona* to what the individual shows about himself/herself in public settings. One of the most influential theoretical systems differentiating between personality and persona is *psychoanalysis. Sigmund *Freud, for instance, believed that unconscious processes direct much of people's behavior. Carl *Jung, by contrast, argued that an individual's personality varies with the situation.

personal deixis
[see *deixis]

personal unconscious
[see *unconscious, personal]

personal zone
[see *zone, personal]

personification
[< Greek PERSONA 'mask']
Portrayal or characterization of inanimate objects, animals, or abstract ideas as if they were human beings.

Illustrations: 1. *Hunger sat shivering on the street.* 2. *The roses danced about the lawn.* 3. *My cat speaks German.*

perspective
[< Latin PER 'through' + SPECERE 'to look']
[see also *painting, perspective]
Art of representing objects or a scene in such a way as to show how they would appear to the eye in real three-dimensional space.

perspective painting
[see *painting, perspective]

persuasion techniques in advertising
[see *advertising, use of persuasion techniques in]

petroglyph
[< Greek PETRA 'rock' + GLYPHĒ 'carving']
Carving or line drawing on rocks or cave walls, especially one made by prehistoric people.

phatic function
[< Greek PHATOS 'spoken']
In Roman *Jakobson's model of communication, function of discourse characterized by formulaic talk, serving to establish social contact rather than to communicate ideas.

Illustrations: 1. *Hi, how's it going?* 2. *What's happening?*

phenomenology
[< Greek PHAINOMENON 'appearance']
Twentieth-century philosophical movement aiming to describe the forms and manifestations of experience as they present themselves to consciousness, without recourse to any theoretical or explanatory framework.

Note: The founder of phenomenology was the German philosopher Edmund *Husserl, who described the abstract content of mental activities such as remembering, desiring, and perceiving as meanings that enabled someone to direct an act towards an object. German philosopher Martin *Heidegger claimed that phenomenology was particularly useful for explaining the structure of everyday experience. In the mid-20th century French existentialist Jean-Paul Sartre (1905–80) agreed with Husserl that consciousness is always directed at objects, but criticized his claim that such directedness is possible only through special mental entities called meanings. Today, phenomenology remains an important movement within philosophy attracting many adherents (see also *Merleau-Ponty, Maurice).

phenotype
[< Greek PHAINEN 'to show' Greek + TYPOS 'a figure']
[see also *genotype]
Salient characteristics of an organism, including anatomical and perceptual traits, that result from both its heredity and its environment.

philology

[< Greek PHILEIN 'to love' + LOGOS 'word']
Science that studies written texts in order to determine their meaning, to analyze their language, and to establish their value in the history of a culture.

Note: In the 19th century, this term was used specifically to designate the general study of language (oral and written), especially the patterns of change that characterized specific languages and language generally. In the 20th century, the purview of philology was refined to the activities of reconstructing and analyzing the texts of imperfect or mutilated manuscripts and inscriptions, often by comparing variant readings in surviving copies of lost texts.

philosophy

[< Greek PHILOSOPHOS 'lover of wisdom']
Theory or logical analysis of the principles underlying conduct, thought, knowledge, and the nature of the universe.

phoneme

[< Greek PHONĒ 'voice, sound']
Unit of sound in language that native speakers recognize as distinctive in the comprehension and production of words.

Note: What keeps words such as *sip* and *zip* distinct is a difference between *s* and *z*: the former is articulated without vibration, and hence called *voiceless* /s/; the second is articulated with vibration and is thus called *voiced* /z/. The two sounds are otherwise articulated in the same way. This difference is said to be *phonemic* because it is the feature that keeps words such as *sip* vs. *zip* or *sap* vs. *zap* distinct.

Phonemic distinctions are perceived by the hearing center of the brain and actualized through its motor pathways via a complex system of coordination between brain and vocal organs. There are twelve cranial nerves. Seven of these link the brain with the vocal organs. Some perform a motor function, controlling the movement of muscles, while others perform a sensory function, sending signals to the brain. The larynx controls the flow of air to and from the lungs, so as to prevent food, foreign objects, or other substances from entering the trachea on their way to the stomach. The ability to control the vocal folds makes it possible to build up pressure within the lungs and to emit air not only for expiration purposes, but also for the production of sound.

phonetics

[< Greek PHONĒ 'voice, sound']
[see also *acoustic phonetics; *articulatory phonetics, *auditory phonetics]
Branch of linguistics concerned with the classification and description of speech sounds.

Note: The main subfields of phonetics are *articulatory*, *acoustical*, and *auditory*. Articulatory phonetics is concerned with describing the ways whereby the vocal organs modify the airstream in the mouth, nose, and throat in order to produce speech sounds; acoustical phonetics is concerned with describing the characteristics of speech waves; and auditory phonetics is concerned with how speech sounds are perceived by the human ear.

phonology

[< Greek PHONĒ 'voice, sound' + LOGOS 'word']
1. system of sounds in a language; 2. systematic study of linguistic sound systems.

Note: Linguists distinguish *phonetic analysis* from *phonological analysis*. The former is concerned with cataloguing and describing the raw speech sounds that humans are capable of making; the latter is concerned instead with studying the ways in which these sounds are used by the languages of the world to create words and meanings.

photograph

[< Greek PHOS 'light' + GRAPHĒ 'drawing']
Image recorded by a camera and reproduced on a photosensitive surface.

photographic art

[< Greek PHOS 'light' + GRAPHĒ 'drawing']
Art involving representation with photography.

Note: The first chapter in the history of photographic art was written in the 1860s by the Englishman Henry Peach Robinson (1830–1901), who pioneered the method of creating one print from several different negatives. Portraits made by Robinson's compatriot Julia Margaret Cameron (1815–79) were designed to emulate the painting styles of her era. English-American photographer Edward Muybridge (1830–1904) developed photographic art by capturing images of animals and people in motion.

The approach to photography as a substitute for the pictorial arts was also challenged by English photographer Peter Henry Emerson (1856–1936), who believed photography to be an art in itself, independent of painting. In 1902 Alfred Stieglitz (1864–1946), an American photographer whose work put into practice Emerson's views, founded the *Photo-Secession movement*, which championed photography as an independent art form. After the Photo-Secessionists disbanded, Stieglitz organized important photo exhibitions at his gallery, 291, in New York City.

The counter-orthodox notions of the *dada movement found photographic expression in the work of artists László Moholy-Nagy (1895–1946) of Hungary and Man Ray (1890–1976) of the United States. In the 1930s, several California photographers formed the *Group f/64* (f/64 is the lens aperture that gives great depth of field), developing a style based on straightforward images of natural objects, people, and landscapes. In the 1950s a tendency towards introspection characterized the work of such photographers as Americans Minor White (1908–76) and Aaron Siskind (1903–91). Beginning in the 1960s photographers started reviving many earlier printing devices, making composite prints, retouching, and painting over photographs. The best-known champion of this style is William Wegman (1943–).

photography

[< Greek PHOS 'light' + GRAPHĒ 'drawing']
Process of producing images of objects on photosensitive surfaces by means of a camera.

Photo-Secession movement

[see *photographic art]

phylogenesis

[see *phylogeny]

phylogeny

[< Greek PHYLON 'tribe' + -GENY 'generation, development']
[also called phylogenesis; see also *ontogeny]
1. term referring to the evolutionary development and history of any plant or animal species (e.g. the *phylogenesis* of the human species); 2. term referring to the evolutionary development of any system or process (e.g. the *phylogenesis* of language).

physical anthropology

[see *anthropology, physical]

physicalism

[< Greek PHYSIS 'nature']
View that all psychic reality, including human emotions and intelligence, can be studied and understood in terms of physical processes.

Note: Although it has ancient roots, this view became widespread in Western theories of mind with the advent of Darwinian

photo 175

evolutionary biology in the 19th century. Physicalists view human consciousness as a product of evolutionary processes. Even human rituals and peculiar behaviors such as kissing and flirting, for instance, are explained as modern-day reflexes of animal mechanisms.

phytosemiosis
[< Greek PHYTON 'plant' + SEMEION 'sign']
*Semiosis (sign processes) in plants.

Illustrations: 1. pollination; 2. budding.

phytosemiotics
[< Greek PHYTON 'plant' + SEMEION 'sign']
Branch of *semiotics studying *semiosis in plants.

Piaget, Jean
[1896–1980]
Swiss psychologist, best known for his work on the development of mental skills in children. Piaget divided human development into four stages: 1. the *sensorimotor stage*, which lasts up to age 2, is marked by the gaining of motor control and learning about physical objects; 2. the *preoperational stage*, from ages 2 to 7, is characterized by the development of verbal skills; 3. the *concrete operational stage*, from 7 to 12, is distinguished by the emergence of highly abstract concepts; 4. the *formal operational stage*, from 12 to 15, is marked by the advent of the ability to reason logically and systematically.

picaresque novel
[see *novel]

pictogram
[see *pictograph]

pictograph
[< Latin PICTURA 'drawing' + GRAPHĒ 'drawing']
1. picture or picture-like symbol represent-

ing an idea; 2. diagram of an object conveying an idea, information, etc.

Illustrations: 1. •• •• = footprints;

2. 🖌 = wet paint.

pictoreme
[< Latin PICTURA 'drawing']
Minimal unit of visual representation (a line or shape). Pictoremes can be straight, round, curved, etc. and used in various combinations to make up all kinds of recognizable forms.

Illustrations: The circle and line are two kinds of pictoremes that can be conjoined in several ways to create figures of different kinds.

1. dumbbells   2. eyeglasses

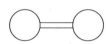

picture plane
[see *painting, perspective]

pidgin
[see also *creole]
Language that results from contact with a dominant language, adapting and simplifying its forms.

Note: Pidgins have a much smaller vocabulary (often 700 to 2000 words) and fewer grammar categories than the dominant language. Pidgins develop when people who speak different languages are brought together and required to develop a common means of communication without having sufficient time to learn each other's native languages.

Plato
[c. 428–347 BC]
One of the most famous philosophers of all time, Plato was the first to use the term *philosophy*, meaning 'love of wisdom.' Chief among his ideas was the Doctrine of Forms

(see *Platonic Forms), by which he proposed that objects in the physical world merely resemble perfect forms innate in the mind. Plato soundly rejected the claim that knowledge is derived from sense experience. True knowledge, he claimed, is attained through the use of reason.

Plato wrote his books in dialogue form, with *Socrates as a central participant, so that ideas could be discussed and criticized through imaginary conversation or debate. His writings include the *Republic*, the *Apology* (Socrates' defense of himself at his trial against the charges of atheism and corrupting Athenian youth), *Phaedo* (the death scene of Socrates, in which he discusses the Doctrine of Forms), and the *Symposium*. Plato's ideas have had a crucial role in the development of modern ideas and science.

Platonic forms

*Plato's view that patterns of thought existed on two levels: one inhabited by invisible ideas or forms, and another by concrete familiar objects. The latter are imperfect copies of the ideas because they are always in a state of flux.

Note: Plato rejected any philosophy that claimed to explain knowledge on the basis of sensory experience. For Plato true knowledge was attained by reasoning about Ideal Forms. A *circle*, for instance, is an Ideal Form that no one has ever seen in Nature. What people actually see are approximations of the ideal circle. When geometers define a circle as a series of points equidistant from a given point, they are referring, in effect, to logical ideas, not actual points. 'Circularity' is an innate mental Form that has greater reality than do circular objects. An object existing in the physical world may be called a 'circle' insofar as it resembles the Form 'circularity.'

Plato's Cave

In his *Republic*, *Plato portrayed humanity as imprisoned in a cave where it mistook shadows on the wall for reality. Only the person with the opportunity to escape from the cave – the true philosopher – had the perspicacity to see the real world outside. The shadowy environment of the cave symbolizes the realm of physical appearances. This contrasts with the perfect world of ideas outside.

play

[see *drama]

plot

[Old English for 'piece of land']
1. unfolding of events in a *narrative;
2. main story of a piece of writing (novel, play, etc.)

Note: The *plot* of a novel is what happens to whom, how it happens, when it happens, etc.

Plotinus

[AD 205–270]
Egyptian-born Roman philosopher who believed that art reveals the form of an object more precisely than ordinary experience does, thus raising the mind to a mystic contemplation of the universal forms of existence. Plotinus's works include 54 treatises in Greek, called the *Enneads*.

poem

[< Greek POIEIN 'to make']
Arrangement of words written or spoken in *verse form, expressing experiences, ideas, or emotions in a style more concentrated, imaginative, and powerful than that of ordinary speech or *prose.

poetic function

[< Greek POIEIN 'to make']
In Roman *Jakobson's model of communication, tailoring a message to deliver meanings effectively.

Illustrations: 1. *Roses are red, violets are blue, and how's it going with you?* 2. *He likes bikes.*

poetic logic
[< Greek POIEIN 'to make'; LOGOS 'word']
Term used by philosopher Giambattista
*Vico referring to the innate capacity of all
human beings to invent symbols, expressions, etc. to represent the world that show
direct connection with the properties of the
sensible world.

poetics
[< Greek POIEIN 'to make']
Branch of *semiotics and literary criticism
concerned with the study of *poetry and
poetic communication generally.

poetry
[< Greek POIEIN 'to make']
Art of writing *poems, characterized by
the use of *meter, *verse, and *rhyme and
thus based on the acoustic, rhythmic, and
imagistic properties of words. Poetry is
divided into *lyric*, *narrative* (including *epics*,
ballads, *metrical romances*, and *verse tales*),
and *dramatic* (direct speech in specified
circumstances).

Note: Poetry and music are two sides of the
same evolutionary coin. Although poetry
eventually gained an independent existence
in some cultures, in others the two are still
conceived as identical. Poetry began as a
form of ritualistic communal expression of
the religious spirit, in tandem with chanting
and dancing. This original function has left
its residues in gospel and other forms of
religious singing, as well as in the fact that,
to this day, the poet like the shaman is considered a soothsayer, a prophet, the conscience of a society. Wherever poetry exists
apart from music, it has substituted its own
purely linguistic rhythms for musical
rhythms. The poet's words reverberate in
our minds, stimulating in us latent memories of how primordial attempts at meaning
making must have 'sounded.'

Most English poetry is *iambic*, i.e. made
up of divisions that alternate an unstressed
and a stressed syllable in rising rhythm.

Lines in poetry are frequently connected by
rhyme into *stanzas* that typically have a
traditional form or structure. Poets may use
other techniques besides rhyme to structure
stanzas. A poet writing in a language in
which pitch is *phonemic, such as Chinese,
can create patterns of contrast and repetition that are impossible to form in English.
Stressed syllables may be linked by repeat-
ing their initial consonants, a form of *alliteration. In poetry, the sound shapes the
sense to a much greater degree than in
prose. The position of a word in the line, a
shift in meter, and the use of rhyme and
sound echoes to highlight key words are
tools relatively unavailable to the prose
writer. A poem generally has a very different rhythm from that of ordinary literary
prose.

The poems, stories, and plays that individuals throughout the world have created,
and continue to create, are testaments to the
need for poetic art in human life. Poets use
words to reproduce natural sounds, to
evoke feelings, to provide insight into the
intrinsic nature of things. The philosopher
Giambattista *Vico saw poetry as the primordial form of language. He called the
first speakers 'poets,' because they formed a
concept poetically as the image of a god or a
hero – e.g. the ancient Greeks formed the
concept of 'valor' poetically through the
character of the hero Achilles in the *Iliad*.
This same pattern is noticeable in children,
who invariably acquire concepts in poetic
ways – through reading about god-like
and heroic story characters who embody
them.

pointillism
[< French POINTILLE 'dot']
Method of painting, in which a white
ground is systematically covered with tiny
points of pure color that blend together
when seen from a distance, producing a
luminous effect.

Illustration: The best examples of pointillist style can be seen in the works of the post-impressionist Georges Seurat (1859–91) and his followers in late 19th-century France.

political map

[see *map]

Polo, Marco

[c. 1254–1324]

Italian adventurer who became fascinated by the customs of the peoples he met on his travels through China and other parts of Asia. His chronicles of his voyages provided medieval Europeans with a wide range of information about the cultures of the Far East. To this day, his diary remains perhaps the most famous and influential travel book in history. With a wealth of vivid detail, Marco Polo gave medieval Europe its first glimpse into the culture of the Eastern world. His work also became the source for some of the first maps of Asia made in Europe. And it helped to arouse in Christopher Columbus (1451–1506) an interest in the Orient that culminated in 1492 with his exploration of America, while attempting to reach the Far East by sailing due west from Europe, as Polo had suggested. The all-sea route from Europe to the Far East around Africa outlined in Polo's book was verified by the Portuguese navigator Vasco da Gama (1460?–1524) in 1497–8.

polychrome

[< Greek POLY 'many' + CHROMA 'color']
Made or decorated in various colors.

polyphony

[< Greek POLY 'many' + PHONE 'voice, sound']
Music with two or more independent *melodic parts sounded together.

polysemy

[< Greek POLY 'many' + SEMA 'signs']
Process by which a *sign bears multiple meanings.

Illustration: The word *play* is polysemous because it has distinct meanings: e.g. 1. to occupy oneself in amusement, sport, or other recreation (*playing with toys*); 2. to take part in a game (*No minors are eligible to play*); 3. to act in jest or sport (*They're not serious about it, they're just playing*); 4. a dramatic production (*That was a great play we saw the other night*); 5. to perform on an instrument (*Can you play Beethoven's piano sonatas?*); 6. to be received or accepted (*That was a speech that played poorly with the voters*); 7. to unfold (*Let's see how it plays out*).

polytonality

[<Greek POLY 'many' + TONOS 'a stretching']
Simultaneous use of two or more *tonalities in a musical composition.

pop art

[abbreviation of *popular art*]
Visual-art movement that began in the 1950s, principally in the United States and Great Britain, whereby scenes and objects from mass culture were represented in painting or sculpture, sometimes with actual objects incorporated into the artwork.

Note: This movement began as a reaction against the abstract art style of the 1940s and 1950s. Pop artists sought to depict everyday life and to provide an impersonal and immediate perception of reality. Pop-art practice was expanded in the 1960s to include brand-name commercial products, fast-food items, and comic-strip frames in art displays and forms. Several pop artists produced *happenings*, or theatrical events staged as art objects. Perhaps the best-known exponent of pop art was the American artist Andy Warhol (1928–87).

pop culture

[abbreviation of *popular culture*]
Form of culture, characteristic of 20th-century technological societies, that emphasizes the trivial and the routine in its artistic and

various other forms of representation. Pop culture includes television programs, advertising, comic books, popular music (rock n' roll, hip hop, etc.), fashion, and the like.

Popper's Worlds 1,2,3

Interconnectionist model of the relation between the brain (World 1), thought (World 2), and culture (World 3) put forward by the philosopher Karl Popper (1902–94).

Note: Popper classified human experience into three 'worlds.' 'World 1' is the experience of physical objects and states as processed by neuronal synapses – electrical impulses between brain cells – transmitting messages along nerve paths that cause muscles to contract or limbs to move, and sensory systems to respond to perceptual input. 'World 2' is the domain of subjective experiences related to these messages. This is the level at which the concept of self emerges, and where perception, planning, remembering, dreaming, and imagining shape the individual's experience. 'World 3' is the domain of culture-specific knowledge that mediates the individual's worldview.

portrait

[< Latin PROTRAHERE 'to draw forth']
Artistic or photographic depiction of a person, focusing on the face.

Note: The first portraits, dating from about 3100 BC in Egypt, were stone carvings of pharaohs seated in rigid poses, conveying eternal authority. Later portraits were more naturalistic. The earliest Greek portrait busts, dating from the 5th century BC, are vivid and lifelike, although they were frequently idealized. Roman sculptors captured the individuality of their subjects with great skill. In China portraits are found as early as the Han Dynasty (206 BC–AD 220). The Chinese artists used clothing and pose to convey the subject's character. Japanese portraits, mainly commemorating Buddhist monks, were first produced in the Nara period (AD 710–84). Portraiture has also played a significant role in African and Native American cultures. The stone heads by the Maya, for example, display powerful images of individuality. Throughout the region of Oceania, representation of the human form plays a large role in art. In that society, skulls are remolded with the original facial features of an ancestor and are used for commemoration and consultation.

Early Christian art, from the 3rd to the 7th century AD, included mosaic and sculpted portraits of the deceased. Medieval gospel books often contained flat, sometimes formulaic, portraits of the gospel authors. During the Renaissance, artists made portrait busts of those who commissioned them. The first self-portraits in Western art developed during this period, when artists started depicting their own faces. During the 17th and 18th centuries, portrait art became even more important. Many of those who had their portraits made did so to put on display their power and wealth, and to assert authority. In the 19th century, romantic artists painted portraits of moody subjects. Early in the 20th century, many painters made psychological studies of subjects through portraiture. But portrait production declined in the middle of the 20th century, a result of the increasing interest in abstraction and non-representational art. Early photographic portraits at the turn of the 20th century were stilted and formal, requiring long, laborious sittings, but as technology advanced, photographers started to experiment creatively with photographic portraiture to explore personality through the many expressions and moods of the human face.

pose

[< Latin PAUSARE 'to place, put']
Bodily position that conveys something about the person's mood, attitude, social class, etc.

positioning

[< Latin PAUSARE 'to place, put']
Placing or targeting of a product for the appropriate market segment.

Illustrations: 1. The perfume *Drakkar Noir* is positioned for a male audience, *Chanel* for a female audience. 2. The marketing of *Audis* and *BMWs* is aimed at upper-class, or aspiring up-scale consumers, the marketing of *Dodge vans* at middle-class suburban dwellers.

positron emission tomography

[abbreviated to PET]
Brain-scanning technique developed in the 1970s for mapping and collecting data on brain functioning, by providing images of brain activities.

postmodern architecture

[see *architecture, postmodern]

postmodern art

[see *art, postmodern]

postmodernism

[literally 'after the modern']
Movement in philosophy and the arts that took hold in the latter part of the 20th century, attacking traditions and value systems as being concoctions of human fancy rather than systems reflecting a teleological purpose. The term *postmodernism* was coined by architects to designate an architectural response against the earlier *Bauhaus style (characterized by box-like skyscrapers, tall apartment buildings, etc.), which had degenerated into sterile and monotonous formulas, reintroducing traditional or classical elements of architectural design in an eclectic way. Postmodern architects called for greater individuality, complexity, and eccentricity in design, while also demanding acknowledgment of historical precedent and continuity – through an innovative reinterpretation of traditional ornamental symbols and patterns. Shortly after its adoption in architecture, the notion of *postmodernism* started to catch on more broadly, becoming a more general movement in philosophy and the arts.

Note: One of the first writers to prefigure postmodern technique was the Irish-born playwright and novelist Samuel Beckett (1906–89), a leading figure of the movement known as the 'theater of the absurd.' In his novels and plays, Beckett focused on the wretchedness of living in an attempt to expose the essence of the human condition, which he ultimately reduced to the solitary self, or to nothingness. His late 1940s play (published in 1952) *Waiting for Godot* is a remarkable work of dramatic art in more ways than one. Above all else, it reflected, in the theatrical medium, an emerging form of artistic representation that a few decades later would be called *postmodern*. People reacted strongly to the play, which became an instant classic of the Western theater. It caught the modern imagination because, like the two tramps it portrays, people in the late 20th century seemed to have literally 'lost faith,' having become skeptical and cynical about the 'meaning' of human existence. Even today, *Godot* challenges our ingrained belief that there is a 'meaning to life,' insinuating that all our meaning structures and systems (language, religious concepts, etc.) are no more than illusory screens we have set up to avoid the 'truth' – that life is an absurd moment of consciousness on its way to extinction.

Many trace the roots of the postmodern outlook to the advent of evolutionary theory in the 19th century, when British biologist Charles *Darwin introduced the controversial notion of *natural selection. Darwin claimed that each generation of a species improves adaptively over the preceding generations, and that this gradual and continuous process was the source of the species's evolution as a whole. Natural selection was only part of Darwin's radical theory; he also introduced the idea that all organisms are descended from common ancestors.

The most publicized and scathing attacks on Darwin's ideas came at first not from academia but, understandably, from the religious sphere. The very thought that human beings could have evolved through natural processes denied, to the shocked minds of the religious people of the era, the special creation of humankind by God and seemed to place humanity on a plane with brute animals. Simply put, Darwin's ideas posed a serious challenge to the Christian narrative. But the potency of the early religious opposition to evolutionary theory was weakened by a discovery made, ironically, by an Augustinian monk, Gregor Johann Mendel (1822–84). Mendel cultivated and tested more than 28,000 pea plants. His tedious experiments showed, for instance, that by crossing tall and dwarf parents of peas hybrid offspring would result that resembled the tall parent rather than being a medium-height blend. To explain this he conceived of hereditary units, now called *genes*, which he claimed were responsible for passing on dominant or recessive characteristics.

The final damaging blow to any religiously motivated opposition to Darwin's theory came in 1953, nearly a century after the publication of his *On the Origin of Species*, when biologists James Watson (1928–) and Francis Crick (1916–) demonstrated that the genetic fabric of all organisms is composed of two nucleic-acids, deoxyribonucleic acid (DNA) and ribonucleic acid (RNA). Nucleic acid molecules contain genetic codes that dictate the manufacture of proteins, and the latter direct the biochemical pathways of development and metabolism in an organism. Watson and Crick's work showed that mutations in the position of a gene in its molecular chain, or in the information coded in the gene, can affect the function of the protein for which the gene is responsible. Natural selection operates by favoring or suppressing a particular gene according to how strongly its protein product contributes to the reproductive success of the organism. In a phrase, the discovery of DNA and RNA verified, conclusively, that physical evolution is a matter of genetic reorganization, not of Divine will.

By the end of the 19th century, the now famous assertion by German philosopher Friedrich *Nietzsche that 'God is dead' acknowledged the paradigm shift that Darwinian evolutionary theory had brought about. Nietszche meant, of course, that the grip which the Christian worldview had on Western society had finally become loosened. By the middle part of the 20th century, the critique of all aspects of that worldview had started in full earnest.

With the advent of TV and advertising in the 1950s, a new secular, consumerist outlook and lifestyle took hold of the modern imagination. Viewing the world through a television camera or through advertisements leads to a gazing upon the world as if it were a montage of purposeless skits, docudramas, or commercials.

Above all else, postmodernism in art and philosophy is an outlook questioning traditional assumptions about certainty, identity, and truth, based on the belief that words can only refer to other words, and that statements about anything subvert their own meanings. In postmodern art, there is no meaning to be found in the actual text, but only in the various, often mutually irreconcilable, interpretations of readers in their search for meaning. Postmodern art assails the traditional assumptions we have about the nature of texts: that language can express ideas without changing them, that writing is secondary to speech, and that a text's author is the source of its meaning.

Postmodernism is, according to many, an outgrowth of the mid-20th-century dramatic genre known as *absurdism*. Absurdist art tended to eliminate much of the cause-and-effect relationship among events, reduce language to a game and minimize its communicative power, reduce characters to archetypes, make place nonspecific, and portray the world as alienating and incomprehensible. Human history has no beginning or end. Human beings fulfill no particular purpose in being alive.

postmodernity
[literally 'after the modern']
Generally a synonym for *postmodernism, but sometimes used to refer to the state of the world, rather than to the artistic or philosophical aspects of the postmodern movement.

poststructuralism
[literally 'after structuralism']
Anti-structuralist movement in *semiotics based on a denial of the fundamental structuralist tenet that human signifying systems, including culture, manifest regularity, systematicity, patterning, predictability, and, above all else, a central system of meanings.

Note: The poststructuralist trend was started by the psychoanalyst Jacques *Lacan and the philosopher Jacques *Derrida. In structuralism *signs are implicitly assumed to be the bearers of innate meaning structures; in poststructuralism it is claimed that only the individual maker of meanings is the central agent in all forms of *signification.

posture
[< Latin POSITURA 'a position']
Position or carriage of the body in standing or sitting that conveys a particular attitude or intent.

potassium-argon method
Archeological technique used to measure the age of ancient fossil remains, based on the fact that radioactive potassium (potassium-40) breaks down extremely slowly, yielding argon-40.

pragmatics
[< Greek PRASSEIN 'to do']
Branch of linguistics concerned with how language is used in social situations. The pragmatic study of language deals with *who* says *what* to *whom* in specific situations.

Illustration: An example of what such a study would focus on is the common conversational device known as a gambit. A gambit is a word, phrase, etc. used to open a conversation, to keep it going, to make it smooth, etc. In English, the following are gambits with three different functions: 1. *Uh huh ... ya ... hmm ... aha ...*; 2. *You agree with me, don't you?* 3. *May I ask you a question?* The grunt-like sounds uttered in (1) constitute a strategy for acknowledging that one is listening, especially on the phone. Total silence in this pragmatic situation is not an appropriate gambit in English, although it is in other languages. The question in (2) is called a *tag question*, i.e. one added on at the end of the sentence through which approval, agreement, consent, etc. are sought. Utterance (3) is an opening gambit – i.e. a strategy for starting a conversation, or for taking a turn in a conversation.

pragmatism
[< Greek PRASSEIN 'to do']
Philosophical movement developed by Charles S. *Peirce and William *James distinguished by the tenet that the validity of an idea or a proposition lies in its observable practical consequences.

predicate
[< Latin PRAE 'before' + DICARE 'to proclaim']
1. an assertion about the subject of a proposition. 2. verb or verb phrase that asserts something about the subject.

Illustration: 1. *The grass is <u>greener on the other side</u>*. 2. *Alexander ate <u>the cake voraciously</u>*.

prefix
[< Latin PRAE 'before' + FIXUS 'fastened']
Affix that is added before a *morpheme.

Illustrations: 1. the *ir-* in *irregular*; 2. the *un-* in *unhappy*; 3. the *re-* in *replay*; 4. the *pre-* in *preview*.

premise
[< Latin PRAE 'before' + MITTERE 'to send']
[see also *syllogism]
Proposition upon which an argument is based or from which a conclusion is drawn. Premises are classified as *major* (general) and *minor* (specific).

Illustration: All living things are mortal (major premise); *my cat is a living thing* (minor premise); *therefore, my cat is mortal* (conclusion).

preoperational stage
[see Jean *Piaget]

preposition
[< Latin PRAE 'before' + POSITUS 'placed']
Word placed before a noun, noun phrase, or substantive, indicating its relation to a verb, an adjective, or another noun.

Illustrations: 1. *I'm going* <u>with</u> *you.* 2. *She's coming* <u>in</u> *the morning.*

prescriptive grammar
[see *grammar]

presentational form
[< Latin PRAE 'before' + ESSE 'to be']
Term used by philosopher Susanne *Langer referring to the form of an artwork that conveys meaning through feeling.

Note: Langer distinguished between the *discursive symbols used in conventional language and the presentational ones used in various art forms. Discursive forms have the property of detachment: e.g. one can focus on a word in a sentence or a phrase without impairing the overall understanding of the sentence or phrase. In contrast, *presentational* forms cannot be broken up into their elements without impairing the meaning: e.g. one cannot focus on a note or

phrase in a melody without destroying the sense of the melody.

presupposition
[< Latin PRAE 'before' + SUB 'under' + POSITUS 'placed']
Process whereby a proposition or something uttered is based on certain presumed premises or assumptions.

primary modeling system
[see *modeling system]

primate studies
[< Latin PRIMUS 'first']
1. studies of primate behavior and communication; 2. studies aiming to determine if primates are capable of human language.

Note: Many of the primate experiments have been motivated by the proposition that interspecies communication is a realizable goal. Although there have been reports of some symbolic activity, of some comprehension of humor, and of some control of sentence structure, the primate experiments have not established the capacity for language and for advanced symbolism in primates.

Since gorillas and chimpanzees are incapable of speech because they lack the requisite vocal organs, the first experimenters chose American Sign Language (ASL) as the code for teaching them human language. One of the first subjects was a female chimpanzee named Washoe whose training by a husband-and-wife team named the Gardners began in 1966 when she was almost one year old. Remarkably, Washoe learned to use 132 ASL signs in just over four years. What appeared to be even more remarkable was that she began to put signs together to express a small set of relations. Inspired by the results obtained by the Gardners, others embarked upon an intensive research program throughout the 1970s and most of the 1980s aimed at expanding upon their teaching procedures. The

Premack husband-and-wife team, whose work actually began as far back as 1954 with a five-year-old chimpanzee named Sarah, taught their subject a form of written language. They instructed Sarah to arrange and respond to vertical sequences of plastic tokens on a magnetic board that represented individual words: e.g. *a small pink square =* 'banana'; *a small blue triangle =* 'apple'; etc. Sarah eventually developed the ability to respond to combinations of such symbols, which included references to abstract notions.

private space
[see *space, private]

productivity
[< Latin PRODUCERE 'to bring forth']
In communication theory, term referring to the infinite capacity of language to express new meanings by using old elements in different ways.

program, computer
[< Greek PRO 'before' + GRAPHEIN 'to write'; Latin COMPUTARE 'to reckon']
Set of commands that a computer can perform. A program may be in a high-level language or in the machine code that the computer actually uses; one version is converted to the other by a translation program called a *compiler.

programming language
[< Greek PRO 'before' + GRAPHEIN 'to write'; Latin LINGUA 'tongue']
Any of many sets of verbal and numerical commands and definitions created by computer programmers to communicate instructions to a computer.

Note: Programming languages are often designed to resemble natural languages, in order to make them easier for people to use. Instructions written in programming languages are converted to machine code, which the computer actually uses, by a computer program called a *compiler.

propaganda
[< Latin PROPAGARE 'to propagate']
Any systematic dissemination of doctrines, views, etc. reflecting specific interests and ideologies (political, social, and so on).

proposition
[< Latin PRO 'according to' + POSITUS 'placed']
1. an informative statement whose truth or falsity can be evaluated by means of logic;
2. a theorem to be demonstrated or a problem to be solved.

Illustration:
PROPOSITION: When two straight lines intersect the vertically opposite angles are equal.

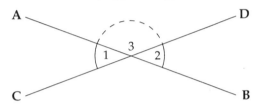

PROOF (that ∠ 1 = ∠ 2, which are vertically opposite)
1. ∠ 1 + ∠ 3 = 180°, because they make up the straight line **CD**
2. ∠ 2 + ∠ 3 = 180°, because they make up the straight line **AB**
3. ∠ 1 + ∠ 3 = ∠ 2 + ∠ 3, things equal to the same thing are equal to each other.
4. ∠ 1 = ∠ 2 (∠ 3 is common to both sides of the equation, and can thus be subtracted).

prose
[< Latin PROVERTERE 'to turn forward']
[see also *poetry]
Ordinary form of written or spoken language, without rhyme or meter.

prosody
[< Greek PROSOIDIA 'tone, accent, song sung to music']
1. art of poetic versification, including metrical structure, stanza form, etc.; 2. features of tone, stress, etc. that accompany speech sounds and words.

prosopopeia
[< Greek PROSOPON 'face, mask, dramatic character']
[see *personification]

Proto-Indo-European
[abbreviated to PIE]
Language reconstructed by linguists, considered to be the original language from which the modern Indo-European languages sprang.

Note: The work on PIE has remained the most useful for theories of language origins, for the simple reason that knowledge about this protolanguage is detailed and extensive. Already in the 19th century, linguists had a pretty good idea both of what PIE sounded like and of what kind of vocabulary it had. PIE had words for animals, plants, parts of the body, tools, weapons, and various abstract notions. It is this stock of reconstructed lexical items that has helped contemporary linguists paint a fairly good picture of the semantic range of one of the first vocabularies utilized by human beings.

The reconstruction is carried out by comparing the forms of the modern-day descendants and then deducing the proto-forms from which they evolved. For example, the words for 'father' in classical Greek, Sanskrit, and Latin show a /p/ in initial position – *pater*, *piter*, and *pater* respectively – but /f/ in Old Gothic (*fadar*). Linguists thus hypothesized that the original form must have had a /p/ and was pronounced more or less like the ancient Greek word. The reconstructed forms are, in effect, best-guess abstract formulas, summarizing the sets of correspondences that are noted among related languages.

protolanguage
[< Greek PROTOS 'first'; Latin LINGUA 'tongue']
Language reconstructed by linguists, considered to be the progenitor of a group or family of languages. Protolanguages are reconstructed by a careful, minute comparison of the sounds and forms of the languages considered to be related (see *Proto-Indo-European).

prototype
[see *concept, basic]

proverb
[< Latin PRO '(put) forth' + VERBUM 'word']
Short, traditional saying that expresses some obvious truth or familiar experience.

Illustrations: Proverbs are used cross-culturally to provide practical advice when it is required in certain situations: e.g. *You've got too many fires burning* (= advice to not do so many things at once); *Rome wasn't built in a day* (= advice to have patience); *Don't count your chickens before they're hatched* (= advice to be cautious); *An eye for an eye and a tooth for a tooth* (= equal treatment is required in revenge of a wrong). Every culture has such proverbs. They constitute a code of ethics and of practical knowledge that anthropologists call 'folk wisdom.' Most proverbs are rooted in folklore and preserved by oral and written traditions.

proxeme
[< Latin PROXIMUS 'nearest']
[see also *proxemic code]
Minimal unit of socially determined space maintained by people when interacting.

Illustrations: 1. A distance of under 18 inches between two people is perceived to be an 'intimate proxeme.' 2. A distance of 12 ft. and beyond between two people is perceived instead to be a 'public proxeme.'

proxemic code
[< Latin PROXIMUS 'nearest']
Social *code regulating how people maintain spaces between each other when interacting, and how they orient their bodies in social situations.

Illustrations: Anthropologist Edward T. *Hall

was among the first to investigate the patterns and dimensions of the zones people establish and maintain between each other when interacting in social situations. He noted that these could be measured very accurately, allowing for predictable statistical variation, and that the boundary dimensions varied from culture to culture. In North American culture, Hall found that a distance of under 6 inches between two people was perceived as an 'intimate' distance, while one of 1.5 to 4 feet was the minimum perceived 'safe' distance. A stranger intruding upon the limits set by this boundary causes considerable discomfort. If the 'safe' distance is breached by some acquaintance, on the other hand, it would be interpreted as a sexual or aggressive advance.

More specifically, Hall identified four types of culturally elaborated zones, called *proxemes: *intimate, personal, social,* and *public.* He further subdivided these into 'far' and 'close' phases. At intimate distance (0–18 in.), all the senses are activated and the presence of the other person or persons is unmistakable. The close phase (0–6 in.) is an emotionally-charged zone reserved for lovemaking, comforting, and protecting; the far phase (6–18 in.) is the distance where family members and close friends interact. Touch is frequent at both phases of intimate distance.

The personal zone (1.5–4 ft.) is the minimum comfortable distance between non-touching individuals. In the close phase (1.5–2.5 ft.), one can grasp the other by extending the arms. The far phase (2.5–4 ft.) is set as anywhere from one arm's length to the distance required for both individuals to touch hands. Beyond this distance the two must move to make contact (e.g. to shake hands). In essence, this zone is reserved for informal contact between friends. It constitutes a small protective space that separates the Self from the Other.

The social distance (4–12 ft.) is considered non-involving and non-threatening by most individuals. Its close phase (4–7 ft.) is typical of impersonal transactions and casual social gatherings. Formal social discourse and transactions are characteristic of the far phase (7–12 ft.). This is the minimum distance at which one could go about one's business without seeming rude to others.

Finally, the public zone (12 ft. and beyond) is the distance that permits one to take either evasive or defensive action if physically threatened. Hall notes that people tend to keep at this distance from important public figures or from anyone participating at a public function. Discourse at this distance will be highly structured and formalized (lectures, speeches, etc.).

proxemics

[< Latin PROXIMUS 'nearest']
Term coined by anthropologist Edward T. *Hall in reference to the systematic study of the cultural, behavioral, and sociological aspects of spatial distances between individuals.

pseudonym

[< Greek PSEUDES 'false' + ONOMA 'name']
[also called pen name]
Fictitious name assumed by an author.

Illustrations: 1. *Mark Twain* (= pseudonym of *Samuel Clemens*). 2. *Lewis Carroll* (= pseudonym of *Charles Dodgson*).

psychoanalysis

[< Greek PSYCHE 'breath, spirit, soul' + ANA 'throughout' + LYSIS 'a loosing']
1. field studying so-called *unconscious mental processes; 2. method, developed by Sigmund *Freud, of treating neuroses, based on the assumption that mental disorders are the result of the rejection by the conscious mind of factors that persist in the unconscious.

Note: Freud believed behavior to be determined by sexual drives (the *libido). Carl *Jung rejected Freud's view as too narrow, feeling that the libido is a composite of all creative instincts and impulses. According to Jung, the unconscious is composed of two parts: the *personal unconscious*, the repository of the individual's entire life experiences; and the *collective unconscious*, the repository of the experiences of the human race. In the collective unconscious exist a number of primordial *archetypes common to all individuals of a given culture or period. These primitive images and modes of though tend to personify natural processes and human traits in symbolic and mythic terms.

Crucial to modern psychoanalytic theory and practice is the concept of anxiety, which actuates the defense mechanisms against certain danger situations. Freud described these situations as the fear of abandonment by, or the loss of, the loved one (the object), the risk of losing the object's love, the danger of retaliation and punishment, and the hazard of reproach by one's own conscience.

psycholinguistics

[< Greek PSYCHE 'spirit, mind' + Latin LINGUA 'tongue']
Branch of linguistics concerned with such topics as language acquisition by children, speech perception, aphasia, and others that involve psychological aspects of language.

psychology

[< Greek PSYCHE 'spirit, mind' + LOGOS 'word, reasoning']
Field studying human thinking, behavior, experience, development, and learning.

Note: The science of psychology developed from many diverse sources, but its origins as a science can be traced to ancient Greek philosophers such as *Plato and *Aristotle. The roots of modern psychological theory are found in the 17th-century ideas of French philosopher René *Descartes and British philosophers Thomas *Hobbes and John *Locke. Descartes maintained that minds have certain inborn ideas that are

crucial in organizing people's experience of the world. Hobbes and Locke, by contrast, stressed the role of experience as the source of human knowledge.

The field that contributed most to the development of scientific psychology was *physiology* – the study of the functions of the various organ systems of the body. The first true experimental psychologists were German physicist Gustav Theodor Fechner (1801–87) and German physiologist Wilhelm Wundt (1832–1920), inspired by the ideas of Hermann *Helmholtz (1821–94). Wundt founded in 1879 the first laboratory of experimental psychology in Leipzig, training students in this new science. Physicians who became concerned with mental illness also contributed to the development of modern psychological theories. The Austrian Sigmund *Freud, who devised the system of investigation and treatment known as *psychoanalysis, subsequently called attention to instinctual drives and unconscious motivational processes that determine people's behavior.

In the United States, psychology was influenced greatly by a strong practical orientation. American psychologists from about 1920 to 1960 showed little concern with mental processes, focusing their attention instead on behavior itself, in a movement known as *behaviorism, which distinguished between two major kinds of learning: *classical conditioning* and *instrumental learning*. Classical conditioning was discovered by Russian physiologist Ivan *Pavlov, who showed that animals could be trained, or conditioned, to respond to a particular stimulus by associating that stimulus with something already familiar to them. For example, a dog was conditioned to salivate at the sound of a bell after repeatedly being fed just after hearing the bell ring. In instrumental learning, emphasis is placed on what the animal does and what outcomes follow its actions. In general, if some action is followed by a reward, the action will be repeated the next time the animal is in the same situation. Since the 1970s, psychological research has tended to focus on the role of cognition in human learning, and especially on the role of attention, perception, pattern recognition, and language in learning processes.

psychology, evolutionary
[< Greek PSYCHE 'spirit, mind' + LOGOS 'word, reasoning'; Latin EVOLUTIO 'an unfolding']
Contemporary school of psychology that is concerned with studying human behaviors and symbolic phenomena in terms of evolutionary theories.

Note: Taking their impetus from *sociobiology, evolutionary psychologists attempt to explain human behaviors in terms of evolutionary patterns by comparison with primate behaviors. According to this perspective, human rituals such as kissing and flirting, for instance, are explained as modern-day reflexes of primate and early hominid behaviors. Aggression in males is viewed as a residue of animal territoriality, one of several mechanisms by which animals control access to critical resources. Males are described as competing for territories, either fighting actual battles or performing ritual combats as tests of their strength. Weaker males are portrayed as incapable of holding a territory or as being forced to occupy less-desirable locations. Accordingly, aggression in modern human males is seen as a reflex of this mechanism.

This kind of reasoning is extended to explaining all feelings, thoughts, urges, artistic creations, etc., which are said to result from the evolutionary processes started by our hunter-gatherer ancestors. Using population statistics, and making correlations between selected sets of facts, evolutionary psychologists aim to show that human traits of all kinds are inherited through the genetic code, not formed by individual experiences in cultural contexts.

public broadcasting service
[< Latin PUBLICUS, from POPLICUS 'of the people']
In the United States the Public Broadcasting Act of 1967 created a source of funding for noncommercial television stations and resulted in the formation of the Public Broadcasting Service (PBS). Stations affiliated with PBS need not adhere to any network time frame and may schedule programs as they wish. Public stations operate on contributions from viewers, corporate gifts, foundation grants, and support from the Corporation for Public Broadcasting. Similar services exist in other countries.

publicity
[< Latin PUBLICUS, from POPLICUS 'of the people']
Craft of disseminating any information that concerns a person, group, event, or product through public media.

public relations
[< Latin PUBLICUS, from POPLICUS 'of the people']
Activities and techniques used by organizations and individuals to establish favorable attitudes and responses in their behalf on the part of the general public or of special groups.

public space
[see *space, public]

public zone
[see *zone, public]

pun
[< Italian PUNTIGLIO 'fine point']
Word or words that sound alike, juxtaposing, connecting, or bringing out two or more of the possible applications of the word or words. The word *pun* was first recorded in a work of 1662 written by English poet John Dryden (1631–1700).

Illustrations: 1. *Our word is your <u>bond</u>* = advertisement for an adhesive tape based on a pun on the word *bond*. 2. *My psychologist's name is Anna List* = *Anna List* is a pun on *analyst*)

puzzle

[< Middle English POSELEN 'to bewilder, confuse']
Baffling question or problem designed to test cleverness or ingenuity.

Note: One of the oldest known puzzles is a Sumerian *cipher – a message laid out in secret code – written in *cuneiform (i.e. by means of wedge-shaped markings carved in soft clay tablets) that dates back to around 2500 BC. Puzzles from the Old Babylonian period (1800–1600 BC), Egypt (1700–1650 BC), and the ancient civilizations of the Orient and the Americas have also been discovered by archeologists.

Pythagoras

[c. 530 BC]
Greek philosopher who founded a movement, known as *Pythagoreanism*, that had religious, political, and philosophical aims. In geometry, the great discovery of the school was the *Pythagorean theorem*, which states that the square of the hypotenuse of a right triangle is equal to the sum of the squares of the other two sides. In astronomy, the Pythagoreans were the first to consider the earth a globe revolving with the other planets around a central fire.

Q

qualisign

[< Latin QUALIS 'of what kind']
In Charles *Peirce's theory, type of *sign that refers to a quality: i.e. a sign that draws attention to, or singles out, some *quality* of its *referent.

Illustrations: 1. In language, an adjective is a qualisign since it draws attention to the qualities (color, shape, size, etc.) of things. 2. In other codes, qualisigns include the colors used by painters, the harmonies and tones used by composers, and various graceful movements made by ballet dancers.

Quintilian

[c. AD 35–c. 96]
Roman rhetorician who prefigured the notion of *index, which he called *indicium* (suggestion) and *vestigium* (trace). His reputation is based on his 12-volume work *The Training of an Orator* (AD 95?) in which he recommends reading as an important part of an orator's training. The work had great influence on humanist theories of education during the Renaissance.

R

Radcliffe-Brown, Alfred

[1881–1955]
British anthropologist who emphasized the social-functional nature of many human emotions. He noted, for instance, that in a specific cultural context a physical response such as weeping could hardly be explained in purely psychobiological terms. Among the Andaman Islanders, situated in the east Bay of Bengal, he found that it was not primarily an expression of joy or sorrow, but rather a response to social situations characterizing such meaningful events as peace-making, marriage, and the reunion of long-separated intimates. In crying together, the people renewed their ties of solidarity.

radio

[abbreviation of radiotelegraphy]
1. communication over a distance via the transmission of sounds or signals converted into electromagnetic waves directly through space to a receiving set, which changes them

back into sounds or signals; 2. broadcasting by radiotelegraphy.

radio broadcasting

Broadcasting of radio programs, as an entertainment and information industry.

Note: In 1837, the *telegraph* was patented, establishing the first system of international communications. However, telegraphic communication was soon found to be inefficient because it depended on the building and maintenance of a complex system of receiving stations wired to each other along a fixed route. In the latter half of the 1800s, communications engineers in many countries devised a system that could overcome these limitations. In 1895, Guglielmo Marconi (1874–1937) transmitted a message in Morse code that was picked up about 3 km away by a receiving device that had no wired connection to his transmitting device, thus demonstrating that an electronic signal could be transmitted through space so that devices at random points could receive it. The invention was called a *radiotelegraph* (later shortened to *radio*), because its signal moved outward in all directions, or radially, from the point of transmission. After the First World War, the Westinghouse Electric Corporation established what many historians consider the first commercially owned radio station to offer programming to the general public, known by the call letters KDKA.

Another early radio broadcaster was the American Telephone and Telegraph Company (AT&T) which, as early as 1922, began exploring the possibilities of charging fees in return for airing commercial advertisements on its stations. In contrast, in Great Britain, radio owners paid yearly license fees, collected by the government, which were turned over directly to an independent state enterprise, the British Broadcasting Corporation (BBC). The BBC produced news and entertainment programming for

its network stations. Radio broadcasting reached the height of its influence and prestige during the Second World War. carrying war news directly from the battlefront into the homes of millions of listeners throughout the world.

radio-carbon technique

Technique used by archeologists to establish the age of objects, human remains, or the time sequence of activities found at a site.

Note: The scientific basis of this technique is that plants, animals, and certain substances contain fixed ratios of a radioactive form of carbon, known as carbon-14. This deteriorates at a constant rate, leaving ordinary carbon. Measuring the traces of carbon in pieces of charcoal, the remains of plants, cotton fibers, wood, and so forth permits the dating of substances to within approximately 50,000 years, although the method is sometimes extended to 70,000 years. Uncertainty in measurement increases with the age of the sample.

RAM

[acronym for random-access memory]
[see also *computer memory, *ROM]
Computer memory based on chips within the computer containing information that can change as the computer functions. The contents are held temporarily, not permanently, and can be read or inputted in any order.

rapid fading

In communication theory, term referring to the fact that auditory signals are transitory and do not await the hearer's convenience.

ratings

System for determining the popularity of a radio or TV program, which arose from sponsors' desire to know how many people they were reaching with their advertising.

rationalism
[< Latin RATIO 'reasoning']
System of thought emphasizing the pivotal role of reason in obtaining knowledge. It contrasts with *empiricism, which emphasizes instead the role of experience, especially sense perception.

Note: Rationalism is primarily identified with 17th-century French philosopher and scientist René *Descartes, who believed that geometry represented the ideal for all sciences and philosophy. He suggested that universal truths could be discovered by reason alone, and that all knowledge could be derived from these truths.

raw vs. cooked
Distinction introduced into anthropology and semiotics by Claude *Lévi-Strauss, emphasizing the role played by the cooking of food in the evolution of culture.

Note: Lévi-Strauss traced the origin of food as a symbolic system to the evolutionary distinction that he termed 'the raw' vs. 'the cooked.' Cooked food is food that has been transformed by culture into something more than a survival substance. According to Lévi-Strauss this transformation was accomplished by two processes – roasting and boiling – both of which were among the first significant technological advances made by humans. Roasting is more primitive than boiling because it implies a direct contact between the food and a fire. So, it is slightly above 'the raw' in evolutionary terms. But boiling reveals an advanced form of thinking, since the cooking process in this case is mediated by both a pot and a fire. This dichotomy has hardly disappeared. In some parts of the world it has been imprinted into the social system to connote class relations. In the Hindu caste system, for instance, the higher castes may receive only raw food from the lower castes, whereas the lower castes are allowed to accept any kind of cooked food from any caste.

reader
[see also *author]
Person decoding or interpreting a text, especially a literary text such as a novel, a play, or a poem.

Note: Traditional literary analysis has focused on how a reader can figure out what the author of a work intended. In recent critical approaches, however, the meaning of a work is portrayed instead as a system of connotations to which a reader responds in kind, according to his/er personal experiences and the particular context (social, historical, psychological) in which the reading occurs.

read-only memory
[see *ROM]

realism
[< Latin REALIS 'real']
1. Doctrine of *scholasticim, opposed to *nominalism, positing that universals exist independently of the particular systems of thought that have generated them; 2. in modern philosophy, term applied to the view that ordinary objects of sense perception have an existence independent of their being perceived.

Note: The term today is generally restricted to naming a movement that began in the mid-19th century, in reaction to the extreme forms of subjectivity of romantic art and philosophy. In art and literature it implies the depiction of everyday scenes of humble life, and a critique of social conditions. Realist writers include the French novelists Gustave Flaubert (1821–80) and Guy de Maupassant (1850–93), the Russian author Anton Chekhov (1860–1904), the English novelist George Eliot (1819–80), and American writers Mark Twain (1835–1910) and Henry James (1843–1916).

rebus
[< Latin REBUS 'from things']
Puzzle that is solved by figuring out the

word(s) or phrase(s) suggested by a combination of pictures, signs, letters, etc.

Illustration:

🐟 + L + & = a picture of an *eye* followed by an L followed by an *ampersand* = *island*.

recall

[see *memory]

receiver

1. person or mechanism capable of receiving and decoding a signal; 2. entity or system, organic or mechanical, to which/whom a message is directed.

recitative

[see *opera]

recognition

[see *memory]

recollection

[see *memory]

reductionism

[< Latin RE 'back' + DUCERE 'to lead']
View that complex phenomena or structures, including mental ones, are reducible to relatively simple chemical and physical systems.

redundancy

[< Latin REDUNDARE 'to flow']
In communication systems, feature that counteracts *noise. In many systems, such as language, redundancy can be seen in the predictability built into certain structures (forms, sentences, etc.).

Illustrations: 1. the high predictability of certain words in many sentences (*Roses are red, violets are ...*); 2. the patterned repetition of elements (*Yes, yes, I'll do it; yes, I will*).

reference

[< Latin RE 'back' + FERRE 'to bear']
Process of directing attention to something or someone in the world.

referent

[< Latin RE 'back' + FERRE 'to bear']
What a *sign (a word, a symbol, a drawing, etc.) stands for (a thing, an idea, an event, etc.).

Illustrations: 1. The referent of *mitten* is something that looks, more or less, like this: 🔔. 2. The referent of C# is a specific tone (note) on a piano keyboard, a violin string, etc. 3. The referent of 9 is 'nine units (objects).' 4. The referent of the word *there* is a particular location.

referential function

[< Latin RE 'back' + FERRE 'to bear']
In Roman *Jakobson's model of communication, function whereby a message is constructed to convey information.

Illustrations: 1. *Main Street is two blocks north of here.* 2. *It is cold outside.*

refrain

[< Vulgar Latin REFRANGERE 'to break off']
Phrase, *verse, or group of verses repeated at intervals throughout a song or *poem, especially at the end of each stanza.

register

[< Latin RE 'back' + GERERE 'to bear']
Aspect of verbal usage having to do with vocabulary, pronunciation, punctuation, level of formality, etc., chosen by a speaker or writer in a particular social or literary context.

Illustrations: 1. *Would you be so kind as to tell me where Mulberry Street is?* (= high/formal register). 2. *Hey, where's Mulberry Street?* (= low/informal register).

reification

[< Latin RES 'thing' + FACERE 'to make']
1. process by which an idea, an abstraction, or a concept is made real either as an artifact, as a word, or as some physically real object; 2. treatment of something imagined as substantially existing, or as a concrete material object.

relativism

[< Latin RELATUS 'borne out']
1. view in anthropology and semiotics that an individual's actions and behaviors are shaped primarily in relation to the culture in which she/he has been reared; 2. philosophical view that there is no absolute, universal moral or ethical code.

relearning

[see *memory]

relief

[< Latin RE 'back' + LEVARE 'to raise']
Projection of figures or forms from a flat background, as in sculpture, or a projection that is apparent only, as in painting.

repetition in advertising

[see *advertising, use of repetition in]

representamen

[literally 'something that does the representing']
Charles *Peirce's term referring to the strategy of representation itself (the use of sounds, hand movements, etc. for some representational purpose).

Illustration: The word *cat* is a representamen if one focuses on the sounds with which it is made, /kæt/. These sounds are associated with a meaning that Peirce called the *object*, and an interpretation of it in personal and social terms, which he called the *interpretant*.

Note: Peirce proposes that there were three kinds of *representamina* in human representational systems. He called these *qualisigns*, *sinsigns*, and *legisigns*. A *qualisign* is a representamen that draws attention to, or singles out, some *quality* of its referent. In language, an adjective is a qualisign since it draws attention to the qualities (color, shape, size, etc.) of referents. In other codes, qualisigns include the colors used by painters, the harmonies and tones used by composers. A *sinsign* is a representamen that

draws attention to, or singles out, a particular object in time-space: e.g. a pointing finger, the words *here* and *there*. A *legisign* is a representamen that designates something by convention: e.g. words referring to abstract concepts, symbols, etc.

representation

[< Latin RE 'again, back' + PRAESENTARE 'to place before']
Activity of using *signs to capture, portray, simulate, or relay impressions, sensations, perceptions, or ideas that are felt or deemed to be identifiable, knowable, and/or memorable.

Illustrations: 1. A portrait of a person is a representation of that person (of his/her personality) from the standpoint of the artist. 2. A map drawn to show someone how to get to a specific place is a representation of the path that must be undertaken.

Note: Representation is a deliberate use of signs to probe, classify, and hence know the world. When an infant comes into contact with an object, his/her first reaction is to explore it with the *senses*, i.e. to handle it, taste it, smell it, listen to any sounds it makes, and visually observe its features. This exploratory phase of knowing, or cognizing, an object can involve the use of the *sensory* apparatus to cognize it in terms of how it feels, tastes, smells, etc. The resulting sensory units of knowing apparently allow the child to *recognize* the same object subsequently without having to examine it over entirely again with his/her sensory system. Now, as the infant grows, she/he starts to engage more and more in behavior that clearly transcends this sensory cognizing phase; i.e. she/he starts to point to the object and/or imitate the sounds it makes and, at some time around the second year of life, can represent it in drawing or by describing it with words. The word *represent* means, literally, 'to present again,' i.e. to present some referent again in terms of signs.

rheme

Charles *Peirce's term designating the meaning that is derivable from a sign that captures some quality (known technically as a *qualisign).

Illustrations: 1. the general meanings derivable from adjectives such as *green, happy, innocent*, etc. are rhemes; 2. the meanings derivable by observing the use of color in a painting, the use of notes to color a melody, etc. are all rhemes.

rhetoric

[< Greek RHETOR 'orator']
[see also *figures of speech]
1. art of using words effectively in speaking or writing 2. branch of philosophy and semiotics studying the various verbal techniques used in all kinds of discourses, from common conversation to poetry.

Note: The founder of rhetoric as a discipline is thought to be Corax of Syracuse, who in the 5th century BC composed the first handbook on the art of rhetoric. With Isocrates in the 4th century BC, the art of rhetoric was broadened to become a cultural study.

*Plato satirized the more technical approach to rhetoric. *Aristotle saw rhetoric as the means to mount effective argumentation skills. The Roman masters of rhetoric were Cicero (106–43 BC) and Quintilian (c. AD 35–c. 9). The study of rhetoric was stressed in both medieval and Renaissance education. Since the Renaissance, the Western world has seen a gradual decline in interest in the formal study of rhetoric. Only in the 20th century has there been a revival of its study, encouraged largely by the work of linguists and psychologists on *metaphor.

The essence of rhetorical study inheres in understanding how figures of speech work, as strategies to be used to give particular emphasis to an idea or sentiment. This is typically accomplished by the user's conscious deviation from the strict literal sense of a word, or from the more commonly used form of word order or sentence construction.

rhetorical question

[< Greek RHETOR 'orator']
1. question that is asked not to gain information, but to assert more emphatically the obvious answer to what is asked; 2. question asked only for effect, as to emphasize a point, no answer being expected.

Illustrations: 1. *You know what I mean, don't you?* 2. *Of course, you agree with me, needless to say?* 3. *Have you ever heard such nonsense?*

rhyme

[< Greek RHYTHMOS 'measure, measured motion']
Feature of *verse in which there is a regular recurrence of corresponding sounds, especially at the ends of lines.

Illustrations: 1. *bold* and *cold*; 2. *hot* and *not*; 3. *simple* and *dimple*; 4. *right* and *light*.

rhythm

[< Greek RHYTHMOS 'measure, measured motion']
In music or poetry, regular recurrence of grouped strong and weak beats, or heavily and lightly accented tones, in alternation.

Note: Rhythm usually is organized in recurring patterns. Such patterns regulate the motion of the words or music. The basic rhythmic unit is the *beat* – a recurring time pattern that resembles the ticking of a clock. The *tempo* determines the speed of the beat. Beats themselves are regulated by larger recurring units called *measures*, which are formed by stressing the first in a series of beats, so that the beats group themselves into a pattern.

Just as beats are grouped into measures, measures are themselves grouped into larger units. These produce the more extended segments of time that determine the form. A motive (shortest melodic idea that forms a relatively complete musical unit) may consist of more than one measure. One or more motives may be repeated and varied to form a phrase (a still larger unit with a more definite sense of ending).

Richards, I.A.

[1893–1979]

English literary critic and educator who emphasized the importance of *metaphor in ordinary, everyday discourse. Richards defined the parts of the metaphor as the *tenor* (what the metaphor is about), the *vehicle* (what delivers the meaning of the tenor), and the *ground* (the meaning generated by the metaphor). For instance, in the metaphor *Alexander is a sly fox, Alexander* is the tenor, *fox* the vehicle, and the ground is something like 'Alexander is a shrewd, crafty person.'

riddle

[< Old English RAEDELS 'guess']

Puzzle in the form of a question or statement so formulated that some ingenuity is required to solve it.

Note: One of the oldest puzzles known to the Western world is the *Riddle of the Sphinx.* In Greek mythology, the Sphinx was a monster with the head and breasts of a woman, the body of a lion, and the wings of a bird. Lying crouched on a rock, she accosted all who were about to enter the city of Thebes by asking them a riddle: 'What is it that has four feet in the morning, two at noon, and three at night?' Those who failed to answer the riddle correctly were killed on the spot. If, however, anyone were ever to come up with the correct answer, the Sphinx vowed to destroy herself. When the hero Oedipus solved the riddle by answering, 'Man, who crawls on four limbs as a baby [in the morning of life],' walks upright on two as an adult [at the noon hour of life], and walks with the aid of a stick in old age [at the twilight of life],' the Sphinx killed herself. For ridding them of this terrible monster, the Thebans made Oedipus their king.

ritual

[< Latin RITUALIS 'ritual']

Performance, ceremony, set of actions, discourse, and/or procedures intended to symbolize some event that bears great meaning.

Illustrations: 1. In Java, masked dramas and spirit-possession dances remain a part of village ritual life. 2. Sub-Saharan African societies engage in masked ritual dances to exorcise spirits. 3. In Western society dance serves to celebrate marriage and coming-of-age rituals (youth dances).

rococo

[< French ROCAILLE 'rock work']

Style of art (especially architecture and painting) that originated in France in the early 18th century, characterized by elaborate ornamentation, especially by arabesques, shells, elaborate curves, and iridescent pastel colors.

role

[French RÔLE, 'roll of parchment' on which an actor's part was written]

Character or part played by a performer.

Note: The word *role* is first recorded in English in 1606, from the French *rôle*, with the sense 'a part one has to play.' From such use it also came to refer to the text from which an actor learned a part. This use brought the word into the world of the theater.

ROM

[acronym for read-only memory]

[see also *computer memory, *RAM]

Computer memory that allows fast access to permanently stored data, but prevents addition to, or modification of, the data.

romance

[< Old French 'to write in Roman']

Long medieval *narrative in verse or prose, originally written in one of the Romance tongues (languages derived from Latin), about the adventures, love affairs, and challenges of knights and other chivalric heroes.

Rousseau, Jean-Jacques

[1712–1778]

French philosopher who linked a life of happiness to the attainment of a state of 'natural life' similar to that of indigenous tribes and of children. Rousseau advocated the elimination of the corrupting influences of Western civilization. He is also well known for his ideas on 'child-centered' education, and for having proposed a theory of language origins by which the gestures and accompanying 'savage cries' of early humans eventually developed into the units of meaning that we now call words. His works include *Discourse on the Sciences and the Arts* (1750), *Discourse on the Origin of Inequality among Mankind* (1755), *The Social Contract* (1762), the novel *Émile* (1762), *Confessions* (1782), and the *New Eloise* (1760).

rune
[possibly Old Norse or Old English RÚN] Alphabetic character used by ancient Germanic peoples from the 3rd to the 13th century; a character sometimes believed to have magic powers.

Russell, Bertrand
[1872–1970]
British philosopher, mathematician, social critic, and writer who influenced the development of symbolic logic, logical positivism, and the set theory of mathematics in the early 20th century. Russell developed a formal, propositional system for representing thought that, he claimed, could be 'verified' simply by experience, and thus could 'purify' language – i.e. eliminate from it all its ambiguity. His works include *The Principles of Mathematics* (1902), *Principia Mathematica* (with A.N. Whitehead, 1910–13), and *The Problems of Philosophy* (1912).

Russian formalism
School of semiotic analysis prominent from 1916 to about 1930, which emphasized the power of poetic thinking in shaping all of discourse and literature.

S

sacred space
[see *space, sacred]

saga
1. prose narrative originating in Iceland, and popular between 1120 and 1400, dealing with the families that first settled in Iceland and their descendants, told with reference to the myths and legends of Germanic gods and heroes; 2. modern prose narrative that resembles a saga.

Santayana, George
[1863–1952]
American poet and philosopher who argued that the pleasure derived from a work of art was a quality of the thing that was represented, rather than a subjective response to the work. Santayana attempted to unify science, art, and religion, considering each as a different but equally valid mode of discovering truths. He also maintained that reality is entirely external to consciousness and is known only by inference from sensory experiences within consciousness.

Sapir, Edward
[1884–1939]
American anthropologist and linguist, student of Franz *Boas, who investigated how language shaped the minds and behaviors of its users.

sarcasm
[< Greek SARKAZEIN 'to tear flesh']
Taunting, sneering, cutting, or caustic use of language.

Illustrations: 1. *How nice you look!* (uttered to someone who is poorly dressed for the occasion). 2. *What a cautious driver you are!* (uttered to someone who has just been in a car accident).

satire

[< Latin SATIRA 'satire, poetic medley']
Literary, dramatic, or cinematic work in which vices, follies, stupidities, abuses, etc. are held up to ridicule and contempt.

Note: As a distinct literary form, satire was the creation of the Romans. The poet Horace (65–8 BC) was the first great satirist of human foibles. The satires of Juvenal (AD 60?–140?) were acrid denouncements of the vices of Roman society. Another work from the 1st century AD is the *Satyricon* of Petronius Arbiter, which describes the adventures of two decadent characters who symbolized the society of the times.

In the 14th century, English poet Geoffrey Chaucer (1340?–1400) used satire extensively in his *Canterbury Tales*. During the Renaissance, satire came to be written more often in prose than in verse. The great Renaissance masters of the genre included French writer François Rabelais (1494?–1553), the Dutch theologian Desiderius Erasmus (1466?–1536), and the Spanish master Miguel de Cervantes Saavedra (1547–1616). Satire was used in 17th-century England by such writers as Ben Jonson (1572–1637), Samuel Butler (1612–80), and John Dryden (1631–1700). In France, the dramas of Molière (1622–73) were intended as trenchant satirical attacks on the social hypocrisy of the bourgeoisie. The 18th century was the 'golden age' of satire in England, becoming a dominant literary genre when writers such as Alexander Pope (1688–1744), Joseph Addison (1672–1719), Henry Fielding (1707–54), and Jonathan Swift (1667–1745) turned their pens to the critique of society and social types. In the 19th century satire appears in the work of writers such as Charles Dickens (1812–70), Oscar Wilde (1854–1900), and Mark Twain (1835–1910). In the 20th century George Bernard Shaw (1856–1950), Nathanael West (1903–40), Aldous Huxley (1894–1963), John Cheever (1912–82), Ralph Waldo Ellison (1914–94), and Tom Wolfe (1931–) were even more brutal and direct in their satire of social mores.

Saussure, Ferdinand de
[1857–1913]
Swiss philologist who became a founder of modern-day linguistics and semiotics. Saussure was born in Geneva in 1857. He attended science classes for a year at the University of Geneva before turning to language studies at the University of Leipzig in 1876. As a student he published his only book, *Mémoire sur le système primitif des voyelles dans les langues indo-européennes* (Memoir on the Original Vowel System in the Indo-European Languages, 1879), an important work on the vowel system of *Proto-Indo-European, considered the parent language from which the Indo-European languages descended.

Saussure taught at the École des Hautes Études in Paris 1881–91 and then became a professor of Sanskrit and Comparative Grammar at the University of Geneva. Although he never wrote another book, his teaching proved highly influential. After his death, two of his assistants collated their notes and the lecture notes of some of Saussure's students and other materials into the seminal work *Cours de linguistique générale* (1916), which bears his name. The book reveals Saussure's ground-breaking approach to language that became the basis for establishing both semiotics and linguistics as autonomous scientific disciplines.

In the *Cours*, Saussure defined the *sign as an entity made up (1) of something physical – sounds, letters, gestures, etc. – which he termed the *signifier*; and (2) of the image or concept to which the signifier refers – which he called the *signified*. He called the relation that holds between the two *signification*. Saussure also claimed that these three dimensions were inseparable.

Semiotics was fashioned by Saussure as a *structuralist* science, i.e. as a mode of inquiry aiming to understand the sensory, emotional, and intellectual *structures* that undergird both the production and interpretation of signs. In his *Cours*, Saussure used the term *semiology* to designate the field he proposed for studying these structures. But while his term is still used somewhat today, the term *semiotics* is the preferred one. Saussure emphasized that the study of signs should be divided into two branches – the *synchronic* and the *diachronic*. The former refers to the study of signs at a given point in time, normally the present, and the latter to the investigation of how signs change in form and meaning over time.

Saussurean theory of the sign

Ferdinand de *Saussure's theory of the *sign as consisting of a physical part, the *signifier*, a conceptual part, the *signified*, and the relation that holds between the two, *signification*. Saussure considered signification to be an arbitrary process that human beings and/or societies establish at will. To make his point, he reasoned that there was no evident reason for using, say, *tree* or *arbre* (French) to designate 'an arboreal plant.' Indeed, any well-formed signifier could have been used in either language – a well-formed signifier is one that is consistent with the orthographic, phonological, or other type of structure characteristic of the code to which it appertains (*tree* is well formed in English; *tbky* is not). Saussure did admit, however, that there were some instances whereby the signifier was fashioned in imitation of the signified. Onomatopoeic words (*drip, plop, whack*, etc.), he granted, did indeed attempt to reflect the sound properties that their referents are perceived to have. But Saussure maintained that this was a relatively isolated and infrequent phenomenon. Moreover, the highly variable nature of onomatopoeia across languages demonstrated to him that even this phenomenon was subject to arbitrary cultural perceptions. For instance, the word used to

refer to the sounds made by a rooster is *cock-a-doodle-do* in English, but *chicchirichí* (pronounced 'keekkeereekee') in Italian; the word employed to refer to the barking of a dog is *bow-wow* in English, but *ouaoua* (pronounced *wawa*) in French; etc. Saussure suggested that such onomatopoeic creations were only approximate and more or less conventional imitations of perceived sounds.

Many semioticians have begged to differ with this specific part of Saussurean theory. What Saussure seems to have ignored is that even those who do not speak English, Italian, or French will notice an *attempt* in all the above signifiers to imitate rooster or canine sounds – an attempt constrained by the respective sound systems of the two languages that are, in part, responsible for the different phonic outcomes. Such attempts, in fact, probably went into the making of most words in a language, even though people no longer consciously experience them as physical simulations of their referents – because time and constant usage have made people forget the connection between signifier and signified.

scenario
[Italian 'stage, scene']
Outline or synopsis of the plot of a dramatic or literary work.

schema
[< Greek SCHEMA 'form']
[see also *image schema]
1. diagrammatic representation; 2. pattern used to assist in explaining or mediating perception.

scholasticism
System of logic, philosophy, and theology of certain scholars from the 10th to the 15th century, based upon Aristotelian logic, the writings of the early Christian fathers, and the authority of tradition and dogma.

Note: The scholastics wanted to demonstrate the truth of existing religious beliefs through dialectical reasoning (asking hypothetical questions and providing plausible responses; see *dialectic). Their methods of teaching helped to entrench the use of rational logic in the West as the only reliable way to discover truth. However, within this movement there were some – the so-called *nominalists – who maintained that truth was a matter of subjective opinion.

The outstanding scholastics of the 11th and 12th centuries included French philosopher and theologian St Anselm (1033–1109), and French philosopher and clergyman Roscelin, the founder of nominalism. The scholastics of the 13th century included Italian theologian and philosopher St Thomas *Aquinas, German philosopher St Albertus Magnus (1206?–80), English monk and philosopher Roger Bacon (1214?–92), Italian prelate and theologian St Bonaventure (1217?–74), and Scottish theologian and philosopher John Duns *Scotus.

science fiction

Fiction genre of a highly imaginative or fantastic kind, typically dealing with the effects of science or future events on human beings.

Note: Although this genre has ancient roots – e.g. in his *True History* (AD 160) Lucian of Samosata dealt with a trip to the moon, the 17th-century British prelate and historian Francis Godwin also wrote of travel to the moon, and the English statesman Sir Thomas More (1478–1535) wrote about a futuristic world in Utopia (1516) – *science fiction* as we now know it traces its origins to the Industrial Revolution when, in her novel *Frankenstein* (1818), the British novelist Mary Shelley (1797–1851) explored the potential of science for good and evil. Right after publication of the novel, the science-fiction genre emerged as a new form of popular fiction.

The first writer to specialize in this new genre was French author Jules Verne (1828–1905). His hugely popular novels include *Journey to the Center of the Earth* (1864) and *Around the World in Eighty Days* (1873). The first major English writer of science fiction was H.G. Wells (1866–1946), whose *Time Machine* (1895), *The Island of Dr. Moreau* (1896), and *The War of the Worlds* (1898) became instant classics when they were published. The mass-distribution magazines established in the 1890s also published many science-fiction stories, such as those by Edgar Rice Burroughs (1875–1950).

In the 20th century the popularity of science fiction grew with the publication of *Brave New World* (1932) by Aldous Huxley (1894–1963) and *Nineteen Eighty-four* (1949) by George Orwell (1903–50). Beginning in the 1950s science fiction became enormously popular in the United States. Widely known American writers in the genre are Robert Heinlein (1907–88), Isaac Asimov (1920–92), Ray Bradbury (1920–), Philip K. Dick (1928–82), and Ursula K. Le Guin (1929–). Beginning in the mid-1960s a new concern for humanistic values emerged. Dubbed the *New Wave*, the writings often focused on the near future. In the 1980s a style of science-fiction writing called *cyberpunk* arose to alert people to the dangers of incessant technological and scientific innovation.

In 1902 French filmmaker and magician Georges Méliès made the first science-fiction film, *A Trip to the Moon*. Early German films such as *Metropolis* (1926) by Fritz Lang (1890–1976), also dealt with science-fiction themes. Until the 1980s, unnatural creatures became the primary theme of science-fiction cinema in the United States, giving rise to a subgenre commonly referred to as *horror* or *monster* movies. Common themes of such motion pictures included the fallibility of scientists, the urgency of worldwide cooperation against invaders from outer space, and the evil aspects of technology. Notable science-fiction movies up to the early 1980s include *The Day the Earth Stood Still* (1950), *War of the Worlds* (1953), *Invasion of the Body Snatchers* (1956), *The Time Machine* (1960), *2001: A Space Odyssey* (1968), *Close Encounters of the Third Kind* (1977), *Star Wars* (1977), and *Blade Runner* (1982). Since the 1950s, numerous science-fiction television shows also became popular, including *The Twilight Zone* (1959–64, revived 1985–7), *Lost in Space* (1965–8), *Star Trek* (1966–9), *Star Trek: The Next Generation* (1987–94), and *The X-Files* (1993–). The latter two have enjoyed fan devotion, with thousands of followers attending major conventions.

Scotus, John Duns

[c. 1266–1308]
Scottish theologian and philosopher who held that seeking the truth entailed making use of the insights afforded not only by natural knowledge, but also by divine revelation. He argued that through faith a person may know with absolute certainty that the human soul is incorruptible and immortal; through reason a person may come instead to intellectualize the existence of such qualities of the soul, but cannot strictly prove that they exist.

script theory

[< Latin SCRIPTURA 'a writing']
[also called *frame theory]
Theory which posits that most of human discourse unfolds in a highly formulaic, script-like manner.

Note: This kind of formulaic knowledge is thought to be stored in memory in the form of *frames* that are adapted to fit with present reality, so that they can be altered as required. For example, ordering from a menu at a restaurant constitutes a frame whereby the dialogue between waiter and customer flows in a formula-like fashion.

sculpture

[< Latin SCULPERE 'to carve in stone']
Art of carving wood, chiseling stone, casting or welding metal, molding clay or wax, etc. into three-dimensional representations, known as statues, figures, forms, etc.

Note: The earliest sculpted objects are 20,000 to 35,000 years old. A small ivory horse with graceful, curving lines, found in a cave in Germany, is among the oldest of these objects. Also found in caves are stone female figurines carved with emphasis on the reproductive organs, the breasts, and the buttocks. Among the oldest Egyptian sculptures is a piece of slate carved in low relief, known as the Palette of King Narmer (3100? BC), portraying kings, armies, servants, and various animals. About 2600 BC the Sumerians carved small marble deities noted for their wide, staring eyes. The Greeks were renowned for their sculptures depicting the human form to perfection. The distinctive contribution of the Romans to the art of sculpture was realistic portraiture. In the early Christian era, sculpture was generally prohibited because of the biblical prohibition of graven images. It was revived in the 9th to the 12th century, when Scandinavian artisans started sculpting objects of daily use.

At the beginning of the Renaissance in 15th-century Italy, a demand emerged for large-scale, freestanding statues. In Florence, Donatello (1386?–1466) became the best-known sculptor of the period. However, the towering genius in sculpture, not only during the Renaissance, but perhaps of all time, was Michelangelo (1475–1564). His spectacular sculptures *Bacchus* (1496–98), *Pietà* (1498–1500), and *David* (1501–4) are probably the greatest works in marble of all time. In the 16th century, sculpture became impressive for its realism and technical skill. In the 17th century the art came to be characterized by dynamic intensity. Gianlorenzo Bernini (1598–1680) was the outstanding personality of the baroque age. During the 18th century, sculptors turned to the ancients for inspiration, reviving classical techniques. In the 19th century, by contrast, sculptors freed themselves from past models, creating works designed to appeal to the emotions. The towering figure of 19th-century sculpture – and the most important sculptor since Bernini – was the French artist Auguste Rodin (1840–1917). His sculptures reveal the inner life of the human being through the body's pose.

Much of the sculpture produced in the 20th century differed radically in form and content from that made in the past. In some instances, it explored the same radical techniques as did painting. This is why movements in both media share the same names: e.g. *cubism, *dadaism, *minimalism, *surrealism. Marcel Duchamp (1887–1968), for instance, expressed his aesthetic nihilism by selecting mass-produced objects, designating them as sculpture, and calling them 'ready-mades'; Man Ray (1890–1976) sculpted a metronome with an oscillating stem displaying a photograph of an eye; Aristide Maillol (1861–1944) sculpted a female torso. The most eminent of all 20th-century sculptors was, however, Henry Moore (1898–1986), the British artist whose works are characterized by smooth, organic forms. Many of his elegant, monumental works are found outdoors, enhancing their modern urban architectural settings. Starting in the 1980s, sculptors began moving away from radical techniques, returning to a more realistic style of representation.

Sebeok, Thomas A.
[1920–]
Leading American semiotician and linguist famous for his work on animal communication, sign theory, and the establishment of the fields of *zoosemiotics and *biosemiotics. Sebeok has been instrumental in showing the relevance of semiotics to those

working in cognate disciplines, aptly comparing semiotics to a spider's web because it rarely fails to entrap scientists, educators, and humanists into its intricate loom of insights into human cognition and culture.

secondary modeling system
neural system that allows human beings to engage in verbal and indexical forms of semiosis (speaking and pointing out things in time and space).

secondness
[see also *firstness; *thirdness]
Charles *Peirce's term referring to a second level of meaning derived from verbal processes. Secondness shows an ability to separate sensory knowledge of an object from recognition of the object. It is the awareness of cause and effect.

secretive statements in advertising
[see *advertising, use of secretive statements in]

segmentation
[< Latin SEGMENTUM 'a piece']
Decomposition of a verbal form or a phrase into its minimal elements.

Illustration: The form *illogical* is one word, but it is 'segmentable' into smaller bits that also have meaning: namely, the basic form, *logic*, which has a dictionary meaning, the negative prefix *il-*, which has a recurring functional meaning ('opposite of'), and the suffix *-al*, which also has a functional meaning ('the act or process of being something').

semantic differential
[< Greek SEMA 'signs']
Experimental technique developed by three psychologists, C.E. Osgood, G.J. Suci, and P.H. Tannenbaum, in their 1957 book *The Measurement of Meaning*, to assess the emotional connotations evoked by words or

concepts. This technique consists in posing a series of questions to subjects about a specific concept – *Is it good or bad? weak or strong?* etc. – as seven-point scales, with the opposing adjectives at each end. The answers are then analyzed statistically in order to sift out any general pattern from them.

Illustration: Evaluate the concept of *American president* in terms of the following seven-point scales (see figure below):

An informant who feels that the *president* should be modern would place a mark towards the *modern* end of the *modern-traditional* scale. One who feels that a *president* should not be too young or old would place a mark near the middle of the *young-old* scale. An informant who feels that a *president* should be bland-looking would place a mark towards the *bland* end of the *attractive-bland-looking* scale; and so on.

If a large number of informants were asked to rate the term *president* in this way, then it would be possible to draw an ideal profile of the *presidency* in terms of the statistically significant variations in the connotations that the term evokes. Interestingly, research utilizing the semantic differential has shown that, while the meanings of most concepts are subject to personal interpretation and individual feelings, the variation is not purely based on subjectivity, but tends to reveal a culture-specific pattern. In other words, the experiments have shown that the connotations of concepts are constrained by culture: e.g. the word *noise* turns out to be a highly emotional concept for the Japanese, who rate it consistently at the ends of the scales presented to them; whereas it is a fairly neutral concept for Americans, who place it in the mid-range of the scales.

semantic field
[also called *lexical field]

semanticity
[< Greek SEMA 'sign']
In communication theory, term referring to the fact that linguistic signals convey meaning through their stable reference to real-world situations.

semantic memory
[see *memory]

semantics
[< Greek SEMA 'sign']
In linguistics and semiotics the study of meaning in language.

Note: Semanticists start traditionally by determining what constitutes *denotative* meaning and then by ascertaining how that meaning can be extended to encompass other referents by *connotation*. Determining what kind of meaning a word, phrase, or sentence has entails knowing 1. the purely denotative aspects of the forms; 2. the pragmatic or contextual conditions that hold

modern								traditional
	– 1	– 2	– 3	– 4	– 5	– 6	– 7	
young								old
	– 1	– 2	– 3	– 4	– 5	– 6	– 7	
attractive								bland-looking
	– 1	– 2	– 3	– 4	– 5	– 6	– 7	
practical								idealistic
	– 1	– 2	– 3	– 4	– 5	– 6	– 7	
friendly								stern
	– 1	– 2	– 3	– 4	– 5	– 6	– 7	

between speakers and forms; and 3. the syntactic relations that hold among words and phrases.

The pragmatic aspect of a word's meaning was studied formally by the British philosopher J.L. *Austin, who described speaking in terms of *acting*, because it appeared to him that when a person states something she/he is, in effect, performing an act. The American philosopher John R. Searle extended Austin's ideas in the 1970s, emphasizing the need to relate the functions of words or expressions to their social context. Searle asserted that speech encompasses at least three kinds of acts: 1. *locutionary acts*, in which things are said with a certain sense or reference (as in *The moon is a sphere*); 2. *illocutionary acts*, in which such acts as promising or commanding are performed by means of speaking (*Come here!*); and 3. *perlocutionary* acts, in which the speaker, by speaking, does something to someone else, i.e. angers, consoles, persuades someone (*I understand you completely*). The speaker's intentions are conveyed by the locutionary force that is given to the words – i.e. by the actions implicit in what is said. To be successfully interpreted, however, the words must also be appropriate, sincere, consistent with the speaker's general beliefs and conduct, and recognizable as meaningful by the hearer.

There are several semantic relations that occur among words, phrases, and sentences. First, there is that of *synonymy*. Synonyms are words, phrases, or sentences having the same or nearly the same meaning in one or more senses: e.g. *near-close, far-distant*, etc. Synonymy results from the fact that their complete set of semantic features (*sememes*) are the same. However, there virtually never is a case of *pure synonymy* by which the specifications of the two words, as they occur in isolation or in a phrase, are exactly the same. The opposite of synonymy is *antonymy*. Antonyms are words, phrases, or sentences that are opposite in meaning: *night-day, hot-cold*, etc. But antonymy, like synonymy, is a matter of degree, rather than of categorical difference.

Another semantic relation is that of *homonymy*. Homonyms are words or phrases with the same pronunciation and/or spelling, but with different meanings. If the homonymy is purely phonetic then the items are known as *homophones* (e.g. *aunt* vs. *ant* and *bore* vs. *boar*). If the homonymy is graphic as well, then the words are known as *homographs* (*play* as in *Shakespeare's play* vs. *play* as in *He likes to play*). A fourth semantic relation is known as *hyponymy*. This is the relation by which the meaning of one word or phrase is included in that of another: e.g. the meaning of *scarlet* is included in the meaning of red.

semaphore

[< Greek SEMA 'mark, sign' + PHEREIN 'to carry']
Apparatus for signaling, such as traffic lights, flags, and mechanical arms on railroads.

semasiology

[< Greek SEMA 'mark, sign' + LOGOS 'word, study']
Study of relationships between *signs and *symbols and what they represent.

semeiotics

[< Greek SEMEION 'mark, sign']
Older spelling of *semiotics.

Note: This term was coined by *Hippocrates (460–377 BC), the founder of Western medical science, who established semeiotics as a branch of medicine for the study of *symptoms* – a *symptom* being, in effect, a *semeion* 'mark, sign' that stands for something other than itself. The same term was used also by the physician *Galen of Pergamum. It was introduced into philosophy by John *Locke in his *Essay Concerning Human Understanding* (1690), and much later revived by American philosopher Charles S. *Peirce as the basis for circumscribing an autonomous field of inquiry that he, like Locke, defined as the 'doctrine of signs.' The word *doctrine* was not used by Peirce in its religious sense, but rather in its basic meaning of 'system of principles.'

sememe

[< Greek SEMEION 'mark, sign']
Minimal unit of meaning that goes into the composition of the overall meaning of a word.

Illustration: This term is used equivalently for *semantic feature.* The words *man, woman, child, bull, cow,* and *calf,* for instance, are kept distinct by specific sememes such as [human], [bovine], [adult], [nonadult], [male], and [female]. These are the 'semantic ingredients' that make up the meanings of these words:

	man	woman	child	bull	cow	calf
[human]	+	+	+	−	−	−
[bovine]	−	−	−	+	+	+
[adult]	+	+	−	+	+	−
[nonadult]	−	−	+	−	−	+
[male]	+	−	±	+	−	±
[female]	−	+	±	−	+	±

From the chart, which shows the presence (+), absence (-), or applicability (±) of a sememe, we can see that it is possible to say with precision what differentiates, say, *man* from *woman* or *bull.* Such charts pinpoint exactly what feature or features trigger an opposition in meaning between two forms. It is claimed that these features, like *factors* in arithmetical and algebraic expressions, allow the human mind to keep certain signs distinct by virtue of the fact that they enter with certain other signs into proportional relations. By virtue of these relations a manageable set of signs allows members of a society to represent economically an illimitable array of meanings, in the same way that an infinite set of numbers can be represented in normal decimal notation by different patterns among ten digits.

The problem with this type of analysis, however, lies in determining what universal set of sememes, if such exists, can be established. The difficulty has been to find a small core of sememes that would suffice to keep most words in a language distinct. It would seem that human meaning is characterized by such a high degree of creativity and expansiveness that any attempt to pin it down to a core set of features is a virtually impossible task.

semiology

[< Greek SEMEION 'mark, sign' + LOGOS 'word, study']
[synonym for *semiotics]
Ferdinand de Saussure's term for the science of signs. Although the term is still used by some (especially in Europe), the term semiotics is now the preferred one.

semiosis

[< Greek SEMEION 'mark, sign']
Innate capacity that underlies the comprehension and production of *signs. Semiosis is an activity of the brain that controls the production and comprehension of signs, from simple physiological signals to highly complex symbols.

semiosphere

[< Greek SEMEION 'mark, sign' + SPHAIRA 'sphere']
[see also *biosphere]
Term used to refer to the level of life governed by *semiosis rather than just by biology.

Note: In the human world the semiosphere consists not only of natural signs (like signals and symptoms), but also of the systems of signs, texts, codes, etc. that humans have themselves made throughout their history in order to understand the world.

semiotic method

[< Greek SEMEION 'mark, sign']
Although there have been various proposals as to how to carry out semiotic investigations, there appear to be three basic questions that guide all semiotic inquiry: 1. *What* does something mean? 2. *How* does it represent what it means? 3. *Why* does it mean what it means?

semiotics

[< Greek SEMEION 'mark, sign']
1. discipline considered to be both a *science*, with its own corpus of findings and its theories, and a *technique* for studying meaning in human systems of representation; 2. generally defined as the science of signs.

Note: Charles *Peirce defined semiotics, as did the philosopher John *Locke before him, as the *doctrine* of signs. The word *doctrine* was not used by Peirce in its religious sense, but rather in its basic meaning of 'system of principles.' A perceptive definition of semiotics was put forward much later by Umberto *Eco, as 'the discipline studying everything which can be used in order to lie,' because if 'something cannot be used to tell a lie, conversely it cannot be used to tell the truth; it cannot, in fact, be used to tell at all.' This is, despite its apparent facetiousness, a rather insightful definition, since it implies that we have the capacity to represent the world in any way we desire through signs, even in misleading and deceitful ways. This capacity for artifice is a powerful one indeed. It allows us to conjure up nonexistent referents, or refer to the world without any back-up empirical proof that what we are saying is true.

Interest in *signs reaches back to the dawn of civilization. The first definition of *sign* as a physical *symptom* came from *Hippocrates, the founder of Western medicine. The physician *Galen of Pergamum further entrenched *semeiotics* into medical practice more than a century later, a tradition that continues to this day in various European countries. The study of signs became the prerogative of philosophers around the time of *Aristotle and the *Stoic philosophers, who investigated the sign in non-medical terms, laying down a theory of the sign that has remained basic to this day. They defined the sign as consisting of three dimensions: 1. the physical part of the sign itself; 2. the *referent* to which it calls attention; and 3. its evocation of a *meaning* (what the referent entails psychologically and socially).

The next major step forward in the study of signs was the one taken by St *Augustine, the philosopher and religious thinker who was among the first to distinguish clearly between *natural* (nonarbitrary) and *conventional* (arbitrary) signs, and to espouse the view that there is an inbuilt *interpretive* component to the whole process of representation. St Augustine's idea of an *interpretive* component was consistent with the hermeneutic tradition established by *Clement of Alexandria, the Greek theologian and early Father of the Church. John *Locke, the English philosopher who set out the principles of empiricism, introduced the formal study of signs into philosophy in his *Essay Concerning Human Understanding* (1690), anticipating that it would allow philosophers to understand the interconnection between representation and knowledge. But the task he laid out remained virtually unnoticed until the ideas of the Swiss philologist Ferdinand de *Saussure and the American philosopher Charles S. *Peirce became the basis for circumscribing an autonomous field of inquiry.

Semiotics is often confused with the study of *communication*. Although the two domains share much of the same theoretical and methodological territory, the *communication sciences* focus more on the technical study of how messages are transmitted (vocally, electronically, etc.), and on the mathematical and/or psychological laws governing the transmission, reception, and processing of information, whereas semiotics pays more attention to *what* messages mean, and to *how* they create meaning.

A large part of the increase in the popularity of this field in the late 20th century was brought about by the publication in 1983 of a best-selling medieval detective novel, *The Name of the Rose*, written by one of the most distinguished practitioners of semiotics, Umberto Eco. The American semiotician and linguist Thomas A. *Sebeok has been instrumental in showing the relevance of semiotics to those working in cognate disciplines. Today, semiotics is a flourishing enterprise, with several well-known organizational structures including the International Association of Semiotic Study and various associations based in specific countries (e.g. the Semiotic Society of America, the Canadian Semiotic Association, etc.).

semiotics, applied
[< Greek SEMEION 'mark, sign']
[see also *semiotics]
Use of semiotic theory to study and understand signifying human phenomena and/or human behavior.

semiotics, cultural
[< Greek SEMEION 'mark, sign']
Branch of *semiotics studying culture and cultural behavior.

semiotics, nonverbal
[< Greek SEMEION 'mark, sign']
Branch of *semiotics studying *signs and *codes based on the body: e.g. *gesture, *facial expression, *eye contact, etc.

Note: The study of nonverbal semiosis and representation has become a major branch of semiotics because of its productivity in human social life. It is estimated that humans can produce up to 700,000 nonverbal signs, of which 1000 are different bodily postures, 5000 are hand gestures, and

250,000 are facial expressions. These are not random actions or mere 'trimmings' to verbal discourse. They are bodily signs that communicate meanings both in conjunction with, and independently of, verbal meanings, conforming to the structural properties of the nonverbal codes to which they appertain. Nonverbal communication imbues social interaction with congruity and consistency, so that it can be carried out routinely and non-threateningly.

semiotics, verbal
[< Greek SEMEION 'mark, sign']
Semiotic study of *language and *speech.

semiotics, visual
[< Greek SEMEION 'mark, sign']
[see also *semiotics]
Study of visual *signs, visual *codes, and visual *representation generally.

Note: Representing the world visually involves transferring 'the seen' onto some surface. Virtually everything we see can be represented by a combination of lines and shapes: e.g. a cloud is a shape, a horizon is a line. Other visual signifiers include *value*, *color*, and *texture*. *Value* refers to the darkness or lightness of a line or shape. It plays an important role in portraying dark and light contrasts. *Color* conveys mood, feelings, atmosphere. This is why we speak of 'warm,' 'soft,' 'cold,' 'harsh' colors. Connotatively, color often has culture-specific symbolic value: e.g. in our culture *yellow* connotes cowardice, whereas in China it connotes royalty. *Texture* refers to the sensation of touch evoked imagistically when we look at some surface.

Semiotic Solutions
[< Greek SEMEION 'mark, sign']
Research-based consultancy agency founded in London by Virginia Valentine that assists image-makers, corporate planners, and product makers in the creation of their strategies.

semiotic square

[< Greek SEMEION 'mark, sign']
Semiotician A.J. *Greimas's theory of *signification whereby, given a unit of sense s_1 (e.g. *rich*), its meaning is gleaned only in terms of its relation with its contradictory $-s_1$ (*not rich*), its contrary s_2 (*poor*), and its contradictory $-s_2$ (*not poor*). Greimas claimed that the course of a narrative corresponds to a movement along this square: i.e. the narrative unfolds in terms of operations leading from a given unit to its contrary (or contradictory).

Illustrations: 1. Semiotic square of the concept *life*:

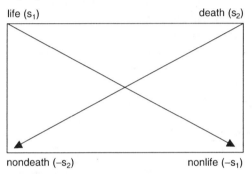

life (s_1)   death (s_2)

nondeath ($-s_2$)   nonlife ($-s_1$)

2. Semiotic square of the concept *appearing*:

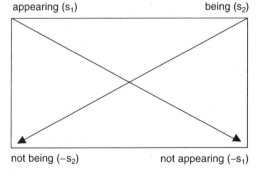

appearing (s_1)   being (s_2)

not being ($-s_2$)   not appearing ($-s_1$)

sender

[< Latin SENTIRE 'to feel, perceive']
Entity or system, organic or mechanical, who/which originates and transmits a message.

sense

[< Latin SENTIRE 'to feel, perceive']
1. ability of the nerves and the brain to receive and react to stimuli through specific bodily organs and the nerves associated with them (sight, touch, taste, smell, and hearing); 2. feeling, impression, or perception through the senses; 3. original sense-based meaning of something.

Note: The German philosopher and mathematician Gottlob *Frege (1848–1925) introduced the distinction between *sense* and *referent* in semantics. The *referent* is the object named, whereas the *sense* is a mode of presentation. In an idiomatic phrase such as *Venus is the Morning Star*, there are two terms with different *senses*, but with the same *referent*. This expression is, in effect, an ornamental version of *Venus is Venus*, involving a reference to an astronomical discovery with terms having different senses.

sense ratio

[< Latin SENTIRE 'to feel, perceive'; RATIO 'a reckoning']
Term coined by Canadian communication theorist Marshall *McLuhan designating the degree to which a physical sense is used in processing information.

Note: McLuhan emphasized that the sense ratios are equally calibrated at birth to process meaningful information. However, in social settings, it is unlikely that all senses will operate at the same ratio. One sense or the other increases according to the representational modes and media employed. In an oral culture, the *auditory sense ratio* dominates information processing and message interpretation; in an alphabetic one, the *visual sense ratio* dominates. This raising or lowering of a sense ratio is not preclusive. Indeed, in contemporary technological cultures, one can have various sense ratios activated in tandem. The ebb of ratios, up and down, in tandem, in opposition, is what defines the *cognitive style* of information processing.

sensorimotor stage
[see Jean *Piaget]

sentence
[< Latin SENTIRE 'to feel, sense']
Word or group of syntactically related words that states, asks, commands, or exclaims something. In writing, a sentence begins with a capital letter and concludes with an end mark (period, question mark, etc.); in speech a sentence begins following a silence and concludes with any of various final pitches and a terminal juncture (as in a statement, a question, etc.).

series
[< Latin SERERE 'to join together']
Popular form of broadcast drama unfolding in episodes (e.g. TV police dramas, private-eye series, westerns, science-fiction series, and series that follow the exploits of lawyers, doctors, and families).

setting
Place and conditions in which a narrative, play, poem, etc. takes place.

sex
[< Latin SECARE 'to cut, divide']
Classification of an organism as *female* or *male* on the basis of reproductive organs and functions.

Note: Humans, like other animals, sense and respond instinctively to the maleness or femaleness of another human. Across the animal realm, such responses are elicited by sexual signals during estrus (going into heat). From an evolutionary perspective, however, the human species has evolved a *sexuality independent of estrus. Other animals experience chemical and physical changes in the body during estrus that stimulate desire. People are different. They normally experience desire first (by some form of stimulation). This then produces changes in the body.

sexuality
[< Latin SECARE 'to cut, divide']
1. behavior associated with *sex; 2. behaving and responding to sexual signals in culture-specific ways.

Note: Sexuality and lovemaking techniques have been studied in various cultures since ancient times. In Europe and the United States, the scientific study of human sexuality began in the late 19th century. Early in the 20th century, German physician Magnus Hirshfeld founded the first sex-research institute. Beginning in the early 1930s, American anthropologist Margaret *Mead and British anthropologist Bronislaw *Malinowski collected data on sexual behavior in other cultures. The most noted scientific studies of sexuality in the 20th century are those of American biologist Alfred Charles Kinsey and his colleagues and those of William H. Masters and Virginia Johnson.

Shannon, Claude
[1916–]
American engineer who demonstrated that information of any kind could be described in terms of binary choices between equally probable alternatives (see *information content)

short story
Short piece of prose fiction, having fewer characters than a novel.

Note: The oldest tales are those of ancient Egypt, the fables of the Greek slave Aesop (6th century BC), and the stories by Roman writers Ovid (43 BC–AD 17) and Lucius Apuleius (2nd century AD). Besides the Indian story collection the *Panchatantra* (4th century AD), the major Asian collection of tales is the *Arabian Nights*, which was compiled over a period of hundreds of years.

Storytelling flourished in Europe during the Middle Ages. Romances, in prose and verse, abounded in France. English poet

Geoffrey Chaucer (1340?–1400), in his *Canterbury Tales*, and Italian writer Giovanni Boccaccio (1313–75), in his *Decameron*, retold and refined many *fables, beast *epics, *romances, *fabliaux, and *legends. After Boccaccio, the short, realistic narrative in prose came to be known as the *novella. The short story, as it is known today, is a development of the 19th century, when writers such as Edgar Allan Poe (1809–49) and Henry James (1843–1916) in the United States, E.T.A. Hoffmann (1776–1822) in Germany, Ivan Turgenev (1818–83), Nikolai Gogol (1809–52), Leo Tolstoy (1828–1910), and Anton Chekhov (1860–1904) in Russia, and Alphonse Daudet (1840–97) and Guy de Maupassant (1850–93) in France perfected the economy and balance necessary to craft short stories successfully.

In the 20th century enormous numbers of short stories were published annually, in almost every language. The short stories of Americans Ernest Hemingway (1899–1961) and William Faulkner (1897–1962) are among the best known in the genre. Other notable 20th-century short-story writers include Irish writer James Joyce (1882–1941), Czechoslovakian-born Franz Kafka (1883–1924), Katherine Mansfield (1888–1923) of New Zealand, Mishima Yukio (1925–70), of Japan, Rabindranath Tagore (1861–1941) of India, Gabriel García Márquez (1928–) of Colombia, Jorge Luis Borges (1899–1986) of Argentina, and Italo Calvino of Italy (1923–85).

short-term memory
[see *memory]

sign
[< Latin SIGNUM 'mark']
Something that stands for something else in some capacity.

Note: A sign consists of three dimensions. First, it involves something physical – sounds, letters, gestures, etc. – that is made to refer to something in the world (a thing, an object, an idea, etc. The word *cat*, for instance, is a sign because it does not stand for the sounds *c-a-t* that constitute it, but rather for 'a carnivorous mammal (*Felis cattus*) domesticated since early times as a catcher of rats and mice.' Similarly, an open hand directed at a person is a sign because it does not stand for itself, the hand, but rather for a warning motion alerting the individual to stop. This physical dimension is called the *signifier or *representamen:

cat stands for

  stands for 'Stop'

The second dimension of the sign is the 'something other than itself' for which it stands (a feline mammal, the action to stop, etc.). This is known as its *referent, *signified, or *object. The third dimension, known as *signification or the *interpretant, is what the sign means in specific uses.

sign, conventional
[< Latin SIGNUM 'mark']
*Sign that has no apparent connection to any perceivable feature of its referent.

Illustrations: 1. the word *tree* for 'arboreal plant'; 2. the letter *x* for 'any number' in algebra.

sign, natural
[< Latin SIGNUM 'mark']
1. sign produced by Nature (e.g. a *symptom, an unwitting *signal); 2. sign that has been constructed to simulate some property of its referent.

Illustrations: 1. The word *chirp* was coined to imitate the sound made by a bird. 2. The visual sign ☺ has been made to resemble the facial features of a boy. 3. A symptom is a natural sign produced by the body.

sign, visual

[< Latin SIGNUM 'mark']
*Sign constructed with a visual *signifier, i.e. with a signifier that can be seen (rather than heard, smelled, etc.).

Illustrations: 1. 🐢 is a visual sign standing for a 'turtle'; 2. 🪣 is a visual sign standing for 'wet paint.'

signal

[< Latin SIGNUM 'mark']
Emission or movement that naturally or conventionally triggers some reaction on the part of a receiver.

Note: All animals are endowed with the capacity to use and respond to species-specific signals for survival. Birds, for instance, are born prepared to produce a particular type of coo, and no amount of exposure to the songs of other species, or the absence of their own, has any effect on their cooing. A bird reared in isolation, in fact, will sing a very simple outline of the sort of song that would develop naturally in that bird born in the wild.

This does not mean, however, that animal signaling is not subject to environmental or adaptational factors. Many bird species have also developed regional cooing 'dialects' by apparently imitating each other. Vervet monkeys, too, have the usual set of signals to express emotional states and social needs, but they also have developed a particular predator signaling system – a specific call alerting the group to eagles, one to four-legged predators such as leopards, another to snakes, and one to other primates. The calls and general categories they represent seem innate, but in actual fact the young of the species learn them only by observing older monkeys and by trial and error. An infant vervet may at first deliver an aerial alarm to signal a vulture, a stork, or even a falling leaf, but eventually comes to ignore everything airborne except the eagle.

Most signals are emitted automatically in response to specific types of stimuli and affective states. Humans are capable as well of deploying witting signals for some intentional purpose – e.g. nodding, winking, glancing, looking, nudging, kicking, head tilting. Artificial and mechanical signaling systems can also be created for conventional social purposes. The list of such systems is extensive, and includes railway signals, smoke signals, semaphores, telegraph signals, Morse code signals, warning lights, flares, beacons, balefires, red flags, warning lights, traffic lights, alarms, distress signals, danger signals, whistles, sirens, beepers, buzzers, gongs, bells, etc.

signification

[< Latin SIGNUM 'mark']
*Meaning of a *sign(s) in specific context(s).

Illustrations: tree = 'arboreal plant' in the phrase *maple tree;* but *tree* = 'family genealogy' in the phrase *family tree.*

significs

[< Latin SIGNUM 'mark']
Lady Victoria *Welby's term for the 'study of the nature of significance in all its forms and relations.'

signified

[see also *signifier]
[also called *referent, *object]
What a sign refers or calls attention to.

Illustrations: 1. The signified of the word *cat* is 'a carnivorous mammal (*Felis cattus*) domesticated since early times as a catcher of rats and mice.' 2. The signified of the visual symbol + is 'plus, positive.'

signifier

[see also *signified]
[also called *representamen]
Physical part of a sign, which can be seen, heard, felt, etc.

Illustrations: 1. The signifier standing for 'a carnivorous mammal (*Felis cattus*) domesticated since early times as a catcher of rats and mice' can be described as the sequence of sounds /k/ + /æ/ + /t/ (= cat). 2. The signifier ☞ standing for 'in this direction,' can be described as the figure of a pointing finger.

signifying order

[also called *semiosphere]

Interconnection of *signs, *codes, *texts, and *contexts, that make up a *culture.

sign language

[< Latin SIGNUM 'mark']

Language code based on gestures and grammatical rules that share some common points with the spoken language, used in place of vocal speech among people lacking a common spoken language, or by people physically incapable of speech or hearing.

Note: An example of a sign language is the one developed by the Plains peoples of North America as a means of communication between tribes that do not share the same language. The gesture signs represent things in Nature, ideas, emotions, and sensations. Sign languages for hearing-impaired people also have been developed. They generally include two types of signs: *natural signs,* which stand for ideas or objects, and *systematic signs,* which are used for word-by-word or letter-by-letter renderings of the written rather than the spoken language.

simile

[< Latin SIMILIS 'similar']

Rhetorical technique by which two ideas are compared explicitly with the words *like* or *as.*

Illustrations: 1. *She sings <u>like</u> a bird.* 2. *He runs <u>as</u> fast <u>as</u> a gazelle.*

simulcast

[< Latin SIMUL 'at the same time']

Simultaneous broadcast of a program by FM and AM radio or by radio and television.

sinsign

term coined by Charles *Peirce to designate a sign that draws attention to, or singles out, a particular object in time-space.

Illustrations: 1. a pointing finger; 2. the words *here* and *there.*

sitcom

[abbreviation of situation comedy]

Humorous recurring program (daily, weekly) made for radio and television.

Note: The *sitcom* has proved the most durable and popular of American broadcasting genres. It uses stock characters and recurring situations to explore life in the home, the workplace, and other common locations. *I Love Lucy* (1951–7), which starred Lucille Ball, was the first hit television sitcom.

situation

[< Latin SITUS 'position, situation']

1. any significant combination of circumstances developing in the course of a novel, play, etc.; 2. physical circumstance that influences the meaning of a *sign or *text.

Skinner, B.F.

[1904–1990]

American psychologist who championed *behaviorism and especially the theory of *conditioning.* Skinner also originated programmed instruction, a teaching technique in which a student is presented with a series of ordered, discrete bits of information. The student must understand each part before proceeding to the next stage.

slang

1. specialized vocabulary used for hiding from outsiders the meaning of what was said and/or to show group identity or solidarity; 2. highly informal speech that is considered to be outside conventional or standard usage.

Note: Although the larger society may find slang undesirable and boorish, it is not immune from it. If the slang-using group has enough contact with the mainstream culture, some of its words and idioms might become forms known to the whole society, usually because they may provide a name needed for an object or action (*walkie-talkie*). Sometimes, slang terms become accepted as standard speech with an altered, tamed meaning (*jazz* originally had sexual connotations). Slang also finds its way into the cultural mainstream through the work of writers who use slang to convey character and ambiance. Shakespeare, for instance, brought into acceptable usage such slang terms as *hubbub*, *to bump*, and *to dwindle*. In the 20th century, the mass media have been instrumental in spreading slang usage. For instance, the words *pot* and *marijuana*, which were part of a secret criminal jargon in the 1940s, became, through media diffusion, common words in the 1960s.

Slang expressions may take form as metaphors, similes, and other figures of speech (*dead as a doornail*). Words may acquire new meanings or they may be abbreviated (*mike* for *microphone*). Slang acronyms may gain currency (*VIP*, *AWOL*). A change in meaning may make a vulgar word acceptable or an acceptable word vulgar.

slapstick

Boisterous form of comedy characterized by chases, collisions, and crude practical jokes.

Note: The word comes from the device for slapping people on-stage that was used in many late-19th- to early-20th-century comedies. The device, called a *slapstick*, was made of two flat pieces of wood fastened at one end. Through its association with *comedy, the term developed the sense in the mid-1920s that encompassed the whole genre of comedy in which a literal slapstick did not necessarily play a role.

slogan

Phrase expressing the aims or nature of an enterprise, an organization, or a candidate.

Illustrations: 1. *McDonald's does it all for you!* 2. *All State – You're in good hands!*

soap opera

Daily serial drama on radio or television, developed originally as a daytime genre aimed specifically at a female audience. It is called *soap opera* because the original sponsors were detergent companies.

Note: Soap operas typically revolve around a romantic plot in which the emotions of the audience are of paramount importance, without regard for character development or logic. Sexual mischief, betrayal, infidelity, and the like are the primary ingredients in soap-opera plots and characterizations.

social zone

[see *zone, social]

society

[< Latin socius 'companion']
Collectivity of individuals who, although they may not all have the same ancestral or tribal origins, nevertheless participate, by and large, in the signifying order of the founding or conquering tribe (or tribes).

Note: The establishment of a dominant signifying order (culture) makes it possible for individuals to interact practically and habitually with each other. Unlike tribes, however, societies can enfold more than one signifying order. As a consequence, individuals may, and typically do, choose to live apart – totally or partially – from the main signifying order. For instance, the modern *society* known as the United States is called loosely, 'American culture.' This culture traces its origins primarily to the signifying order of the British people who settled in the United States a few centuries ago. Since then, American society has also accommodated and sanctioned aboriginal and other parallel cultural systems, each one entailing a different way of life, a different language, a different system of rituals, etc. Moreover, within the dominant signifying order, diversification has come about as a consequence of the tendency of splinter groups – known as *subcultures* – to emerge within large and impersonal societies. Thus, it is possible for an individual living in the United States to remain apart from the dominant signifying order by espousing a parallel one or becoming a participant in a subcultural one. But very much like a tribal person, a city-dwelling individual living in America today who chooses to live apart from the dominant signifying order will typically face social risks, such as exposure to various forms of ridicule or censure and perhaps even exclusion from participation in various institutional systems or communal activities.

sociobiology

[< Latin SOCIUS 'companion' + Greek BIOS 'life' + LOGOS 'word, study']
Science studying the co-dependency of biological factors with social ones in the evolution of all species. The main claim of sociobiology is that there is a high degree of innate control in all social behaviors.

Note: Sociobiologists attempt to describe what caused the change from largely genetically programmed behavior to reflective thought in the human species in terms of a gene-culture coevolution process. This process was purportedly triggered in *Homo habilis* after this species had learned how to use the hands to make tools between 1.5 and 2 million years ago. *Homo habilis* beings were small creatures with a human body and a brain similar to that of an ape. They lived in groups as hunter-gatherers on the savanna plains of Africa. Threatened by larger mammals, but desperately needing to catch game in order to survive, they had to learn how to act cooperatively, to think logically, and to communicate among themselves in some fashion. So, they developed social rules for hunting, food sharing, division of labor, mating, etc. Theirs was the earliest human culture.

As cultures in subsequent *Homo* species (*erectus* and *sapiens*) became more complex, so did the human mind, because humans were forced to make choices that conferred upon them greater survival and reproductive abilities. Gene evolution gradually gave way to cultural evolution. The body's survival mechanisms were eventually replaced by the survival formats provided by culture.

The sociobiological perspective has gained widespread popularity beyond academia in part as a result of the publication of accessibly written books such as those by the contemporary British biologist Richard Dawkins (1941–). With great rhetorical deftness and aplomb, Dawkins portrays cultures as collective adaptive systems that emerged in the human species to enhance its survivability and future progress by replacing the functions of genes with those of mental units that he calls *memes* – a word he coined in direct imitation of the word genes. Dawkins defines memes as replicating patterns of information (ideas, laws, clothing fashions, artworks, etc.) and of behavior (marriage rites, love rituals, religious ceremonies, etc.) that people inherit directly from their cultural environments. Like genes, memes involve no intentionality on the part of the receiving human organism. As part of culture, the human being absorbs memes unreflectively from birth, and then becomes part of a collective system that passes them on just as unreflectively to subsequent generations, allowing the memes to improve adaptively over preceding generations. The memetic code is thus responsible for cultural progress, advancement, and betterment, having become the primary agent in the human species's evolutionary thrust forward.

Many arguments have been put forward against meme theory. Genes can be identified and separated from organisms, and then studied, altered, and even cloned physically. That is a scientific fact. The theory of *memes*, by contrast, is no more than an idea of how cultural systems work. There is no empirical way to verify the reality of memes, as defined by Dawkins; they can only be talked about as if they existed.

The key figure behind sociobiological theory and research is the American biologist E.O. *Wilson, known for his work tracing the effects of natural selection on biological communities, especially on populations of insects, and for extending the idea of natural selection to human cultures. Wilson claims that the psychological capacities and social behaviors that humans manifest are genetically based and that evolutionary processes favor those that enhance reproductive success and survival. Thus, characteristics such as heroism, altruism, aggressiveness, and male dominance, for instance, can be understood as evolutionary outcomes, not in terms of historical, social, or psychic processes. Moreover, Wilson sees the creative capacities undergirding language, art, scientific thinking, etc. as originating in the same pool of genetic responses that help the human organism to solve physical problems of survival.

sociolinguistics
[< Latin SOCIUS 'companion' + LINGUA 'tongue']
Branch of linguistics studying how language functions in society. Sociolinguists study how linguistic forms and uses vary according to age, class, gender, situation, and other social variables.

Socrates
[470?–399? BC]
Greek philosopher, who profoundly affected Western philosophy through his influence on *Plato, in whose works his character and ideas are portrayed. Socrates believed in the superiority of argument over any other form of disclosure, and spent hours in the public places of Athens, engaging in dialogue and argument with anyone who would listen. He emphasized rational argument and the quest for general abstract ideas, and believed in a purely objective understanding of justice, love, and virtue. He thought that wickedness was the result of ignorance and that people are not willingly bad.

Socratic irony
[after Socrates in Plato's *Dialogues*]
Feigning of ignorance in argument, in order to make a point more forcefully.

software
[see also *hardware]
Programs that cause computers to do specific kinds of things.

Note: Software as a whole can be divided into a number of categories based on the types of work done by programs: 1. *operating system software*, which controls the workings of the computer; 2. *application software*, which addresses the multitude of tasks for which people use computers; 3. *network software*, which enables groups of computers to communicate; 4. *language software*, which provides programmers with the tools they need to write programs.

soliloquy
[see *monologue]

solipsism
[< Latin SOLUS 'alone' + IPSE 'oneself']
View that the self is the only thing that can be known and verified, and thus the only reality.

something-for-nothing lure in advertising
[see *advertising, use of the something-for-nothing lure in]

sonnet
[< Italian SONETTO 'little sound']
A 14-line *verse form usually having a conventional *rhyme scheme.

Sophists
[5th century BC]
Group of traveling teachers who became famous throughout Greece towards the end of the 5th century BC. The Sophists denied the existence of objective knowledge, and were notorious for their clever, specious arguments.

sound symbolism
Process by which referents (objects, ideas, events, actions, etc.) are represented through some form of vocal simulation.

Illustrations: 1. in the language of cartoons and comic books: *Zap!*, *Boom!*, *Pow!*, etc. 2. in many of the world's languages [i]-type vowels are used to express 'nearness,' in contrast to [a]-, [o]-, and [u]-type vowels to express the opposite notion of 'distance' (as in English *near* vs. *far*).

source domain
[see *target domain]
Part of a *conceptual metaphor that delivers the meaning of the metaphor.

Illustrations: In the conceptual metaphor *people are animals*, a general formula that summarizes the use of animal vehicles to describe people (*That man is a snake*; *Alexander is a fox*; *Sarah is a pussy cat*; etc.), there are two domains. *People* is the *target domain* because it is what the conceptual metaphor is all about; and *animals* is the *source domain* because it entails the class of vehicles that deliver the metaphor (the 'source' of the metaphorical concept).

space
[< Latin SPATIUM 'space']
Area with definite or indefinite boundaries, studied by semioticians because of the meanings that such an area entails.

space, private
[< Latin SPATIUM 'space']
Space felt typically to be an extension of self.

Illustration: A home provides a private space that has a straightforward denotative meaning – it is a shelter providing protection from weather and intruders. In semiotic terms, shelters are human-made extensions of the body's protective armor. They constitute privately bounded spaces that are designed to ensure safety and preserve sanity. A home is thus an extension of the body.

The forms of shelters are *signifiers with personal meanings. In tribal societies the house tends to be a single volume, a room for all activities, reflecting a holistic experience of persona. It is usually built directly against neighboring structures and often close to the tribal meeting-house or religious site as well. In China, by contrast, the walled-in form of the courtyard house, which has persisted for centuries, reflects the need for privacy that is inherent in Chinese social traditions and perceptions of self. But rows of single-volume dwellings, each with a small court or garden, are also found in China, reflecting a different type of persona. At the other end of the scale are the imperial palace compounds, of which the Forbidden City in Beijing is the outstanding example. The various buildings of these compounds, laid out to form a vast, symmetrical complex, constitute a symbolic text supporting the divine claims of the emperors and the society they governed.

space, public
[< Latin SPATIUM 'space']
Site where communal or social interactions of various kinds take place.

Note: In the wilderness, spaces are perceived by all species as providing sustenance and shelter. But in cultural contexts, the territory appropriated by a tribe or society is felt typically by its members to be a communal organism. This is why societies are often described by people as being *healthy*, *sick*, *vibrant*, *beautiful*, *ugly*, etc. in their respective languages. And, indeed, outsiders habitually judge a society at first sight on how the public spaces appear to the eye – as *neat*, *dirty*, *organized*, *disorganized*, etc. This is why when someone defaces public places, s/he is felt, literally, to have violated the entire community. Conflicts between tribes or nations are, in actual fact, often triggered by such acts against the communal body.

space, sacred
[< Latin SPATIUM 'space']
Site that is believed to put humans in contact or proximity with the divinities.

Note: Churches, synagogues, mosques, temples, etc. are buildings that generate a sense of sacredness within them. In tribal societies, one building was enough to host the congregation; but in large urban societies, many such buildings are needed. These all have the same goal of making the individuals of a culture feel that they have entered a special place.

The salient characteristic of all sacred spaces is the feeling that they do not belong to the real world, that they are places where the divinities can be reached and where miracles and supernatural events are occasionally expected to take place. After the Madonna appeared to Bernadette at Lourdes, the grotto where she carried out her dialogue with the peasant girl has ever since become sacred and thought to be able to cure disease and bring spiritual healing. Similar places exist throughout the world.

spatial code
[< Latin SPATIUM 'space']
Set of meanings and rules of conduct ascribed systematically to spaces in buildings and in other physical spaces of a society.

Note: Each building or place is a *text with a broad range of meanings. The rules that govern private and public spaces are thus socially coded: e.g. one must knock on the door of a house to announce one's presence, but one does not knock on the door of a retail store; one may sit and wait for some-

one in a foyer, atrium, or lobby, but one does not normally wait for someone in a public washroom; one can walk on a public sidewalk, but one cannot walk on someone's porch without permission; and the list could go on and on. When one enters a sacred space like a church or chapel, one feels and behaves differently than when one enters a bank, a stadium, etc. – in such a space one tends to speak with a lower voice, to be more careful with the walking noises made, and so on.

spatial deixis
[see *deixis]

specialization
[< Latin SPECIES 'kind']
In communication theory, term referring to the fact that the sound waves of speech have no function other than to signal meaning.

speech
Vocalized, articulated, or written language.

Note: Although in colloquial parlance people rarely distinguish between *language* and *speech*, in actual fact the two are different. Vocal *speech* is a physiological phenomenon. It involves the use of the organs of the vocal apparatus – the tongue, the teeth, the epiglottis, etc. – to deliver *language*, which is a mental code. Language can also be expressed through pictorial, alphabetic, and gestural (e.g. sign language) modes. One can have language without speech (as do individuals with impaired vocal organs), because it exists in the mind. But one cannot have speech without language, because speech depends on the language code for its physical transmission.

speech act
View that an utterance can replace an actual physical act or desire for some action.

Illustrations: 1. The utterance *Be careful!* has the same effect as the act of putting a hand in front of someone to block him/her from, say, crossing the road carelessly. 2. A judge's statement *I sentence you to life imprisonment* has the same effect as if the judge had marched the accused to prison and locked him/her up.

Spencer, Herbert

[1820–1903]
English philosopher who conceived of societies and cultural institutions as rankable on the exact same scale as living things, from the most simple to the most complex. In *Principles of Psychology* (1855) he wrote that individual characteristics gradually develop from simple to more complex and diverse states. Spencer was an influential proponent of social Darwinism, an application of the natural-selection theory of British scientist Charles *Darwin to human societies. The theory holds that only the most well-adapted individuals in a population will survive and reproduce. Spencer was, in fact, the one who coined the phrase *survival of the fittest* to describe the competition among human individuals and groups.

split-brain experiments

[called, more technically, commisurotomy experiments]
Widely publicized studies conducted during the 1950s and 1960s by the American psychologist Roger Sperry (1913–94) and his associates on epilepsy patients who had had their two cerebral hemispheres separated by surgical section.

Note: The split-brain studies showed that both hemispheres, not just a dominant left one, were needed in a neurologically cooperative way to produce complex thinking; they also provided a detailed breakdown of the main psychological functions according to hemisphere; and they confirmed that the left hemisphere was the primary site for language.

stanza

[see also *verse]
One of the divisions of a *poem, composed of two or more lines usually characterized by a common pattern of *meter or *rhyme.

statistical map

[see *map]

stereotype

[< Greek STEREOS 'hard, solid' + Latin TYPUS 'model, symbol']
Fixed or conventional notion, or conception, of a person, group, idea, etc., held by a number of people, and allowing for no critical judgment.

Illustrations: 1. Elderly Americans are the neglected sector of the fashion industry, characterized by an image of blue hair and polyester pantsuits. 2. 'Teenagers are all stir-crazy.'

Stoics

[c. 300 BC]
Members of a Greek school of philosophy, founded by Zeno around 308 BC, holding that all things are governed by unvarying natural laws, and that the wise person should follow virtue alone, obtained through reason, remaining indifferent to passions or emotions. The Stoics held that all reality is material, but that this is to be distinguished from *logos, the unvarying order manifested in nature. In particular, the rational part of the soul was considered by the Stoics to be a spark of the divine logos in the individual human being. The four cardinal virtues of the Stoic philosophy are wisdom, courage, justice, and temperance.

storage hardware

Computer devices like disk drives and *memory.

Note: Disk drive types include hard, floppy, magneto-optical, and compact. Magnetic hard disk drives are usually part of a computer, able to store much information and retrieve it quickly. *Memory* refers to computer chips that store information for quick retrieval. *Random-access memory* (RAM) stores both information and instructions that operate the computer's programs. *Read-only memory* (ROM) contains permanent information and programs such as the operating system that directs the computer.

stratigraphic analysis
[< Latin STERNERE 'to lay out'; Greek ANA 'throughout' + LYSIS 'a loosing']
Archeological technique for establishing the chronology of things at a site through an analysis of the time-ordered deposits of soil, organic materials, and remains of human activity.

Note: Deposits gradually build up and cover each preceding phase in human sites. The primary task of stratigraphic analysis lies in piecing together the remains of floors, storage pits, and other constructions in a way that is consistent logically with the deposit sequences or layers found at the site.

stream of consciousness
Literary technique by which a novel, film, or play is structured to unfold through the thoughts and feelings of a character as they develop.

Note: The term *stream of consciousness* was first used by American psychologist William James (1842–1910) in his book *The Principles of Psychology* (1890). In fiction it constitutes a powerful technique for revealing a character's feelings and thoughts. The plot is made to unfold by means of an associative rather than a logical sequence, without commentary by the narrator. Notable exponents of this form of writing are Irish novelist James Joyce (1882–1941), American writer William Faulkner (1897–1962), and British novelist Virginia Woolf (1882–1941).

strophe
[< Greek STROPHĒ 'a twist']
First of a pair of *stanzas of alternating form on which the structure of a given poem is based.

structuralism
[< Latin STRUCTURA ' arrangement']
Mode of inquiry in semiotics, linguistics, anthropology, and other human sciences aiming to understand the sensory, emotional, and intellectual *structures* that undergird both the production and interpretation of *signs. The basic tenet of structuralism is that signs and concepts beget their meanings and functions through binary oppositions.

Illustrations: 1. The words *tip* and *rip* bear meaning through a minimal difference in sound (as seen in the initial consonants). 2. At the level of concept-formation, *good* is understood in contrast with *evil*, *night* with *day*, and so on.

Note: Structuralists emphasize techniques to be used to determine the underlying, abstract system of structures in representation that is distinguishable from actual instances of representation. This approach began in 1916 with the posthumous publication of the work of Ferdinand de *Saussure. Saussure distinguished between the concepts of *langue* (French for 'language') and *parole* ('word'). By langue he meant the knowledge that speakers of a language share about what is grammatical in that language. Parole referred to the actual spoken utterances of the language.

Beginning in the late 1940s anthropologist Claude *Lévi-Strauss, semiotician Roland *Barthes, and other mid-century thinkers initiated 'French structuralism' by applying linguistically based formal methods to literature and cultural behaviors. These structuralists attempted to investigate the 'structure' of a culture as a whole by 'decoding' or interpreting its interactive systems of signs. These systems include literary texts and genres as well as other cultural texts, such as advertising, fashion, and taboos on certain forms of behavior.

structural grammar
[see *grammar]

structural schema
[see *image schema]

structure
[< Latin STRUCTURA ' arrangement']
Any repeatable or predictable aspect of *signs, *codes, and *texts.

Illustrations: 1. In Italian word structure can be seen in the fact that nouns end typically in a vowel (*gatto* 'cat,' *donna* 'woman,' etc.). 2. In music a 'perfect cadence' is a structure because it has a recognizable 'sound' to it (made up of the dominant-to-tonic chord movement).

Sturm und Drang
[German 'storm and stress,' after a drama by Friedrich Maximilian von Klinger (1752–1831)]
Late-18th-century German romantic literary movement depicting the struggles of a highly emotional character against conventional society.

Note: The movement was inspired in large part by the ideas of the contemporary French philosopher Jean-Jacques Rousseau (1712–78) and the German philosopher Johann Gottfried von Herder (1744–1803). Elements of *Sturm und Drang* are found in works of Johann Wolfgang von Goethe (1749–1832), notably his novel *The Sorrows of Young Werther* (1774), and in Friedrich von Schiller's (1759–1805) plays, especially *The Robbers* (1781). The *Sturm und Drang* movement is viewed as a prelude to romanticism in the arts.

style
[< Latin STYLUS 'spike, writing instrument']
1. manner or mode of expression in language, as distinct from the ideas expressed; 2. way of using words to express thoughts; 3. in any art, period, or work, the way in which anything is made or done; 4. in clothing, a synonym for *fashion.

stylistics
[< Latin STYLUS 'spike, writing instrument']
1. branch of linguistics studying *style in language; 2. study of style as a means of analyzing works of literature and their effects.

subject
[< Latin SUB 'under' + IACERE 'to throw']
[see also *predicate]
1. something dealt with in a discussion or work; 2. noun or other form that is one of the two immediate constituents of a sentence and about which something is said in the predicate; 3. in logic that part of a proposition about which something is said.

Illustrations: 1. The <u>boy</u> is reading a book. 2. <u>It</u> is true.

subliminal technique
[< Latin SUB 'under' + LIMEN 'threshold']
In advertising, technique that is designed to communicate a hidden meaning below the threshold of consciousness or apprehension.

Note: The most common type of subliminal technique is to embed images in a photograph of a product. Sexual images, for instance, can be worked into the shape of spaghetti on a plate or into the puff of exhaled cigarette smoke. The theory behind such a technique is that the unconscious mind will pick up the image and make an association between eating the spaghetti or smoking a cigarette and sexuality; hence, an association that increases the allure of the product.

subordinate concept
[see *concept, subordinate]

subplot
[< literally 'below the plot']
Plot subordinate to the main *plot of a literary work, play, or film, added for various reasons: e.g. to complicate the plot (in a mystery story), to provide diversion or comic relief (in a tragedy), to shed light on the personality of a key character, etc.

subtext
[< literally 'below the text']
Text (message) hidden within a *text, alluding to mythical themes (good vs. evil), narratives, etc.: e.g. an allusion to eating a forbidden fruit or to the figure of a snake constitutes a biblical subtext.

suffix
*Affix added to the end of a *morpheme.

Illustrations: 1. -*ly* in *regularly*; 2. -*ness* in *happiness*; 3. -*ed* in played; 4. -*ish* in *boyish*.

supercomputer
[see *computers]

superego
In psychoanalytic theory, the element of personality that automatically modifies and inhibits instinctual impulses that tend to produce antisocial actions and thoughts.

Note: According to psychoanalysts, the superego is one of the three basic constituents of human character, the others being the *ego and the *id. The superego develops as the child gradually and unconsciously adopts parental and social values and standards.

superordinate concept
[see *concept, superordinate]

surface structure
[see also *deep structure]
Linguist Noam *Chomsky's notion referring to the structure of a sentence as it appears to observation, which is often different from its underlying structure, known as *deep structure.*

Illustration: The two sentences *John is eager to please* and *John is easy to please* have the same *surface structure*, i.e. they can be put in a one-to-one structural mapping. However, the meanings of the sentences are rather different. In effect, the surface structure does not tell the whole syntactic story. A paraphrase of the two sentences reveals that they have different *deep structures: John is eager to please = John is eager to please someone; John is easy to please = It is easy for someone to please John.* The conflation of both these deep structures into homologous surface structures is due to the operation of what Chomsky called *transformational rules*, which move around, delete, and add elements to deep structure forms.

surname
[literally 'the name added on top of a name']
[also called family name]
*Name shared by the members of a family, as distinguished from each member's given name. In the late Middle Ages, one personal (given) name was generally sufficient as an identifier. Duplications, however, began to occur so often that additional differentiations became a necessity. Hence, *surnames* were given to individuals.

Illustrations: 1. In England, a person living near or at a place where apple trees grew might be called 'John where-the-apples-grow,' hence, *John Appleby* (regional or place names, such as *Wood* or *Woods, Moore, Church,* or *Hill*, constitute a large number of English surnames). 2. Descendant surnames were often formed with the use of prefixes such as *Mac-, Mc-* in Scotland or Ireland, or *Ap-* in Wales (e.g. *Macintosh, McInnis,* etc.); the suffixes -*son* in English names and -*sen* and -*dottir* in Scandinavian names were also used commonly (e.g. *Johnson* or *Jensen,* 'son of John,' *Maryson* 'son of Mary,' *Jakobsdottir*, 'daughter of Jacob'). 3. Surnames reflecting medieval life and occupations include *Smith* – with equivalents in Spanish (*Ferrer*), German (*Schmidt*), and Hungarian (*Kovacs*) – *Farmer, Carpenter, Tailor, Weaver*, etc.

surrealism

[literally 'above the real']
20th-century literary and artistic movement, founded by French poet and critic André Breton (1896–1966) in Paris in 1924, which wanted artists to express the imagery of their unconscious mind through fantastic and incongruous juxtaposition of subject matter in their works.

Note: Surrealists aimed to express in an overt fashion the unconscious symbols that induce creative activity. The movement spread all over the world and flourished in the United States during the Second World War. Surrealists often employed abstract and fantastic shapes and forms. Members of the movement included Max Ernst (1891–1976), René Magritte (1898–1967), and Salvador Dalí (1904–89). Dalí's earlier paintings depicted dream imagery and everyday objects in unexpected forms. His later ones often portrayed religious themes and were characterized by brilliant colors.

syllabary

[< Greek SYLLABĒ 'syllable']
Set of graphic characters, each character representing a syllable.

syllable

[< Greek SYLLABĒ 'syllable']
Word or part of a word pronounced with a single, uninterrupted sounding of the voice (usually a vowel) and generally one or more sounds of lesser sonority (usually consonants).

Illustrations: 1. The word *cover* is made up of two syllables: *co-* and *-ver*. 2. The word *our* is a single-syllable word. 3. The word *converter* is made up of three syllables: *con-*, *ver-*, and *-ter*.

syllogism

[< Greek SYLLOGIZESTHAI 'to reckon together, sum up']
Deductive reasoning formula, developed by *Aristotle, consisting of two premises (a major and a minor one) and a conclusion logically derived from them.

Illustration: 1. *Major premise*: 'All humans are mortal.' 2. *Minor premise*: 'I am human.' 3. *Conclusion*: 'I am mortal.'

symbol

[< Greek SYN 'together' + BALLEIN 'to throw']
1. *sign that represents or refers to something in an arbitrary, conventional way;
2. any sign referring to an abstract notion.

Note: Symbol use is what sets human representation apart from that of all other species. Words in general are symbolic signs. But any *signifier – object, sound, figure, etc. – can be symbolic. A cross figure can stand for the concept 'Christianity'; a V-sign made with the index and middle fingers can stand symbolically for the concept 'peace'; *white* is a color that can be symbolic of 'cleanliness,' 'purity,' 'innocence,' and *dark* of 'uncleanness,' 'impurity,' 'corruption.'

symbolicity

[< Greek SYN 'together' + BALLEIN 'to throw']
Production, comprehension, and utilization of *symbols.

Note: The claim of many semioticians is that symbolicity is a derivative of the more fundamental *iconic and *indexical modes of representation. Symbols are 'residues' of icons and indexes. The anecdotal evidence to support this view is substantial: e.g. the child first learns to represent something by pointing to it (indexicality) and then naming it (symbolicity) later; people instinctively resort to iconicity (gesturing, making imitative sounds, etc.) and indexicality (pointing) when communicating with someone who does not speak the same language.

The debate on symbolicity goes back to the Greek philosopher *Plato, who viewed symbolic representation as separate from sensory imitation (iconicity). The French philosopher René *Descartes reinforced this view by claiming that nonverbal forms of thought proceeded without logic, and so could not be studied scientifically. But abstract forms of reasoning, such as those used in mathematics and science, are not purely symbolic. The use of diagrams to 'demonstrate' a theory is, in effect, an iconic strategy.

symbolism
[< Greek SYN 'together' + BALLEIN 'to throw']
Property of something that has highly symbolic features (e.g. symbolist poetry, painting, etc.).

Note: In literature, symbolism started in the late 19th century as an aesthetic movement that encouraged writers to express their ideas, feelings, and values by means of symbols or suggestions rather than by direct statements. Symbolist writers, in reaction to earlier 19th-century trends, proclaimed that the imagination was the true interpreter of reality. The symbolist movement traces its origin in the poetry of Charles Baudelaire (1821–67), whose *Flowers of Evil* (1857) and *Le spleen de Paris* (1869) were judged as decadent by his contemporaries. Stéphane Mallarmé (1842–98) followed Baudelaire's symbolism with *The Afternoon of a Faun* (1876) and the treatise *Ramblings* (1897), which formed the most important statement of symbolist aesthetics. Other examples of symbolist poetry are *Songs without Words* (1874) by Paul Verlaine (1844–96) and *The Drunken Boat* (1871) and *A Season in Hell* (1873) by Arthur Rimbaud (1854–91).

symbology
[< Greek SYN 'together' + BALLEIN 'to throw']
1. study of symbols and their uses; 2. use of symbols for specific purposes (e.g. the symbology of teenage gangs).

sympathetic magic
[see *magic]

symptom
[< Greek SYMPTOMA 'a happening']
Bodily *sign that indicates the presence of some altered physical state (an ailment, disease, etc.).

Note: *Semiotics arose from the scientific study of the physiological symptoms induced by particular diseases or physical states. It was Hippocrates (460–377 BC), the founder of Western medical science, who established semeiotics as a branch of medicine for the study of *symptoms* – a symptom being, in effect, a *semeion* 'mark, sign' that stands for something other than itself. The physician's primary task, Hippocrates claimed, was to unravel what a symptom stands for.

As the biologist Jakob von *Uexküll argued, the symptom is a reflex of anatomical structure. Animals with widely divergent anatomies will manifest virtually no symptomatology in common. The term symptom is often extended metaphorically to refer to intellectual, emotional, and social phenomena that result from causes that are perceived to be analogous to physical processes: *Their behavior is a symptom of our times; Their dislike of each other is a symptom of circumstances;* etc.

synapse
[< Greek SYN 'together' + APSIS 'a joining']
Junction point of two *neurons, across which a nerve impulse passes.

synchrony
[< Greek SYN 'with, together' + CHRONOS 'time']
[see also *diachrony]
Study of *signs, *codes, and *texts at a specific point in time (usually the present).

Illustration: The difference between *synchronic* and *diachronic* analysis can be seen when considering the meaning of a word such as *duomo* in Italian. Synchronically, the word is characterizable as a noun meaning 'dome.' This meaning can be seen in such expressions as *il Duomo di Milano* 'the Dome of Milan,' *il duomo della cattedrale* 'the dome of the cathedral,' etc. A diachronic analysis of this term reveals, however, that it derives from Latin DOMUS 'house.' This implies that its original meaning narrowed in Italian to become, more specifically, a type of house (a religious house).

synecdoche

[< Greek SYN 'together' + EKDECHESTHAI 'to receive']
Type of *metonymy whereby a part is used to represent the conceptual whole to which it belongs, or vice versa.

Illustrations: 1. *bread* for *food*; 2. *the White House* for *the presidency*; 3. *Kleenex* for *tissue paper*; 4. *wheels* for *automobile*.

synesthesia

[< Greek SYN 'together' + AISTHESIS 'perception, sense-impression']
1. sensation felt in one part of the body when another part is stimulated; 2. fusion of two sensory forms of representation (sight and hearing, touch and sight, etc.).

Illustrations: 1. *loud red* (= hearing + sight); 2. *smooth melody* (= touch + hearing).

synonym

[< Greek SYN 'together' + ONOMA 'name']
[see also *antonym]
Word having the same or nearly the same meaning as another in the same language.

Illustrations: 1. *near-close*; 2. *far-distant*.

synonymy

[< Greek SYN 'together' + ONOMA 'name']
[see also *antonymy]

Relation by which the meanings of different signs overlap.
1. *hide-conceal*; 2. *big-large*.

syntagm

[< Greek SYN 'together' + TASSEIN 'to arrange']
[see also *paradigm]
Structural pattern by which *signs or *texts are composed.

Note: Signs beget their forms and meanings in *structured* ways. In pairs such as *pin-bin*, *fun-run*, and *duck-luck*, the initial consonant is sufficient to keep these words distinct. This differentiation feature of signs is known as *paradigmatic* structure – i.e. the relation whereby some minimal feature in a sign is sufficient to keep it differentiated from all other signs of the same kind. Now, these words are legitimate signs, not only because they are differentiable in a specific way, but also because the combination of sounds with which they are constructed is consistent with English syllable structure. By contrast, *tpin, tbin, tfun, tpun, tduck, tluck* would not be legitimate signs in English because they would violate its syllable structure. Syllable structure is an example of *syntagmatic* structure – i.e. the relation whereby signs are constructed in some definable sequence or combination. Syntagmatic structure is found in all human representational systems. In music, for instance, a melody is recognizable as such only if the notes follow each other in a certain way (e.g. according to the rules of classical harmony).

syntax

[< Greek SYN 'together' + TASSEIN 'to arrange']
1. arrangement of words, phrases, and clauses in language-specific ways to form sentences; 2. study of how words are combined in a language to make sentences.

Note: Sentences are characterized by the

presence, explicit or implicit, of a *subject* (usually a noun or noun phrase) and a *predicate* (consisting of a verb and optional complements). A general characteristic of syntactic systems is that words are not directly combined into sentences, but rather into intermediate units, called *phrases*, which then are combined into *sentences*. The study of syntax is more precisely an examination of the hierarchical rules that group words into phrases, and phrases into sentences.

synthetic language

[< Greek SYN 'together' + TITHENAI 'to place'; Latin LINGUA 'tongue']
Language that is characterized largely by the fact that it depends on inflections to convey meaning.

Illustration: In English the two sentences *The boy loves the girl* and *The girl loves the boy* mean different things. English is thus classified as an *analytic language*, namely, a language that is dependent largely on word order to deliver meaning. By contrast, in Latin, a *synthetic language*, the sentence *The boy (PUER) loves (AMAT) the girl (PUELLAM)* could have been rendered in any one of six ways, because the ending on each word would have told the speaker what relation the word has to the others: PUER is in the nominative case and is thus the subject of the sentence; PUELLAM is in the accusative case (nominative = PUELLA) and thus will always be interpreted as the object of the sentence, no matter where it occurs in it.

system

[< Greek SYN 'together' + HISTANAI 'to set up, establish']
Group of interacting, interrelated, or interdependent elements forming a complex whole.

Illustration: A computer is a hardware system consisting of a microprocessor and allied chips and circuitry, plus an input device (keyboard, mouse, disk drive), an output device (monitor, disk drive), and any peripheral devices (printer, modem). Within this system is an operating system, often called system software, which is an essential set of programs that manage hardware and data files and work with application programs. External to the computer are any collection or combination of programs, procedures, data, and equipment utilized in processing information: an accounting system, a billing system, a database management system, etc.

T

taboo

[< Tongan TABU 'under prohibition']
1. among some Polynesian cultures, a sacred prohibition put upon certain people, things, or acts that makes them untouchable and/or unmentionable; 2. by extension, any social prohibition or restriction that results from convention or tradition; 3. in language, the substitution of one word or phrase for another because of such a restriction.

Tacitus, Cornelius

[c. AD 55–117]
Roman historian who described the character, manners, and geographical distribution of the German tribes he studied. Only portions of his two major works survive: *The Histories* (AD 104?–109?) and *The Annals* (AD 115?–117?). The power of Tacitus as a historian lies in his psychological insight and the brilliance of his character portrayals.

tacteme

[< Latin TANGERE 'to touch']
Minimal unit of touch that embodies some specific meaning.

Illustrations: 1. a pat on the back = approval; 2. a handshake = greeting.

tactile code

[< Latin TANGERE 'to touch']
Social *code that regulates the patterns of touch in social interpersonal situations.

Note: In public places the amount of touching varies considerably from culture to culture: e.g. in San Juan (Puerto Rico) research has found that the rate of couples touching is 180 times per hour, in Paris 110, and in London 0. In many modern urban cultures, such as the North American one, people rarely touch each other. Some clinical psychologists have attributed many modern anxieties and emotional syndromes to this apparent fear and abhorrence of touch. The fields of *touch* and *dance therapy* have been developed, in fact, as a means to help people express themselves and relate to others through touch.

Tactile codes are made of specific touch *signifiers that allow people to make appropriate social contact texts. The minimal units of touch (where to touch, duration of the touch, etc.) are called *tactemes*. The study of tactemes and tactile communication is known more technically as *haptics* (from Greek for 'grasp, touch'). The most common form of haptic communication is handshaking, which is an intrinsic component of formal greeting rituals. Cross-culturally, the form that handshaking assumes varies considerably. People can give a handshake by squeezing the hand, shaking the other's hand with both hands, shaking the other's hand and then patting the other's back or hugging him/her, leaning forward or standing straight while shaking, and so on. But handshaking is not universal. Southeast Asians, for instance, press their palms together in a praying motion when greeting each other.

tactile icon

[see *iconicity]

tactile image

[see *image, mental]

tactile mode

[< Latin TANGERE 'to touch']
Mode of communication based on touch.

tag question

Word, phrase, or clause added to the end of a sentence to emphasize a point, to seek approval, to ascertain some reaction.

Illustrations: 1. *She's coming tomorrow, isn't she?* 2. *That's true, don't you agree?*

target domain

Part of a conceptual *metaphor constituting the abstract topic (the 'target' of the conceptual metaphor).

Illustrations: In the conceptual metaphor *people are animals*, a general formula that summarizes the use of animal vehicles to describe people (*John is a snake; That woman is a fox; Your friend is a pussy cat;* etc.), there are two domains. *People* is the *target domain* because it is what the conceptual metaphor is all about; and animals is the source domain because it entails the class of vehicles that deliver the metaphor (the 'source' of the metaphorical concept).

taxonomy

[< Greek TAXIS 'arrangement' + NOMOS 'law, method']
Ordered system of classification designed to indicate some natural relationship among the elements in the classification.

Illustrations: 1. in biology, arranging animals and plants into natural, related groups based on some factor common to each, such as anatomical structure, embryology, or biochemistry; 2. in linguistics, arranging forms according to level: e.g. *sentences* are made up of *phrases*, which in turn are made up of *lexemes*, which, in their turn, are made up of *morphemes*, which, finally, are made up of *phonemes*.

technology

[< Greek TEKHNĒ 'art, craft' + LOGOS 'area of study']

1. made objects, what they imply and how they contribute to social development; 2. processes by which human beings fashion objects and machines to increase their understanding of, and control over, the material environment.

Note: Many historians of science argue not only that technology has become an essential condition of advanced, industrial civilization, but also that the rate of technological change has developed its own momentum in recent centuries. Innovations now seem to appear at a rate that increases geometrically, without respect to geographical limits or social systems. These innovations tend to transform traditional cultural systems, frequently with unexpected social consequences. For this reason, social critics see technology as both a creative and a destructive process.

telecast

[< Greek TELĒ 'far off']
Abbreviation of *television broadcast*.

telegraphic speech

[< Greek TELĒ 'far off' + GRAPHEIN 'to write']
Pattern of speech that emerges at around 18 months of age, when children start constructing sentences using only key words (as in telegraphic communication).

Illustrations: 1. *Sarah hungry* (= *I, Sarah, am hungry*); 2. *Alex eat* (= *I, Alex, want to eat*).

teleology

[< Greek TELOS 'end' + LOGIA 'study']
1. philosophical study of final causes;
2. belief that natural phenomena are determined not only by mechanical causes but by an overall metaphysical design or purpose.

television

[< Greek TELĒ 'far off'; Latin VIDERE 'to see']
Broadcasting by means of electronically transmitted visual signals received by a television set.

Note: In 1884 the German engineer Paul Nipkow designed a scanning disk that created crude television images. Nipkow's scanner was used from 1923 to 1925 in experimental television systems. Then, in 1926, the Scottish scientist John Logie Baird (1888–1946) perfected the scanning method, and in 1931 the Russian-born engineer Vladimir Zworykin (1889–1982) built the electronic scanning system that became the prototype of the modern TV camera.

The first home television receiver was exhibited in Schenectady, New York, in 1928 by American inventor Ernst F.W. Alexanderson. The images were small, poor, and unsteady, but the set was instantly recognized as having commercial potential. By the late 1930s, television service was in place in several Western countries. The British BBC, for example, started a regular service in 1936. The Radio Corporation of America (RCA) unveiled television to the American public at the 1939 New York World's Fair, with live coverage of opening ceremonies. Immediately following the Second World War four companies stood ready to initiate network television broadcasting in the United States – network broadcasting takes place when local stations covering different regions agree to simultaneously transmit the same signal. Two of the companies, the National Broadcasting Company (NBC) and the Columbia Broadcasting System (CBS), had made vast fortunes in radio broadcasting. The remaining two were the American Broadcasting Company (ABC) and the DuMont Television Network (DuMont went out of business in 1955). By the mid-1950s NBC, CBS, and ABC – collectively known as the Big Three – had successfully secured American network television as their exclusive domain. It was not until the mid-1980s that a fourth company, News Corporation, owned by Australian-born executive Rupert Murdoch, broke their monopoly with the establishment of the Fox television network. Today, there are many private channels, pay channels, and various other viewing options.

Socially, television has become a powerful medium. Today, 98% of North American households own a television set, and a large portion of these have more than one. People glean much of their information, intellectual stimulation, and recreation from television. Television personages are household names, looming larger than life. TV actors and announcers are lifestyle trend-setters. Many people even plan their daily lives around television programs.

television, effects of

[< Greek TELĒ 'far off'; Latin VIDERE 'to see'] View that television produces effects on behavior, lifestyle, and cognition.

Note: Marshall McLuhan (1911–80) was among the first to descry that electronic media have an impact far greater than that of the material they communicate. He argued that in each cultural era the medium in which information is recorded and transmitted is decisive in determining the character of that culture. An oral culture is vastly different in organization and outlook than an alphabetic one. McLuhan also believed that the worldwide linking of electronic information media would create an interconnected 'global village.' And indeed, just as he predicted, through advances in satellite communications, television now allows viewers even to see themselves as 'participants' in wars and conflicts going on in some other part of the world. The world has become a TV village.

There are three main psychological effects that TV has had on society at large. These have been called various things by different social scientists. One effect can be seen in the fact that television personages are perceived as mythic figures, larger than life. Like any type of privileged space – a platform, a pulpit, etc. that is designed to impart focus and significance to someone – television creates mythic heroes by simply 'containing' them in electronic space, where they are seen as suspended in time and space, in a mythic world of their own. This is why meeting actors, musical stars, etc. causes great enthusiasm and excitement in many people.

Another effect can be seen in the fact that TV literally fabricates history by inducing the impression in viewers that some ordinary event – an election campaign, an actor's love affair, a fashion trend, etc. – is a momentous happening. People make up their minds about the guilt or innocence of others by watching news and interview programs; they see certain behaviors as laudable or damnable by tuning into talk shows or real-life docudramas; and the list could go on and on. In effect, the events that receive air time are felt as being more significant and historically meaningful to society than those that do not. Sports events like the *World Series*, the *Super Bowl*, or the *Stanley Cup Playoffs* are transformed on television into Herculean struggles of mythic heroes. Events such as the John Kennedy and Lee Harvey Oswald assassinations, the Vietnam War, the Watergate hearings, the Rodney King beating, the O.J. Simpson trial, and the Bill Clinton sex scandal are transformed into portentous and prophetic historical occurrences. They are imbued with the same emotional power that comes from watching the great classical dramas. TV is both the *maker* of history and its *documenter* at the same time. People now *experience* history through TV, not just read about it in a newspaper or a chronicle. And, as a result, television *shapes* history. The horrific scenes coming out of the Vietnam War that were transmitted into people's homes daily in the late 1960s and early 1970s brought about an end to the war, mobilizing social protest. Significantly, an MTV flag was hoisted by East German youths over the Berlin Wall as they tore it down in 1989. More people watched the wedding of England's Prince Charles and

Princess Diana, and later Diana's funeral, than had ever before in human history observed such events at the same time.

A third effect results from the fact that the TV medium presents its stories, information, and events by compacting them for time-constrained transmission. This leaves little time for reflection on the topics, implications, words, etc. contained in a segment, and effect that has fostered a psychological dependency on information and visual stimulation for their own sake. The amount of information presented in a news program, for instance, is edited and stylized for effortless mass consumption. The camera moves in to select aspects of a situation, to show a face that cares, that is suffering, that is happy, that is angry, and then shifts to the cool handsome face of an anchorman or to the attractive one of an anchorwoman to tell us what it's all about. The news items, the film footage, the commentaries are all fast-paced and brief. They are designed to be visually dramatic snippets of easily digestible information. Within such a stylistic environment, the news information is beyond comprehension. The facts of the news are subjected to the stylized signature of the specific news program – the same story will be interpreted differently according to whoever the television journalist is.

television, as social text

[< Greek TELĒ 'far off'; Latin VIDERE 'to see'] View that television, like a religious (e.g. biblical) narrative, constitutes a *social text that is directive of behavior and lifestyle.

television culture

[< Greek TELĒ 'far off'; Latin VIDERE 'to see'] View that since the 1950s the history of television has become the history of many cultures.

Note: TV has showcased racial protests, riots, and other significant social events, thus forcing the hand of change several

times. Without it, there probably would have been no civil-rights legislation, no Vietnam War protests, no cynical reaction to politics after Watergate. Moreover, many TV programs were pivotal in bringing about a change in social mindset vis-à-vis certain issues. For example, in 1977 the miniseries *Roots* was among the first to deal forcefully with the enduring problem of racism; in 1968 *Star Trek* featured the first interracial kiss in an episode titled *Plato's Stepchildren*; in 1970 the first divorced couple appeared on the *Odd Couple*; in 1971 *All in the Family* cast the first homosexual characters in prime time; in 1973 the same program dealt with the topic of rape; in 1991 the first scene of women kissing was aired on an episode of *L.A. Law*; in 1992 an episode of *Seinfeld* dealt with one of the more taboo subjects of our society, masturbation; and the list could go on and on.

With the advent of satellite transmission, television has also become a powerful medium for inducing radical social, moral, and political changes in all cultures. When asked about the stunning defeat of communism in eastern Europe in the late 1980s, the Polish leader Lech Walesa was reported by the newspapers as saying that it 'all came from the television set,' implying that television had undermined the stability of the communist world's relatively poor and largely sheltered lifestyle with images of consumer delights seen in Western programs and commercials. Marshall *McLuhan's phrase of the 'global village' rings true today more than ever before. Television has indeed shrunk the world into a village.

Like the automobile did at the turn of the century, television has changed the general shape of world culture. Demographic surveys now show consistently that people spend more time in front of television sets than they do working, that watching TV is bringing about a gradual decline in reading, that television's particular form of textuality is leading to the demise of the nation-state concept as ideas and images cross national boundaries daily through television channels. The medium has induced a kind of insatiability for entertainment, variety, and visual stimulation in society at large. With the barrage of TV images that assail people daily, individuals are conditioned to crave constantly for sensory stimulation and variety.

television mythologies

[< Greek TELĒ 'far off'; Latin VIDERE 'to see'] [see also *mythologie]

View that television shows are often based around a *mythologie*, the term used by semiotician Roland *Barthes in reference to the fact that the original mythic themes continue to reverberate residually in modern-day societies, especially in discourse, rituals, and performances.

Illustration: Early television programming genres were derived from radio. The situation comedy, or sitcom, which uses recurring characters and conditions to explore life in the home, the workplace, and other common locations has remained to this day a framework where modern-day mythologies are made, developed, and eventually discarded. Consider, as a case in point, the mythology of fatherhood that TV constructed and developed from the 1950s to the late 1990s.

In the 1950s television programs like *Father Knows Best* and *The Adventures of Ozzie and Harriet* sculpted the father figure to fit the requirements of the traditional patriarchal family structure. Most of these early sitcoms painted the family in a rosy-colored fashion. The father was in charge of the family, with his wife working behind the scenes to maintain harmony through subservience. This mythology of fatherhood reflected the social mindset of the 1950s. TV reinforced it and gave it a narrative form for people to enjoy on a weekly basis, allowing them to evaluate their own family situations in terms of plot, character, and setting. There were several exceptions to this: e.g. *The Honeymooners* and *I Love Lucy*, both of which revolved around strong-willed wives who were, in effect, precursors of later TV feminist characters. But, in general, the subtext to the 1950s TV sitcom was *father = know-all* and *be-all*.

In the 1960s and early 1970s the situation changed drastically, and the mythology was changed to reflect new times. The TV father was becoming more and more of a ludicrous character. The sitcom that reflected this new subtext the most was *All in the Family*. The North American continent was divided, ideologically and emotionally, into two camps – those who supported the views and attitudes of the TV father, Archie Bunker, a staunch defender of the Vietnam War, and those who despised the war and thus the persona of Archie Bunker. What was happening inside the TV Bunker family was apparently happening in families across the continent. North American society had entered into a period of emotional turmoil and bitter debate over such controversial issues as the Vietnam War, racism, the role of women in society, and the hegemony of the patriarchal family. The new subtext that was informing the sitcoms of the late 1960s and early 1970s was *father = opinionated, ludicrous character.*

The total 'deconstruction' of the 1950s mythology of fatherhood became apparent in many of the 1980s and 1990s sitcoms. A typical example was *Married ... with Children*, a morbid parody of fatherhood and of the nuclear family. The father on this program, Al Bundy, was little more than a physical brute, a reprehensible character who was hardly deserving of the title of *father*. Indeed, as the title of the sitcom suggested, he was merely 'married' and just happened to have 'children,' who were about as shallow and despicable as he was – Bud, his boorish, sex-crazed son, and Kelly, his empty-headed and over-sexed daughter.

There was no sugar-coating in that sitcom. *Married ... with Children* was implanted on a new parodic subtext: *father = moron*.

Married ... with Children and similar sitcoms (e.g. the cartoon *The Simpsons*) constituted a scathing indictment of traditional family values and roles. The fathers on those sitcoms were antiheroes who had all the wrong answers to family problems, and who always felt sorry for themselves. The television programs of the 1950s and 1960s had built up a patriarchal mythology of fatherhood. This mythology was challenged not only by *All in the Family*, but also throughout the 1970s by programs such as *The Mary Tyler Moore Show*, *Wonder Woman*, *Rhoda*, *Maude*, *The Days and Nights of Molly Dodd*, *Cagney and Lacey*, and others that portrayed strong, independent women who were attempting to survive, socially and professionally, in a world that was disassembling patriarchal structures.

It is interesting to note that in the midst of that mythological reconfiguration, a program like the *Bill Cosby Show* achieved unexpected success throughout the 1980s. In hindsight, there were a number of reasons for the success of that apparent throwback to the patriarchal programs of the 1950s. First and foremost, Bill Cosby himself was a great comedian who could easily endear himself to a large audience. But, more important, the *Cosby Show* was appropriate for the 1980s. In the 1970s, programs like *All in the Family* and *The Jeffersons* reflected an iconoclastic movement to tear down authority models and figures. But during the 1980s, with the ascendancy of a new right-wing moralism, as evidenced by the election of conservative governments in Canada and the United States, the mythology of patriarchal authority was making a comeback. Once more, audiences were searching for TV father figures who were gentle and understanding at the same time. Bill Cosby fit this image perfectly – with a difference.

Unlike the wife in *Father Knows Best*, Cosby's wife had a more assertive role to play in the family. This 'new-look' patriarchal family provided reassuring in traditional values in a world that was, and continues to be, in constant moral doubt and flux.

By contrast, *Roseanne* (featuring Roseanne Barr) portrayed a boisterous working-class family in a constant state of upheaval. Brash and often controversial, this 1990s sitcom was praised for its honesty and groundbreaking discussion of current social issues.

tempo
[see *rhythm]

temporal deixis
[see *deixis]

tenor
[see *topic]

territoriality
[< Latin TERRA 'earth']
Mechanism by which animals seek out territories for survival.

Note: Each species has the biological means for seeking out appropriate territories for its survival, of marking them, and of defending them. Intrusion into the territory is perceived instinctively as a signal of aggression. Cats, for example, mark the boundaries of their proclaimed territory by urination, and are prepared to challenge any intrusions into the territory aggressively.

In the mid part of the 20th century the territoriality mechanism became the target of behavioral psychologists, whose experiments received much media attention because of the implications they seemed to have at the time for life in modern crowded urban centers. The gist of these experiments can be outlined as follows. When two laboratory rats were enclosed in the same cage, the researchers found that each one would instinctively seize an area of approximately equal dimensions. When a third rat would be introduced into the same cage, then a tripartite arrangement of subdivided areas would seem to be negotiated among the three rats. However, there always seemed to be some initial reluctance to do so, as signaled by minor altercations among the three rats at the beginning of the negotiations. As each extra rat would be introduced progressively into the same environment, more reluctance and aggression would ensue until a 'critical mass' would apparently be reached, whereupon the rats in the cage would either fight aggressively and relentlessly or demonstrate some form of aberrant behavior. The implications for 'urban overcrowding' that those experiments apparently had were not missed by journalists and reporters. The experiments also seemed to provide an explanation as to why some people 'snap,' as the expression goes, when this critical mass is surpassed, and why others seek rational solutions such as escaping into the suburbs, moving to the country, etc.

tertiary modeling system
Highly complex neural system that allows human beings to engage in abstract forms of *semiosis, which in turn permit symbolic representational activities (narration, art, etc.).

text
[< Latin TEXTUS 'fabric']
Anything put together with *signs to represent or communicate something – conversations, letters, speeches, poems, myths, novels, television programs, paintings, scientific theories, musical compositions, etc.

Illustrations: 1. A novel, for instance, is a *verbal text* constructed with language signs according to the rules of the language's orthographic and grammatical systems.
2. A map is a *nonverbal text* constructed with shapes, symbols, etc. to show where places are in relation to each other.

text, social
Any text that is known, explicitly or implicitly, by a group of people (society, tribe, etc.).

Note: A *social text* is an overriding *text that informs a society. The Christian social text, for example, is based on biblical and specific theological traditions. This is why religious dates such as Christmas and Easter are regularly planned yearly events when many people in Western society organize significant social activities. In medieval Europe, the Christian text probably regulated one's entire day. In that era, people emphasized going to church regularly during the day and the week, lived by strict moral codes derived from the Bible, and listened conscientiously to the dictates of clergymen. The underlying *subtext of the medieval Christian social text was that each day brought one closer and closer to one's true destiny – salvation and an afterlife with God. Living according to this text no doubt imparted a feeling of security, emotional shelter, and spiritual meaning to life.

After the Renaissance, the Enlightenment, and the Industrial Revolution, the Christian social text came gradually to be replaced by a more secular form of textuality. Today, people organize their day typically around work commitments, social appointments, etc. that have hardly anything to do with salvation; and only at those traditional 'points' in the calendar (Christmas, Easter, etc.) do they synchronize their secular text with the more traditional religious one. Outside of special cases – such as in certain cloisters and monasteries – the textual organization of the day is hardly ever conscious.

texture
[< Latin TEXTUS 'fabric']
Sensation of touch evoked imagistically when one looks at some drawn figure.

Illustration: A wavy figure produces a pleasant sensation, a jagged one does not:

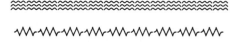

By increasing the number of edges, and hence the jaggedness of the shape, the unpleasant sensation one feels would increase proportionately.

theater
[see *drama]
1. reenactment of some event in nature, in life, in society in some carefully scripted way, involving actors and a spatial location, such as a raised stage, around which an audience can view and hear the performance; 2. building, room, or platform for the presentation of plays; 3. audience assembled for a dramatic performance.

theorem
[< Greek THEOREIN 'to look at']
1. idea that is demonstrably true or assumed to be so; 2. in mathematics, a *hypothesis that has been proved, or can be proved, on the basis of explicit assumptions and *axioms.

Illustrations: 1. *In a right-angle triangle the square of the hypotenuse is equal to the sum of the squares of the other two sides.* 2. *The sum of the angles in any triangle is 180°.*

theory
[< Greek THEORIA 'a looking at']
1. speculative idea or plan as to how something might be done; 2. systematic formulation of apparent relationships or underlying principles of certain observed phenomena that has been verified to some degree.

thesaurus
[< Greek THESAUROS 'a treasure']
Alphabetic listing of *synonyms, often including *antonyms.

Illustrations: 1. A thesaurus might list as synonyms for *love* such words as *devotion, passion, tenderness, liking, affection, fondness,* etc. 2. As antonyms for *love* the thesaurus might include such words as *hatred, detestation, revulsion, repugnance, abhorrence,* etc.

thirdness
[see *firstness, *secondness]
Term coined by Charles *Peirce to designate an abstract system of knowing derived from symbolic processes.

timbre
[< Greek TYMPTEIN 'to strike']
1. in music, the characteristic quality of sound that distinguishes one voice or musical instrument from another; 2. in language, the characteristic quality of sound that distinguishes one vowel sound from another.

tonality
[< Greek TONOS 'a stretching']
1. in music, system of composition based on the relationship between the seven tones of a tonic key; 2. in painting, scheme or interrelation of the color tones.

tone
[< Greek TONOS 'a stretching']
1. vocal or musical sound; 2. pitch or modulation of the voice that expresses a particular meaning or feeling; 3. manner of speaking or writing that shows a certain attitude on the part of the speaker or writer; 4. quality or value of color; 5. relative height of pitch with which a syllable or word is pronounced; 6. any one of the full intervals of a diatonic scale.

tool use
Distinguishing characteristic of the species *Homo.

Note: Although other species, including some non-primate ones, are capable of a limited degree of tool use, only in the human species did complete bipedalism free the hand sufficiently to allow it to become a supremely sensitive and precise manipulator and grasper, thus permitting proficient tool making and use. The earliest stone tools date back to about 2.5 million years ago. Sites in various parts of eastern Africa, from 1.5 million years ago, contain not only many stone tools, but also animal bones with scratch marks that research has shown could only have been left by human-like cutting actions.

topic

[also called *tenor; see also *vehicle]
What a metaphor is about; also called the *A-domain* in the formula [*A* is *B*], which shows the general (explicit or implicit) form of metaphor.

Illustrations: 1. In *John is a snake*, *John* is the topic (= A-domain) and *snake* the vehicle (= B-domain). 2. In *That woman is a computer*, *That woman* is the topic (= A-domain) and *computer* the vehicle (= B-domain).

topographic map

[see *map]

toponym

[< Greek TOPOS 'place' + ONOMA 'name']
Name given to a geographical place.

Note: Toponyms are assigned typically (1) to honor famous personages (*Washington, Lincoln*), (2) to describe some salient topological characteristic (*Black Creek, Niagara Falls*), or (3) to recall a different place seen to have some connection with it (*Syracuse, Paris* in New York State).

total feedback

In communication theory, term referring to the fact that speakers of a language hear and can reflect upon everything that they say (unlike the visual displays often used in animal courtship signaling).

totem

Animal, plant, or natural object serving among certain tribal or traditional peoples as the emblem of a clan or family and often revered as its founder, ancestor, or guardian.

trade advertising

[see *advertising, trade]

trademark

[see *brand name]

traditional transmission

In communication theory, term referring to the fact that language is transmitted from one generation to the next primarily by a process of teaching and learning (not by genetic inheritance).

tragedy

[< Greek TRAGOIDIA 'tragedy']
Serious *drama typically dealing with the problems of a central character, leading to an unhappy or disastrous ending brought on by fate, a tragic character flaw, moral weakness, psychological maladjustment, or social pressure.

Illustrations: Two classic tragedies of Western culture are *Oedipus Rex* by Sophocles (496?–406? BC), considered one of the greatest of all Greek dramatists, and *King Lear* by William Shakespeare (1564–1616). In *Oedipus Rex* (Oedipus the King), Sophocles dramatized the famous story of Oedipus, the Greek mythological figure who unwittingly killed his father, the king, and married his own mother; in *King Lear*, Shakespeare deals with the consequences of the irresponsibility and misjudgment of a father who gives power to his evil children, rather than to his good child.

transformational-generative grammar

[see *grammar]

translation

[< Latin TRANSLATARE 'to transfer']
1. conversion of writing or speech from one language to another; 2. in computer science,

conversion of one type of *programming language into another.

transliteration

[< Latin TRANS 'across' + LITTERA 'letter, character']
Writing of words with characters of another *alphabet that represent the same sound or sounds: e.g. writing Russian words, written in Cyrillic, with letters of the English alphabet.

transmission

[< Latin TRANS 'across' + MITTERE 'to send']
1. physical process of sending messages to a receiver; 2. the physical conveyance of broadcast signals.

tribalism

[< Latin TRIBUS 'one of the three groups into which Romans were originally divided']
Characteristic form of human group life marked by a communal system of signs (language, rituals, etc.).

Note: Like most other species, humans have always lived in groups. Group life enhances survivability by providing protection, shelter, and other safeguards against both enemies and abrupt changes in the surroundings. But at some phase in their evolutionary history – probably around 100,000 years ago – as bipedal hominids became adept at tool making, communicating, and thinking in symbols, they also became aware of the advantages of a group life based on a communal form of living and communicating. The archeological evidence suggests that, by around 30,000 to 40,000 years ago, hominid groups became increasingly characterized by communal customs, language, and the transmission of technological knowledge through a *signifying order (system of signs).

Known as the *tribe*, this form of communal living remains the type of collectivity to which human beings instinctively relate even in modern times. In complex city-societies, where various cultures, subcul-

tures, countercultures, and parallel cultures exist in constant competition with each other, where the shared territory is so large that it becomes an abstraction or figment of mind, the tendency for individuals to relate to tribal-type groupings or arrangements that exist within the larger societal context manifests itself regularly and predictably. People continue to perceive their membership in smaller groups as more directly meaningful to their lives than allegiance to the larger society or nation. This inclination towards *tribalism*, as Marshall *McLuhan emphasized, reverberates constantly within modern-day humans, and may be the source of the angst and sense of alienation that many city-dwelling individuals feel living in large, impersonal social systems.

tribe

[< Latin TRIBUS 'one of the three groups into which Romans were originally divided']
Collectivity of human beings sharing a *signifying order, a territory, and a tradition.

trope

[< Greek TROPOS 'turn, figure of speech']
1. word used in a figurative sense; 2. figure of speech (*metaphor, *metonym, etc.); 3. figurative language in general.

Note: Since the early 1980s the practice has been to use the term *metaphor* to refer to the study of all tropes. Within this framework, *personification*, for instance (*My cat speaks Spanish*), would be seen as a particular kind of metaphor, one in which the *topic of the metaphor is an animal or inanimate object and the *vehicle a referent that applies to human beings.

Turing, Alan Mathison

[1912–1954]
British mathematician who envisioned a device, referred to as the *Turing machine, that could, in theory, perform any calculation. He also devised what has come to be known as the *Turing test, a procedure de-

signed to show that a computer can 'think' essentially like a human.

Turing machine
[named for British mathematician Alan *Turing]
*Algorithm for carrying out a specific computation.

Note: Turing showed that by putting four simple operations on a tape – *move to the right, move to the left, erase the slash, print the slash* – a machine could execute any kind of *program that could be expressed in a binary code (as, for example, a code of blanks and slashes). So long as one could specify the steps involved in carrying out a task and translating them into the binary code, the Turing machine would be able to scan the tape containing the code and carry out the instructions.

Turing test
[named for British mathematician Alan *Turing]
Logical argument devised by mathematician Alan Turing to show that one could program a computer in such a way that it would be virtually impossible to discriminate between its answers and those contrived by a human being.

Illustration: Suppose someone is in a room that hides on one side a programmed computer and, on the other, a human being. The computer and the human being can only respond to the person's questions typed on pieces of paper that both pass on to the observer through slits in the wall. If the observer cannot identify, on the basis of the written responses, who is the computer and who the human being, then she/he must logically conclude that the machine is 'intelligent.' It has passed the *Turing test.*

Tylor, Edward B.
[1832–1917]
British founder of cultural *anthropology who started up the first department of anthropology at Oxford University in 1884. Tylor's studies on the role of religion in cultures, along with his definition of culture, were important early contributions to the field of anthropology.

type vs. token
[< Latin TYPUS 'a model, symbol']
Distinction between a general form, a *type,* and a specific manifestation of that form, a *token.*

Illustrations: 1. A *tree* is a type of plant; a *maple* is a token example of this type. 2. *Blue* is a type of color; *celeste* is a token example of this type.

typological classification
[< Latin TYPUS 'a model, symbol']
Classification of languages according to type of grammatical system they display.

Illustrations: 1. English is classified as an *analytic* or word-order language because it depends mainly on word-order in order to deliver meaning: e.g. *The boy loves the girl* has a different meaning from *The girl loves the boy.* 2. Latin is classified as a *synthetic* language because it delivers meaning through a change in the form of words: e.g. the words in *The boy* (PUER) *loves* (AMAT) *the girl* (PUELLAM) can be arranged in any order and the result would not alter the meaning.

U

Uexküll, Jacob von
[1864–1944]
Estonian biologist who established a point of contact between biology and *semiotics; i.e. between studying the *biosphere and the *semiosphere. For von Uexküll every organism has different inward and outward 'lives.' The key to understanding this duality is in the anatomical structure of the organism itself. Animals with widely divergent anatomies do not share common

forms (perceptions, symptoms, etc.) equally. An organism does not perceive an object in itself, but according to its own particular kind of *Bauplan* – the pre-existent mental modeling system that allows it to interpret the world in a biologically set way. For von Uexküll, each system is grounded in the organism's body, which routinely converts the external world of experience into an internal one of representation in terms of the particular features of the Bauplan with which it is endowed.

Umwelt
[German for 'outside world']
[see *Umwelt* vs. *Innenwelt*]

Umwelt vs. *Innenwelt*
Distinction introduced by biologist Jakob von *Uexküll, implying essentially that the inner mental processes (*Innenwelt*) with which a species is endowed allows it to cope with the outside world (*Umwelt*) in its own particular way.

uncertainty principle
[see *Heisenberg's principle]

unconscious
[< Latin CUM 'with' + SCIRE 'to know']
In psychoanalytic theory, hypothetical region of the mind containing wishes, memories, fears, feelings, and ideas that are prevented from coming to conscious awareness, but that manifest themselves by their influence on conscious processes and, most strikingly, by how they influence dreams and neurotic states. The concept of the unconscious was developed in the period 1895–1900 by Austrian physician and neurologist Sigmund *Freud, the founder of psychoanalysis.

unconscious, collective
[< Latin CUM 'with' + SCIRE 'to know']
In the psychoanalysis of Carl *Jung, the area of the unconscious mind containing the accumulated inherited feelings, thoughts, and memories shared by all humanity.

unconscious, personal
[< Latin CUM 'with' + SCIRE 'to know']
In psychoanalysis, the area of the unconscious mind containing the accumulated feelings and thoughts developed by an individual during his/her lifetime.

universal grammar
[abbreviated to UG]
Linguist Noam *Chomsky's notion that the human brain is endowed at birth with a set of grammatical principles that undergird the development of specific languages.

Note: The role of the linguist, according to Chomsky, is to establish the nature of the UG that makes up the speech faculty. The differences in basic structure that exist in the world's languages are explained by UG theory as due to the different *parameters (instantiations of universal rule types) that lead to variation in specific language grammars. Parameters are defined as different choices of rule types from a fairly small inventory of possibilities. On this view, the child only has to 'set these parameters' on the basis of parental input, and the full richness of grammar will ensue when those parametrized rules interact with one another and with universal principles. According to Chomsky, the parameter-setting view can help explain the universality and rapidity of language acquisition: when the child learns one fact about his/her language, he/she can deduce that other facts are also true without having to learn them one by one.

Chomsky's universalist theories are related to the ideas of philosopher René *Descartes, the *Enlightenment philosophers, and the 18th- and early-19th-century grammarians who urged that grammar be considered a part of logic. Universal grammarians such as the British philosopher John Stuart Mill (1806–73), for instance, believed rules of grammar to be linguistic manifestations of universal thought forms. Chomsky has attempted to make good on Mill's claim, suggesting that the correspondence between language and thought is due to the presence in the human brain of a universal grammar and of a capacity for realizing the rules of grammar for particular languages. This view has been highly criticized, however, for its restrictiveness to syntactic phenomena. UG theory cannot explain the presence of *iconicity in language development and, especially, of the child's strategic use of imitation.

unlimited semiosis

Term used in semiotics to refer to the fact that a *sign when deciphered produces further signs, resulting in a chain of associations that eventually seem quite removed from the initial sign.

unmarked category

[see *markedness]

utterance

Word or words (written or spoken) used in a specific social communicative situation.

V

value

[< Latin VALERE 'to be worth']
1. Ferdinand de *Saussure's term designating the relation that holds between signs; 2. darkness or lightness of a line or shape.

vanishing point

[see *painting, perspective]

vehicle

[< Latin VEHICULUM 'carriage']
Part of a metaphor to which a *topic (what the metaphor is about) is connected; also called the *B-domain* in the formula [A is B], which shows the general (explicit or implicit) form of metaphor.

Illustrations: 1. In *Jerry is a snake*, *Jerry* is the topic (= A-domain) and *snake* is the vehicle (= B-domain). 2. In *My sister is a computer*, *my sister* is the topic (= A-domain) and *computer* is the vehicle (= B-domain).

verb

[< Latin VERBUM 'word']
Words that refer to some form of action; verbs are generally recognized by the form of *inflection known as conjugation, which generally involves changes of form according to person and number, tense, voice, and mood.

Illustrations: 1. *Alexander is eating the candy* (*is eating* = verb in the present progressive tense). 2. *Sarah ate the candy yesterday* (*ate* = verb in the simple past tense).

verbality

[< Latin VERBUM 'word']
In communication theory, term referring to the fact that language is unique to the human species.

Note: All other communication systems in Nature are nonverbal. *Language* is verbal, but not necessarily only *vocal*, since it can be expressed and transmitted also by means of alphabet characters, gestures, etc.

verbal semiotics

[see *semiotics, verbal]

verse

[< Latin VERSUS 'a turning, verse']
Single line in a poem, marked by rhythm, accent, and other kinds of patterns.

Note: In the English language the basic system of versification is known as accentual-syllabic. In this system the parts are the number of syllables in a line of verse and the arrangement of these according to whether they are accented or unaccented. Rhyme, or duplication of sound, is also a characteristic of English verse. Most poems are constructed with end rhyme – i.e. duplicating of sound at the ends of lines. Un-rhymed verse is called *blank verse*. A pattern of rhymes, or rhyme scheme, extending beyond two or three lines, is called a *stanza*.

Poets often use variations and unpat-terned effects to achieve a unique style. The most important variation is *stress*, or differ-entiation in the degree of accent. Another kind of variation from the standard versifi-cation pattern is the length and phonetic character of the *pauses*, or intervals, between syllables of verse. A third variation is vowel and consonant quality. Harsh sounds may suggest pain or striving; soft ones joy or calm.

verum factum
[Latin 'the truth is made']
Notion made popular by Giambattista *Vico that knowledge is a figment of the human imagination: i.e. humans can only under-stand what they have themselves made, including theories of the world; they can never really grasp what they have not made (such as Nature).

Vico, Giambattista
[1688–1744]
Italian philosopher who sought to unravel the origins of mind, language, and culture by analyzing the meanings of the first words. Vico proposed a cyclical theory of history, according to which human societies progressed through a series of stages from sensory barbarism to civilization and then back to barbarism, but of a reflective kind. Vico argued that the human imagination is the faculty that underlies the invention of everything that is human-made, including rationalistic systems of thought like math-ematics and science.

videme
[variant of *viseme]

video display
[see *output hardware]

virtual reality
[abbreviated as VR]
System of devices that enables users to move and react in a computer-simulated environment, sensing and manipulating virtual objects (objects in computer *cyberspace) much as they would real objects.

Note: Virtual worlds are created by math-ematical models and computer programs. These differ from other computer simul-ations in that they require special interface devices that transmit the sights, sounds, and sensations of the simulated world to the user. These devices also record and send the speech and movements of the participants to the simulation program. In effect, the human subject is interacting with a world totally made up, a kind of *representational space* where the user is interacting with the representation.

To see in the virtual world, the user wears a head-mounted display (HMD) with screens directed at each eye. The HMD contains a position tracker to monitor the location of the user's head and the direction in which the user is looking. Using this information, a computer recalculates images of the virtual world to match the direction in which the user is looking and displays these images on the HMD. Users hear sounds in the virtual world through ear-phones in the HMD. Currently, with the use of a glove and position tracker, the user can reach into the virtual world and 'handle' objects.

viseme
[< Latin VISUALIS 'of seeing']
Minimal unit of *eye contact with a specific meaning.

Illustrations: 1. a glance = sign of interest in someone; 2. a wink = a signal of acknowl-edgment.

visual art
[see *art]

visual icon
[see *iconicity]

visual image
[see *image, mental]

visual representation
[see *representation]

visual semiotics
[see *semiotics, visual]

visual sign
[see *sign, visual]

vocable
[< Latin VOCALIS 'of the voice']
Word considered only as a sequence of sounds or letters rather than as a unit of meaning (= verbal *signifier).

Illustrations: 1. *plunt* (= a word with no meaning); 2. *joip* (= a word with no meaning).

vocabulary
[see *lexicon]

vocal icon
[see *iconicity]

vocality
[< Latin VOCALIS 'of the voice']
In communication theory, term referring to the fact that *signals and *messages can be transmitted vocally or nonvocally. Bird communication, for instance, is vocal; bee-dancing is nonvocal.

voice-recognition module
[see *input hardware]

vowel
[< Latin VOCALIS 'of the voice']
[see also *consonant]
Vocal sound produced with no significant obstruction to the airstream emanating from the lungs.

Illustrations: 1. c*o*ld; 2. *u*p; 3. l*i*ve; 4. c*a*t.

Vygotskij, Lev S.
[1896–1934]
Russian psychologist who described human development as a process governed by physical and social actions. For Vygotskij the child first employs nonverbal symbols (action, play, drawing, painting, music, etc.), then imaginative constructs (narratives, fables, dramatizations, etc.), and finally oral expression and creative writing on the way to the development of abstract thought.

W

Warhol, Andy
[1928?-1987]
American pop artist and cinematographer who produced paintings and silk-screen prints of commonplace objects and images, such as soup cans and photographs of celebrities. Warhol's films were characterized by improvised dialogue, lack of plot, and extreme eroticism. In 1994 the Andy Warhol Museum was opened in Pittsburgh.

Watson, John B.
[1878–1958]
American psychologist, founder and leading exponent of the school of psychology known as *behaviorism. Watson believed that the only legitimate and realizable goal for psychology was the study of objectively observable behavior.

Welby, Lady Victoria
[1837–1912]
British semiotician who put forward the theory of *significs, a branch of semiotics dealing with meaning in all its forms and manifestations, verbal and nonverbal. Lady Welby's correspondence with Charles *Peirce has become a key source for understanding the development of the ideas of both scholars.

Wernicke's area
[see *Broca's area]
Area of the left hemisphere responsible for the comprehension of verbal forms.

Note: This area of the brain was discovered in 1874 by the German neurologist Carl Wernicke (1848–1904) after he noticed that damage to this area consistently produced a recognizable pattern of impairment to the faculty of *speech comprehension.

Whitehead, Alfred North
[1861–1947]
British philosopher who revived the theory of *Platonic forms to show the failure of mechanistic science as a way of fully interpreting reality. Together with Bertrand *Russell, he co-authored the *Principia Mathematica* (1910–13), a pivotal text for the modern study of mathematical and logical systems.

Whorf, Benjamin Lee
[1897–1941]
American linguist and anthropologist, student of Edward *Sapir, who kindled widespread interest among culture theorists in the view that language, thought, and culture are interdependent systems.

Whorfian hypothesis
[see *linguistic relativity hypothesis]

Wiener, Norbert
[1894–1964]
Mathematician who pioneered the field of *cybernetics. Wiener's approach to control systems was adopted by the information-control industry to manufacture the first true modern-day computers.

William of Ockham
[c. 1285–c. 1349]
English Franciscan theologian who acerbically denounced *scholasticism, stressing that abstract entities were merely the result of words referring to other words, rather than to actual things. He also rejected St *Augustine's emphasis on the study of conventional signs and differentiated between mental and private signs and those that are spoken/written in order to be made public.

Wilson, Edward Osborne
[1929–]
American evolutionary biologist, founder of *sociobiology, who claims that many human behavioral characteristics should be understood as evolutionary outcomes. Since the mid-1950s, Wilson has constantly maintained that the psychological capacities and social behaviors that humans manifest are genetically based and that cultural-evolutionary processes favor those characteristics that enhance reproductive success and survival. Thus, heroism, altruism, aggressiveness, and male dominance, for instance, should be understood as adaptations, and not simply as consequences of historical, social, or psychic processes. Moreover, Wilson sees the creative capacities undergirding language, art, scientific thinking, etc. as originating in the same pool of genetic adaptive responses that have helped humankind solve physical problems of survival and species continuity.

Wittgenstein, Ludwig
[1889–1951]
Austrian-born British philosopher who developed a 'picture theory' of meaning by which he claimed that verbal propositions represented features of the world in the same way that pictures did. Wittgenstein argued that the words in sentences showed how things were related to each other in the same way that the lines and shapes of drawings did.

  Wittgenstein had serious misgivings about his theory of language later in life. In his posthumously published *Philosophical Investigations* (1953), he expressed perplexity at the fact that language was used by people to do much more than just construct propositions about the world. So, he introduced the idea of 'language games,' by which he claimed that there existed a variety of linguistic games (describing, reporting, guessing riddles, making jokes, etc.) that went beyond simple reference to the world.

wittingness

In communication theory, term referring to the fact that certain messages have been constructed purposefully and intentionally, rather than emitted spontaneously (as in animal signaling behavior).

word

[< Indo-European root WER- 'speak, say' via early Germanic WORDAM]
[see also *morpheme]
Unit of meaning in a language that is recognized as separable from other parts of a sentence.

Note: A word is not the smallest unit of meaning. For example, words such as spearhead, loveboat, etc. are made up of two other words. Also, forms such as illegitimate and irregular, can be decomposed into smaller units: il + legitimate and ir + regular.

word magic

Belief that words evoke magic or can cause things to happen magically.

Illustrations: Techniques of word magic typically include chants and spells (special gestures and actions). Throughout the world, naming objects and artifacts is felt to bestow upon them a mysterious life force. When a name is given to a brand product or a tropical storm, for instance, these seem to take on an identity, a personality.

Word magic is a common theme in literature. A well-known example is the Open Sesame formula used by Ali Baba in Arabian Nights to open the door of the robbers' cave. The word abracadabra derives from the letters, arranged in the inverted pyramid design, of an amulet worn around the neck several centuries ago. In each line of the pyramid there was a letter. Each letter was supposed to vanish magically until only the A remained to form the vertex of the triangle. As the letters disappeared, so purportedly did the disease or problem of its wearer.

In tribal societies, shamans are thought to possess knowledge of magical words that allows them to control objects, people, spirits, and natural events, and thus cure disease, ward off evil, and bring good or harm to another person. In some cultures, knowing the name of God is thought to give the knower great power. Such knowledge is often a closely guarded secret, if indeed it is allowed to be known by anyone but a select few. In Native American cultures, the given *name is thought to bring with it all the spiritual qualities of the individuals who have shared that name. These are thought to cast a magical, protective spell on the child given the name.

word square
[see *acrostic]

World Wide Web
[abbreviated to www]
Information server on the Internet composed of interconnected sites and files developed in 1989.

writing
[see *alphabet]
1. process of representing speech with graphic characters; 2. written work, especially a literary composition.

Note: In evolutionary terms writing did not develop as a simple substitute for speech. Alphabets are late developments. The earliest writing systems were all independent of speech and not alphabetic or syllabic in nature. They were pictographic. In the ancient civilization of Sumer around 3500 BC, for instance, *pictographs were used to represent nouns such as 'star' and 'animal,' with a few for such qualifying adjectives as 'small,' 'big,' and 'bright.' A few centuries later, this pictographic system was expanded to include verbs: 'to sleep,' for example, was represented by a person in a supine position. To facilitate the speed of writing, the Sumerians eventually streamlined their pictographs and transformed them into symbols for the actual sounds of speech. These were written down on clay tablets with a stylus in a form of writing known as cuneiform.

By about 3000 BC the Ancient Egyptians also used a pictographic script – known as *hieroglyphic*. But in their case, the pictographs were more symbolic, standing for parts of words. Hieroglyphic writing was used to record hymns and prayers, to register the names and titles of individuals and deities, and to annotate various community activities – *hieroglyphic* derives from Greek *hieros* 'holy' and *glyphein* 'to carve.'

Once writing became a flourishing enterprise in the ancient civilizations, it began to appear without pictures, producing the first wholly verbal written *texts*. It was the ancient Phoenicians who had systematically severed the iconic relationship between pictographs and referents, creating an abstract system for recording sounds. The Greeks adopted the Phoenician alphabet and called each symbol by such words as *alpha, beta, gamma*, etc., which were imitations of Phoenician words: *aleph* 'ox,' *beth* 'house,' *gimel* 'camel,' etc. The Greeks then introduced symbols for vowel sounds, thus producing the first true *alphabet*, in the modern sense of the word.

Wundt, Wilhelm Max
[1832–1920]
German physiologist who, in 1862, offered the first academic course in psychology, and then in 1879 established the first laboratory for conducting experimental research in psychology in Leipzig.

Z

Zeno of Elea
[5th century BC]
Greek philosopher who discredited the senses as potential sources of thought, laying the foundation for the development of the science of logic. He is famous for his paradoxes.

Zeno's paradoxes
[named for *Zeno of Elea, 5th century BC]
*Paradoxes devised by Zeno of Elea to show how the senses can betray and mislead.

Illustration: One of Zeno's most famous paradoxes asserts that a runner cannot reach a finish line because, as our sense of sight would have it, the runner must first traverse half the distance to the line; then half of that distance; then half of that new distance; and so on ad infinitum. Because of the infinite number of bisections that exist in such linear paths, Zeno concluded that the runner could never travel any given linear distance in a finite period of time. This thus demonstrated to him the logical impossibility of motion as perceived by the senses.

zeugma
[Greek for 'a bond']
Sentence in which a single word, especially a verb or an adjective, is applied to two or more nouns even though its sense is appropriate to only one of them or to both in different ways.

Illustrations: 1. *The room was not light, but his fingers were.* 2. *He took my advice and my wallet.*

zone, interpersonal
[Greek ZONĒ 'a belt']
[see also *proxeme, etc.]
Culturally determined distance that people keep when interacting with one other. The presence and statistical predictability of

interpersonal zones was discovered by anthropologist Edward T. *Hall in the 1950s.

Illustration: In North American culture, Hall found that a distance of under 6 inches between two people was perceived as an 'intimate' zone; while one at from 1.5 to 4 feet was the minimum one perceived to be a safe zone.

zone, intimate
[Greek ZONĒ 'a belt']
[see also *proxme, etc.]
Interpersonal *zone, measured by anthropologist Edward T. *Hall at 0–18 in., which tends to activate all the senses. The close phase (0–6 in.) is an emotionally charged zone reserved for lovemaking, comforting, and protecting; the far phase (6–18 in.) is the zone where family members and close friends interact. Touch is frequent at both phases.

zone, personal
[Greek ZONĒ 'a belt']
[see also *proxeme, etc.]
Interpersonal *zone, measured by anthropologist Edward T. *Hall at 1.5–4 ft., which is the minimum comfortable zone between non-touching individuals. In the close phase (1.5–2.5 ft.), one individual can grasp the other by extending the arms. The far phase (2.5–4 ft.) is anywhere from one arm's length to the minimum distance at which both individuals can touch hands. Beyond this distance the two must move towards each other to make contact (e.g. to shake hands).

zone, public
[Greek ZONĒ 'a belt']
[see also *proxeme, etc.]

Interpersonal *zone, measured by anthropologist Edward T. *Hall at 12 ft. and beyond, which constitutes the distance at which one can take either evasive or defensive action if physically threatened. People tend to keep at this distance from important public figures or from anyone participating at a public function. Discourse at this distance will be highly structured and formalized (lectures, speeches, etc.).

zone, social
[Greek ZONĒ 'a belt']
[see also *proxeme, etc.]
Interpersonal *zone, measured by anthropologist Edward T. *Hall at 4–12 ft., which is perceived as non-involving and non-threatening by most individuals. The close phase (4–7 ft.) is typical of impersonal transactions and casual social gatherings. Formal social discourse and transactions are characteristic of the far phase (7–12 ft.). This is the minimum distance at which one could go about one's business without seeming rude to others.

zoosemiosis
[Greek ZOION 'an animal' + SEMEION 'mark, sign']
Term coined by Thomas A. *Sebeok to refer to *semiosis in and across animal species.

zoosemiotics
[Greek ZOION 'an animal' + SEMEION 'mark, sign']
Term coined by Thomas A. *Sebeok referring to the branch of *semiotics studying semiosis in and across animal species.

BIBLIOGRAPHY

Note: The following is not complete in any sense of the word. It is simply a compilation for in-depth reading and/or consultation of the technical literature for research purposes.

Abercrombie, N. 1996. *Television and Society*. Cambridge: Polity Press.

Adatto, K. 1993. *Picture Perfect: The Art and Artifice of Public Image Making*. New York: Basic Books.

Aitchison, J. 1996. *The Seeds of Speech: Language Origin and Evolution*. Cambridge: Cambridge University Press.

Allert, B., ed. 1996. *Languages of Visuality: Crossings between Science, Art, Politics, and Literature*. Detroit: Wayne State University Press.

Andersson, L., and Trudgill, P. 1990. *Bad Language*. London: Blackwell.

Andren, G.L., L. Ericsson, R. Ohlsson, and T. Tännsjö. 1978. *Rhetoric and Ideology in Advertising*. Stockholm: AB Grafiska.

Andrews, E. 1990. *Markedness Theory*. Durham: Duke University Press.

Andrews, E., and Y. Tobin, eds. 1996. *Toward a Calculus of Meaning: Studies in Markedness, Distinctive Features and Deixis*. Amsterdam: John Benjamins.

Argyle, M. 1988. *Bodily Communication*. New York: Methuen.

Armstrong, D.F., W.C. Stokoe, and S.E Wilcox. 1995. *Gesture and the Nature of Language*. Cambridge: Cambridge University Press.

Arnheim, R. 1969. *Visual Thinking*. Berkeley: University of California Press.

– 1986. *New Essays on the Psychology of Art*. Berkeley: University of California Press.

Ashley, L.R.N. 1984. *The History of the Short Story*. Washington: U.S. Information Agency.

Atwan, R. 1979. *Edsels, Luckies and Frigidaires: Advertising the American Way*. New York: Dell.

Austin, J.L. 1962. *How to Do Things with Words*. Cambridge, Mass.: Harvard University Press.

Axtell, R.E. 1991. *Gestures*. New York: John Wiley.

Ayer, A.J. 1968. *The Origins of Pragmatism: Studies in the Philosophy of Charles Sanders Peirce and William James*. London: Macmillan.

Baigrie, B.S., ed. 1996. *Picturing Knowledge: Historical and Philosophical Problems Concerning the Use of Art in Science*. Toronto: University of Toronto Press.

Bal, M. 1997. *Narratology: Introduction to the Theory of the Narrative*. 2nd ed. Toronto: University of Toronto Press.

Barbe, K. 1995. *Irony in Context*. Amsterdam: John Benjamins.

Barkow, J.H., L. Cosmides, and J Tooby, eds. 1992. *The Adapted Mind: Evolutionary Psychology and the Generation of Culture*. Oxford: Oxford University Press.

Barlow, H., C. Blakemore, and M. Weston-Smith, eds. 1990. *Images and Understanding*. Cambridge: Cambridge University Press.

Barnes, J.A. 1994. *A Pack of Lies: Towards a Sociology of Lying*. Cambridge: Cambridge University Press.

Baron, N. 1992. *Growing Up with Language: How Children Learn to Talk*. Reading, Mass.: Addison-Wesley.

Barthel, D. 1988. *Putting on Appearances: Gender and Advertising*. Philadelphia: Temple University Press.

Barthes, R. 1957. *Mythologies*. Paris: Seuil.

– 1967. *Système de la mode*. Paris: Seuil.

– 1968. *Elements of Semiology*. London: Cape.

– 1970. *S/Z*. Trans. R. Miller. New York: Hill and Wang

– 1977. *Image-Music-Text*. London: Fontana.

Basso, K.H. 1976. *Meaning in Anthropology*. Albuquerque: University of New Mexico Press.

Bateson, G. 1968. *Animal Communication: Techniques of Study and Results of Research*. Bloomington: Indiana University Press.

Battistella, E.L. 1990. *Markedness: The Evaluative Superstructure of Language*. Albany: State University of New York Press.

Baudrillard, J. 1981. *For a Critique of the Political Economy of the Sign*. St Louis: Telos Press.

Bauman, Z. 1992. *Intimations of Postmodernity*. London: Routledge.

Beaken, M. 1996. *The Making of Language*. Edinburgh: Edinburgh University Press.

Bechtel, W. 1988. *Philosophy of Mind: An Overview for Cognitive Science*. Hillsdale, NJ: Lawrence Erlbaum Associates.

Bellack, L., and S.S. Baker. 1983. *Reading Faces*. New York: Bantam.

Bennett, T.J.A. 1988. *Aspects of English Colour Collocations and Idioms*. Heidelberg: Winter.

Benveniste, E. 1971. *Problems in General Linguistics*. Coral Gables: University of Miami Press.

Berger, A.A. 1996. *Manufacturing Desire: Media, Popular Culture, and Everyday Life*. New Brunswick, NJ: Transaction Publishers.

Berger, J. 1972. *Ways of Seeing*. Harmondsworth: Penguin.

Berlin, B., and P. Kay. 1969. *Basic Color Terms*. Berkeley: University of California Press.

Bernardelli, A., ed. 1997. *The Concept of Intertextuality Thirty Years On: 1967–1997*. Special issue of *Versus 77/78*. Milano: Bompiani.

Bettelheim, B. 1989. *The Uses of Enchantment: The Meaning and Importance of Fairy Tales*. New York: Vintage.

Bickerton, D. 1995. *Language and Human Behavior*. Seattle: University of Washington Press.

Bierlein, J.F. 1994. *Parallel Myths*. New York: Ballantine.

Birdwhistell, R. 1970. *Kinesics and Context: Essays on Body Motion Communication*. Harmondsworth: Penguin.

Black, M. 1962. *Models and Metaphors*. Ithaca: Cornell University Press.

Bloomfield, L. 1933. *Language*. New York: Holt.

Blumenberg, H. 1985. *Work on Myth*. Cambridge, Mass.: MIT Press.

Boas, F. 1940. *Race, Language, and Culture*. New York: Free Press.

Bonner, J.T. 1980. *The Evolution of Culture in Animals*. Princeton: Princeton University Press.

Bouissac, P., M. Herzfeld, and R. Posner, eds. 1986. *Iconicity: Essays on the Nature of Culture. Festschrift for Thomas A. Sebeok on His 65th Birthday*. Tübingen: Stauffenburg.

Bouissac, P., et al., eds. 1986. *Iconicity: Essays on the Nature of Culture*. Tübingen: Stauffenberg.

Bremer, J., and H. Roodenburg, eds. 1991. *A Cultural History of Gesture*. Ithaca: Cornell University Press.

Brent, J. 1994. *Charles Sanders Peirce: A Life*. Bloomington: Indiana University Press.

Britton, B.K., and A.D. Pellegrini, eds. 1990. *Narrative Thought and Narrative Language*. Hillsdale, NJ: Lawrence Erlbaum Associates.

Brown, R.L. 1967. *Wilhelm von Humboldt's Conception of Linguistic Relativity*. The Hague: Mouton.

Brown, R.W. 1958. *Words and Things*. New York: Free Press.

Brunning, J., and P. Forster, eds. 1997. *The Rule of Reason: The Philosophy of Charles Sanders Peirce*. Toronto: University of Toronto Press.

Burke, K. 1966. *Language as Symbolic Action: Essays on Life, Literature, and Method*. Berkeley: University of California Press.

Bybee, J., R. Perkins, and W. Pagliuca, eds. 1994. *The Evolution of Grammar: Tense, Aspect, and Modality in the Languages of the World*. Chicago: University of Chicago Press.

Campbell, J. 1949. *The Hero with a Thousand Faces*. New York: Pantheon.

– 1969. *Primitive Mythology*. Harmondsworth: Penguin.

Carlson, M. 1989. *Places of Performance: The Semiotics of Theatre Architecture*. Ithaca: Cornell University Press.

Carnap, R. 1942. *Introduction to Semantics*. Cambridge, Mass.: Harvard University Press.

Caron, J. 1992. *An Introduction to Psycholinguistics*. Toronto: University of Toronto Press.

Casad, E.H., ed. 1996. *Cognitive Linguistics in the Redwoods: The Expansion of a New Paradigm in Linguistics*. Berlin: Mouton de Gruyter.

Cashmore, E. 1994. *And There Was Television*. London: Routledge.

Cassirer, E. 1944. *An Essay on Man: An Introduction to a Philosophy of Human Culture*. New Haven: Yale University Press.

– 1946. *Language and Myth*. New York: Dover.

– 1957. *The Philosophy of Symbolic Forms*. New Haven: Yale University Press.

Cavalli-Sforza, L., and M. Feldman. 1981. *Cultural Transmission and Evolution*. Princeton: Princeton University Press.

Chamberlain, E.N., and C. Ogilvie. 1974. *Symptoms and Signs in Clinical Medicine*. Bristol: Wright.

Chao, Y.R. 1968. *Language and Symbolic Systems*. Cambridge: Cambridge University Press.

Cherry, C. 1966. *On Human Communication*. Cambridge, Mass.: MIT Press.

Cherwitz, R., and J. Hikins. 1986. *Communication and Knowledge: An Investigation in Rhetorical Epistemology*. Columbia: University of South Carolina Press.

Chomsky, N. 1957. *Syntactic Structures*. The Hague: Mouton.

– 1965. *Aspects of the Theory of Syntax*. Cambridge, Mass.: MIT Press.

– 1966b. *Cartesian Linguistics*. New York: Harper and Row.

– 1975. *Reflections on Language*. New York: Pantheon.

– 1995. *The Minimalist Program*. Cambridge, Mass.: MIT Press.

– 1987. *Principles of Semiotic*. London: Routledge and Kegan.

– 1990. *Sources of Semiotic: Readings with Commentary from Antiquity to the Present*. Carbondale: Southern Illinois University Press.

Classen, C. 1993. *Worlds of Sense: Exploring the Senses in History and across Cultures*. London: Routledge.

Classen, C., D. Howes, and A. Synnott. 1994. *Aroma: The Cultural History of Smell*. London: Routledge.

Colapietro, V., and T. Olshewsky. 1995. *Peirce's Doctrine of Signs: Theory, Applications, and Connections*. Berlin: Mouton de Gruyter.

Colton, H. 1983. *The Gift of Touch*. New York: Putnam.

Cooper, B.L., and W.S. Haney. 1995. *Rock Music in American Popular Culture*. New York: Harrington Park Press.

Coulmas, F. 1989. *The Writing Systems of the World*. Oxford: Blackwell.

Cox, M. 1992. *Children's Drawings*. Harmondsworth: Penguin.

Craig, C., ed. 1986. *Noun Classes and Categorization*. Amsterdam: John Benjamins.

Craik, J. 1993. *The Face of Fashion: Cultural Studies in Fashion*. London: Routledge.

Crawford, M. 1995. *Talking Difference: On Gender and Language*. Thousand Oaks: Sage.

Crispin Miller, M. 1988. *Boxed In: The Culture of TV*. Evanston: Northwestern University Press.

Croft, W. 1991. *Syntactic Categories and Grammatical Relations*. Chicago: University of Chicago Press.

Crystal, D. 1987. *The Cambridge Encyclopedia of Language*. Cambridge: Cambridge University Press.

Culler, J. 1983. *Roland Barthes*. New York: Oxford University Press.

– 1983. *On Deconstruction*. London: Routledge.

Dance, F., and C. Larson. 1976. *The Functions of Communication: A Theoretical Approach*. New York: Holt, Rinehart and Winston.

D'Andrade, R. 1995. *The Development of Cognitive Anthropology*. Cambridge: Cambridge University Press.

Dane, J.A. 1991. *The Critical Mythology of Irony*. Athens: University of Georgia Press.

Danesi, M. 1993. *Vico, Metaphor, and the Origin of Language*. Bloomington: Indiana University Press.

– 1994. *Cool: The Signs and Meanings of Adolescence*. Toronto: University of Toronto Press.

– 1999. *Of Cigarettes, High Heels, and Other Interesting Things: An Introduction to Semiotics*. New York: St Martin's.

Danesi, M., and P. Perron. 1999. *Analyzing Cultures*. Bloomington: Indiana University Press.

Daniels, H., ed. 1996. *An Introduction to Vygotsky*. London: Routledge.

Daniels, P.T., and W. Bright, eds. 1995. *The World's Writing Systems*. Oxford: Oxford University Press.

Danna, S.R. 1992. *Advertising and Popular Culture: Studies in Variety and Versatility*. Bowling Green, Ohio: Bowling Green State University Popular Press.

Davies, R. 1989. *How to Read Faces*. Woolnough: Aquarian.

Davis, F. 1992. *Fashion, Culture, and Identity*. Chicago: University of Chicago Press.

Dawkins, R. 1976. *The Selfish Gene*. Oxford: Oxford University Press.

De Toro, F. 1995. *Theatre Semiotics: Text and Staging in Modern Theatre*. Toronto: University of Toronto Press.

Deacon, T.W. 1997. *The Symbolic Species: The Co-Evolution of Language and the Brain*. New York: Norton.

Deane, P. 1992. *Grammar in Mind and Brain: Explorations in Cognitive Syntax*. Berlin: Mouton de Gruyter.

Deely, J. 1980. *The Signifying Animal: The Grammar of Language and Experience*. Bloomington: Indiana University Press.

– 1982. *Introducing Semiotics*. Bloomington: Indiana University Press.

– 1990. *Basics of Semiotics*. Bloomington: Indiana University Press.

– 1994. *New Beginnings: Early Modern Philosophy and Postmodern Thought*. Toronto: University of Toronto Press.

– Forthcoming. *Four Ages of Understanding*. Toronto: University of Toronto Press.

Dennett, D.C. 1991. *Consciousness Explained*. Boston: Little, Brown.

Derrida, J. 1976. *Of Grammatology*. Trans. G.C. Spivak. Baltimore: Johns Hopkins Press.

Dissanayake, E. 1992. *Homo Aestheticus: Where Art Comes from and Why*. New York: Free Press.

Docker, J. 1994. *Postmodernism and Popular Culture: A Cultural History*. Cambridge: Cambridge University Press.

Dondis, D.A. 1986. *A Primer of Visual Literacy*. Cambridge, Mass.: MIT Press.

Dubois, P. 1988. *L'acte photographique*. Brussels: Labor.

Duchan, J.F., G.A. Bruder, and L.E. Hewitt, eds. 1995. *Deixis in Narrative: A Cognitive Science Perspective*. Hillsdale, NJ: Lawrence Erlbaum Associates.

Dunbar, R. 1997. *Grooming, Gossip, and the Evolution of Language*. Cambridge, Mass.: Harvard University Press.

Dunning, W.V. 1991. *Changing Images of Pictorial Space: A History of Visual Illusion in Painting*. Syracuse: Syracuse University Press.

Durkheim, E. 1912. *The Elementary Forms of Religious Life*. New York: Collier.

Dyer, G. 1982. *Advertising as Communication*. London: Routledge.

Eagleton, T. 1983. *Literary Theory: An Introduction*. Minneapolis: University of Minnesota Press.

Eco, U. 1976. *A Theory of Semiotics*. Bloomington: Indiana University Press.

– 1979. *The Role of the Reader: Explorations in the Semiotics of Texts*. Bloomington: Indiana University Press.

– 1984. *Semiotics and the Philosophy of Language*. Bloomington: Indiana University Press.

– 1990. *The Limits of Interpretation*. Bloomington: Indiana University Press.

Eco, U., and T.A. Sebeok, eds. 1983. *The Sign of Three: Dupin, Holmes, Peirce*. Bloomington: Indiana University Press.

Edie, J.M. 1976. *Speaking and Meaning: The Phenomenology of Language*. Bloomington: Indiana University Press.

Efron, D. 1972 (1941). *Gesture, Race, and Culture*. The Hague: Mouton.

Eichler, E., et al. 1995. *Namensforschung*. Berlin: Mouton de Gruyter.

Ekman, P. 1985. *Telling Lies*. New York: Norton.

Ekman, P., and W. Friesen. 1975. *Unmasking the Face*. Englewood Cliffs, NJ: Prentice-Hall.

Eliade, M. 1963. *Myth and Reality*. New York: Harper and Row.

– 1972. *A History of Religious Ideas*. Chicago: University of Chicago Press.

Emmorey, K., and J. Reilly, eds. 1995. *Language, Gesture, and Space*. Hillsdale, NJ: Lawrence Erlbaum Associates.

Engen, T. 1982. *The Perception of Odours*. New York: Academic.

Ewen, S. 1976. *Captains of Consciousness*. New York: McGraw-Hill.

– 1988. *All Consuming Images*. New York: Basic Books.

Fauconnier, G. 1985. *Mental Spaces*. Cambridge: Cambridge University Press.

– 1997. *Mappings in Thought and Language*. Cambridge: Cambridge University Press.

Fauconnier, G., and E. Sweetser, eds. 1996. *Spaces, Worlds, and Grammar*. Chicago: University of Chicago Press.

Feher, M., R. Naddaf, and N. Tazi, eds. 1989. *Fragments for a History of the Human Body*. New York: Zone.

Fernandez, J.W., ed. 1991. *Beyond Metaphor: The Theory of Tropes in Anthropology*. Stanford: Stanford University Press.

Fillmore, C.J. 1997. *Lectures on Deixis*. Stanford: CSLI Publications.

Fiske, J. 1979. *Introduction to Communication Studies*. London: Methuen.

– 1987. *Television Culture.* London: Methuen.

Fleming, D. 1996. *Powerplay: Toys as Popular Culture.* Manchester: Manchester University Press.

Forceville, C. 1996. *Pictorial Metaphor in Advertising.* London: Routledge.

Foucault, M. 1972. *The Archeology of Knowledge.* Trans. A.M. Sheridan Smith. New York: Pantheon.

– 1976. *The History of Sexuality.* London: Allen Lane.

Freud, S. 1913. *Totem and Taboo.* New York: Norton.

Fridlund, A.J. 1994. *Human Facial Expression: An Evolutionary View.* New York: Academic.

Friedberg, A. 1993. *Window Shopping: Cinema and the Postmodern.* Berkeley: University of California Press.

Friedrich, P. 1986. *The Language Parallax: Linguistic Relativism and Poetic Indeterminacy.* Austin: University of Texas Press.

Frutiger, A. 1989. *Signs and Symbols.* New York: Van Nostrand.

Frye, N. 1981. *The Great Code: The Bible and Literature.* Toronto: Academic Press.

– 1990. *Words with Power.* Harmondsworth: Penguin.

Gallagher, W. 1993. *The Power of Place: How Our Surroundings Shape Our Thoughts, Emotions, and Actions.* New York: HarperCollins.

Gardner, H. 1985. *The Mind's New Science: A History of the Cognitive Revolution.* New York: Basic Books.

Garza-Cuarón, B. 1991. *Connotation and Meaning.* Berlin: Mouton de Gruyter.

Geertz, C. 1973. *The Interpretation of Cultures.* New York: Harper Torch.

Genette, G. 1988. *Narrative Discourse Revisited.* Ithaca: Cornell University Press.

Gibbs, R.W. 1994. *The Poetics of Mind: Figurative Thought, Language, and Understanding.* Cambridge: Cambridge University Press.

Gibson, K.R., and T. Ingold, eds. 1993. *Tools, Language and Cognition in Human Evolution.* Cambridge: Cambridge University Press.

Gill, A. 1994. *Rhetoric and Human Understanding.* Prospect Heights, Ill.: Waveland.

Gill, J.H. 1991. *Merleau-Ponty and Metaphor.* Atlantic Highlands, NJ: Humanities Press.

Goatly, A. 1997. *The Language of Metaphors.* London: Routledge.

Goffman, E. 1959. *The Presentation of Self in Everyday Life.* New York: Anchor.

– 1963. *Stigma: Notes on the Management of Spoiled Identity.* Englewood Cliffs, NJ: Prentice-Hall.

– 1979. *Gender Advertisements.* New York: Harper and Row.

Goldblatt, D., and L.B. Brown, eds. 1997. *Aesthetics: A Reader in the Philosophy of the Arts.* Upper Saddle River, NJ: Prentice-Hall.

Goldman, R., and R. Papson. 1996. *Sign Wars: The Cluttered Landscape of Advertising.* New York: Guilford.

Goldwasser, O. 1995. *From Icon to Metaphor: Studies in the Semiotics of the Hieroglyphs.* Freiburg: Universtätsverlag.

Goode, J. 1992. 'Food.' In R. Bauman, ed., *Folklore, Cultural Performances, and Popular Entertainments,* 233–45. Oxford: Oxford University Press.

Goody, J. 1982. *Cooking, Cuisine and Class.* Cambridge: Cambridge University Press.

Goossens, L., et al. 1995. *By Word of Mouth: Metaphor, Metonymy and Linguistic Action in a Cognitive Perspective.* Berlin: Mouton de Gruyter.

Gordon, W.T. 1997. *Marshall McLuhan: Escape into Understanding, A Biography.* New York: Basic.

Gottdiener, M. 1995. *Postmodern Semiotics: Material Culture and the Forms of Postmodern Life.* London: Blackwell.

Green, K., ed. 1996. *New Essays in Deixis, Discourse, Narrative, Literature.* Amsterdam: Rodopi.

Greenbie, B. 1981. *Spaces: Dimensions of the Human Landscape.* New Haven: Yale University Press.

Greimas, A.J. 1987. *On Meaning: Selected Essays in Semiotic Theory*. Trans. P. Perron and F. Collins. Minneapolis: University of Minnesota Press.

Greimas, A.J., and J. Courtés. 1979. *Semiotics and Language*. Bloomington: Indiana University Press.

Haley, M.C. 1989. *The Semeiosis of Poetic Metaphor*. Bloomington: Indiana University Press.

Hall, E.T. 1966. *The Hidden Dimension*. New York: Doubleday.

– 1973. *The Silent Language*. New York: Anchor.

Hall, K., and M. Bucholtz. 1996. *Gender Articulated: Language and the Socially Constructed Self*. London: Routledge.

Hall, M.B. 1992. *Color and Meaning*. Cambridge: Cambridge University Press.

Halliday, M.A.K. 1975. *Learning How to Mean: Explorations in the Development of Language*. London: Arnold.

– 1985. *Introduction to Functional Grammar*. London: Arnold.

Hardin, C.L., and L. Maffi, eds. 1997. *Color Categories in Thought and Language*. Cambridge: Cambridge University Press.

Hardwick, C.S., ed. 1977. *Semiotic and Significs: The Correspondence between Charles S. Peirce and Victoria Lady Welby*. Bloomington: Indiana University Press.

Harris, R. 1986. *The Origin of Writing*. London: Duckworth.

Harris, R., and T.J. Talbot. 1989. *Landmarks in Linguistic Thought: The Western Tradition from Socrates to Saussure*. London: Routledge.

Harvey, D. 1990. *The Condition of Postmodernity: An Enquiry into the Origins of Cultural Change*. Cambridge: Blackwell.

Harvey, K., and C. Shalom, eds. 1997. *Language and Desire: Encoding Sex, Romance, and Intimacy*. London: Routledge.

Hatcher, E.P. 1974. *Visual Metaphors: A Methodological Study in Visual Communication*. Albuquerque: University of New Mexico Press.

Hauser, M.D. 1996. *The Evolution of Communication*. Cambridge, Mass.: MIT Press.

Hausman, C.R. 1989. *Metaphor and Art*. Cambridge: Cambridge University Press.

– 1993. *Charles S. Peirce's Evolutionary Philosophy*. Cambridge: Cambridge University Press.

Hawkes, T. 1977. *Structuralism and Semiotics*. Berkeley: University of California Press.

Heine, B. 1997. *Cognitive Foundations of Grammar*. Oxford: Oxford University Press.

Hjelmslev, L. 1963. *Prolegomena to a Theory of Language*. Madison: University of Wisconsin Press.

Hodge, R., and G. Kress. 1988. *Social Semiotics*. Ithaca: Cornell University Press.

Hoek, K. van. 1997. *Anaphora and Conceptual Structure*. Chicago: University of Chicago Press.

Hoffmeyer, J. 1996. *Signs of Meaning in the Universe*. Bloomington: Indiana University Press.

Holbrook, M.B., and E.C. Hirschman. 1993. *The Semiotics of Consumption: Interpreting Symbolic Consumer Behavior in Popular Culture and Works of Art*. Berlin: Mouton de Gruyter.

Hollander, A. 1978. *Seeing through Clothes*. Harmondsworth: Penguin.

– 1994. *Sex and Suits: The Evolution of Modern Dress*. New York: Knopf.

Honeck, R.P., and R. Hoffman, eds. 1980. *Cognition and Figurative Language*. Hillsdale, NJ: Lawrence Erlbaum.

Howes, D., ed. 1991. *The Varieties of Sensory Experience*. Toronto: University of Toronto Press.

Hughes, G. 1991. *Swearing*. London: Blackwell.

Humboldt, W. von. 1836 (1988). *On Language: The Diversity of Human Language-Structure and Its Influence on the Mental Development of Mankind*. Trans. P. Heath. Cambridge: Cambridge University Press.

Hymes, D. 1971. *On Communicative Competence*. Philadelphia: University of Pennsylvania Press.

Indurkhya, B. 1992. *Metaphor and Cognition*. Dordrecht: Kluwer.

Ingham, P. 1996. *The Language of Gender and Class*. London: Routledge.

Innis, R.E. 1994. *Consciousness and the Play of Signs*. Bloomington: Indiana University Press.

Jackendoff, R. 1994. *Patterns in the Mind: Language and Human Nature*. New York: Basic Books.

– 1997. *The Architecture of the Language Faculty*. Cambridge, Mass.: MIT Press.

Jackson, B.S. 1985. *Semiotics and Legal Theory*. London: Routledge and Kegan Paul.

Jackson, J.B. 1994. *A Sense of Place, A Sense of Time*. New Haven: Yale University Press.

Jacobson, M.F., and L.A. Mazur. 1995. *Marketing Madness*. Boulder: Westview.

Jakobson, R. 1974. *Main Trends in the Science of Language*. New York: Harper & Row.

– 1980. *The Framework of Language*. Ann Arbor: Michigan Studies in the Humanities.

– 1985. *Selected Writings VII*. Ed. S. Rudy. Berlin: Mouton.

Jameson, F. 1991. *Postmodernism or the Cultural Logic of Late Capitalism*. Durham: Duke University Press.

Jarvella R.H., and W. Klein, eds. 1982. *Speech, Place and Action: Studies in Deictic and Related Topics*. New York: John Wiley and Sons.

Jhally, S. 1987. *The Codes of Advertising*. New York: St Martin's Press.

Johansen, J.D. 1993. *Dialogic Semiosis: An Essay on Signs and Meaning*. Bloomington: Indiana University Press.

Johnson, M. 1987. *The Body in the Mind: The Bodily Basis of Meaning, Imagination and Reason*. Chicago: University of Chicago Press.

Jung, C. 1956. *Analytical Psychology*. New York: Meridian.

Kaplan, J., and A. Bernays. 1996. *The Language of Names: What We Call Ourselves and Why It Matters*. New York: Simon and Schuster.

Kay, P. 1997. *Words and the Grammar of Context*. Cambridge: Cambridge University Press.

Kellner, D. 1995. *Media Culture*. London: Routledge.

Kennedy, J.M. 1993. *Drawing and the Blind: Pictures to Touch*. New Haven: Yale University Press.

Ketner, K.L. 1995. *Peirce and Contemporary Thought*. New York: Fordham University Press.

Kevelson, R. 1988. *The Law as a System of Signs*. New York: Plenum.

– 1993. *Peirce's Esthetics of Freedom: Possibility, Complexity, and Emergent Value*. New York: Peter Lang.

Key, W.B. 1972. *Subliminal Seduction*. New York: Signet.

– 1976. *Media Sexploitation*. New York: Signet.

– 1980. *The Clam-Plate Orgy*. New York: Signet.

– 1989. *The Age of Manipulation*. New York: Holt.

Kinzle, D. 1982. *Fashion and Fetishism: A Social History of the Corset, Tight-Lacing and Other Forms of Body-Sculpture in the West*. Totowa, NJ: Rowman and Littlefield.

Kitcher, P. 1985. *Vaulting Ambition: Sociobiology and the Quest for Human Nature*. Cambridge, Mass.: MIT Press.

Koch, W.A. 1986. *Evolutionary Cultural Semiotics*. Bochum: Brockmeyer.

– 1993. *The Biology of Literature*. Bochum: Brockmeyer.

Kosslyn, S.M. 1994. *Image and Brain*. Cambridge, Mass.: MIT Press.

Kövecses, Z. 1986. *Metaphors of Anger, Pride, and Love: A Lexical Approach to the Structure of Concepts*. Amsterdam: Benjamins.

– 1988. *The Language of Love: The Semantics of Passion in Conversational English*. London: Associated University Presses.

– 1990. *Emotion Concepts*. New York: Springer.

Krafft-Ebing, R. von. 1886. *Psychopathia sexualis*. Stuttgart.

Krampen, M. 1991. *Children's Drawings: Iconic Coding of the Environment*. New York: Plenum.

Kristeva, J. 1989. *Language: The Unknown*. New York: Columbia University Press.

Kubey, R., and M. Csikszentmihalyi. 1990. *Television and the Quality of Life*. Hillsdale, NJ: Lawrence Erlbaum Associates.

Lakoff, G. 1987. *Women, Fire and Dangerous Things: What Categories Reveal about the Mind*. Chicago: University of Chicago Press.

Lakoff, G., and L. Johnson. 1980. *Metaphors We Live By*. Chicago: Chicago University Press.

Lakoff, G., and M. Johnson. 1999. *Philosophy in Flesh: The Embodied Mind and Its Challenge to Western Thought*. New York: Basic.

Lakoff, G., and M. Turner. 1989. *More than Cool Reason: A Field Guide to Poetic Metaphor*. Chicago: University of Chicago Press.

Lamb, T., and J. Bourriau, eds. 1995. *Colour: Art and Science*. Cambridge: Cambridge University Press.

Landau, T. 1989. *About Faces: The Evolution of the Human Face*. New

Landsberg, M.E., ed. 1988. *The Genesis of Language: A Different Judgement of Evidence*. Berlin: Mouton.

Langacker, R.W. 1987. *Foundations of Cognitive Grammar*. Stanford: Stanford University Press.

– 1990. *Concept, Image, and Symbol: The Cognitive Basis of Grammar*. Berlin: Mouton de Gruyter.

Langer, S. 1948. *Philosophy in a New Key*. Cambridge, Mass.: Harvard University Press.

– 1957. *Problems of Art*. New York: Scribner's.

Layton, R. 1991. *The Anthropology of Art*. Cambridge: Cambridge University Press.

Le Guérer, A. 1992. *Scent: The Essential and Mysterious Powers of Smell*. New York: Kodansha.

Leach, E. 1976. *Culture and Communication: The Logic by Which Symbols Are Connected*. Cambridge: Cambridge University Press.

Lee, P. 1996. *The Whorf Theory Complex: A Critical Reconstruction*. Amsterdam: John Benjamins.

Leech, G. 1981. *Semantics: The Study of Meaning*. Harmondsworth: Penguin.

Leiss, W., S. Kline, and S. Jhally. 1990. *Social Communication in Advertising: Persons, Products and Images of Well-Being*. Toronto: Nelson.

Leitch, T.M. 1986. *What Stories Are: Narrative Theory and Interpretation*. University Park: Pennsylvania State University Press.

Levenstein, H. 1993. *Paradox of Plenty: A Social History of Eating in Modern America*. Oxford: Oxford University Press.

Lévi-Strauss, C. 1958. *Structural Anthropology*. New York: Basic Books.

– 1962. *La pensée sauvage*. Paris: Plon.

– 1962. *Le totémisme aujourd'hui*. Paris: Presses Universitaires de France.

– 1964. *The Raw and the Cooked*. London: Cape.

– 1978. *Myth and Meaning: Cracking the Code of Culture*. Toronto: University of Toronto Press.

Levin, S.R. 1988. *Metaphoric Worlds*. New Haven: Yale University Press.

Levine, R. 1997. *A Geography of Time: The Temporal Misadventures of a Social Psychologist or How Every Culture Keeps Time Just a Little Bit Differently*. New York: Basic.

Liebert, R.M., and J.M. Sprafkin. 1988. *The Early Window: Effects of Television on Children and Youth*. New York: Pergamon.

Linden, E. 1986. *Silent Partners: The Legacy of the Ape Language Experiments*. New York: Signet.

Liszka, J.J. 1989. *The Semiotic Study of Myth: A Critical Study of the Symbol*. Bloomington: Indiana University Press.

– 1989. *The Semeiotic of Myth: A Critical Study of the Symbol*. Bloomington: Indiana University Press.

Logan, R.K. 1987. *The Alphabet Effect*. New York: St Martin's Press.

Lotman, Y. 1991. *Universe of the Mind: A Semiotic Theory of Culture*. Bloomington: Indiana University Press.

Lucente, G.L. 1981. *The Narrative of Realism and Myth*. Baltimore: Johns Hopkins University Press.

Lucid, D.P., ed. 1977. *Soviet Semiotics: An Anthology*. Baltimore: The Johns Hopkins Press.

Lucy, J.A. 1992. *Language Diversity and Thought: A Reformulation of the Linguistic Relativity Hypothesis*. Cambridge: Cambridge University Press.

– 1994. *Grammatical Categories and Cognition: A Case Study of the Linguistic Relativity Hypothesis*. Cambridge: Cambridge University Press.

Lyle, J. 1990. *Body Language*. London: Hamylin.

Lyons, J. 1977. *Semantics*. Cambridge: Cambridge University Press.

Lyotard, J.-F. 1984. *The Postmodern Condition: A Report on Knowledge*. Minneapolis: University of Minnesota Press.

MacCannell, D., and J.F. MacCannell. 1982. *The Time of the Sign: A Semiotic Interpretation of Modern Culture*. Bloomington: Indiana University Press.

MacCormac, E. 1976. *Metaphor and Myth in Science and Religion*. Durham, NC: Duke University Press.

– 1985. *A Cognitive Theory of Metaphor*. Cambridge, Mass.: MIT Press.

Mallery, G. 1972. *Sign Language among North American Indians Compared with That among Other Peoples and Deaf-Mutes*. The Hague: Mouton.

Maritain, J. 1943. *Sign and Symbol: Redeeming the Time*. London: Geoffrey Bles.

Markel, N. 1997. *Semiotic Psychology: Speech as an Index of Emotions and Attitudes*. New York: Peter Lang.

May, R. 1991. *The Cry for Myth*. New York: Norton.

McBryde, C.M., and R.S. Backlow. 1970. *Signs and Symptoms: Applied Pathologic Physiology and Clinical Interpretation*. Philadelphia: Lippincott.

McCracken, G. 1988. *Culture and Consumption*. Bloomington: Indiana University Press.

– 1995. *Big Hair: A Journey into the Transformation of Self*. Toronto: Penguin.

McLuhan, M. 1951. *The Mechanical Bride: Folklore of Industrial Man*. New York: Vanguard.

– 1962. *The Gutenberg Galaxy*. Toronto: University of Toronto Press.

– 1964. *Understanding Media*. London: Routledge and Kegan Paul.

McLuhan, M., and E. McLuhan. 1988. *Laws of Media: The New Science*. Toronto: University of Toronto Press.

McNeill, D. 1992. *Hand and Mind: What Gestures Reveal about Thought*. Chicago: University of Chicago Press.

McRobbie, A. 1988. *Zoot Suits and Second-Hand Dresses*. Boston: Unwin Hyman.

Merrell, F. 1995. *Peirce's Semiotics Now: A Primer*. Toronto: Canadian Scholars' Press.

– 1996. *Signs Grow: Semiosis and Life Processes*. Toronto: University of Toronto Press.

– 1997. *Peirce, Signs, and Meaning*. Toronto: University of Toronto Press.

Metz, C. 1974. *Film Language: A Semiotics of the Cinema*. Chicago: University of Chicago Press.

Miller, G.A., and P.N. Johnson-Laird. 1976. *Language and Perception*. Cambridge, Mass.: Harvard University Press.

Miller, J. 1978. *The Body in Question*. New York: Random House.

– 1993. *The Passion of Michel Foucault*. New York: Simon and Schuster.

Miller, M.C. 1988. *Boxed In: The Culture of TV*. Evanston: Northwestern University Press.

Mintz, S.W. 1996. *Tasting Food, Tasting Freedom: Excursions into Eating, Culture, and the Past*. Boston: Beacon.

Montagu, A. 1986. *Touching: The Human Significance of the Skin*. New York: Harper and Row.

Moog, C. 1990. *Are They Selling Her Lips? Advertising and Identity*. New York: Morrow.

Morris, C. 1946. *Signs, Language and Behavior*. New York: Prentice-Hall.

Morris, C.W. 1938. *Foundations of the Theory of Signs*. Chicago: Chicago University Press.

– 1946. *Signs, Language and Behavior*. Englewood Cliffs, NJ: Prentice-Hall.

– 1946. *Writings on the General Theory of Signs*. The Hague: Mouton.

Morris, D., et al. 1979. *Gestures: Their Origins and Distributions*. London: Cape.

Napier, J. 1980. *Hands*. Princeton: Princeton University Press.

Nash, C. 1994. *Narrative in Culture*. London: Routledge.

Nespoulous, J.L., P. Perron, and A.R. Lecours, eds. 1986. *The Biological Foundations of Gestures: Motor and Semiotic Aspects*. Hillsdale, NJ: Lawrence Erlbaum.

Newcomb, H., ed. 1996. *Encyclopedia of Television*. Chicago: Fitzroy Dearborn.

Noble, W., and I. Davidson. 1996. *Human Evolution, Language and Mind*. Cambridge: Cambridge University Press.

Nochimson, M. 1992. *No End to Her: Soap Opera and the Female Subject*. Berkeley: University of California Press.

Norris, C. 1991. *Deconstruction: Theory and Practice*. London: Routledge.

Nöth, W. 1990. *Handbook of Semiotics*. Bloomington: Indiana University Press.

Nöth, W. ed. 1994. *Origins of Semiosis: Sign Evolution in Nature and Culture*. Berlin: Mouton de Gruyter.

Nuessel, F. 1992. *The Study of Names: A Guide to the Principles and Topics*. Westport: Greenwood.

O'Barr, W.M. 1994. *Culture and the Ad*. Boulder: Westview Press.

O'Toole, M. 1994. *The Language of Displayed Art*. London: Leicester University Press.

Ogden, C.K., and I.A. Richards. 1923. *The Meaning of Meaning*. London: Routledge and Kegan Paul.

Ong, W.J. 1977. *Interfaces of the Word: Studies in the Evolution of Consciousness and Culture*. Ithaca: Cornell University Press.

Osgood, C.E., G.J. Suci, and P.H. Tannenbaum. 1957. *The Measurement of Meaning*. Urbana: University of Illinois Press.

Packard, V. 1957. *The Hidden Persuaders*. New York: McKay.

Palmer, G.B. 1996. *Toward a Theory of Cultural Linguistics*. Austin: University of Texas Press.

Parmentier, R.J. 1994. *Signs in Society: Studies in Semiotic Anthropology*. Bloomington: Indiana University Press.

Peck, S.R. 1987. *Atlas of Facial Expression*. Oxford: Oxford University Press.

Peirce, C.S. 1931–58. *Collected Papers of Charles Sanders Peirce*. Vols. 1–8. Ed. C. Hartshorne and P. Weiss. Cambridge, Mass.: Harvard University Press.

Polanyi, L. 1989. *Telling the American Story: A Structural and Cultural Analysis of Conversational Storytelling*. Cambridge, Mass.: MIT Press.

Popper, K. 1976. *The Unending Quest*. Glasgow: HarperCollins.

Popper, K., and J. Eccles. 1977. *The Self and the Brain*. Berlin: Springer.

Posner, R., K. Robering, and T.A. Sebeok. 1997–98. *Semiotics: A Handbook on the Sign-Theoretic Foundations of Nature and Culture*, 2 vols. Berlin: Walter de Gruyter.

Preziosi, D. 1979. *The Semiotics of the Built Environment: An Introduction to Architectonic Analysis*. Bloomington: Indiana University Press.

– 1989. *Rethinking Art History: Meditations on a Coy Science*. New Haven: Yale University Press.

Prince, G. 1982. *Narratology: The Form and Functioning of Narrative*. Berlin: Mouton.

Propp, V.J. 1928. *Morphology of the Folktale*. Austin: University of Texas Press.

Randazzo, S. 1995. *The Myth Makers*. Chicago: Probus.

Rathje, W., and C. Murphy. 1992. *Rubbish! The Archeology of Garbage*. New York: HarperCollins.

Reynolds, R. 1992. *Super Heroes: A Modern Mythology*. Jackson: University of Mississippi Press.

Richards, B. 1994. *Disciplines of Delight: The Psychoanalysis of Popular Culture*. London: Free Association Books.

Richards, I.A. 1936. *The Philosophy of Rhetoric*. Oxford: Oxford University Press.

Ricoeur, P. 1983. *Time and Narrative*. Chicago: University of Chicago Press.

Riggins, S.H., ed. 1994. *The Socialness of Things: Essays on the Socio-Semiotics of Objects*. Berlin: Mouton de Gruyter.

Roberts, D. 1973. *The Existential Graphs of Charles S. Peirce*. The Hague: Mouton.

Robinson, A. 1995. *The Story of Writing*. London: Thames and Hudson.

Robinson, A.H., and B.B. Petchenik. 1976. *The Nature of Maps*. Chicago: University of Chicago Press.

Rollin, L. 1992. *Cradle and All: A Cultural and Psychoanalytic Study of Nursery Rhymes*. Jackson: University of Mississippi Press.

Royce, A.P. 1977. *The Anthropology of Dance*. Bloomington: Indiana University Press.

Rubinstein, R.P. 1995. *Dress Codes: Meanings and Messages in American Culture*. Boulder: Westview.

Ruesch, J. 1972. *Semiotic Approaches to Human Relations*. The Hague: Mouton.

Ruthroff, H. 1997. *Semantics and the Body: Meaning from Frege to the Postmodern*. Toronto: University of Toronto Press.

Saint-Martin, F. 1990. *Semiotics of Visual Language*. Bloomington: Indiana University Press.

Sapir, E. 1921. *Language*. New York: Harcourt, Brace, and World.

Sassienie, P. 1994. *The Comic Book*. Toronto: Smithbooks.

Saussure, F. de 1916. *Cours de linguistique générale*. Paris: Payot.

Schmandt-Besserat, D. 1992. *Before Writing*. Austin: University of Texas Press.

Schogt, H. 1988. *Linguistics, Literary Analysis, and Literary Translation*. Toronto: University of Toronto Press.

Scholes, R. 1982. *Semiotics and Interpretation*. New Haven: Yale University Press.

Schrag, R. 1990. *Taming the Wild Tube*. Chapel Hill: University of North Carolina Press.

Searle, J.R. 1969. *Speech Acts: An Essay in the Philosophy of Language*. Cambridge: Cambridge University Press.

Sebeok, T.A. 1968. *Animal Communication: Techniques of Study and Results of Research*. Bloomington: Indiana University Press.

– 1972. *Perspectives in Zoosemiotics*. The Hague: Mouton.

– 1976. *Contributions to the Doctrine of Signs*. Lanham, Md.: University Press of America.

– 1979. *The Sign and Its Masters*. Austin: University of Texas Press.

– 1981. *The Play of Musement*. Bloomington: Indiana University Press.

– 1986. *I Think I Am a Verb: More Contributions to the Doctrine of Signs*. New York: Plenum.

– 1991. *A Sign Is Just a Sign*. Bloomington: Indiana University Press.

– 1991. *Semiotics in the United States*. Bloomington: Indiana University Press.

– 1994. *Signs: An Introduction to Semiotics*. Toronto: University of Toronto Press.

Sebeok, T.A., and J. Umiker-Sebeok, eds. 1992. *Biosemiotics*. Berlin: Mouton de Gruyter.

– 1994. *Advances in Visual Semiotics*. Berlin: Mouton de Gruyter.

– 1994. *Advances in Visual Semiotics*. Berlin: Mouton de Gruyter.

Seiter, E. 1995. *Sold Separately: Parents and Children in Consumer Culture*. New Brunswick, NJ: Rutgers University Press.

Shands, H.C. 1970. *Semiotic Approaches to Psychiatry*. The Hague: Mouton.

Shapiro, M. 1983. *The Sense of Grammar: Language as Semeiotic*. Bloomington: Indiana University Press.

Shuker, R. 1994. *Understanding Popular Culture*. London: Routledge.

Silverman, K. 1983. *The Subject of Semiotics*. Oxford: Oxford University Press.

Simone, R., ed. 1995. *Iconicity in Language*. Amsterdam: John Benjamins.

Sinclair, J. 1987. *Images Incorporated: Advertising as Industry and Ideology*. Beckenham: Croom Helm.

Singer, B. 1986. *Advertising and Society*. Toronto: Addison-Wesley.

Singer, M. 1991. *Semiotics of Cities, Selves, and Cultures: Explorations in Semiotic Anthropology*. Berlin: Mouton de Gruyter.

Solomon, J. 1988. *The Signs of Our Time*. Los Angeles: J.P. Tarcher.

Sonnesson, G. 1989. *Pictorial Concepts: Inquiries into the Semiotic Heritage and Its Relevance for the Analysis of the Visual World*. Lund: Lund University Press.

Sørensen, H.S. 1963. *The Meaning of Proper Names*. Copenhagen: Gad.

Sparshott, F. 1995. *A Measured Pace: Toward a Philosophical Understanding of the Arts of Dance*. Toronto: University of Toronto Press.

Stahl, S. 1989. *Literary Folkloristics and the Personal Narrative*. Bloomington: Indiana University Press.

Steele, V. 1995. *Fetish: Fashion, Sex, and Power*. Oxford: Oxford University Press.

Stern, J., and M. Stern. 1992. *Encyclopedia of Pop Culture*. New York: Harper.

Sutton-Smith, B. 1986. *Toys as Culture*. New York: Gardner.

Sweetser, E. 1990. *From Etymology to Pragmatics: The Mind-as-Body Metaphor in Semantic Structure and Semantic Change*. Cambridge: Cambridge University Press.

Synnott, A. 1993. *The Body Social: Symbolism, Self and Society*. London: Routledge.

Tannen, D. 1994. *Gender and Discourse*. Oxford: Oxford University Press.

Taylor, J.R. 1995. *Linguistic Categorization: Prototypes in Linguistic Theory*. Oxford: Oxford University Press.

Thom, R. 1975. *Structural Stability and Morphogenesis: An Outline of a General Theory of Models*. Reading: W.A. Benjamin.

Todorov, T. 1977. *Theories of the Symbol*. Ithaca: Cornell University Press.

Toolan, M.J. 1988. *Narrative: A Critical Linguistic Introduction*. London: Routledge.

Tufte, E.R. 1997. *Visual Explanations: Images and Quantities, Evidence and Narrative*. Cheshire: Graphics Press.

Turnbull, D. 1989. *Maps Are Territories*. Chicago: University of Chicago Press.

Uexküll, J. von. 1909. *Umwelt und Innenwelt der Tierre*. Berlin: Springer.

Umiker-Sebeok, J., ed. 1987. *Marketing Signs: New Directions in the Study of Signs for Sale*. Berlin: Mouton.

Ungerer, F., and H.-J. Schmid. 1996. *An Introduction to Cognitive Linguistics*. Harlow: Longman.

Valentine, T., T. Brennen, and S. Brédart. 1996. *The Cognitive Psychology of Proper Names*. London: Routledge.

Vardar, N. 1992. *Global Advertising: Rhyme or Reason?* London: Chapman.

Verene, D.P. 1981. *Vico's Science of the Imagination*. Ithaca: Cornell University Press.

Vestergaard, T., and K. Schrøder. 1985. *The Language of Advertising*. London: Blackwell.

Visser, M. 1991. *The Rituals of Dinner*. New York: HarperCollins.

– 1994. *The Way We Are*. Toronto: HarperCollins.

Vroon, P., and A. van Amerongen. 1996. *Smell: The Secret Seducer*. New York: Farrar, Straus and Giroux.

Way, E.C. 1991. *Knowledge Representation and Metaphor*. Dordrecht: Kluwer.

Weissenborn, J., and W. Klein, eds. 1982. *Here and There: Cross-Linguistic Studies on Deixis and Demonstration*. Amsterdam: John Benjamins.

Wells, G. 1986. *The Meaning Makers: Children Learning Language and Using Language to Learn*. Portsmouth: Heinemann.

Werner, H., and B. Kaplan. 1963. *Symbol Formation: An Organismic-Developmental Approach to the Psychology of Language and the Expression of Thought*. New York: John Wiley.

Wernick, A. 1991. *Promotional Culture: Advertising, Ideology, and Symbolic Expression*. London: Gage.

Wheelwright, P. 1954. *The Burning Fountain: A Study in the Language of Symbolism*. Bloomington: Indiana University Press.

Whiteside, R.L. 1975. *Face Language*. New York: Pocket.

Whorf, B.L. 1956. *Language, Thought, and Reality*. Ed. J.B. Carroll. Cambridge, Mass.: MIT Press.

Williamson, J. 1985. *Decoding Advertisements: Ideology and Meaning in Advertising*. London: Marion Boyars.

Wilson, F.R. 1998. *The Hand: How Its Use Shapes the Brain, Language, and Human Culture*. New York: Pantheon.

Wimsatt, W.R. 1954. *The Verbal Icon: Studies in the Meaning of Poetry*. New York: University of Kentucky Press.

Winner, E. 1982. *Invented Worlds: The Psychology of the Arts*. Cambridge, Mass.: Harvard University Press.

– 1988. *The Point of Words: Children's Understanding of Metaphor and Irony*. Cambridge, Mass.: Harvard University Press.

Wolfe, T. 1981. *From Bauhaus to Our House*. New York: Farrar, Strauss and Giroux.

Wundt, W. 1901. *Sprachgeschichte und Sprachpsychologie*. Leipzig: Eugelmann.

Wundt, W. 1973. *The Language of Gestures*. The Hague: Mouton.

INDEX

This index contains both notions and the names of personages not listed as main entries in the corpus of the dictionary, as well as important additional references to notions and names that do have entries.

ABC, 40
Abelard, Peter, 83
absurdism, 81
acoustic phonetics, 173
actant, 157
action painting, 4
Addison, Joseph, 197
addressee, 58
addresser, 58
advertising agency, 41
Aeschylus, 80
Aesop, 19, 90, 208
Aiken, Howard, 61
Alexanderson, Ernst F.W., 226
Allen, Woody, 50
alliteration, 7
Anaximander, 138
Andersen, Hans Christian, 91
anticlimax, 93
antithesis, 93
Antonioni, Michelangelo, 49, 137, 161
Apollinaire, Guillaume, 136
apologue, 19
apostrophe, 93
Apple Macintosh, 114
Apuleius, 156, 208
Aquinas, St Thomas, 129, 147
archetype, 66, 123–4
Aristides, 156, 160
Aristophanes, 41
Aristotle, 9, 45, 69, 77, 88, 129, 145, 147, 159, 187, 194, 221
articulatory phonetics, 173

artificial intelligence, 120
Asimov, Isaac, 199
atom, 3
atonality, 3
AT&T, 190
Atwood, Margaret, 161
Auden, W.H., 136
auditory phonetics, 4, 173
Augustine, St, 12, 83, 205
Austen, Jane, 160
Austin, John L., 15, 203

Babbage, Charles, 15, 61
Bach, Johann Sebastian, 31, 151
background, 96
Bacon, Francis, 83
Baird, John Logie, 226
ballet, 71
balloon, 57
Balzac, Honoré de, 160
Barrett Browning, Elizabeth, 136
Barthes, Roland, 7, 15, 153, 158
Bates, Henry Walter, 148
Baudelaire, Charles, 136, 222
Bauhaus School, 22, 23
Baum, L. Frank, 49
Baumgarten, Alexander Gottlieb, 9, 10
BBC, 40
Beardsley, Aubrey, 28
beat gesture, 100
Beauchamp, Pierre, 31
Beckett, Samuel, 18, 90, 180
Beethoven, Ludwig van, 151, 162, 165

Bellini, Vincenzo, 165
Berg, Alban, 166
Bergman, Ingmar, 49
Bergson, Henri, 10
Berkeley, George, 116
Berlin, Brent, 56
Berlioz, Hector, 152, 165
Bernini, Gianlorenzo, 23, 200
Bertolucci, Bernardo, 49
biosemiotics, 120
birth and rebirth myth, 154
bit, 42
Bizet, Georges, 166
Blitzstein, Marc, 166
Bloomfield, Leonard, 133
Boas, Franz, 33, 103, 133
Boccaccio, Giovanni, 156, 160, 209
Bogdanovich, Peter, 50
Boole, George, 97
Borges, Jorge Luis, 209
Boswell, James, 35
Bowdler, Thomas, 40
Bradbury, Ray, 199
Brahms, Johannes, 152
brand name, 6, 8
Braque, Georges, 25, 70
Breathed, Berkeley, 57
Breton, André, 221
Broca, Paul, 41
Brunelleschi, Filippo, 23, 116, 168
Buñuel, Luis, 50
Burns, Robert, 136
Burroughs, Edgar Rice, 199
Burroughs, William S., 32
Butler, Samuel, 197
byte, 62

Caccini, Giulio, 163
Callimachus, 84
Calvino, Italo, 91, 209
Camerata, 163
Cameron, Julia Margaret, 174
Camões, Luis (Vaz) de, 87
Campbell, Joseph, 153
Campion, Thomas, 136
Capp, Al, 57
Caravaggio, Michelangelo Merisi da, 47

Cassirer, Ernst, 153
Catullus, 84, 162
Cavafy, Constantine, 136
CBC, 41
CBS, 40
Cervantes Saavedra, Miguel de, 160, 197
Cézanne, Paul, 25
Champollion, Jean François, 109
Chandler, Raymond, 76
character, 156
Charlemagne, 46
Chaucer, Geoffrey, 12, 91, 169, 197, 209
Cheever, John, 197
Chekhov, Anton, 191, 209
Chesterton, G.K., 76
chiaroscuro, 25
Chomsky, Noam Avram, 60, 73–4, 99, 103, 127, 131, 133, 220, 236
Chopin, Frédéric François, 31, 152
Christie, Agatha, 76
Cicero, Marcus Tullius, 194
circumfix, 11
Clement of Alexandria, 205
climax, 93
closed work, 163
code, 58
cognition, 54
cohesive gesture, 100
Coleridge, Samuel Taylor, 88
collective unconscious, 66, 123
color field painting, 3
Columbus, Christopher, 178
Comenius, 83–4
commedia dell'arte, 80, 168
conative function, 59
conceit, 93
connotation, 31
contact, 58
content analysis, 96
context, 58
Corinthian form, 21
cosmogonic myth, 154
Cousin, Victor, 10
Crick, Francis, 181
Croce, Benedetto, 10
cubism, 3, 25
culture-hero myth, 154
Cyrillic, 13

dada, 25–6
Dalí, Salvador, 26, 50, 221
Dallapiccola, Luigi, 166
Dante Alighieri, 12, 43, 69 87, 129
Darwin, Charles, 36, 157, 180
Daudet, Alphonse, 209
Davies, Robertson, 161
da Vinci, Leonardo, 25, 47
Dawkins, Richard, 143, 213
DBS, 41
deconstruction, 75–6
deep structure, 220
Degas, Edgar, 25, 118–19
deictic gesture, 74
Déjerine, Jules, 126
Delacroix, Eugène, 25
DeMille, Cecil B., 49
demotic, 109
Derrida, Jacques, 73, 104, 182
Descartes, René, 44, 83, 147, 187
De Sica, Vittorio, 49
Dewey, John, 10, 84, 98
Dick, Philip K., 199
Dickens, Charles, 197
Dickinson, Emily, 136
Diderot, Denis, 86
Dirks, Rudolph, 57
discursive form, 183
DNA, 181
domain, 146
Donatello, 200
Donizetti, Gaetano, 165
Donne, John, 35, 88
Doric form, 21, 22
Dostoyevsky, Fyodor, 90, 161
Dowland, John, 135
Doyle, Sir Arthur Conan, 76
Dreyer, Carl-Theodor, 50
Dryden, John, 188, 197
dualism, 76
Duchamp, Marcel, 26, 70, 201
DuMont Television Network, 40
Durkheim, Emile, 153

Eckert, J. Presper, 61
Eco, Umberto, 205, 206
ecological theory, 17
El Greco, 137

Eliade, Mircea, 84
Eliot, George, 191
Eliot, T.S., 69, 87
Ellison, Ralph Waldo, 197
Emerson, Peter Henry, 174
emotive function, 59
Epicureans, 88, 107
Epimenides, 169
Erasmus, Desiderius, 83, 197
Eratosthenes, 138
Ernst, Max, 221
eschatological myth, 154
ethnography, 17
ethology, 36
etymology, 89
euphemism, 93
Euripedes, 41, 80
Eyck, Jan van, 25

fabliau, 160
Faulkner, William, 209, 218
fauvism, 25
Fechner, Gustav Theodor, 187
feedback, 71
Feiffer, Jules, 57
Fellini, Federico, 49
Ferlinghetti, Lawrence, 32
Fichte, Johan Gottlieb, 10
Firdwasi, Abu al-Qasim, 87
Fisher, Bud, 57
Flaubert, Gustave, 5, 191
foreground, 30
Foucault, Michel, 14
Fox Television Network, 40
Frankenthaler, Helen, 56
Frege, Gottlob, 97
Freud, Sigmund, 5, 10, 28, 43, 66, 131,
    153, 172, 186–7, 236
Frost, Robert, 136
Funk, Isaac Kaufmann, 131

Galen of Pergamum, 203, 205
Galfridus Grammaticus, 130
Gama, Vasco da, 178
Gardner, Erle Stanley, 76
Gauguin, Paul, 25
gene, 158, 213
general Turing machine, 54

Gershwin, George, 166
Gibson, William, 71
Ginsberg, Allen, 32
Giotto, 24–5
Glass, Philip, 26, 148, 152
Goethe, Johann Wolfgang von, 34, 80, 136
Gogol, Nikolai, 209
Gosse, Edmund, 160
Gounod, Charles, 165
Goya, Francisco, 25, 43
Gray, Thomas, 84, 136
Greimas, Algirdas Julien, 4, 157, 207
Griffith, D.W., 49
Grimm, Jacob, 133
Gropius, Walter, 22, 32
ground, 145
Group f/64, 174
Gutenberg, Johann, 39, 104, 142

Hall, Edward T., 185–6, 242–3
Hammett, Dashiell, 76
Handel, George Frideric, 151, 164
Harris, Joel Chandler, 19
Harris, John, 86
Haydn, Franz Joseph, 151
Hegel, Georg Wilhelm Friedrich, 10, 77, 88, 116
Heidegger, Martin, 6, 172
Heine, Heinrich, 136
Heinlein, Robert, 199
Heisenberg, Werner, 107–8
Heller, Joseph, 18
Helmholtz, Hermann, 4, 187
Hemingway, Ernest, 209
Herder, Johann Gottfried von, 131
Herodotus, 110
Hesse, Hermann, 34
Hippocrates, 203, 205
Hitchcock, Alfred, 50
Hjelmslev, Louis, 102
Hobbes, Thomas, 34, 129, 187
Hockett, Charles, 36
Hoffmann, E.T.A., 209
Hofmannsthal, Hugo von, 136
Hogarth, William, 44
Hollerith, Herman, 61
holophrases, 127

Homer, 87, 122
Horace, 69, 162, 197
Housman, A.E., 136
Humboldt, Wilhelm von, 131
Hume, David, 28, 88
Husserl, Edmund, 88, 172
Huxley, Aldous, 197, 199
hyperbole, 93

IBM, 61, 64
Ibsen, Henrik, 80
icon, 171
iconic gesture, 100
ideograph, 13
image schema, 146
impressionism, 25
index, 33, 171
infix, 11
interpretant, 170–1
intertext, 156
Ionesco, Eugène, 90
Ionic form, 21, 22
irony, 93
Isocrates, 194

Jacquard, Joseph-Marie, 61
Jakobson, Roman, 58–9, 62, 67, 85, 145, 172, 177, 192
James, Henry, 191, 209
James, William, 98, 218
Jenney, William Le Baron, 47
Jespersen, Otto, 133
Johnson, Mark, 118, 146
Johnson, Philip C., 22, 23
Johnson, Samuel, 6, 130
Jones, William, 133
Jonson, Ben, 88, 197
Joyce, James, 43, 122, 161, 163, 209, 218
Jung, Carl Gustav, 21, 43, 66, 131, 153, 172, 186–7, 236
Juvenal, 197

Kafka, Franz, 209
Kandinsky, Wassily, 25
Kant, Immanuel, 10, 88, 116, 147
Kasparov, Garry, 64
Kay, Paul, 56

KDKA, 190
Kerouac, Jack, 32
Kersey, John, 130
Klee, Paul, 25
Koffka, Kurt, 99
Köhler, Wolfgang, 36, 99
Kooning, Willem de, 4, 5
Kuhn, Thomas, 142

Lacan, Jacques, 182
La Fontaine, Jean de, 90
Lakoff, George, 118, 146
Lang, Fritz, 199
Langer, Susanne, 10, 79, 183
langue, 34
Larson, Gary, 57
La Tour, Georges de, 47
Le Guin, Ursula K., 199
legisign, 171
Leibniz, Gottfried Wilhelm, 61, 103, 132
leitmotif, 165
Lenneberg, Eric, 69
Leoncavallo, Ruggero, 166
Lessing, Gotthold Ephraim, 10, 88
Lévi-Strauss, Claude, 95, 152, 191
Lévy-Bruhl, Lucien, 153
literary cameo, 42
litotes, 93
Locke, John, 28, 83, 129, 187, 203, 205
Lockhart, John Gibson, 35
logical positivism, 43–4
Lorca, Federico García, 136
Lorris, Guillaume de, 12
Louis XIV, 31
Lully, Jean Baptiste, 31, 164

Machiavelli, Niccolò, 129
Mackmurdo, Arthur, 28
Magritte, René, 26, 226
Maillol, Aristide, 201
Malinowski, Bronislaw, 153
Mallarmé, Stéphane, 222
Manet, Édouard, 25, 118
Mann, Thomas, 43, 161
mannerism, 22, 23
Mansfield, Katharine, 209
Marconi, Guglielmo, 190

Márquez, Gabriel García, 209
Marx, Karl, 10, 77
Mascagni, Pietro, 166
materialism, 116
Matisse, Henri, 25, 92
Mauchley, John, 61
Maupassant, Guy de, 191, 209
Maurois, André, 35
McLuhan, Marshall, 27, 101, 142, 207, 228
McNeill, David, 99–100
Méliès, Georges, 48, 199
Melville, Herman, 160
meme, 213
Mendel, Gregor Johann, 158
Menotti, Gian-Carlo, 166
Mercator, Gerardus, 138
Mercator projection, 138
Mesmer, Franz, 144
message, 58
metalingual function, 59
metaphor, 93
metaphoric gesture, 100
metonymy, 94
Meung, Jean de, 12
Meyerbeer, Giacomo, 165
Michelangelo, 25, 200
Mill, James, 107
Mill, John Stuart, 107, 236
Miller, Arthur, 81
Milton, John, 84, 87
minimalism, 26
mock epic, 42
modernism, 22, 23, 32
Moholy-Nagy, László, 174
Molière, 42, 92, 197
Monet, Claude, 119
Montaigne, Michel de, 83
Monteverdi, Claudio, 163
Moore, G.E., 15
Moore, Henry, 201
More, Thomas, 199
Morgan, Lewis Henry, 17
Morisot, Berthe, 119
morphology, 132
Morris, Desmond, 100
Morrison, Toni, 161
Motherwell, Robert Burns, 4

Mozart, Wolfgang Amadeus, 151, 165
Müller, Friedrich Max, 152
Muybridge, Edward, 174
myth, 42–3, 65

narratology, 104
Nast, Thomas, 44
natural selection, 73
NBC, 40
neogrammarians, 133
Neumann, John von, 61
news, 40
Newton, Isaac, 130
Nietzsche, Friedrich, 10, 78, 181
nihilism, 107
Nipkow, Paul, 226
Nono, Luigi, 166

object, 171
onomatopoeia, 20
Ortelius, Abraham, 138
Orwell, George, 199
Outcault, Richard Felton, 57
Ovid, 208
oxymoron, 94

painting, 167
painting, perspective, 25, 117
Panini, 103, 132
paradox, 94
parole, 33–4
Pascal, Blaise, 61, 170
Pasolini, Pier Paolo, 49
Pavlov, Ivan, 33, 36, 58, 187
Paxton, Joseph, 22, 23
PBS, 41, 188
Peirce, Charles Sanders, 3, 78, 94, 115, 122,
    129, 171, 189, 193, 194, 201, 203, 205, 211,
    232, 240
Pergolesi, Giovanni Battista, 165
Peri, Jacopo, 163
personal unconscious, 66, 123
personification, 94
Petrarch, 136
Petronius Arbiter, 197
phatic function, 59
phenomenology, 113

phoneme, 125–6
phonetics, 132
physicalism, 66, 74–5
Piaget, Jean, 84
Picasso, Pablo, 3, 25, 70
pictograph, 13
Pindar, 161
Pissarro, Camille, 118
Plato, 9, 24, 69, 77, 88, 116, 159, 176, 187, 194
Platonic forms, 3
Plautus, 41, 80
Pliny the Elder, 86
plot, 156
Plotinus, 10
Plutarch, 35
Poe, Edgar Allan, 76, 209
poetic function, 59
poetic logic, 152
Poincaré, Henri, 46–7
Pollock, Jackson, 4
Pope, Alexander, 88, 197
Popper, Karl, 179
Porter, Edwin S., 48
postmodernism, 22
poststructuralism, 73
pragmatics, 132
pragmatism, 76, 88, 170
prefix, 11
presentational form, 79
Prokofiev, Sergei, 152, 166
Propp, Vladimir, 156
Proto-Indo-European, 132
Proust, Marcel, 161
proxemics, 105
Ptolemy, 138
Puccini, Giacomo, 166
Purcell, Henry, 151, 164

qualisign, 170
Quine, Willard, 15
Quintilian, 83, 194

Rabelais, François, 197
Rachmaninoff, Sergei, 152
Raphael, 25, 47, 137
Rask, Rasmus Christian, 133
rationalism, 85

Ray, Man, 174, 201
Raymond, Alex, 57
realism, 116
referential function, 59
Reggio, Godfrey, 26
Rembrandt van Rijn, 25, 47
Renoir, Pierre Auguste, 25, 119
repetition in advertising, 8
representamen, 170
rhetorical question, 94
Richards, I.A., 10
Rilke, Rainer Maria, 136
Rimbaud, Arthur, 222
RNA, 181
Robbe-Grillet, Alain, 18
Robinson, Henry Peach, 174
rococo, 22, 23, 25
Rodin, Auguste, 201
Rosetta Stone, 109
Rossellini, Roberto, 49
Rossini, Gioacchino, 165
Rothko, Mark, 4
Rousseau, Jean-Jacques, 83, 101
Rubens, Peter Paul, 25
Russell, Bertrand, 15
Rutherford, Ernest, 3

Salinger, J.D., 18
Sallust, 110
Santayana, George, 10
Sapir, Edward, 131, 133
Sartre, Jean-Paul, 10, 172
Saussure, Ferdinand de, 78, 127–8, 132, 133,
    198, 205, 218
Scarlatti, Alessandro, 164
Schikard, Wilhelm, 61
Schiller, Friedrich von, 162
Schiller, Johann Christoph Friedrich von, 10
Schoenberg, Arnold, 152
Schopenhauer, Arthur, 10
Schubert, Franz, 152
Schumann, Robert, 152
scroll, 39
Searle, John, 47–8, 203
Sebeok, Thomas A., 36, 149, 206, 243
segmentation, 150
semantics, 132

semeion, 109
semeiotics, 109
semiology, 198
semiotics, 170, 197–8
semiotic square, 104
Seneca, 80
sense ratio, 142
series, 41
setting, 156
Seurat, Georges, 178
Shakespeare, William, 11, 35, 80, 136
Shannon, Claude E., 59, 120
Shaw, George Bernard, 197
Shelley, Mary Wollstonecraft, 160, 199
Shikibu, Baroness Murasaki, 160
Shostakovich, Dmitri, 152, 166
sign, 197–8
signification, 197–8
signified, 197–8
signifier, 197–8
simile, 94
sinsign, 171
Siskind, Aaron, 174
sitcom, 40
Skinner, B.F., 33
soap opera, 40
sociobiology, 66
Socrates, 176
Sophists, 88
Sophocles, 80
Southey, Robert, 29
Spenser, Edmund, 87
Sperry, Roger, 217
Spielberg, Steven, 50
Stahl, Georg Ernst, 16
Stendhal, 160
Stieglitz, Alfred, 174
Still, Clifford, 56
Stoics, 88
Strauss, Richard, 152, 166
Stravinsky, Igor, 152
Strindberg, August, 81
strophe, 218
structuralism, 133
subtext, 156
suffix, 11, 156
Sullivan, Louis, 22, 23

surface structure, 74
surrealism, 26
Swift, Jonathan, 88, 197
Swinnerton, James Guilford, 57
syllabary, 13
syllogism, 24
symptom, 109
synecdoche, 94
syntagm, 169
syntax, 132

Tacitus, Cornelius, 109
Tagore, Rabindranath, 209
Tasso, Torquato, 87
Tchaikovsky, Peter Ilich, 152
Terence, 80
Thomas, Dylan, 136
Thompson, Virgil, 166
Thrax, Dionysius, 132
Thucydides, 110
Titian, 25
Tolstoy, Leo, 161, 209
topic, 145
Toulouse-Lautrec, Henri de, 25
transcendentalism, 124, 147
travesty, 42
Trudeau, Gary, 57
Turgenev, Ivan, 209
Turing, Alan Mathison, 54, 61
Turing machine, 54
Turing test, 47
Twain, Mark, 160, 191, 197
Tylor, Edward B., 16, 17, 153
Tzara, Tristan, 72

Uexküll, Jacob von, 37
Uldall, Hans Jørgen, 102
unconscious, 66, 97
unconscious, collective, 123
universal grammar, 127
utilitarianism, 107

van Gogh, Vincent, 25
Vasari, Giorgio, 35
vehicle, 145
Verdi, Giuseppe, 152, 165
Verlaine, Paul, 222
Verne, Jules, 199

Vico, Giambattista, 11, 91, 97, 121, 144,
   152, 177
Vincent of Beauvais, 86
Virgil, 87
Vivaldi, Antonio, 151
Voltaire, François Marie Arouet, 88
Vygotskij, Lev S., 239

Wagner, Richard, 130, 165
Walpole, Horace, 160
Walton, Izaak, 35
Warhol, Andy, 26, 178
Watson, James, 181
Watson, John B., 7, 33
Weber, Carl Maria von, 165
Webster, Noah, 131
Wegman, William, 174
Welby, Lady Victoria, 210
Welles, Orson, 49
Wells, H.G., 199
Wernicke, Carl, 126, 240
Wertheimer, Max, 99
Wertmuller, Lina, 49
West, Nathaniel, 197
White, Minor, 174
Whitman, Walt, 86, 136
Whorf, Benjamin Lee, 131
Whorfian hypothesis, 131
Wiener, Norbert, 71
Wilde, Oscar, 9, 88, 197
William of Ockham, 160
Williams, Tennessee, 81
Wilson, Edward Osborne, 214
Winckelmann, Johann Joachim, 10
Wittgenstein, Ludwig, 15
Wolfe, Tom, 197
Woolf, Virginia, 161, 218
word, 150
Wordsworth, William, 87
Wright, Frank Lloyd, 22, 47
Wundt, Wilhelm Max, 54, 187

Yeats, William Butler, 136
Yukio, Mishima, 209

Zappa, Frank, 155
Zweig, Stefan, 35
Zworykin, Vladimir, 226